Seconds

Bryan Lee O'Malley

with

Jason Fischer . . . . Drawing Assistant

Dustin Harbin . . . . Lettering

Nathan Fairbairn . . . . Color

BALLANTINE BOOKS

NEW YORK

Copyright © 2014 by Bryan Lee O'Malley

Published in the United States by Ballantine Books, an imprint of Random House, a division of Random House LLC, a Penguin Random House Company, New York.

BALLANTINE and the HOUSE colophon are registered trademarks of Random House LLC.

Grateful acknowledgment is made to Hal Leonard Corporation for permission to reprint an excerpt from "Over and Over" words and music by Christine McVie, copyright © 1979 by Universal Music-Careers. International copyright secured. All rights reserved. Reprinted by permission of Hal Leonard Corporation.

ISBN 978-0-345-52937-4
Barnes & Noble special edition ISBN 978-0-553-39436-8
Comic-Con International: San Diego special edition (numbered) ISBN 978-0-553-39435-1
Comic-Con International: San Diego special edition (lettered) ISBN 978-0-553-39434-4
eBook ISBN 978-0-345-53878-9

Printed in China on acid-free paper

randomhousebooks.com

Seconds

I felt a kind of vertigo, as if
I were merely plunging from
one world to another, and in
each I arrived shortly after
the end of the world had
taken place

—Italo Calvino,
If on a winter's night a traveler

And I said
Could it be me?
Could it really, really be?
Over and over

—Fleetwood Mac

Seconds

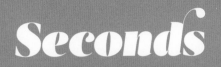

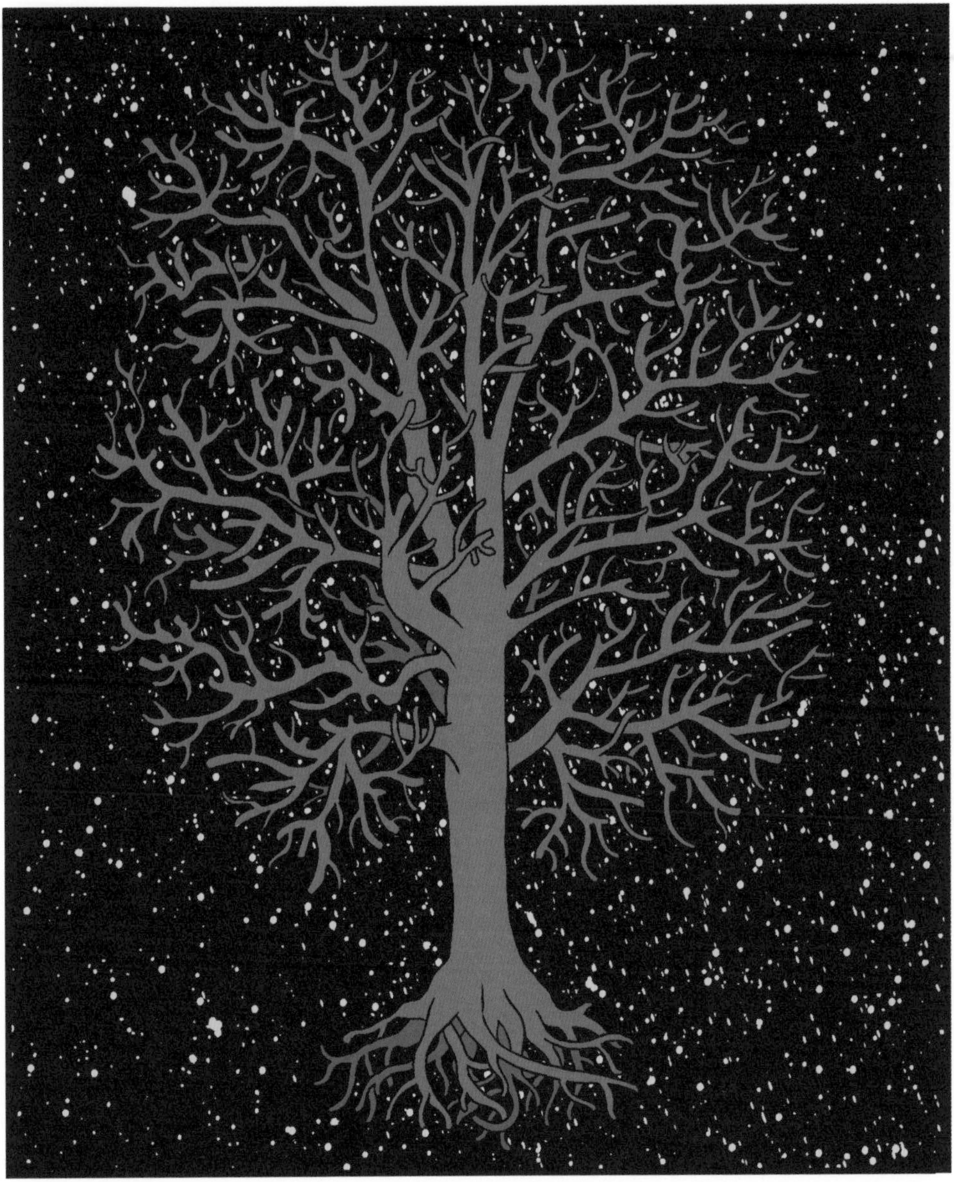

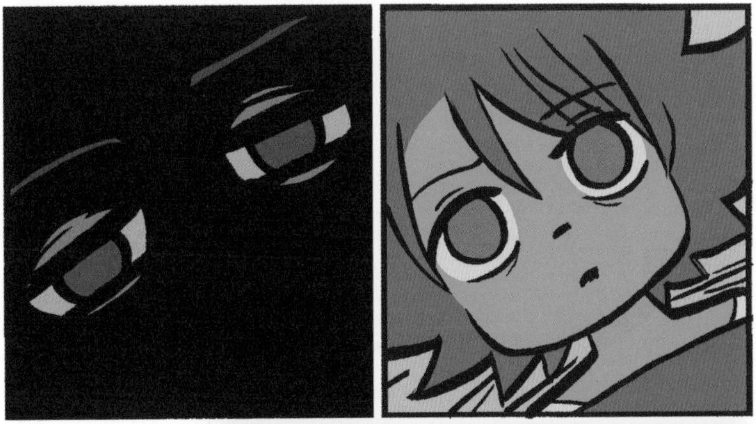

She woke up,

and there was a glow.

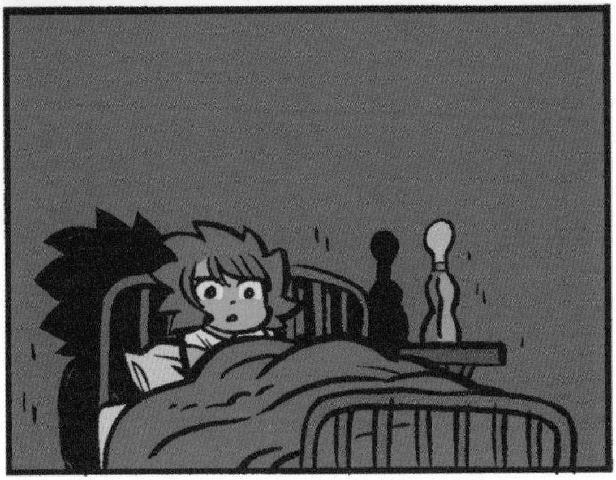

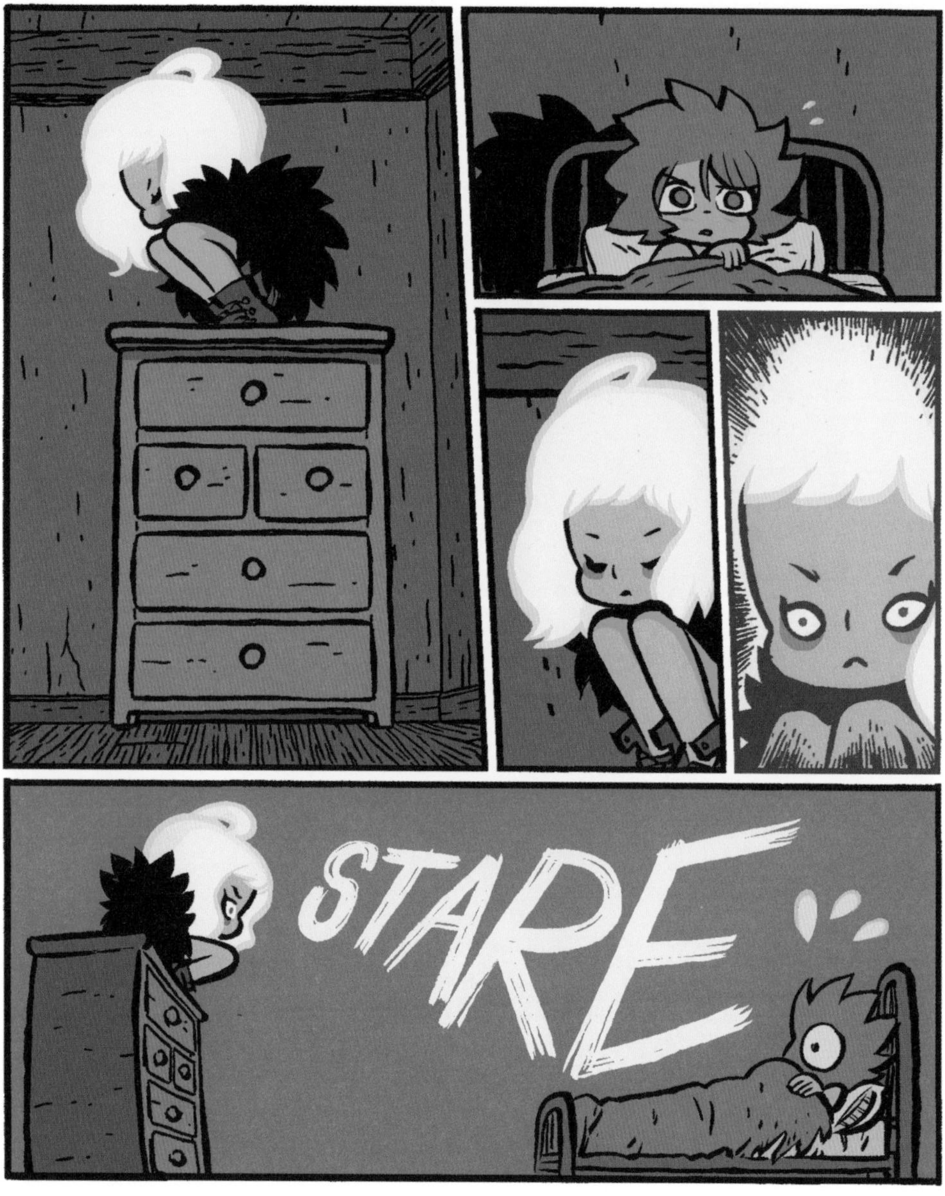
STARE

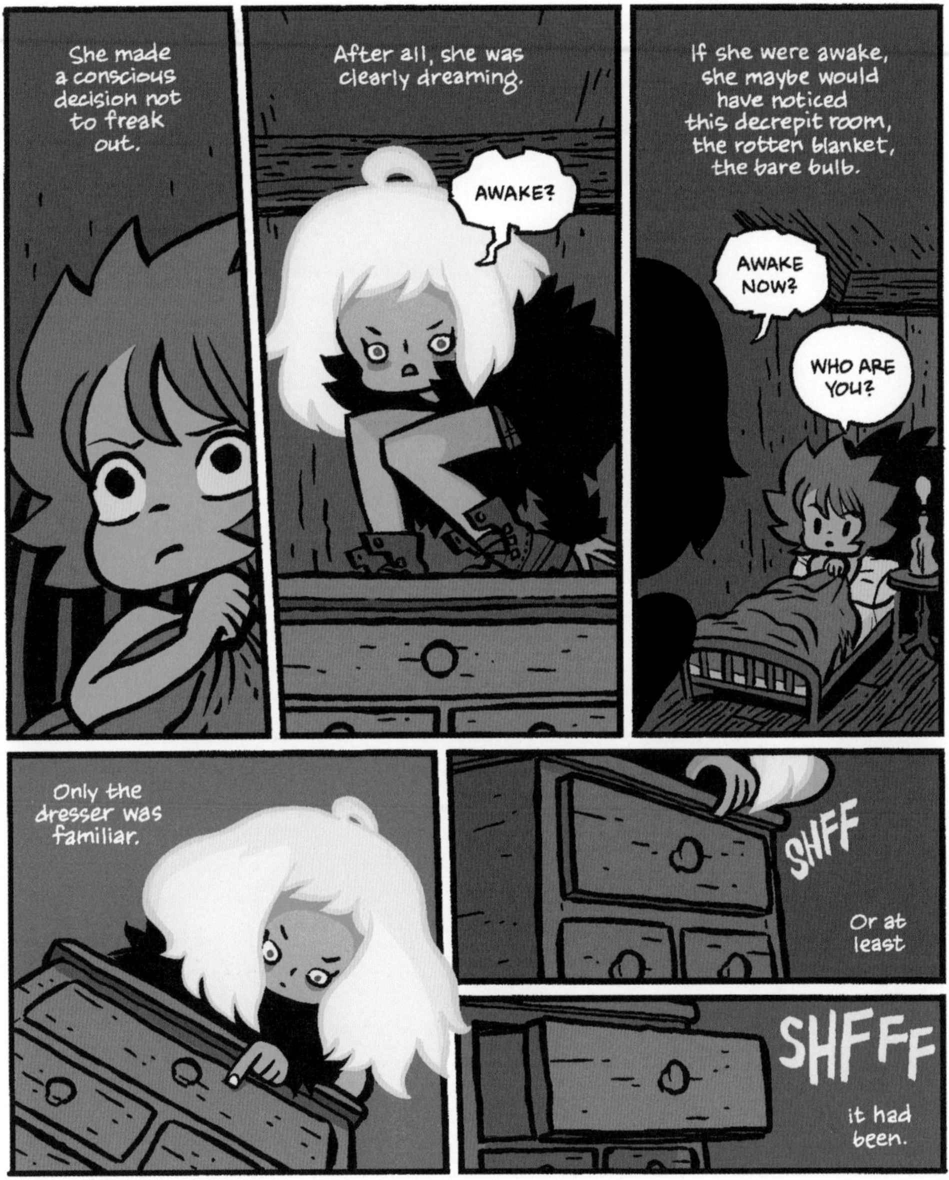

She made a conscious decision not to freak out.
After all, she was clearly dreaming.
AWAKE?
If she were awake, she maybe would have noticed this decrepit room, the rotten blanket, the bare bulb.
AWAKE NOW?
WHO ARE YOU?
Only the dresser was familiar.
SHFF
Or at least
SHFFF
it had been.

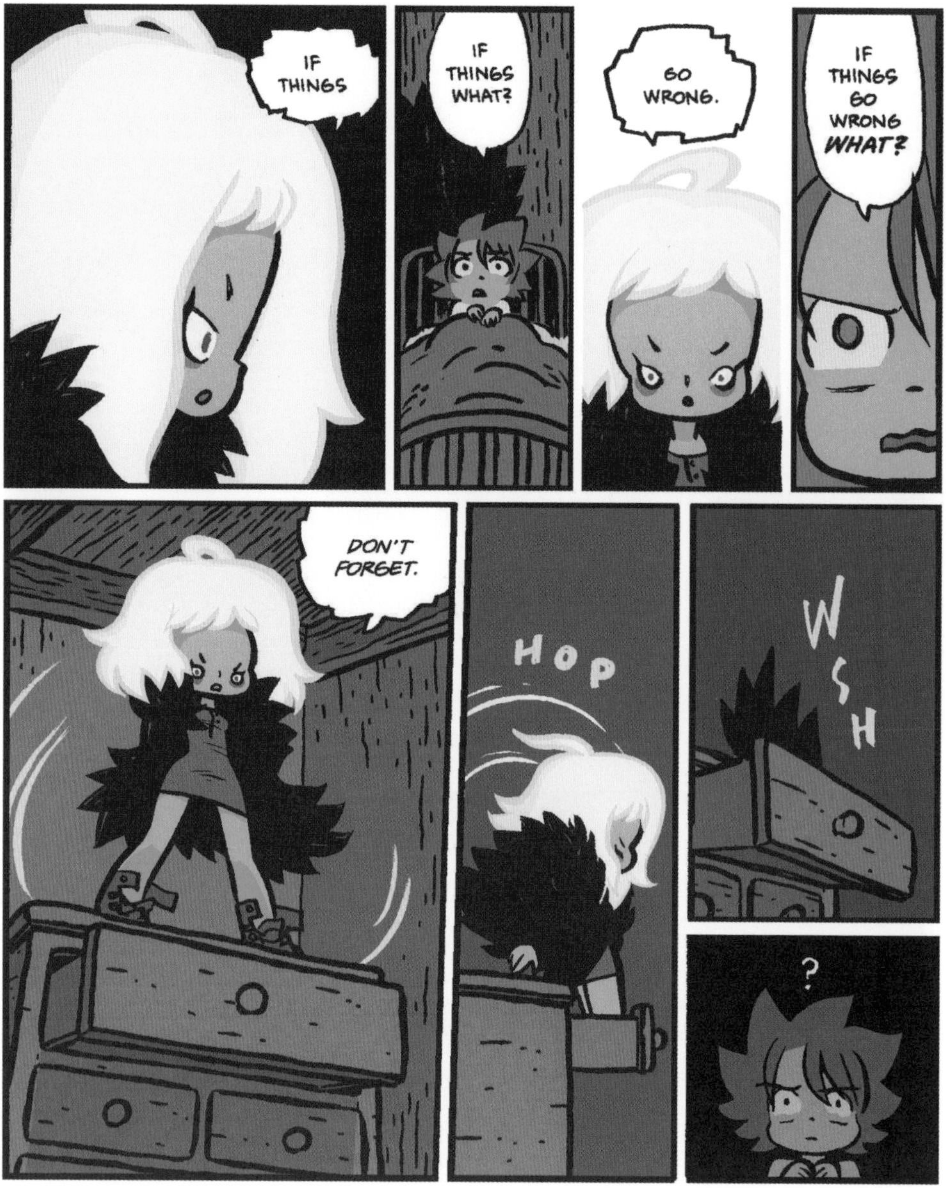
IF THINGS
IF THINGS WHAT?
GO WRONG.
IF THINGS GO WRONG WHAT?
DON'T FORGET.
HOP
WSH
?

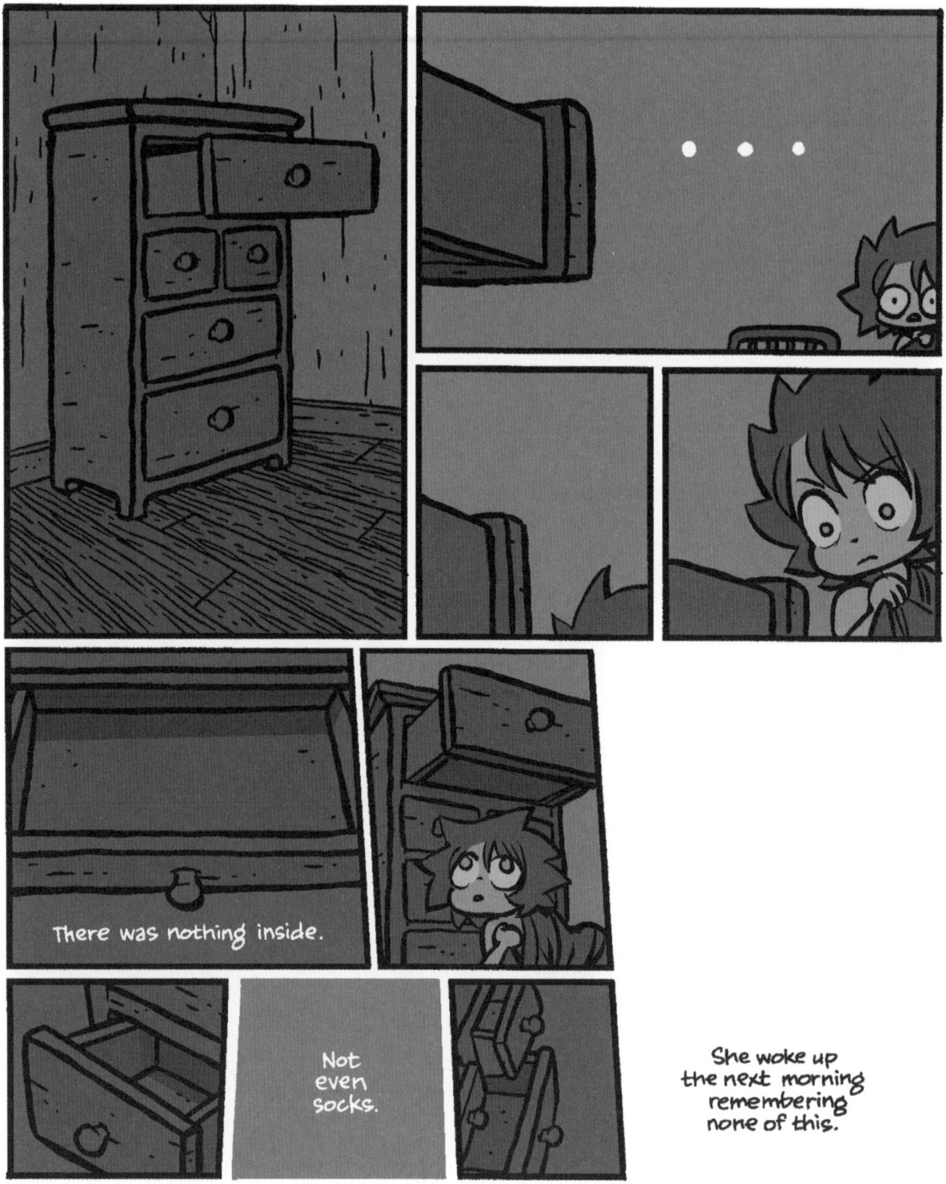
. . .
There was nothing inside.
Not even socks.
She woke up the next morning remembering none of this.

1

Katie

Katie was stressed out.
I'M PERFECTLY FINE.
She was sleeping too little, worrying too much, feeling old.
SHE WAS IN HER TWENTIES AND YOUNG AND TOTALLY GREAT.
At 29, she felt like everything was slipping away.
UM, NO.
...and she was talking to herself more than usual.

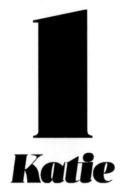

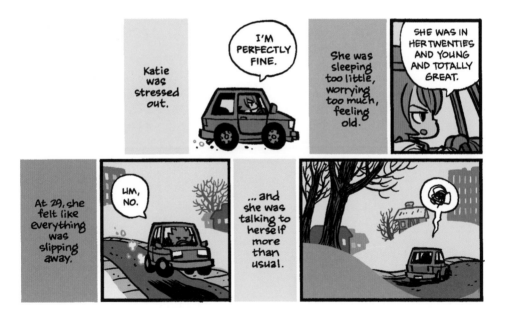

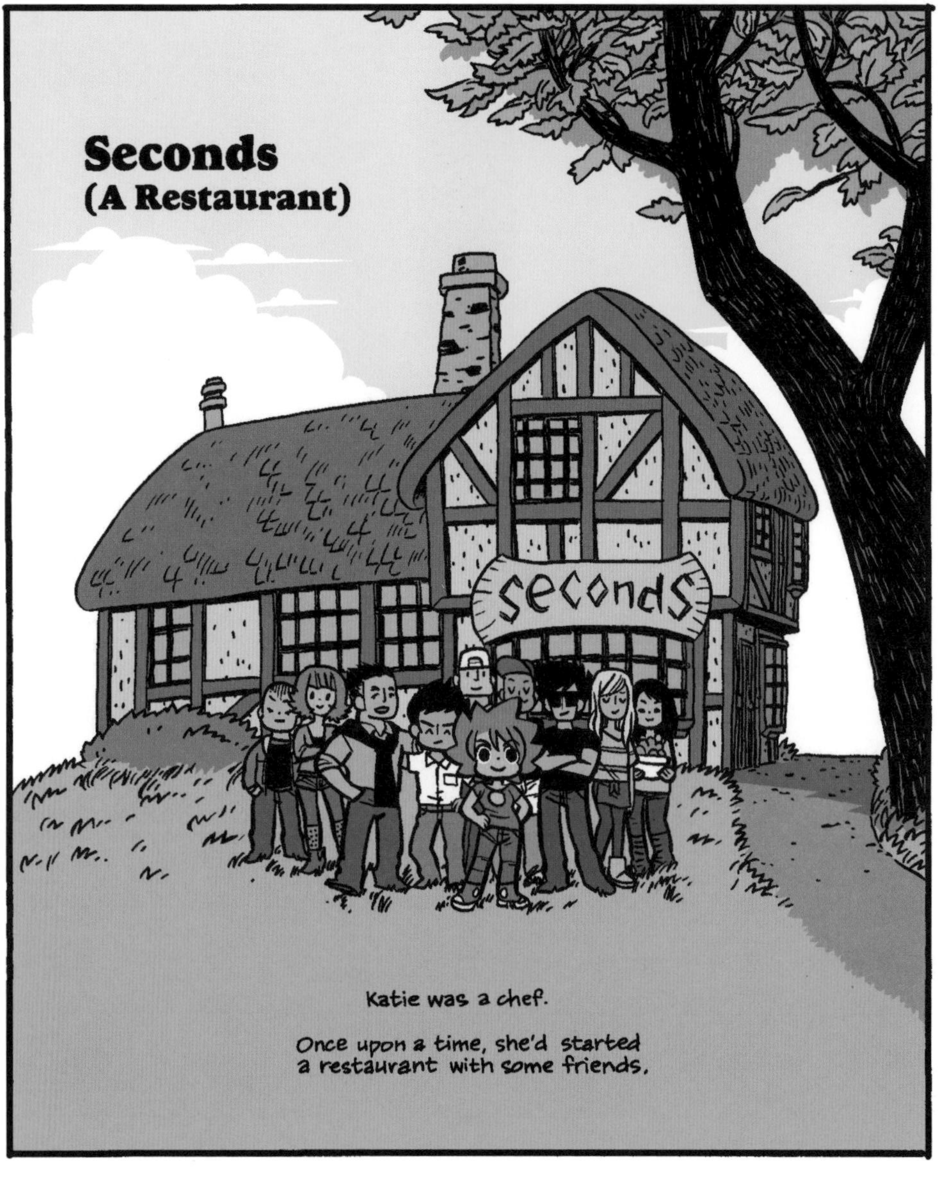
Seconds
(A Restaurant)
seconds
Katie was a chef.
Once upon a time, she'd started a restaurant with some friends.

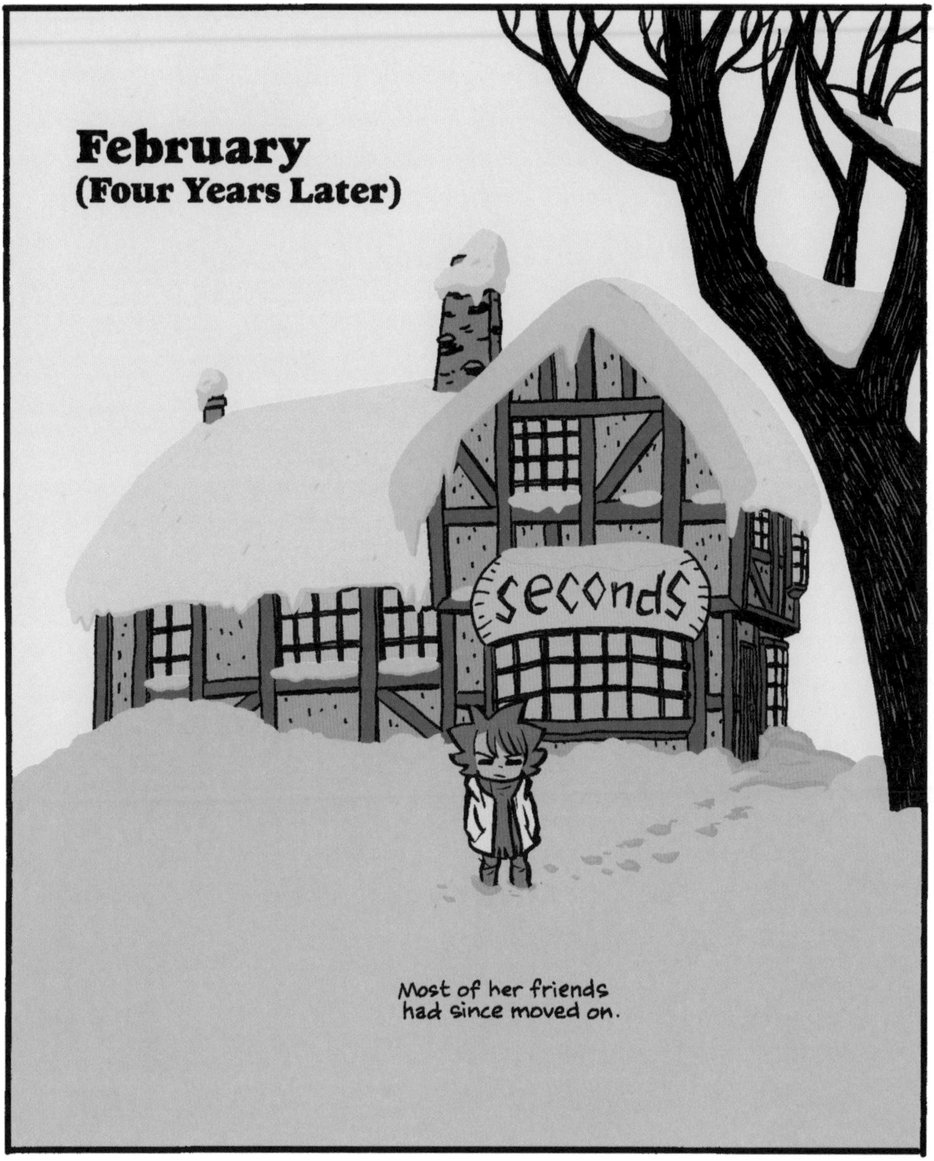
February
(Four Years Later)
seconds
Most of her friends had since moved on.

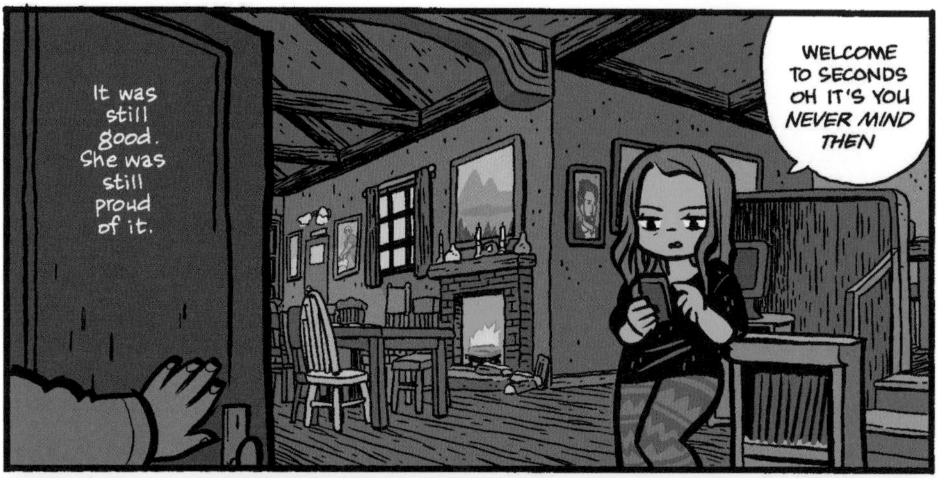
It was still good. She was still proud of it.
WELCOME TO SECONDS OH IT'S YOU NEVER MIND THEN

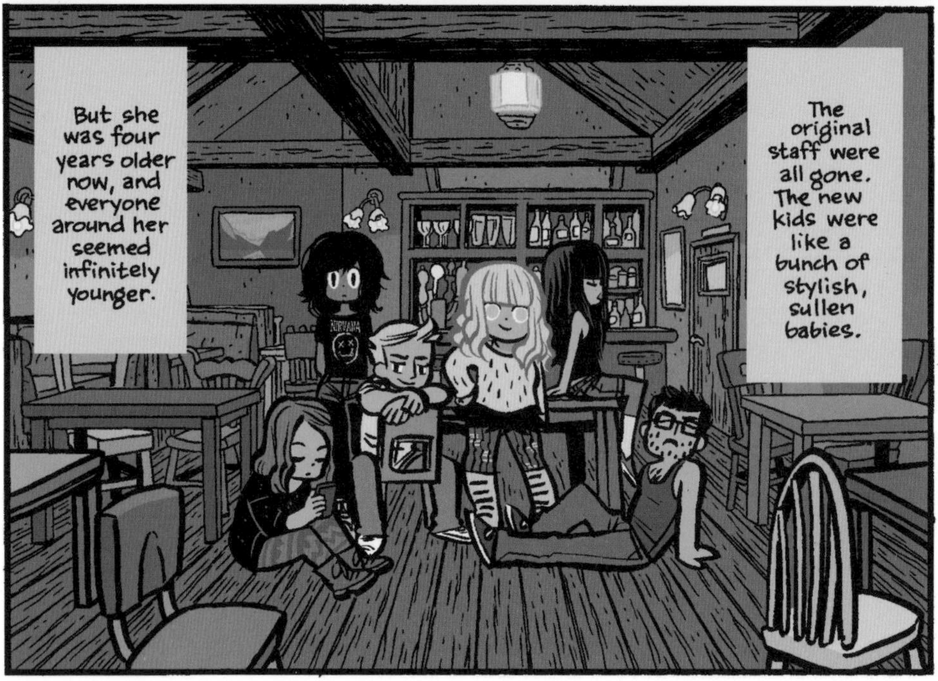
But she was four years older now, and everyone around her seemed infinitely younger.
The original staff were all gone. The new kids were like a bunch of stylish, sullen babies.
NIRVANA

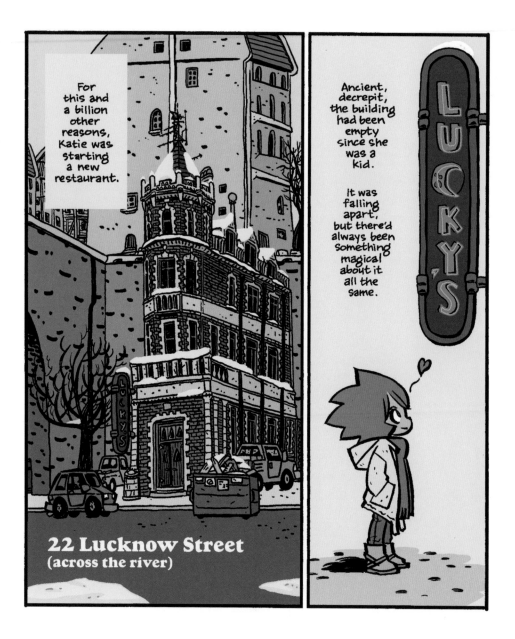

For this and a billion other reasons, Katie was starting a new restaurant.

Ancient, decrepit, the building had been empty since she was a kid.

It was falling apart, but there'd always been something magical about it all the same.

22 Lucknow Street
(across the river)

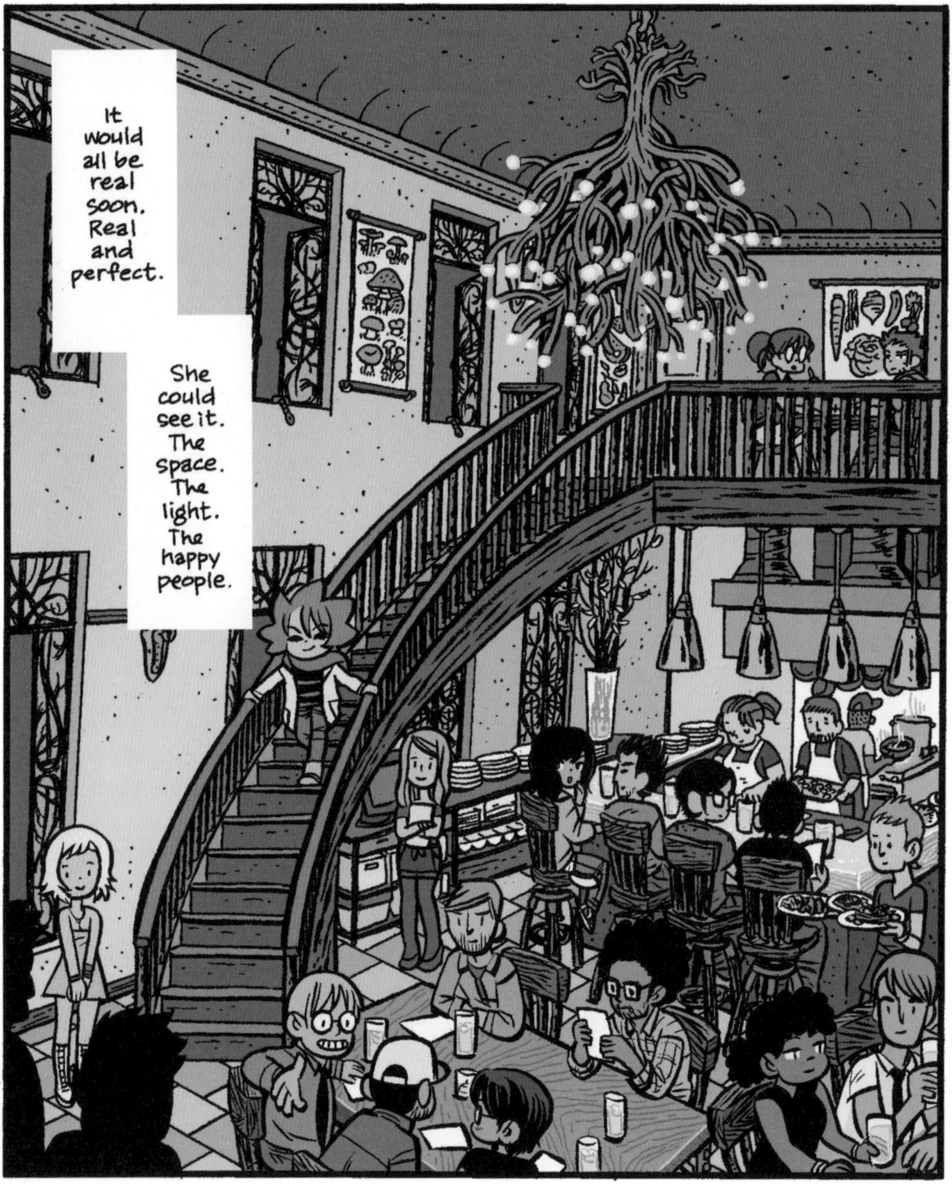
It would all be real soon. Real and perfect.
She could see it. The space. The light. The happy people.

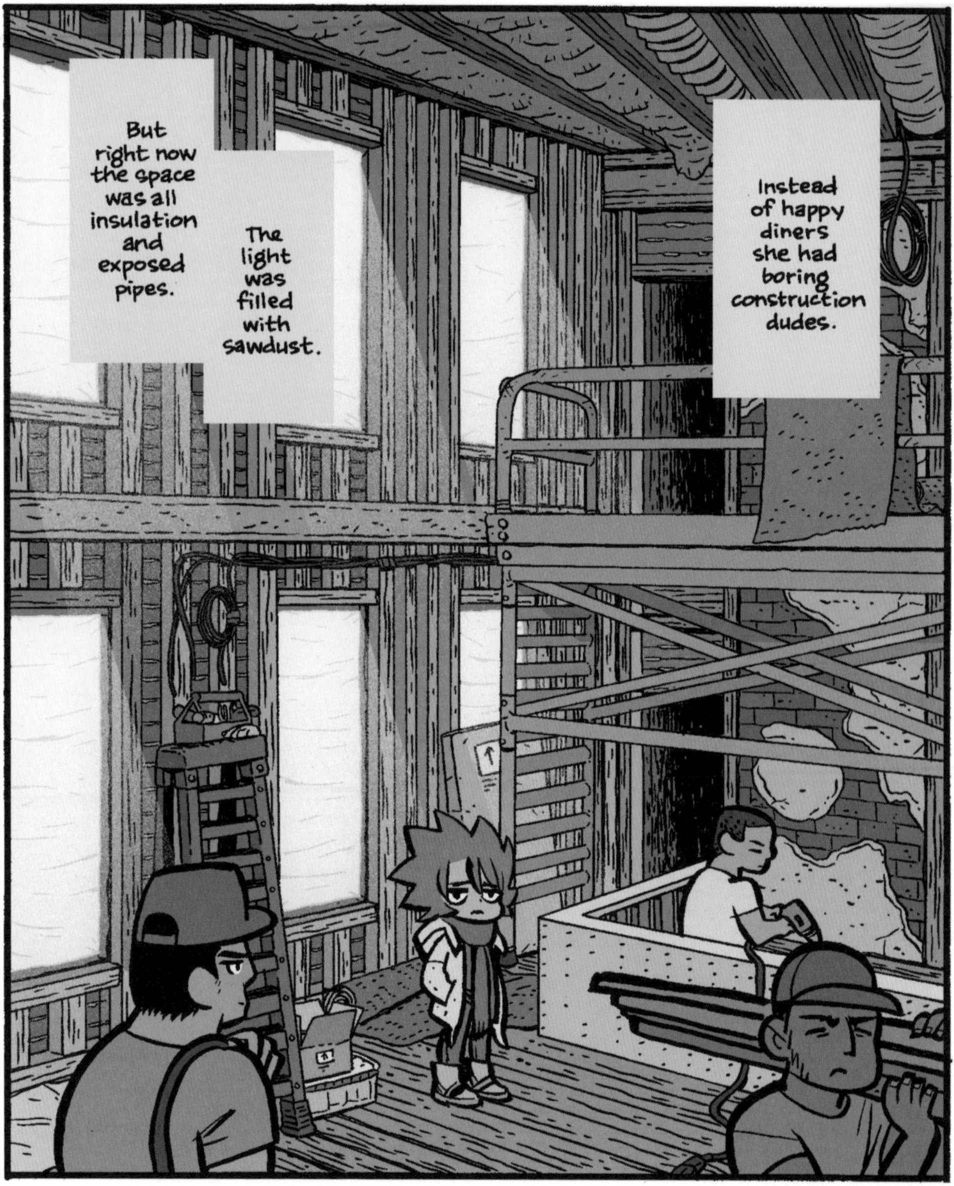
But right now the space was all insulation and exposed pipes.
The light was filled with sawdust.
Instead of happy diners she had boring construction dudes.

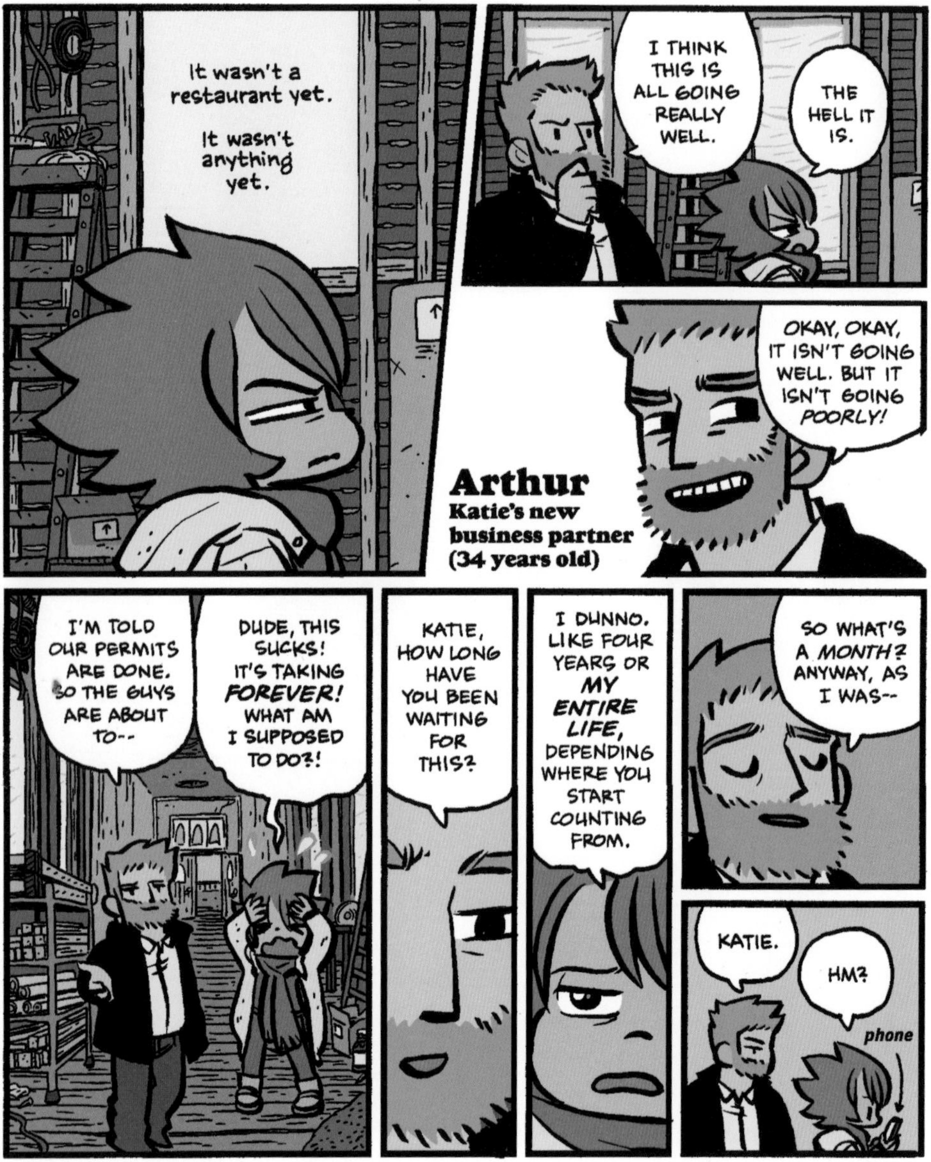
It wasn't a restaurant yet.
It wasn't anything yet.
I THINK THIS IS ALL GOING REALLY WELL.
THE HELL IT IS.
OKAY, OKAY, IT ISN'T GOING WELL. BUT IT ISN'T GOING POORLY!
Arthur
Katie's new business partner (34 years old)
I'M TOLD OUR PERMITS ARE DONE. SO THE GUYS ARE ABOUT TO--
DUDE, THIS SUCKS! IT'S TAKING FOREVER! WHAT AM I SUPPOSED TO DO?!
KATIE, HOW LONG HAVE YOU BEEN WAITING FOR THIS?
I DUNNO. LIKE FOUR YEARS OR MY ENTIRE LIFE, DEPENDING WHERE YOU START COUNTING FROM.
SO WHAT'S A MONTH? ANYWAY, AS I WAS--
KATIE.
HM?
phone

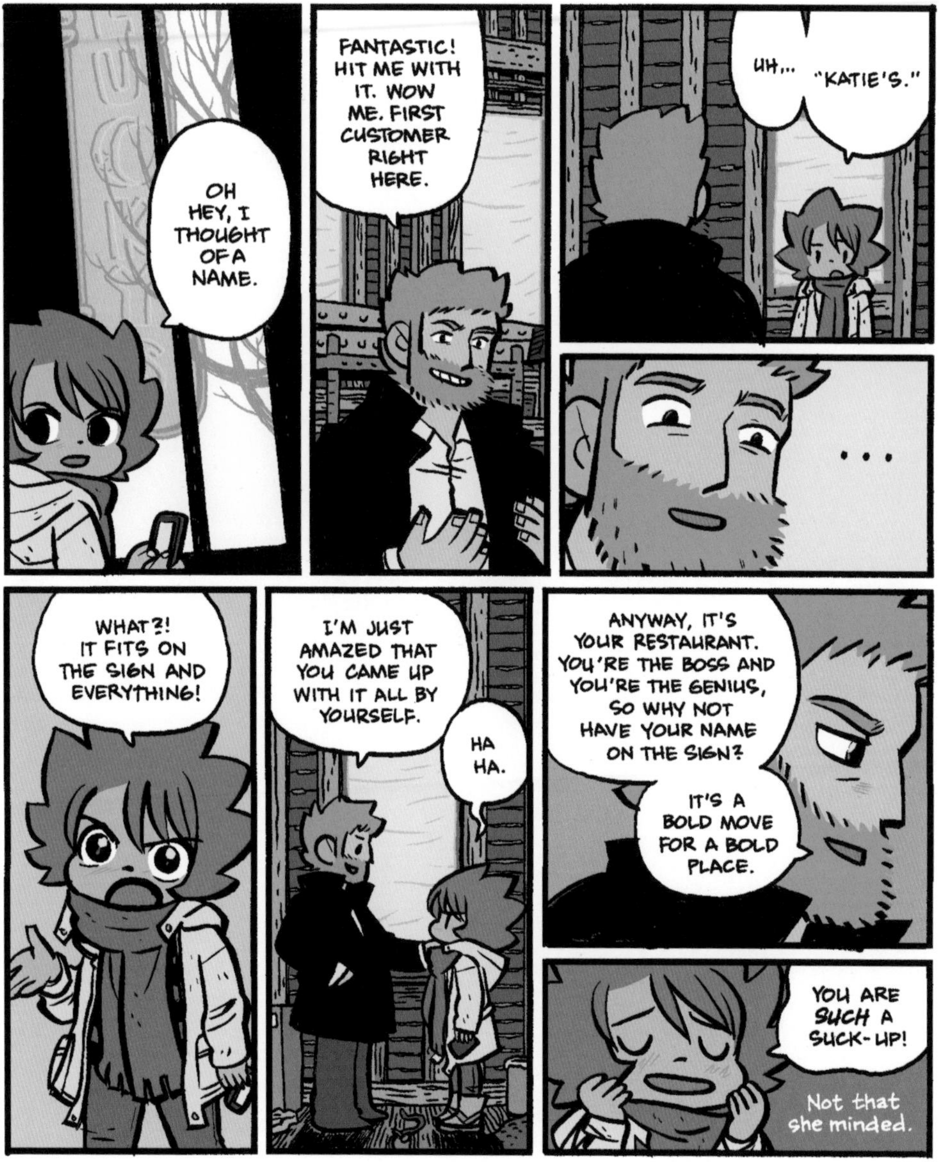
OH HEY, I THOUGHT OF A NAME.
FANTASTIC! HIT ME WITH IT. WOW ME. FIRST CUSTOMER RIGHT HERE.
UH...
"KATIE'S."
...
WHAT?! IT FITS ON THE SIGN AND EVERYTHING!
I'M JUST AMAZED THAT YOU CAME UP WITH IT ALL BY YOURSELF.
HA HA.
ANYWAY, IT'S YOUR RESTAURANT. YOU'RE THE BOSS AND YOU'RE THE GENIUS, SO WHY NOT HAVE YOUR NAME ON THE SIGN?
IT'S A BOLD MOVE FOR A BOLD PLACE.
YOU ARE SUCH A SUCK-UP!
Not that she minded.

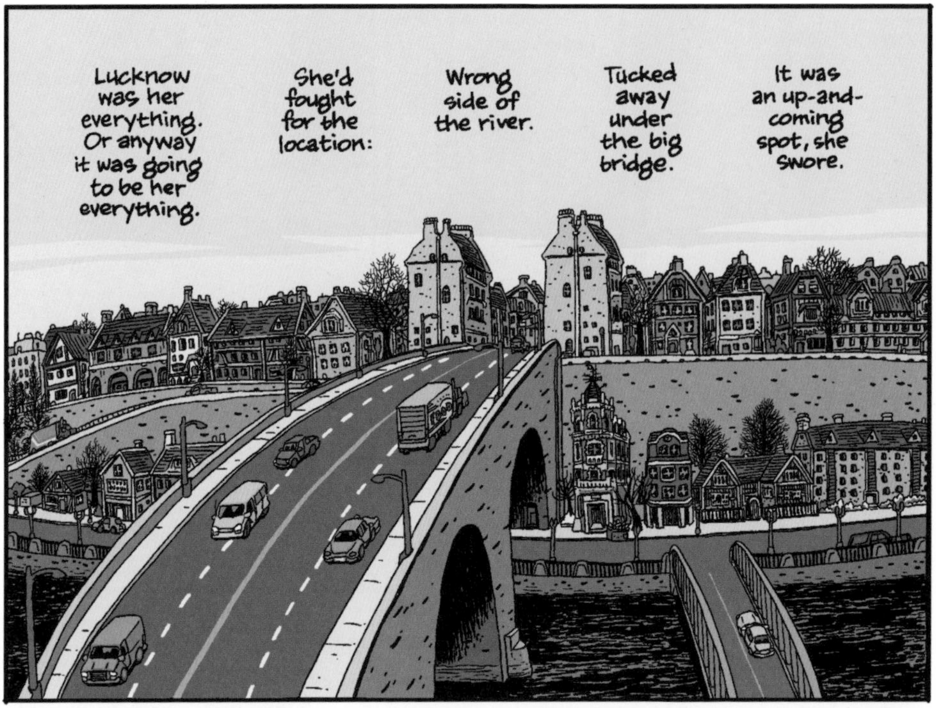
Lucknow was her everything. Or anyway it was going to be her everything.
She'd fought for the location:
Wrong side of the river.
Tucked away under the big bridge.
It was an up-and-coming spot, she swore.

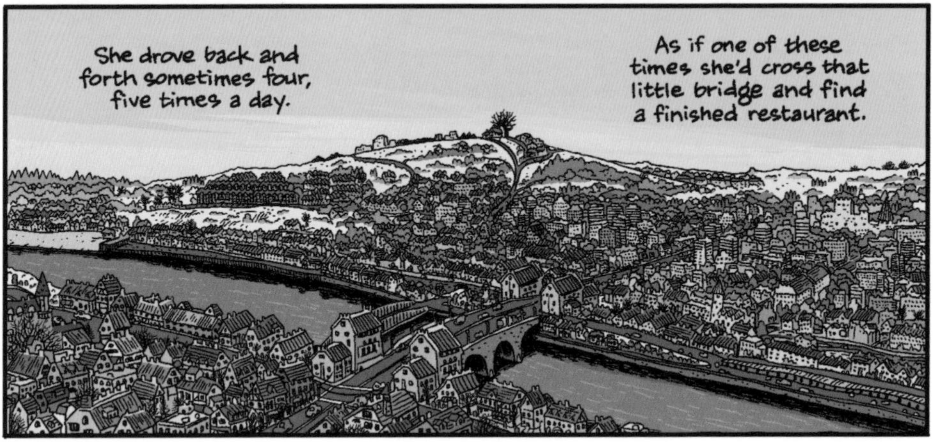
She drove back and forth sometimes four, five times a day.
As if one of these times she'd cross that little bridge and find a finished restaurant.

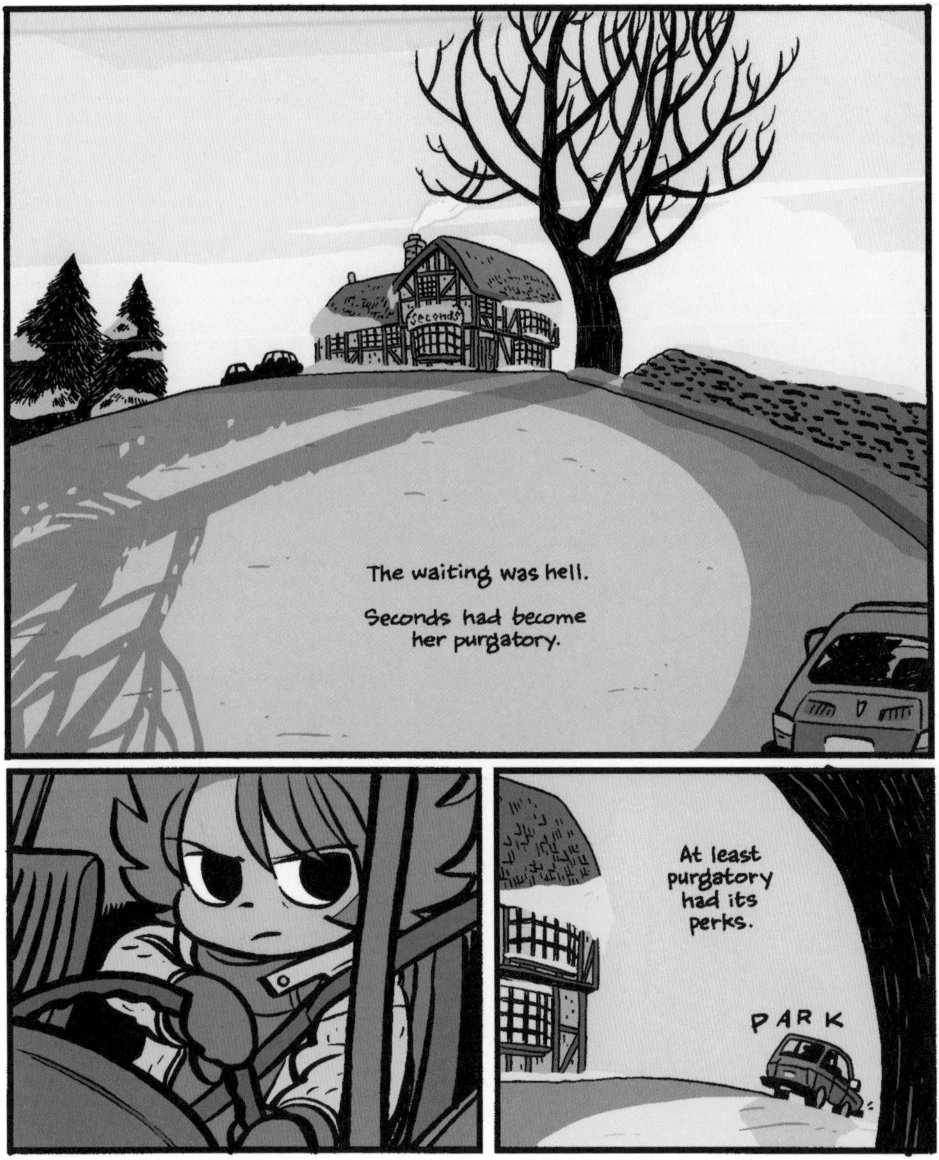

The waiting was hell.
Seconds had become her purgatory.
Seconds
At least purgatory had its perks.
PARK

Seconds was probably the most popular restaurant in town.

The food was beloved.

The food was the star here.

And the food was Katie's...

...so Katie was pretty much the star here.

seconds

Executive Chef
Katie Clay

1. sous vide top sirloin
   + foraged green leaves
   + birch ash vinaigrette

2. smoked cornish hen
   + buttermilk mashed tub
   + whipped pork fat
   + pickled asparagus

   roasted spaghetti
   ch + blistered
   tomato

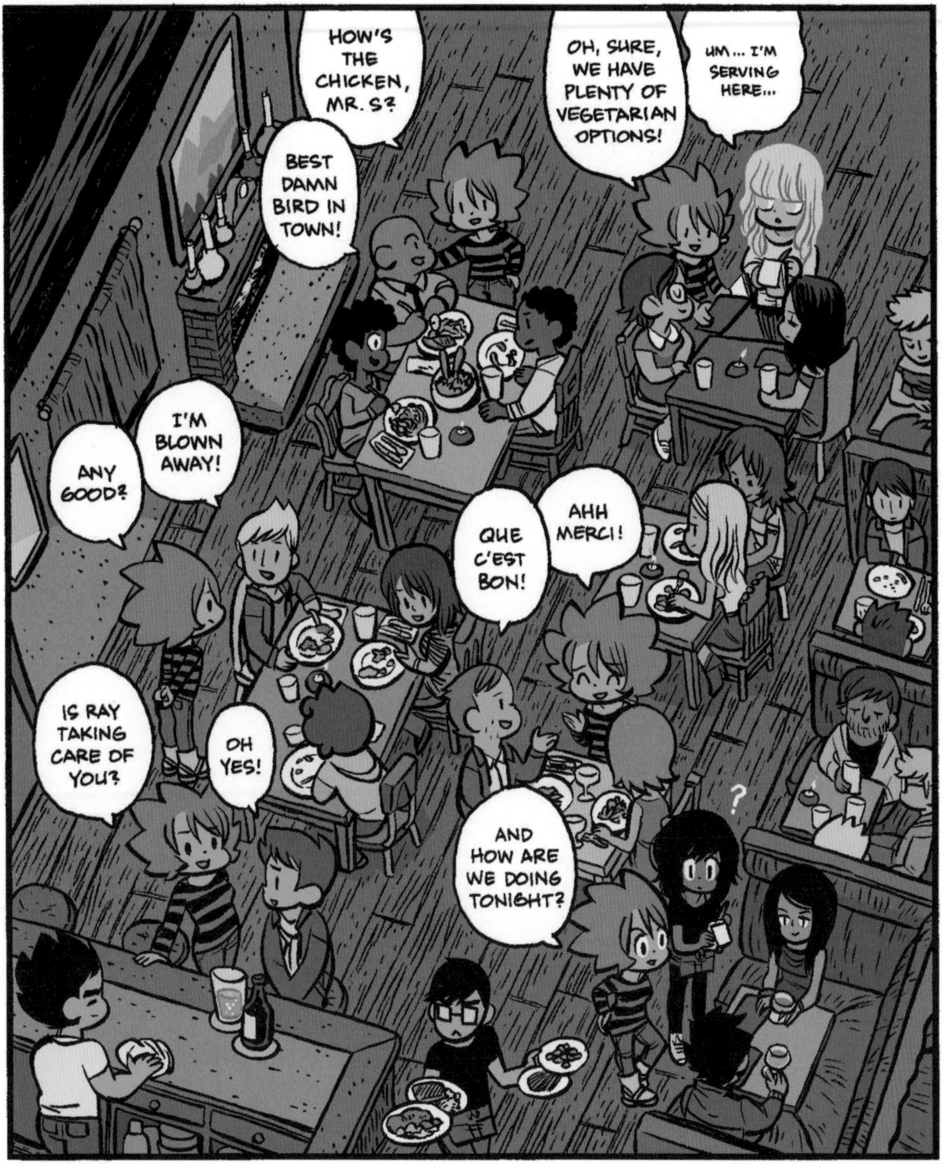
HOW'S THE CHICKEN, MR. S?
BEST DAMN BIRD IN TOWN!
OH, SURE, WE HAVE PLENTY OF VEGETARIAN OPTIONS!
UM... I'M SERVING HERE...
ANY GOOD?
I'M BLOWN AWAY!
QUE C'EST BON!
AHH MERCI!
IS RAY TAKING CARE OF YOU?
OH YES!
AND HOW ARE WE DOING TONIGHT?
?

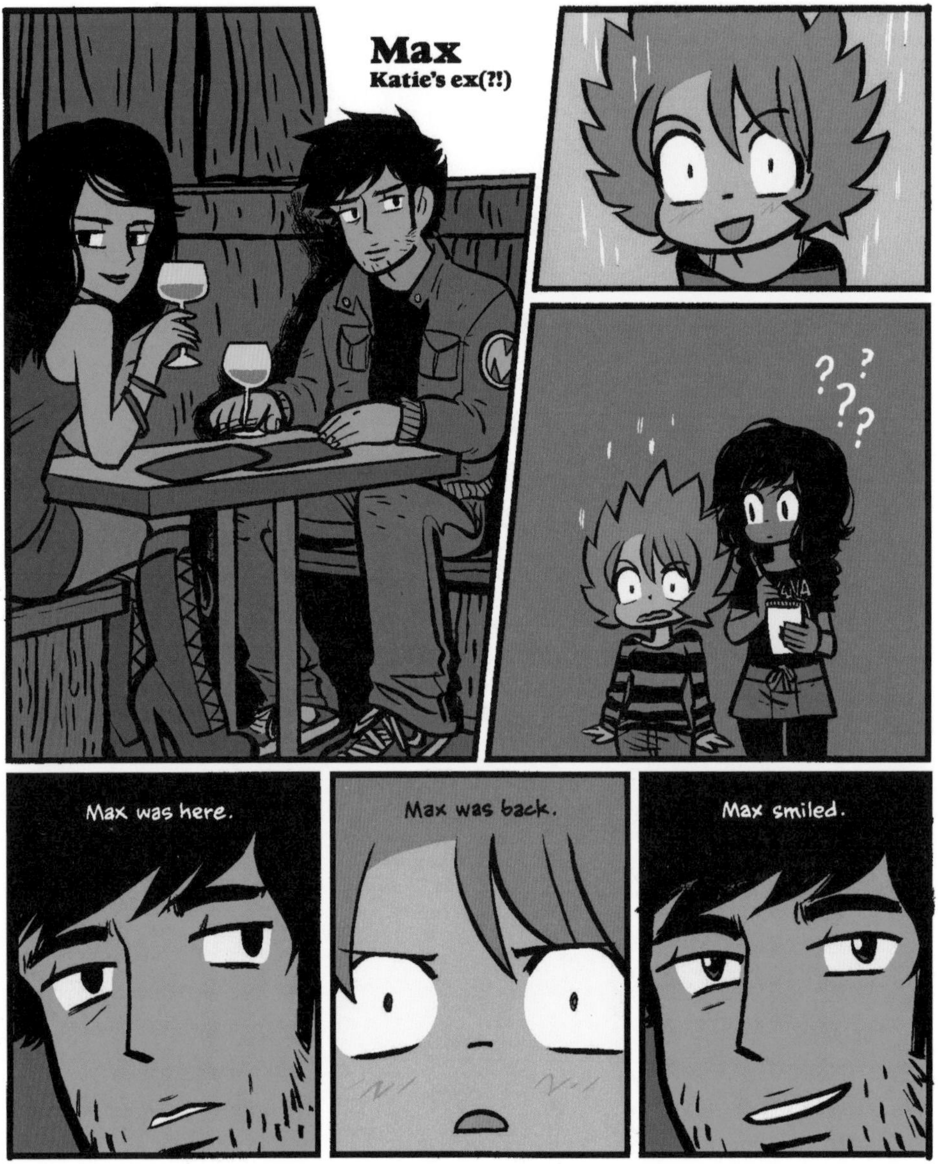
Max
Katie's ex(?!)
???
??
Max was here.
Max was back.
Max smiled.

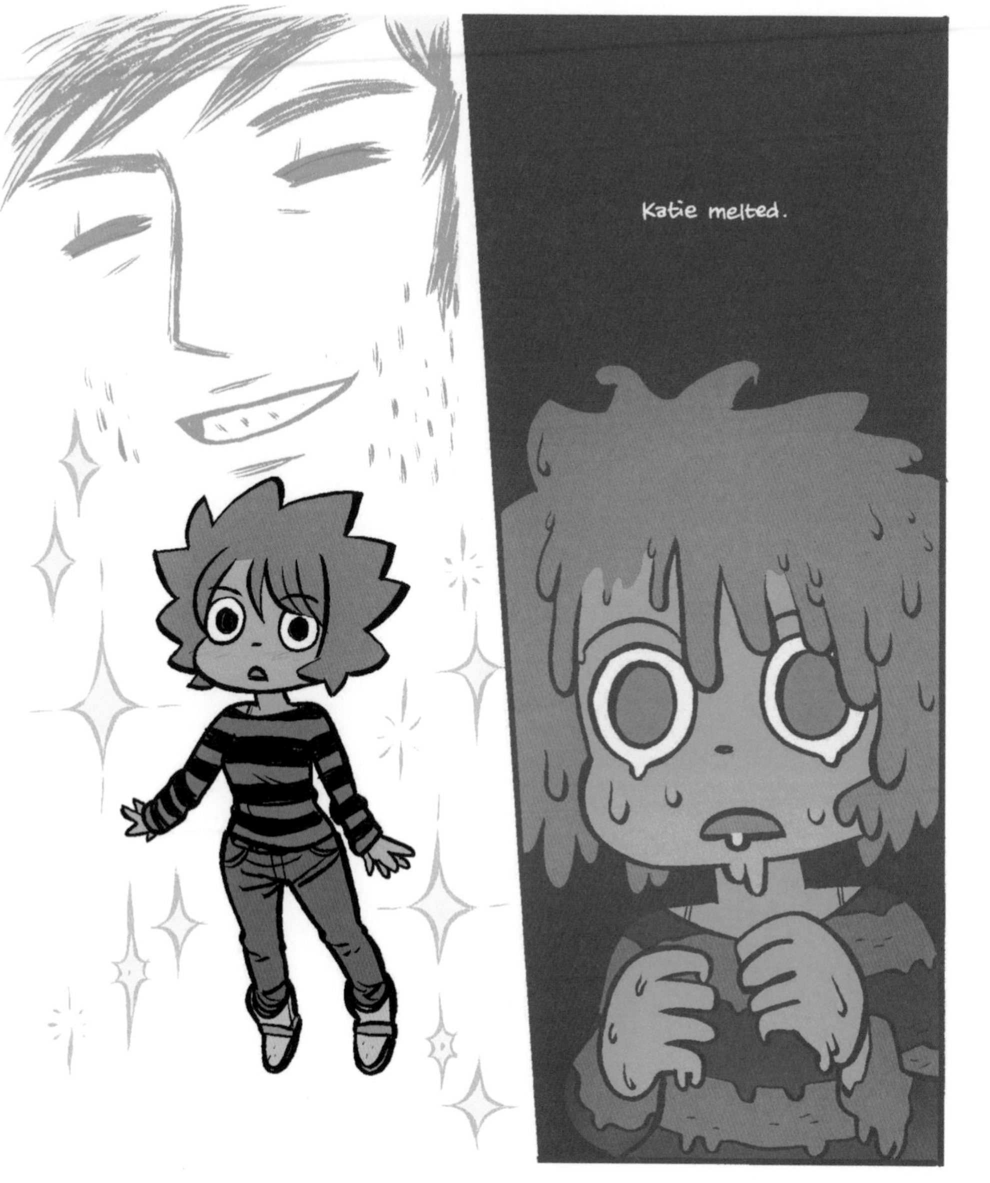
Katie melted.

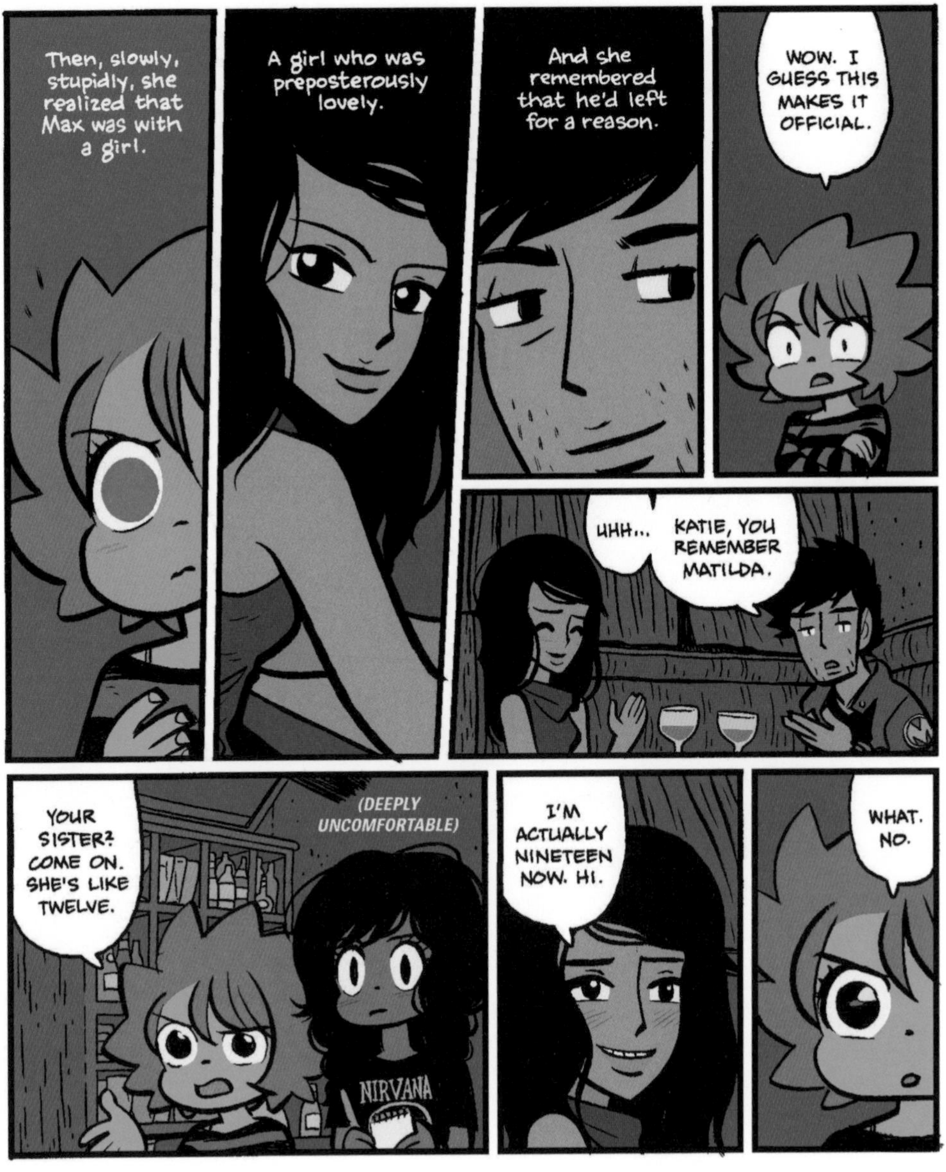
Then, slowly, stupidly, she realized that Max was with a girl.
A girl who was preposterously lovely.
And she remembered that he'd left for a reason.
WOW. I GUESS THIS MAKES IT OFFICIAL.
UHH...
KATIE, YOU REMEMBER MATILDA.
YOUR SISTER? COME ON. SHE'S LIKE TWELVE.
(DEEPLY UNCOMFORTABLE)
NIRVANA
I'M ACTUALLY NINETEEN NOW. HI.
WHAT. NO.

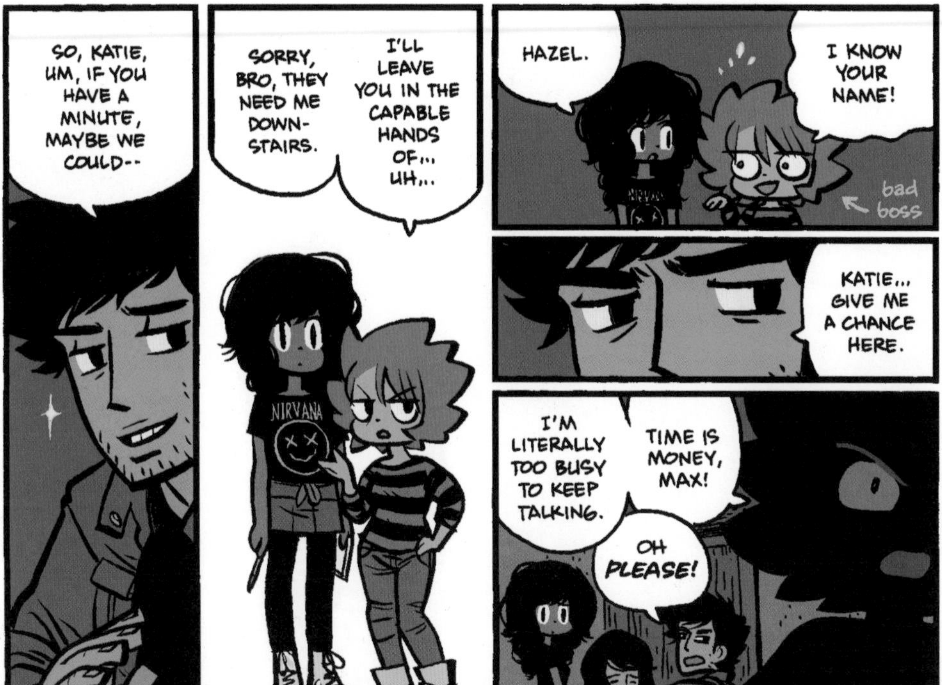
SO, KATIE, UM, IF YOU HAVE A MINUTE, MAYBE WE COULD--
SORRY, BRO, THEY NEED ME DOWN-STAIRS.
I'LL LEAVE YOU IN THE CAPABLE HANDS OF... UH...
NIRVANA
HAZEL.
I KNOW YOUR NAME!
NIRVANA
bad boss
KATIE... GIVE ME A CHANCE HERE.
I'M LITERALLY TOO BUSY TO KEEP TALKING.
TIME IS MONEY, MAX!
OH PLEASE!
Katie was an idiot.
WHAT? NO. THAT WAS SO SMOOTH.
Was that really his sister?
Had so much time passed?
WHO EVEN CARES? NOT ME.

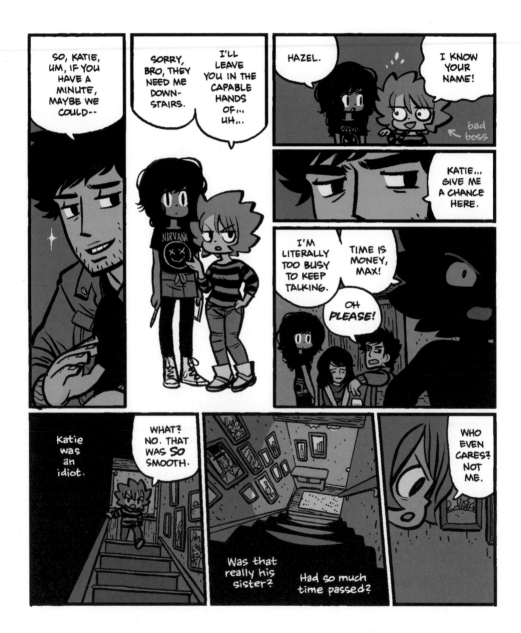

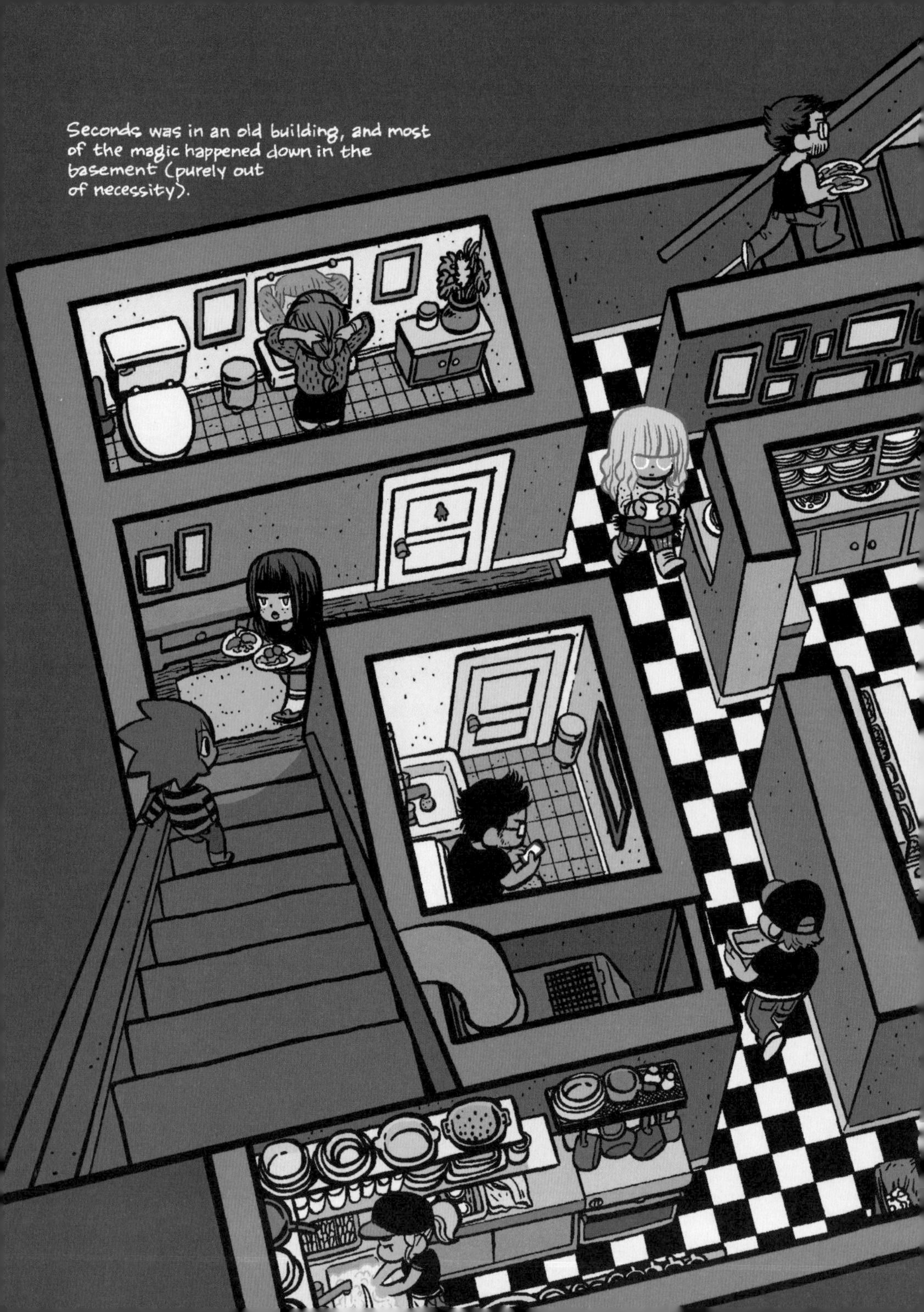
Seconds was in an old building, and most of the magic happened down in the basement (purely out of necessity).

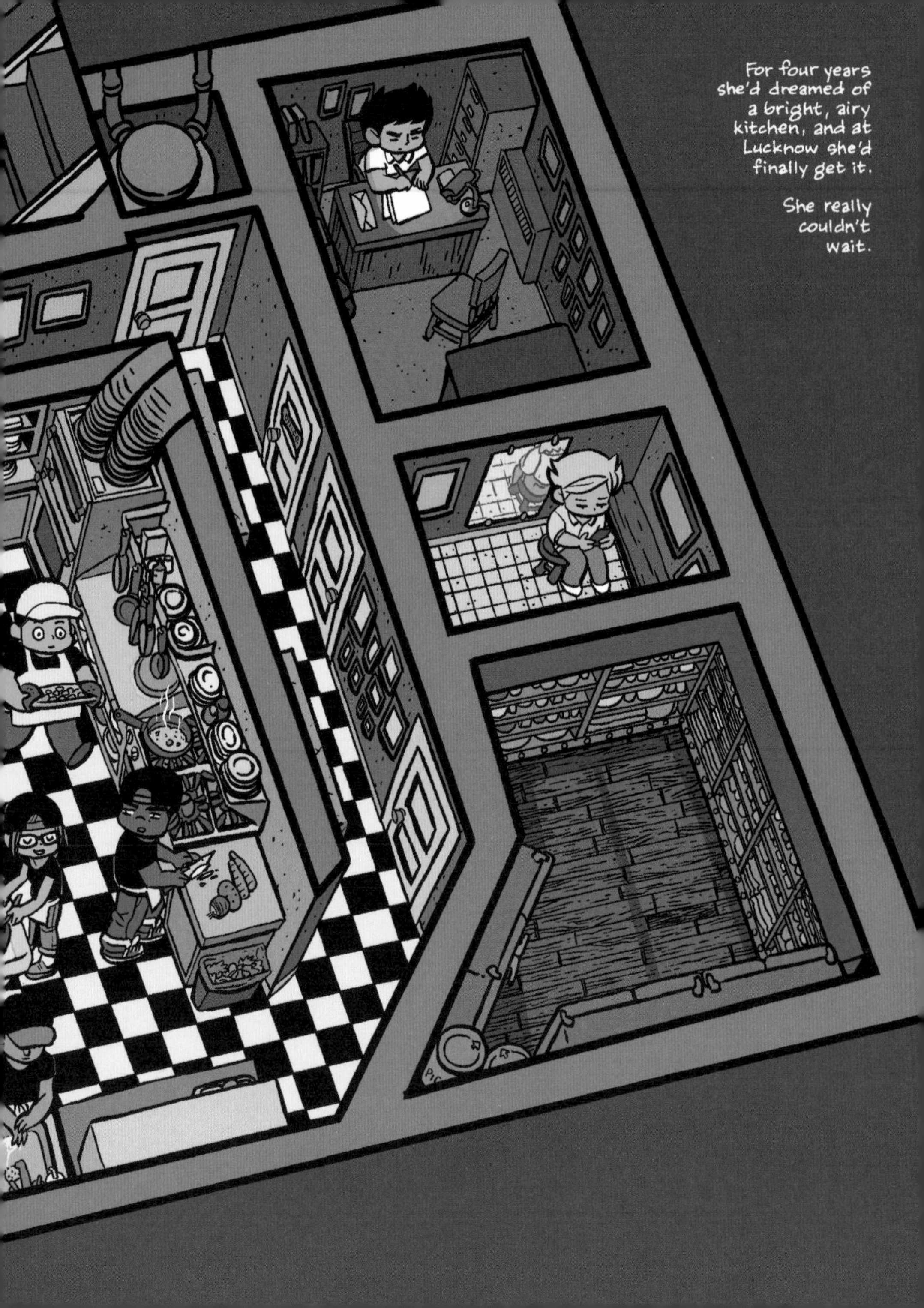
For four years she'd dreamed of a bright, airy kitchen, and at Lucknow she'd finally get it.
She really couldn't wait.

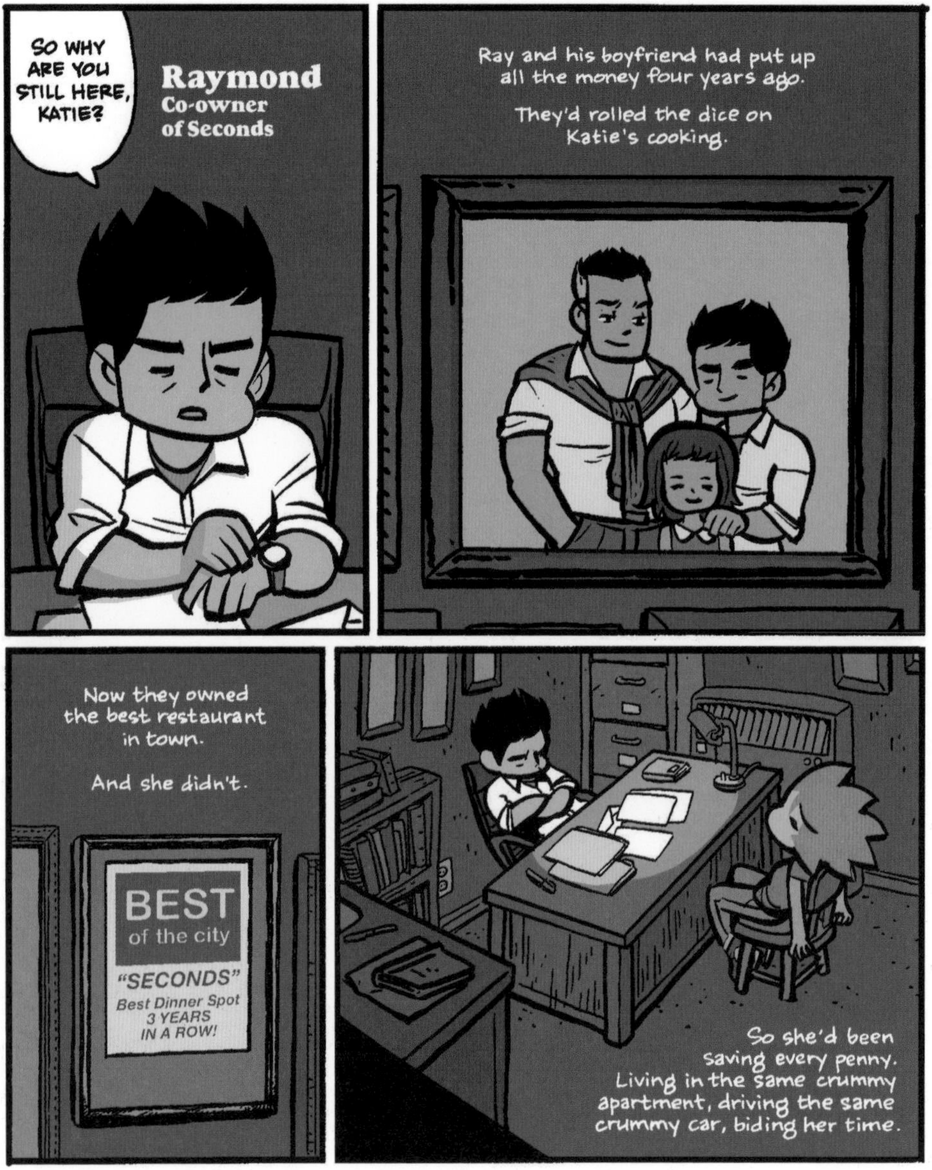
SO WHY ARE YOU STILL HERE, KATIE?
Raymond
Co-owner of Seconds
Ray and his boyfriend had put up all the money four years ago.
They'd rolled the dice on Katie's cooking.
Now they owned the best restaurant in town.
And she didn't.
BEST of the city
"SECONDS"
Best Dinner Spot 3 YEARS IN A ROW!
So she'd been saving every penny. Living in the same crummy apartment, driving the same crummy car, biding her time.

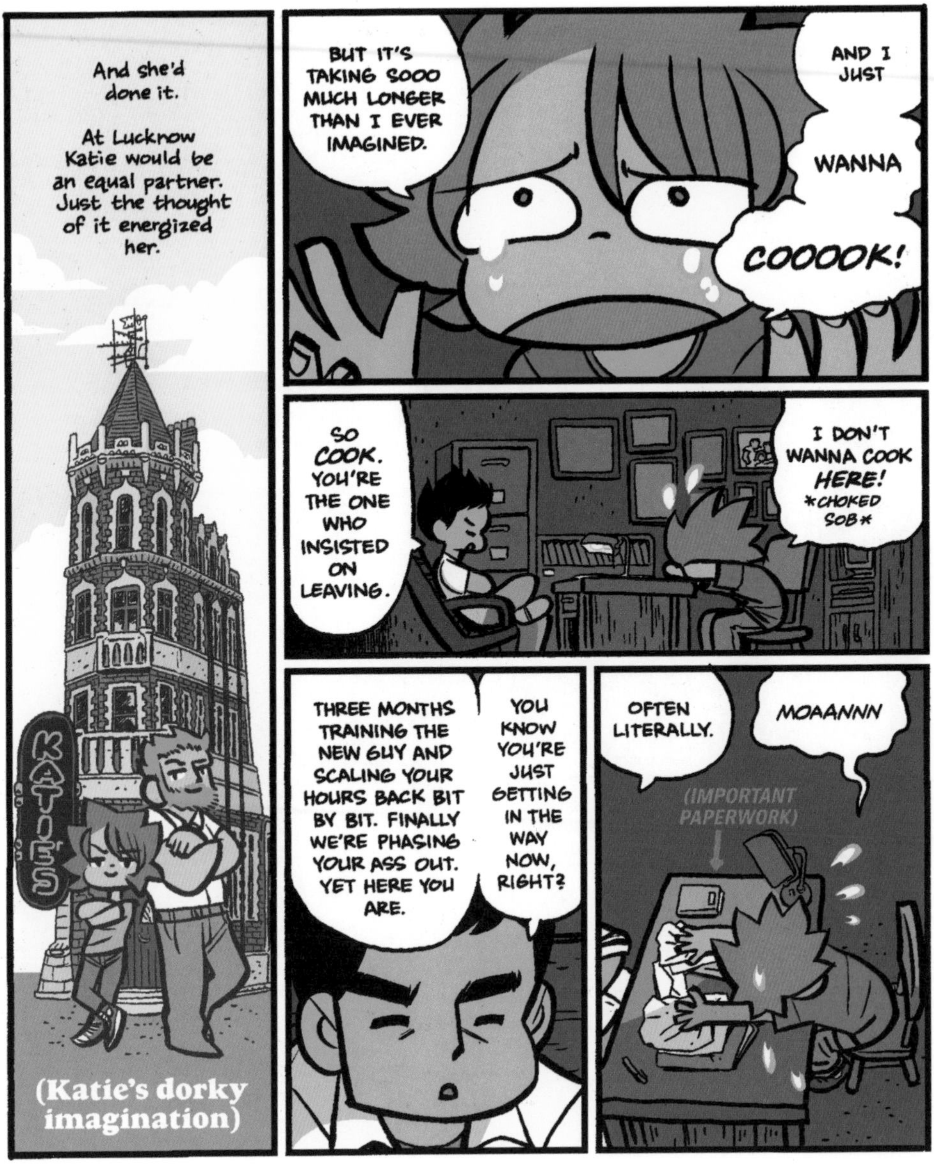
And she'd done it.
At Lucknow Katie would be an equal partner. Just the thought of it energized her.
KATIES
(Katie's dorky imagination)
BUT IT'S TAKING SOOO MUCH LONGER THAN I EVER IMAGINED.
AND I JUST
WANNA
COOOOK!
SO COOK. YOU'RE THE ONE WHO INSISTED ON LEAVING.
I DON'T WANNA COOK HERE! *CHOKED SOB*
THREE MONTHS TRAINING THE NEW GUY AND SCALING YOUR HOURS BACK BIT BY BIT. FINALLY WE'RE PHASING YOUR ASS OUT. YET HERE YOU ARE.
YOU KNOW YOU'RE JUST GETTING IN THE WAY NOW, RIGHT?
OFTEN LITERALLY.
MOAANNN
(IMPORTANT PAPERWORK)

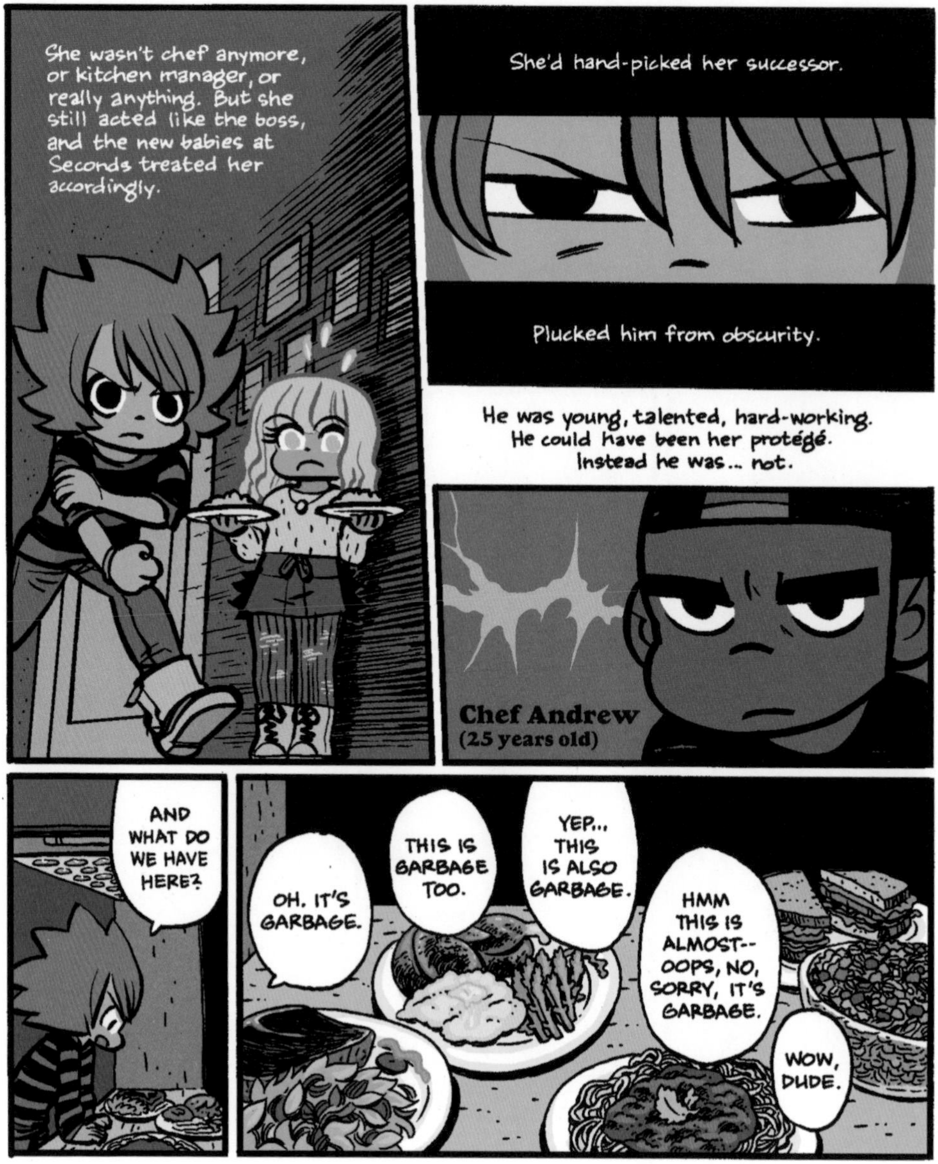
She wasn't chef anymore, or kitchen manager, or really anything. But she still acted like the boss, and the new babies at Seconds treated her accordingly.
She'd hand-picked her successor.
Plucked him from obscurity.
He was young, talented, hard-working. He could have been her protégé. Instead he was... not.
Chef Andrew
(25 years old)
AND WHAT DO WE HAVE HERE?
OH. IT'S GARBAGE.
THIS IS GARBAGE TOO.
YEP... THIS IS ALSO GARBAGE.
HMM THIS IS ALMOST-- OOPS, NO, SORRY, IT'S GARBAGE.
WOW, DUDE.

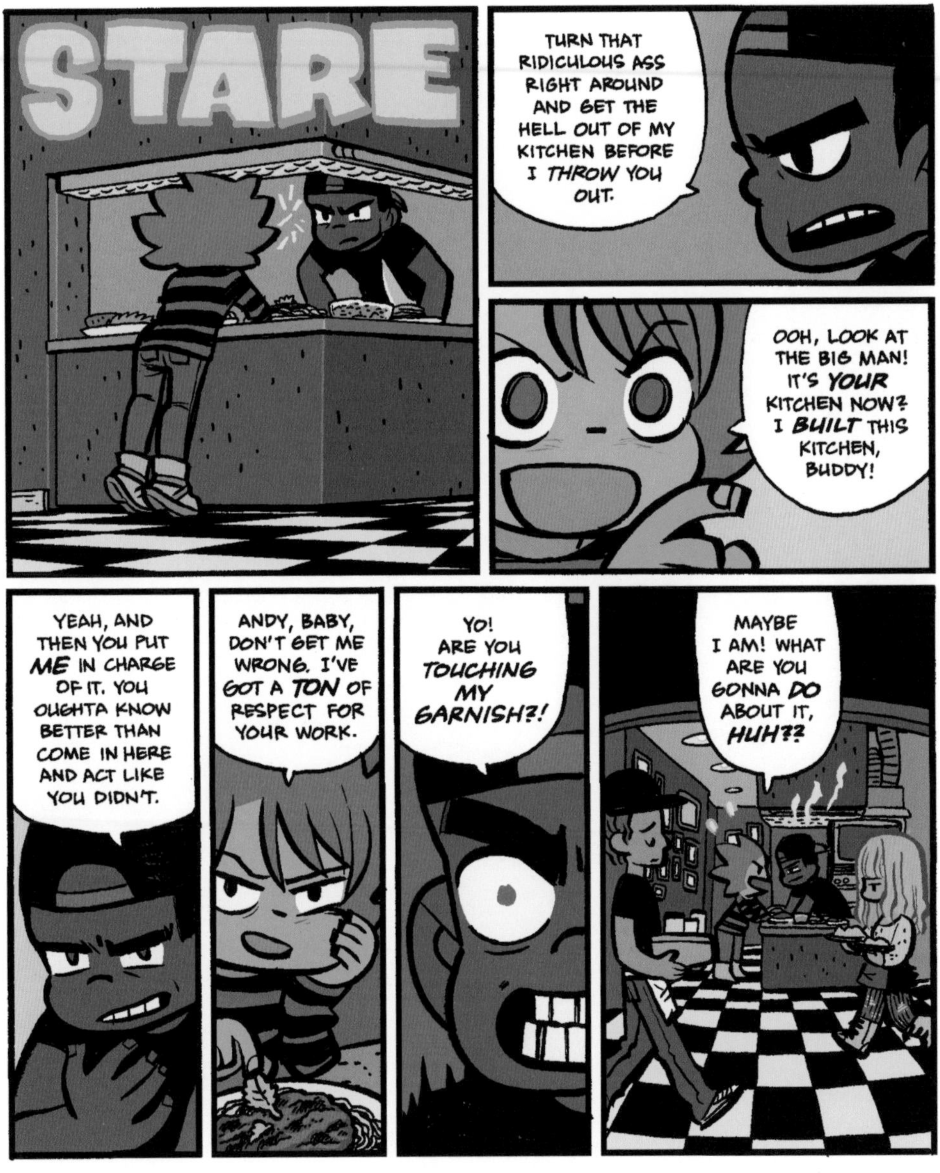
STARE
TURN THAT RIDICULOUS ASS RIGHT AROUND AND GET THE HELL OUT OF MY KITCHEN BEFORE I THROW YOU OUT.
OOH, LOOK AT THE BIG MAN! IT'S YOUR KITCHEN NOW? I BUILT THIS KITCHEN, BUDDY!
YEAH, AND THEN YOU PUT ME IN CHARGE OF IT. YOU OUGHTA KNOW BETTER THAN COME IN HERE AND ACT LIKE YOU DIDN'T.
ANDY, BABY, DON'T GET ME WRONG. I'VE GOT A TON OF RESPECT FOR YOUR WORK.
YO! ARE YOU TOUCHING MY GARNISH?!
MAYBE I AM! WHAT ARE YOU GONNA DO ABOUT IT, HUH??

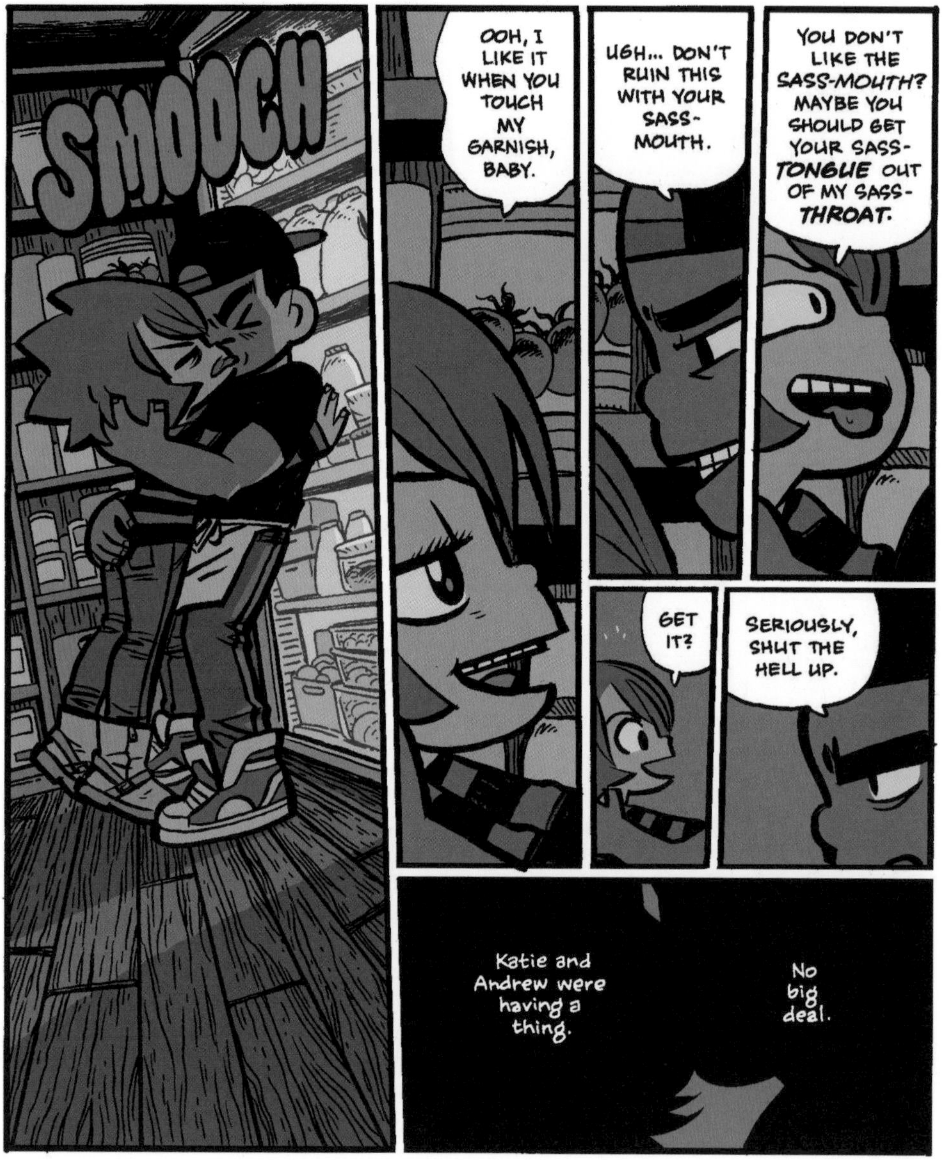
SMOOCH
OOH, I LIKE IT WHEN YOU TOUCH MY GARNISH, BABY.
UGH... DON'T RUIN THIS WITH YOUR SASS-MOUTH.
YOU DON'T LIKE THE SASS-MOUTH? MAYBE YOU SHOULD GET YOUR SASS-TONGUE OUT OF MY SASS-THROAT.
GET IT?
SERIOUSLY, SHUT THE HELL UP.
Katie and Andrew were having a thing.
No big deal.

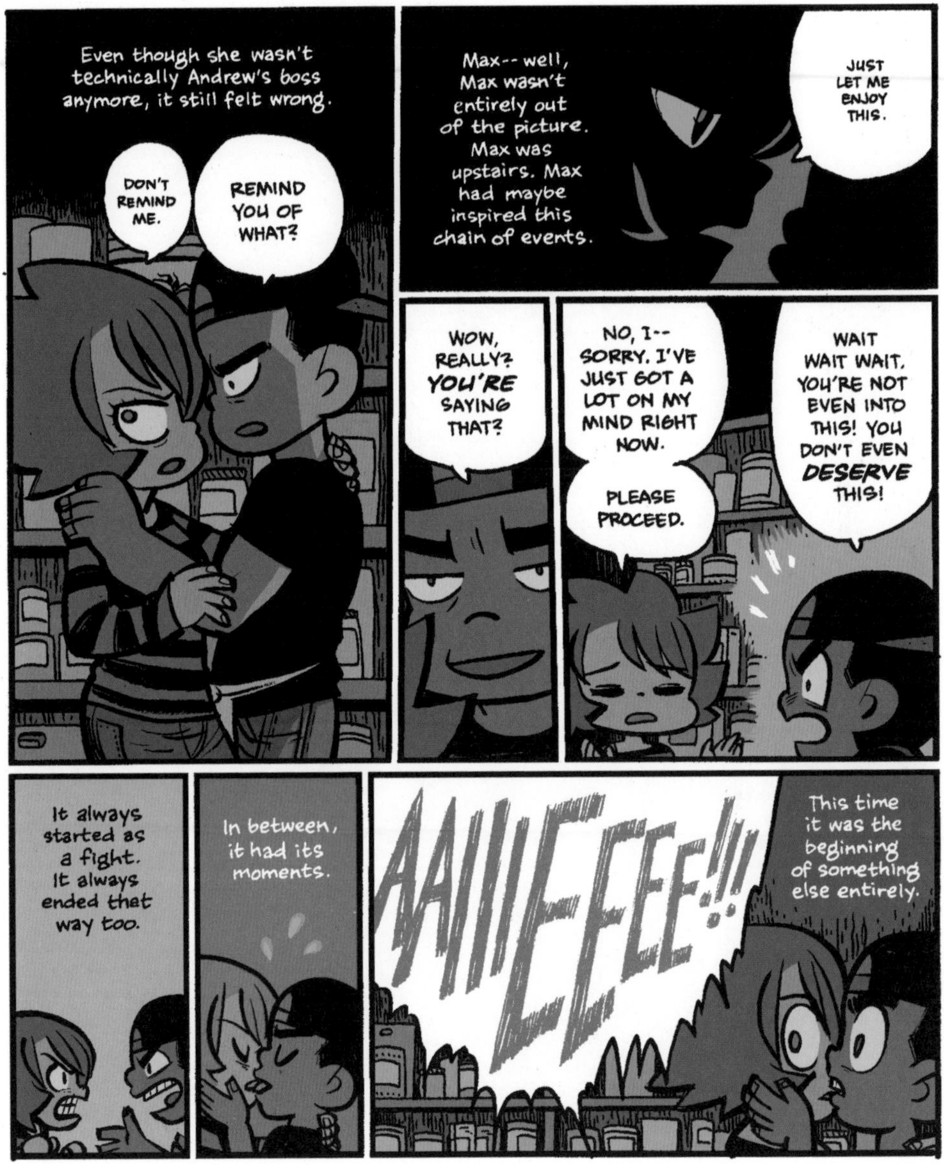
Even though she wasn't technically Andrew's boss anymore, it still felt wrong.
DON'T REMIND ME.
REMIND YOU OF WHAT?
Max-- well, Max wasn't entirely out of the picture. Max was upstairs. Max had maybe inspired this chain of events.
JUST LET ME ENJOY THIS.
WOW, REALLY? YOU'RE SAYING THAT?
NO, I-- SORRY. I'VE JUST GOT A LOT ON MY MIND RIGHT NOW.
PLEASE PROCEED.
WAIT WAIT WAIT. YOU'RE NOT EVEN INTO THIS! YOU DON'T EVEN DESERVE THIS!
It always started as a fight. It always ended that way too.
In between, it had its moments.
AAIIIEEEE!!!
This time it was the beginning of something else entirely.

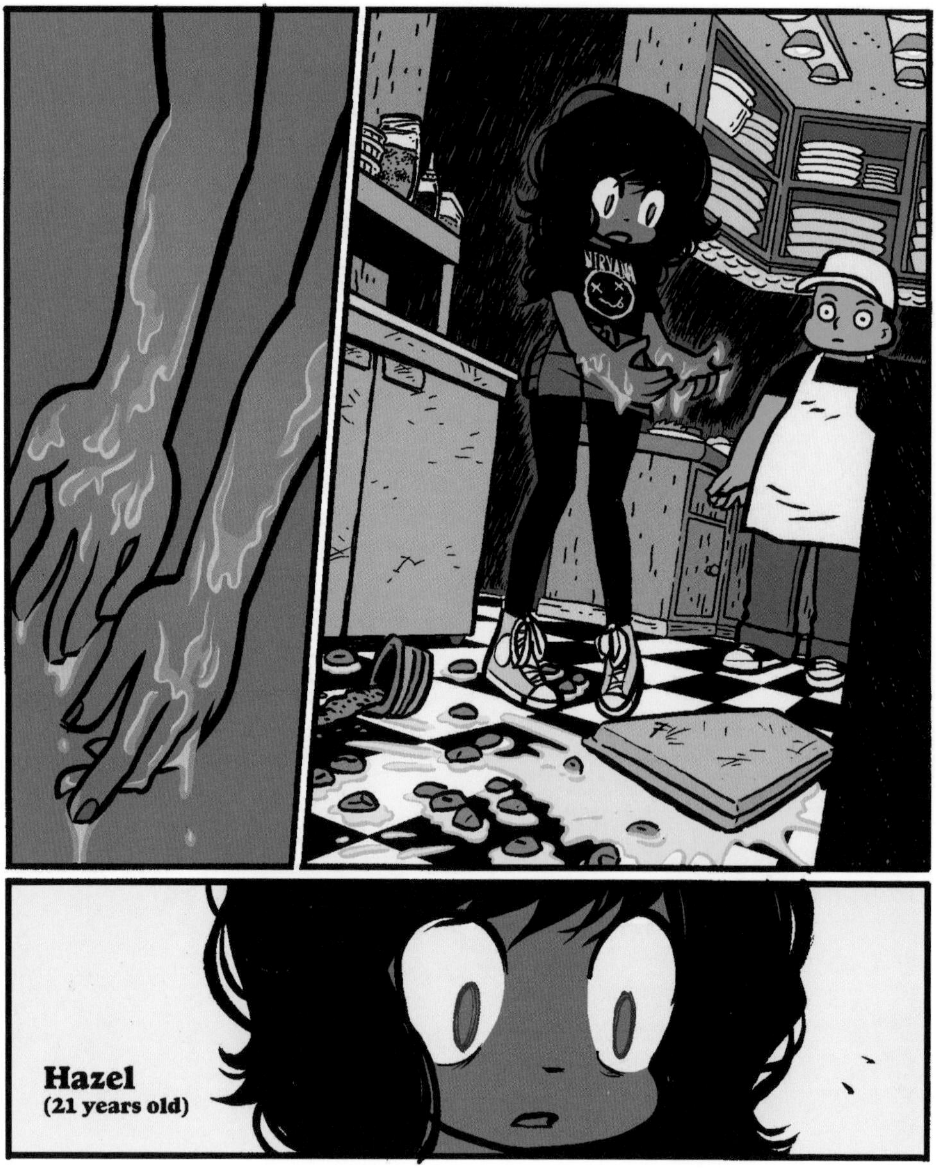
NIRVANA
Hazel
(21 years old)

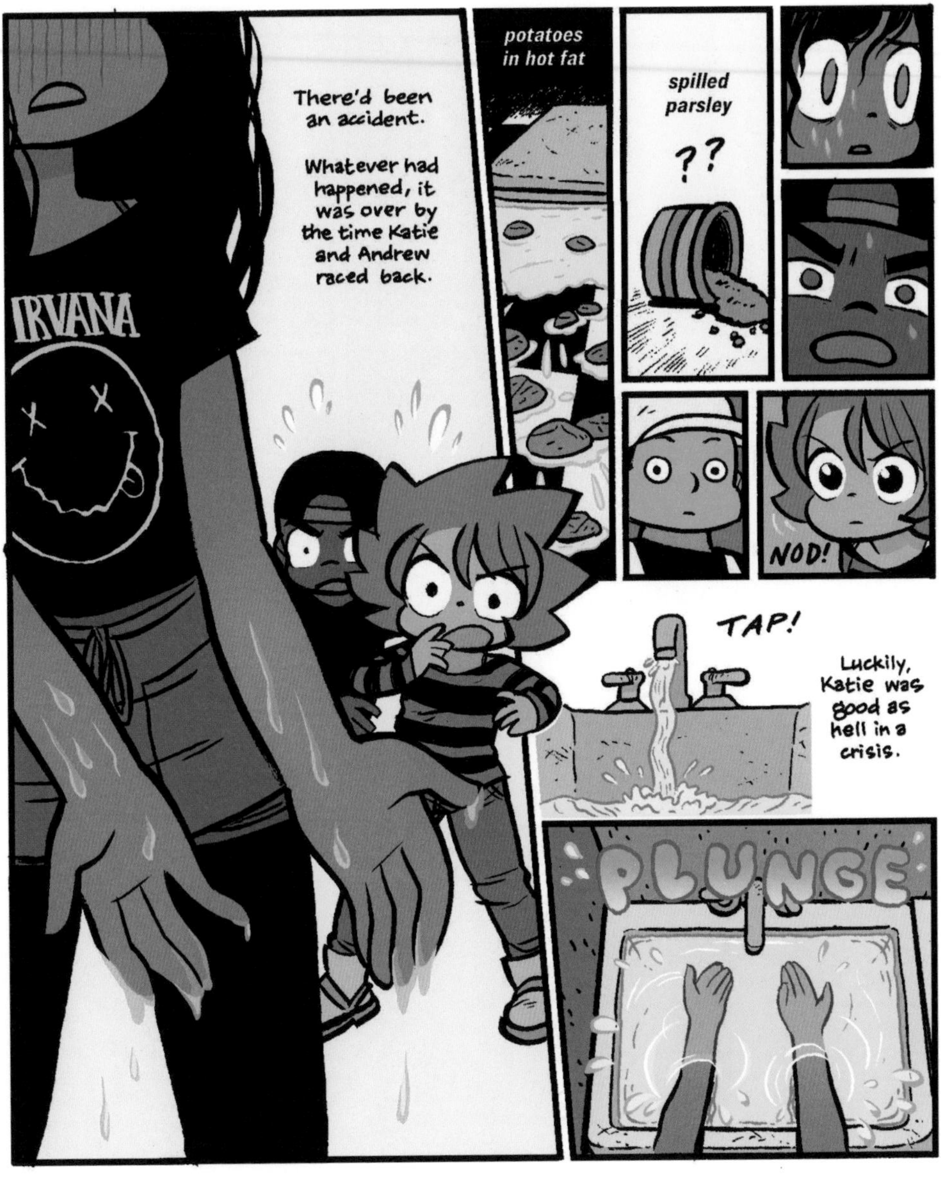
There'd been an accident.
Whatever had happened, it was over by the time Katie and Andrew raced back.
IRVANA
potatoes in hot fat
spilled parsley
??
NOD!
TAP!
Luckily, Katie was good as hell in a crisis.
PLUNGE

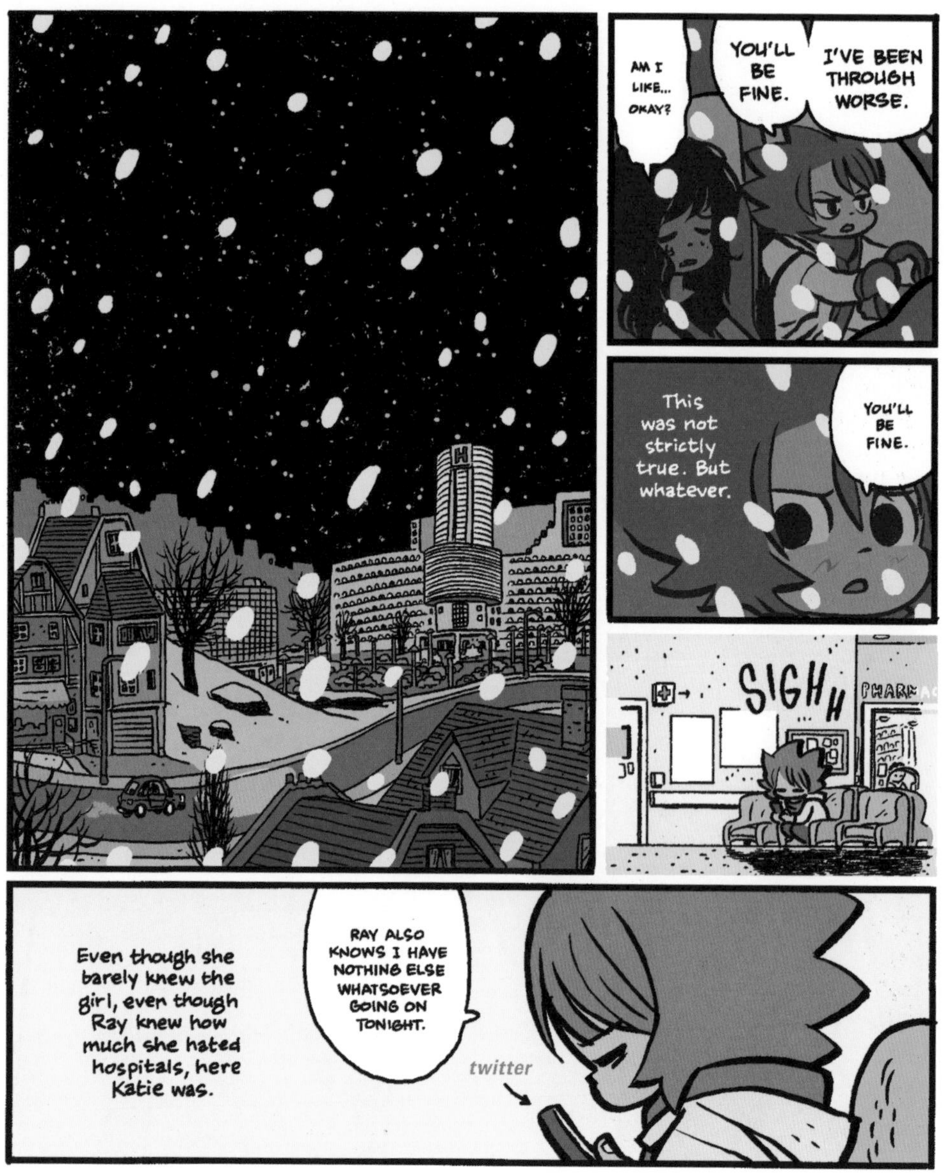
AM I LIKE... OKAY?
YOU'LL BE FINE.
I'VE BEEN THROUGH WORSE.
This was not strictly true. But whatever.
YOU'LL BE FINE.
SIGHH
PHARM
Even though she barely knew the girl, even though Ray knew how much she hated hospitals, here Katie was.
RAY ALSO KNOWS I HAVE NOTHING ELSE WHATSOEVER GOING ON TONIGHT.
twitter

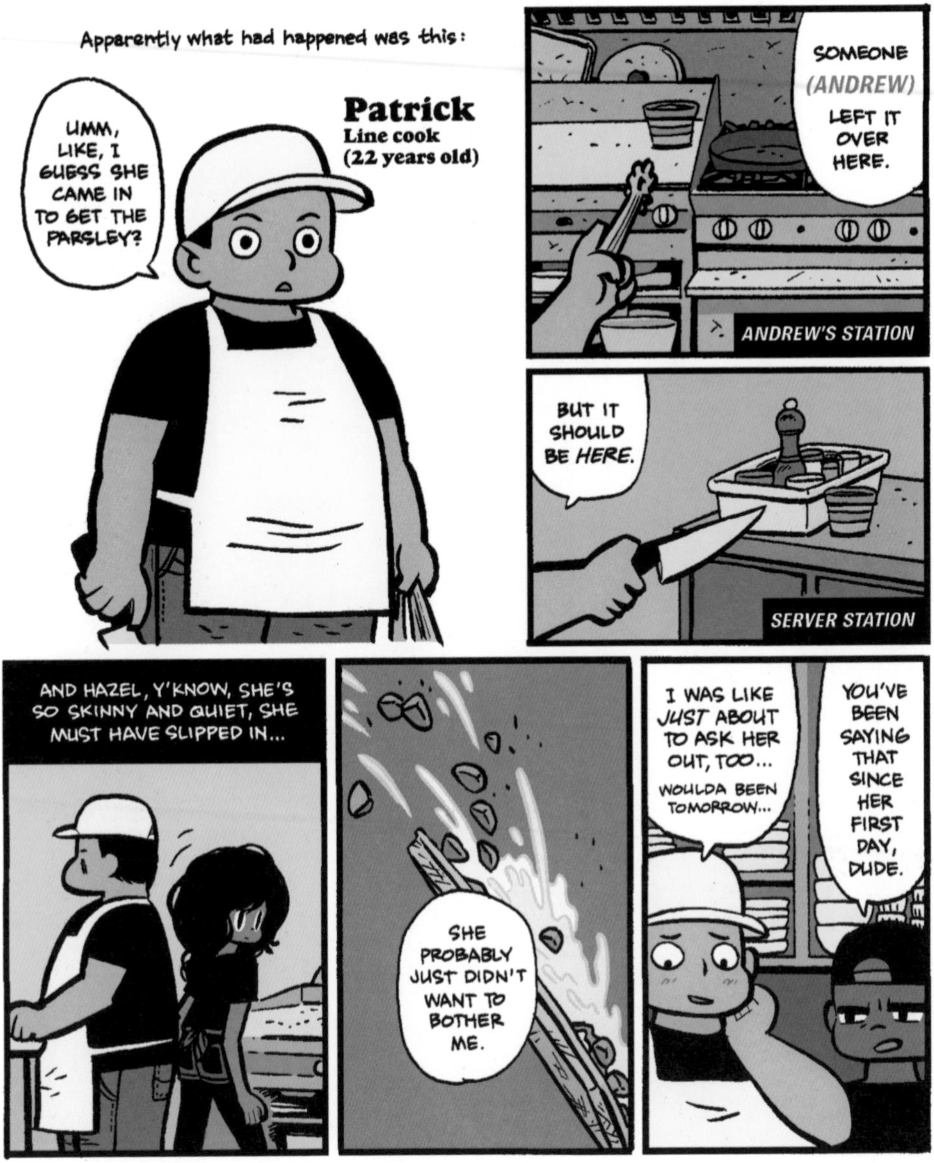

Apparently what had happened was this:
Patrick
Line cook
(22 years old)
UMM, LIKE, I GUESS SHE CAME IN TO GET THE PARSLEY?
SOMEONE (ANDREW) LEFT IT OVER HERE.
ANDREW'S STATION
BUT IT SHOULD BE HERE.
SERVER STATION
AND HAZEL, Y'KNOW, SHE'S SO SKINNY AND QUIET, SHE MUST HAVE SLIPPED IN...
SHE PROBABLY JUST DIDN'T WANT TO BOTHER ME.
I WAS LIKE JUST ABOUT TO ASK HER OUT, TOO...
WOULDA BEEN TOMORROW...
YOU'VE BEEN SAYING THAT SINCE HER FIRST DAY, DUDE.

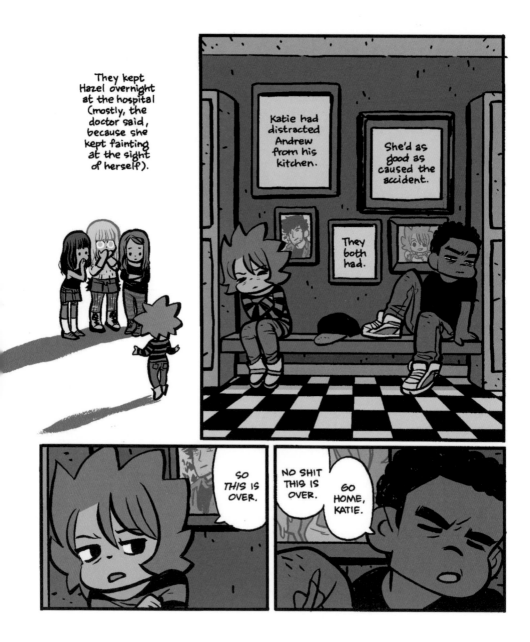

They kept Hazel overnight at the hospital (mostly, the doctor said, because she kept fainting at the sight of herself).

Katie had distracted Andrew from his kitchen.

She'd as good as caused the accident.

They both had.

SO *THIS* IS OVER.

NO SHIT THIS IS OVER.

GO HOME, KATIE.

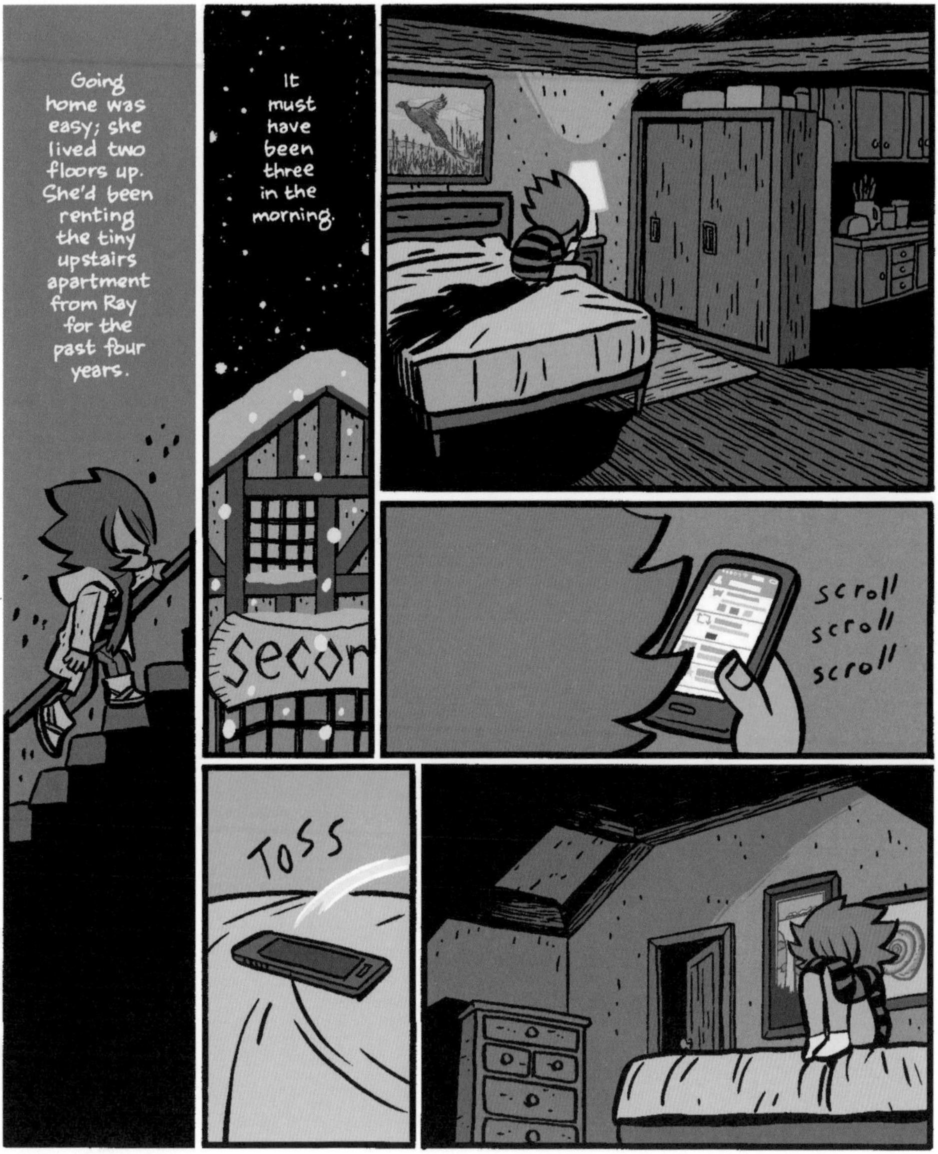
Going home was easy; she lived two floors up. She'd been renting the tiny upstairs apartment from Ray for the past four years.
It must have been three in the morning.
Secon
scroll
scroll
scroll
TOSS

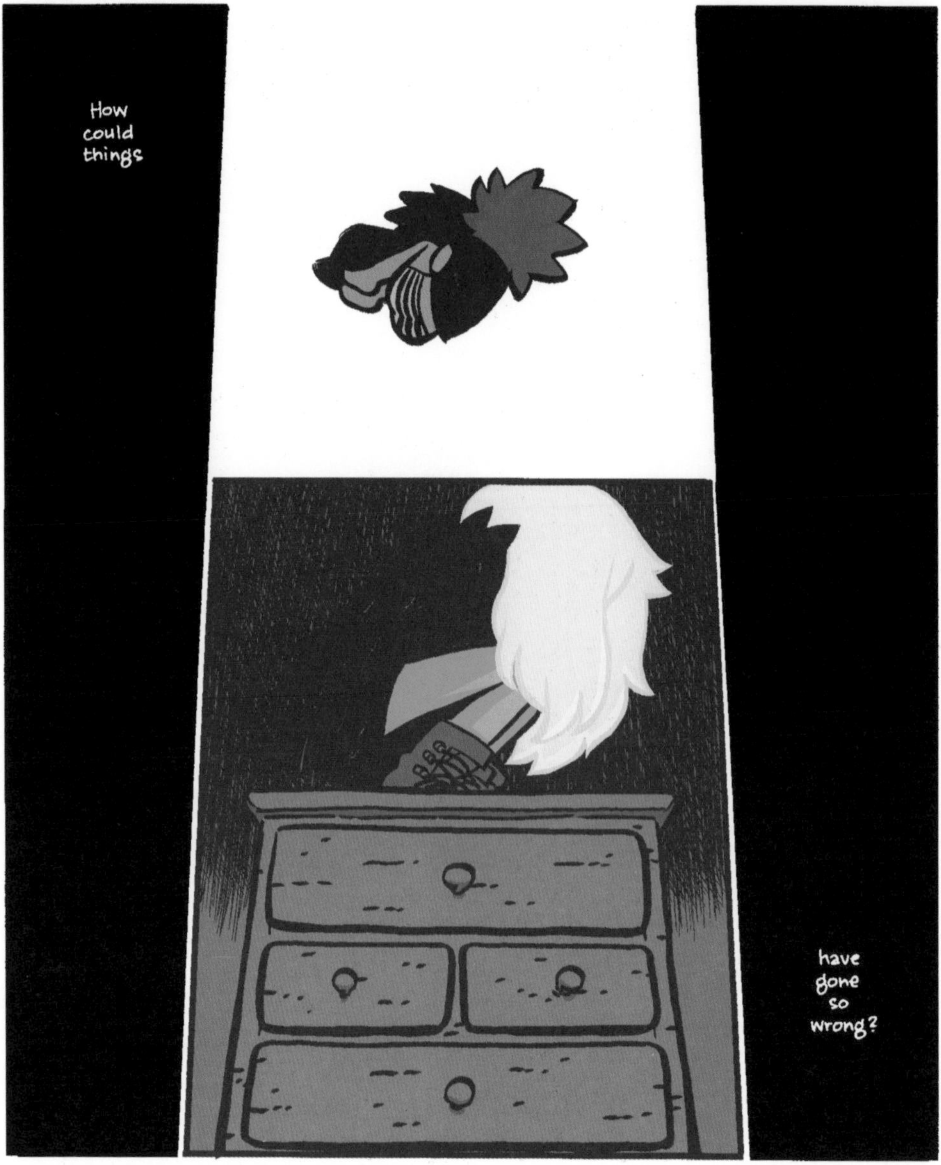
How could things
have gone so wrong?

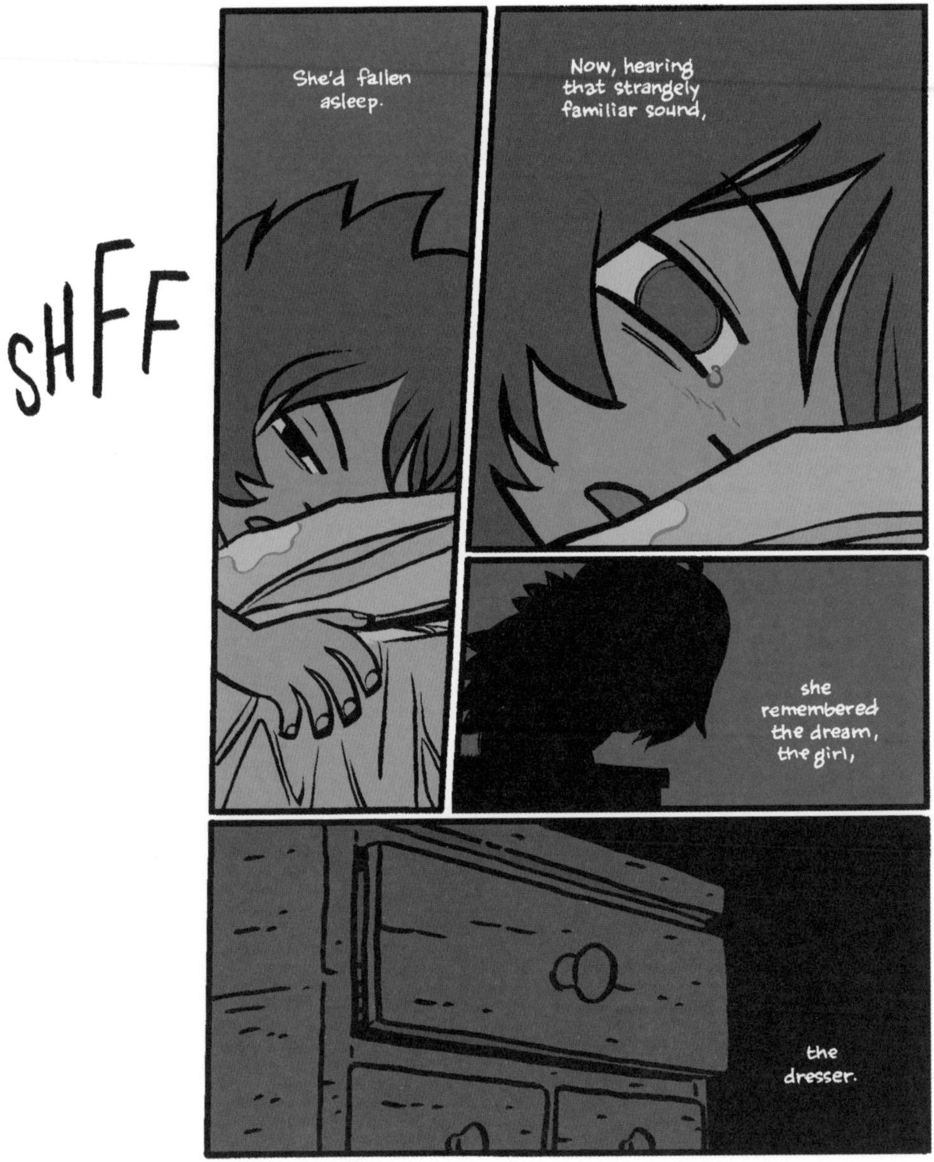
She'd fallen asleep.
SHFF
Now, hearing that strangely familiar sound,
she remembered the dream, the girl,
the dresser.

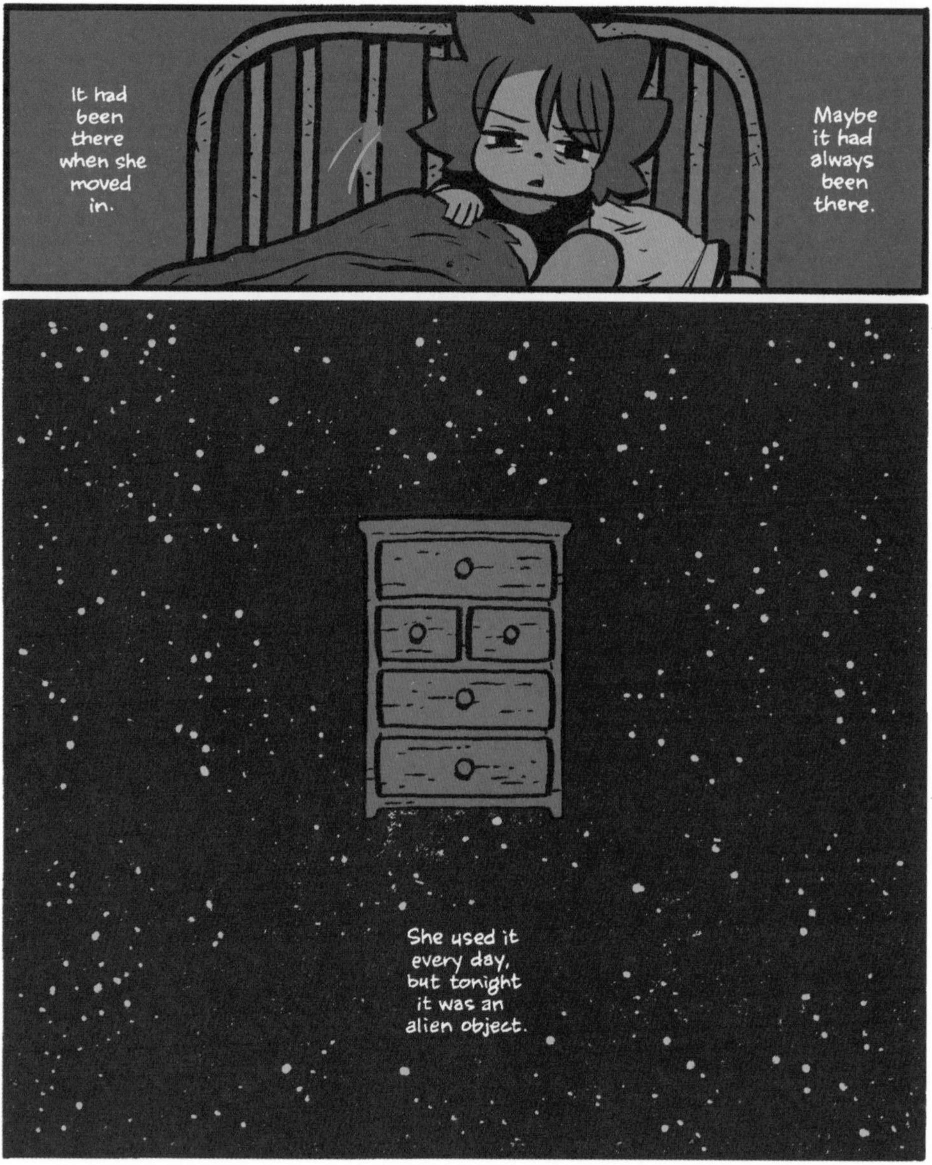
It had been there when she moved in.
Maybe it had always been there.
She used it every day, but tonight it was an alien object.

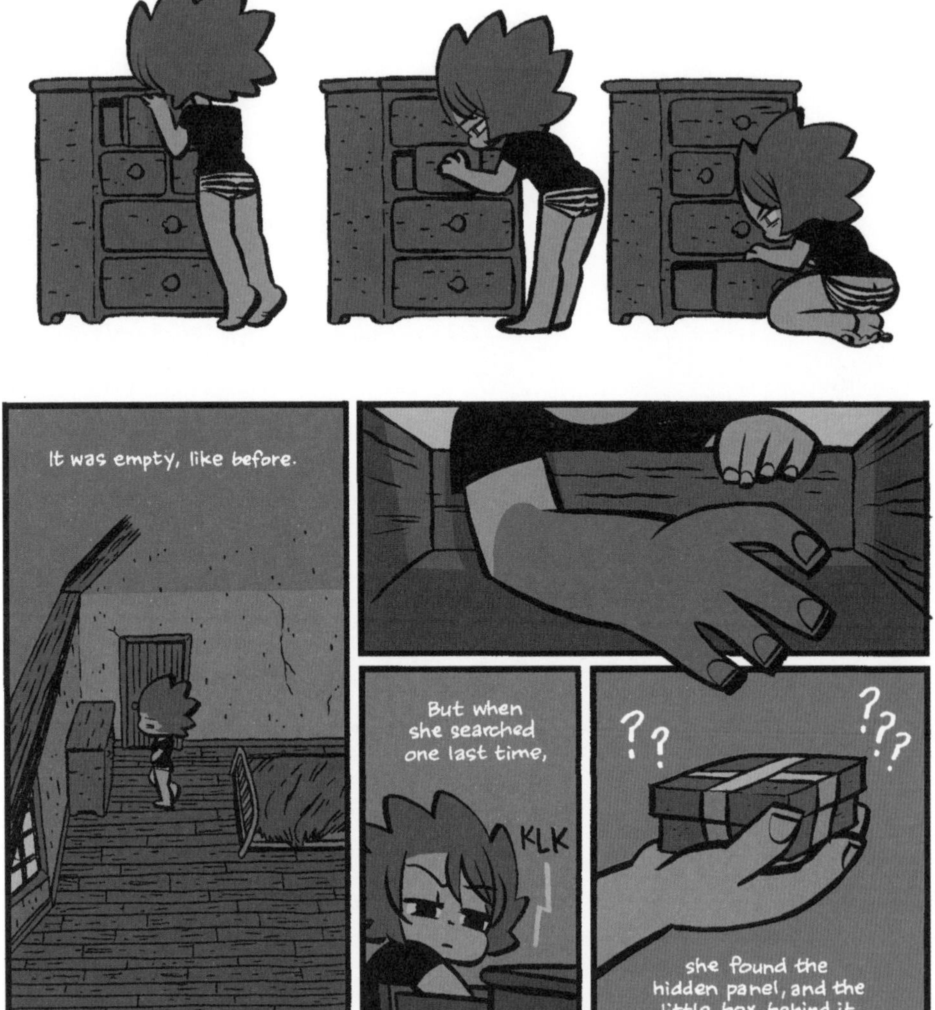
It was empty, like before.
But when she searched one last time,
KLK
??
???
she found the hidden panel, and the little box behind it.

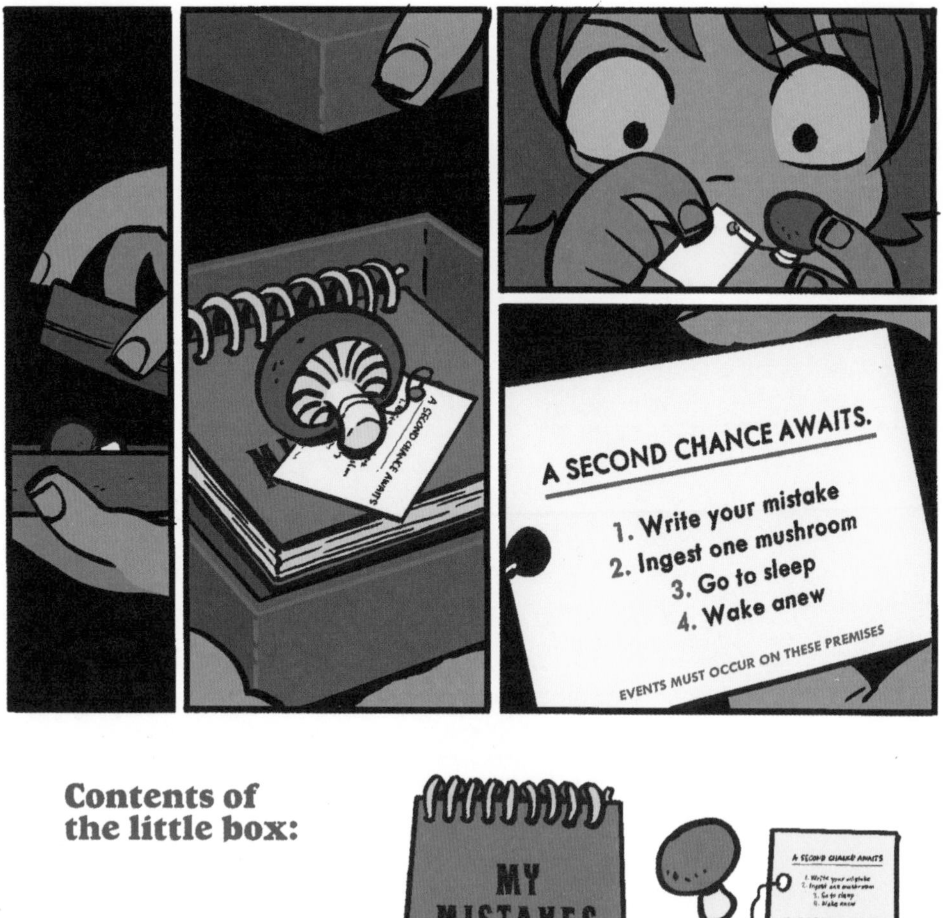
A SECOND CHANCE AWAITS.
1. Write your mistake
2. Ingest one mushroom
3. Go to sleep
4. Wake anew
EVENTS MUST OCCUR ON THESE PREMISES

Contents of the little box:

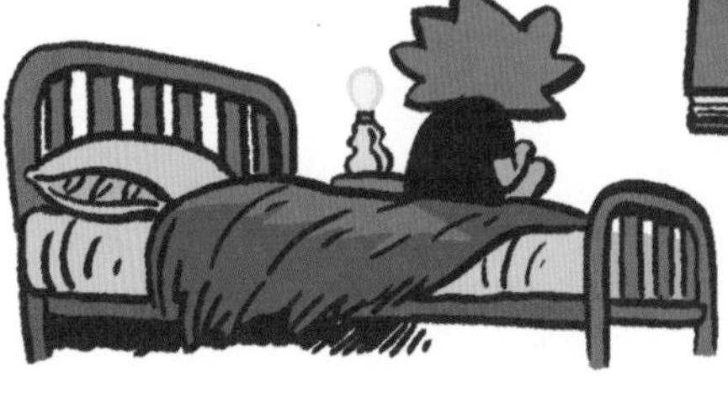

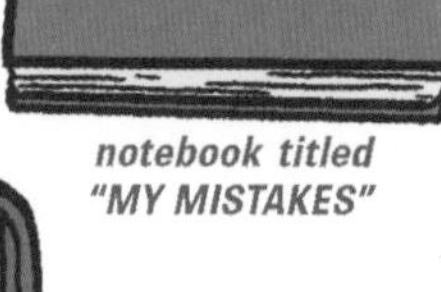
MY MISTAKES

notebook titled "MY MISTAKES"

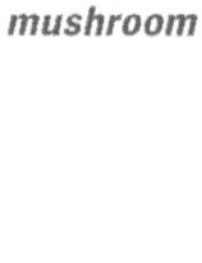

one (1) mysterious red-capped mushroom

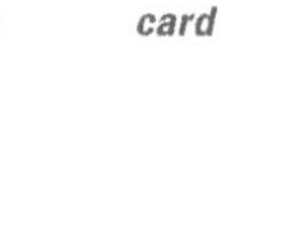

immaculately printed instruction card

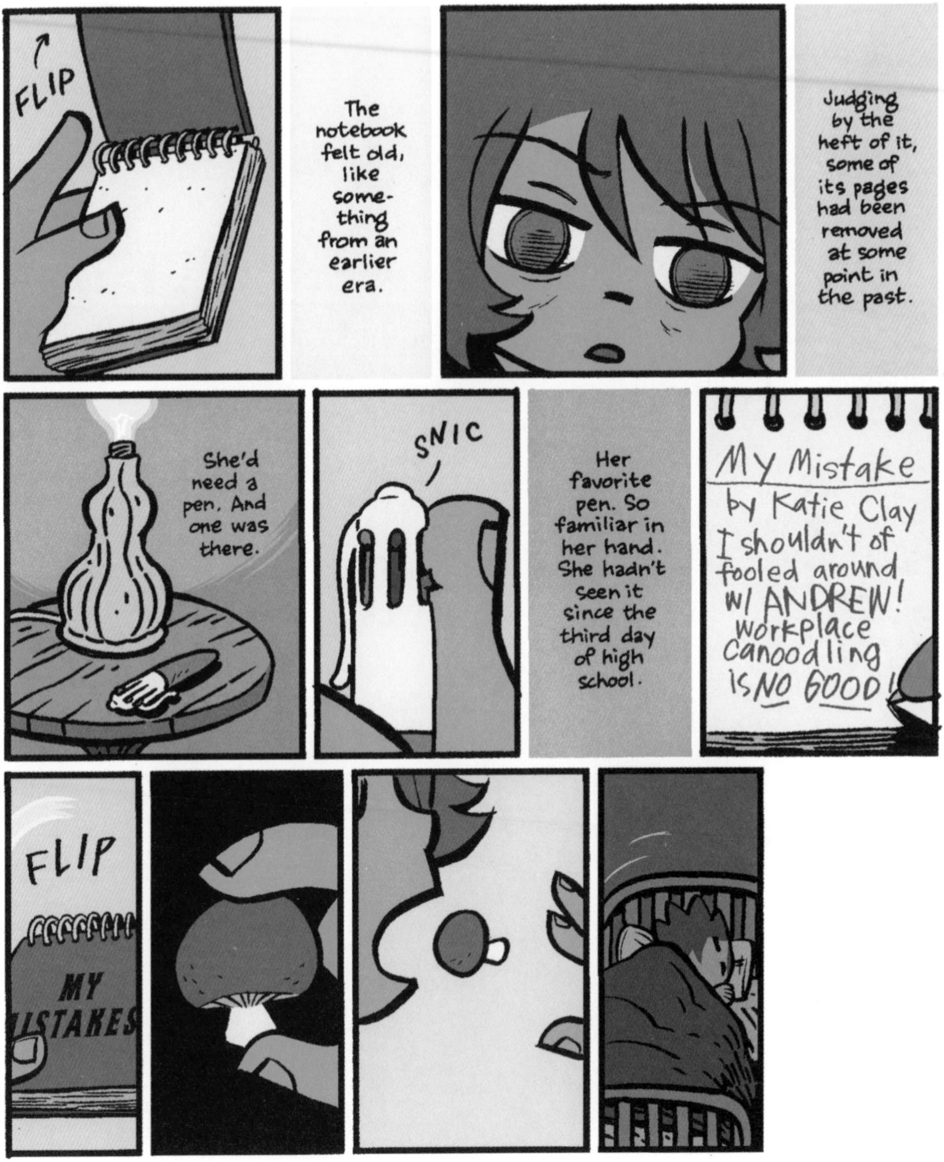
FLIP
The notebook felt old, like something from an earlier era.
Judging by the heft of it, some of its pages had been removed at some point in the past.
She'd need a pen. And one was there.
SNIC
Her favorite pen. So familiar in her hand. She hadn't seen it since the third day of high school.
My Mistake
by Katie Clay
I shouldn't of fooled around w/ ANDREW! workplace canoodling is NO GOOD!
FLIP
MY
ISTAKES

REVISION #1

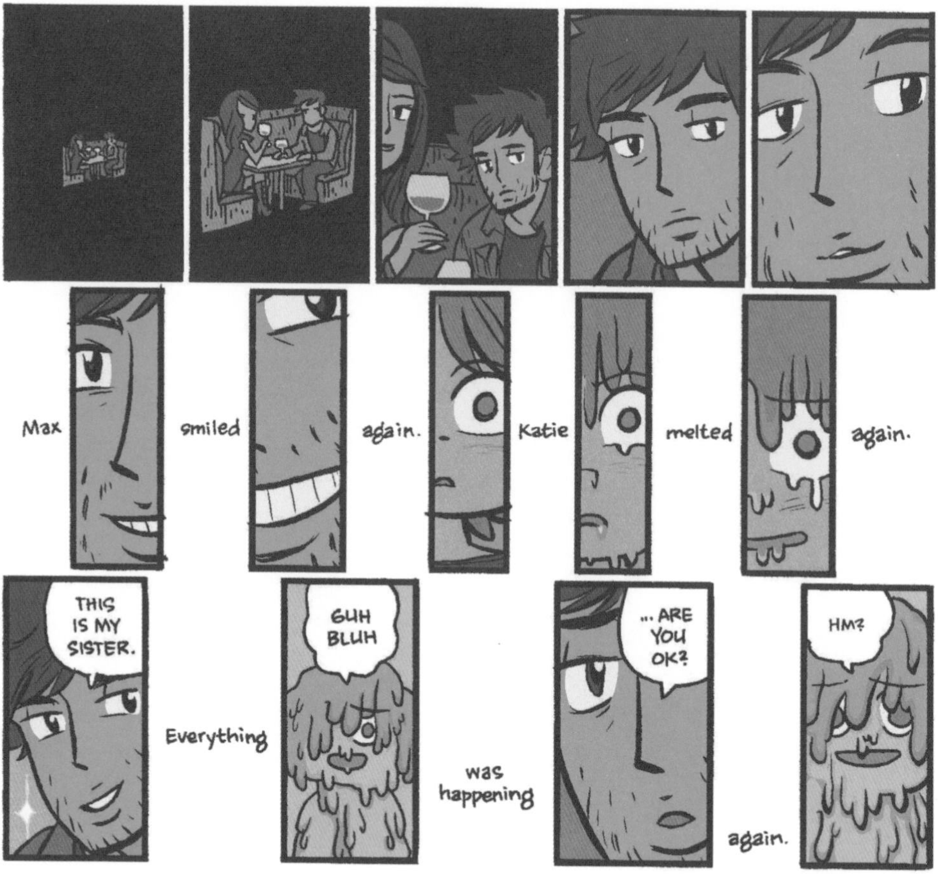
Max
smiled
again.
Katie
melted
again.
THIS IS MY SISTER.
Everything
GUH BLUH
was happening
... ARE YOU OK?
again.
HM?

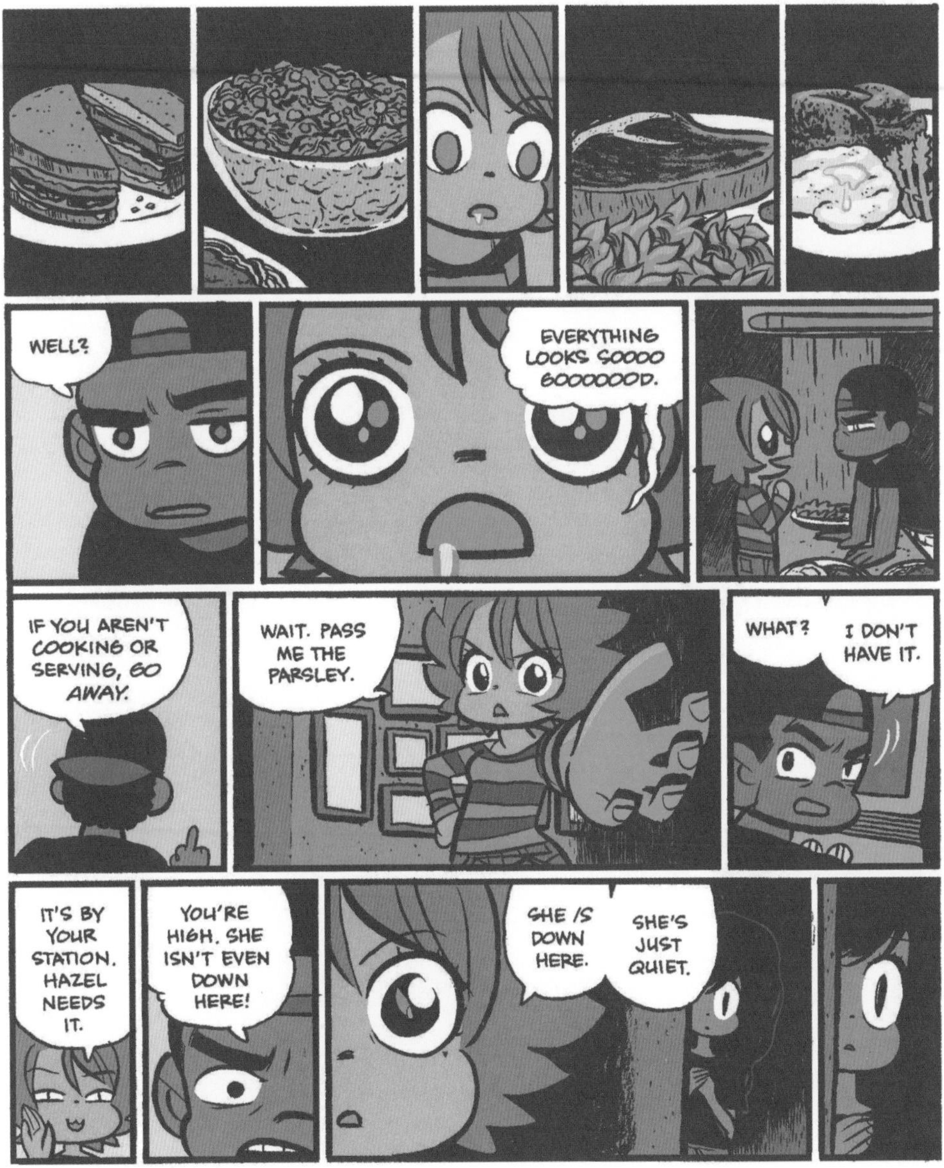
WELL?
EVERYTHING LOOKS SOOOO GOOOOOOOD.
IF YOU AREN'T COOKING OR SERVING, GO AWAY.
WAIT. PASS ME THE PARSLEY.
WHAT?
I DON'T HAVE IT.
IT'S BY YOUR STATION. HAZEL NEEDS IT.
YOU'RE HIGH. SHE ISN'T EVEN DOWN HERE!
SHE *IS* DOWN HERE.
SHE'S JUST QUIET.

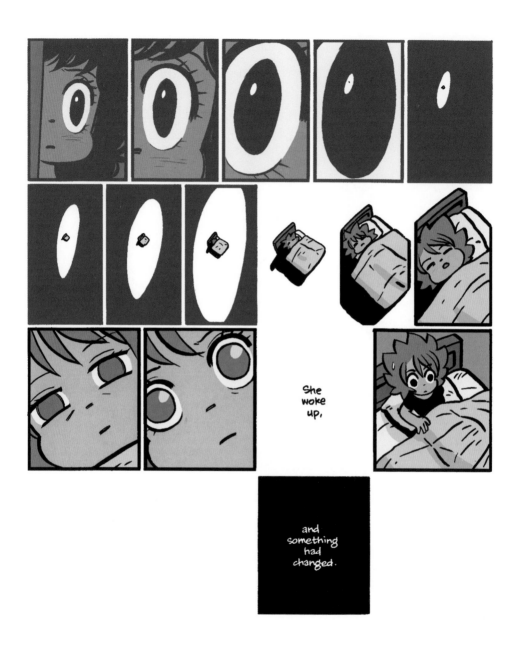

She woke up,

and something had changed.

2
Hazel

That morning, the girl wasn't at the hospital.

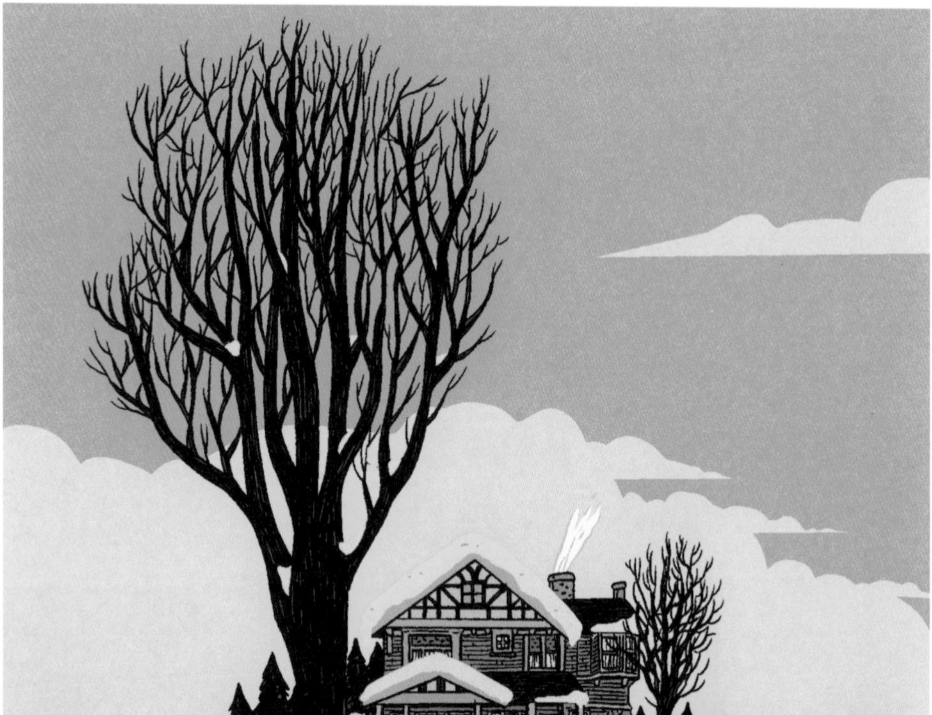
Katie found the girl's address in a three-month-old unread work email (re: new staff).
HAZEL.
HER NAME'S HAZEL.

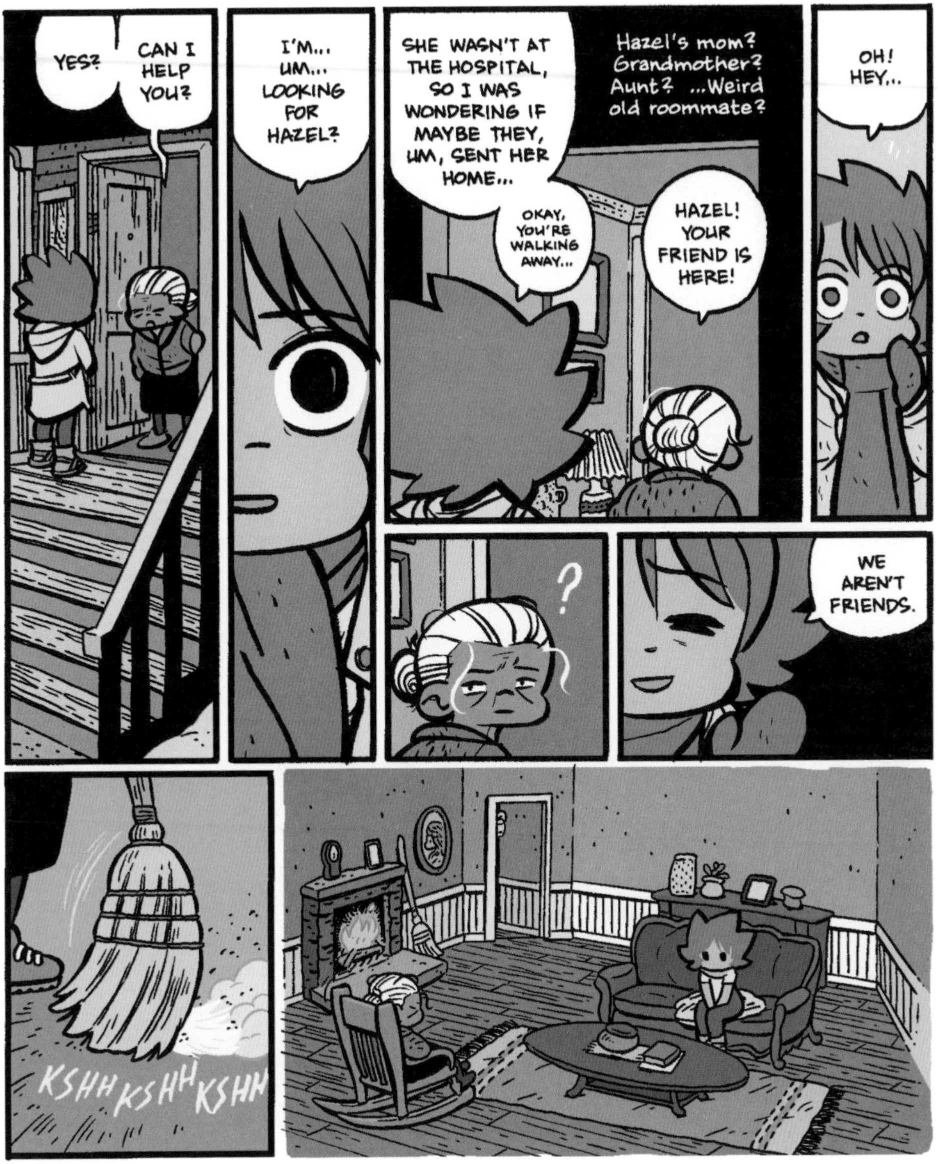
YES?
CAN I HELP YOU?
I'M... UM... LOOKING FOR HAZEL?
SHE WASN'T AT THE HOSPITAL, SO I WAS WONDERING IF MAYBE THEY, UM, SENT HER HOME...
Hazel's mom? Grandmother? Aunt? ...Weird old roommate?
OKAY, YOU'RE WALKING AWAY...
HAZEL! YOUR FRIEND IS HERE!
OH! HEY...
?
WE AREN'T FRIENDS.
KSHH KSHH KSHH

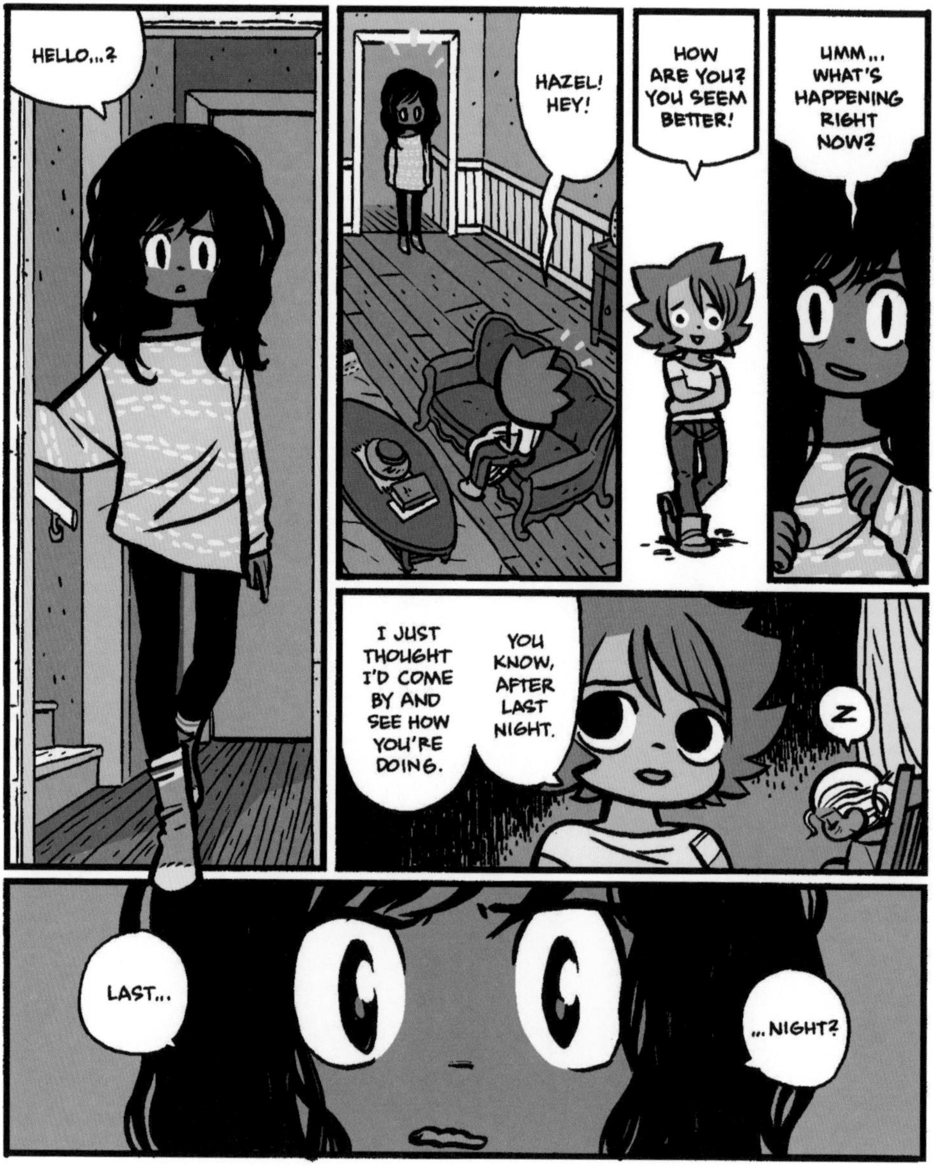
HELLO...?
HAZEL! HEY!
HOW ARE YOU? YOU SEEM BETTER!
UMM... WHAT'S HAPPENING RIGHT NOW?
I JUST THOUGHT I'D COME BY AND SEE HOW YOU'RE DOING.
YOU KNOW, AFTER LAST NIGHT.
Z
LAST...
...NIGHT?

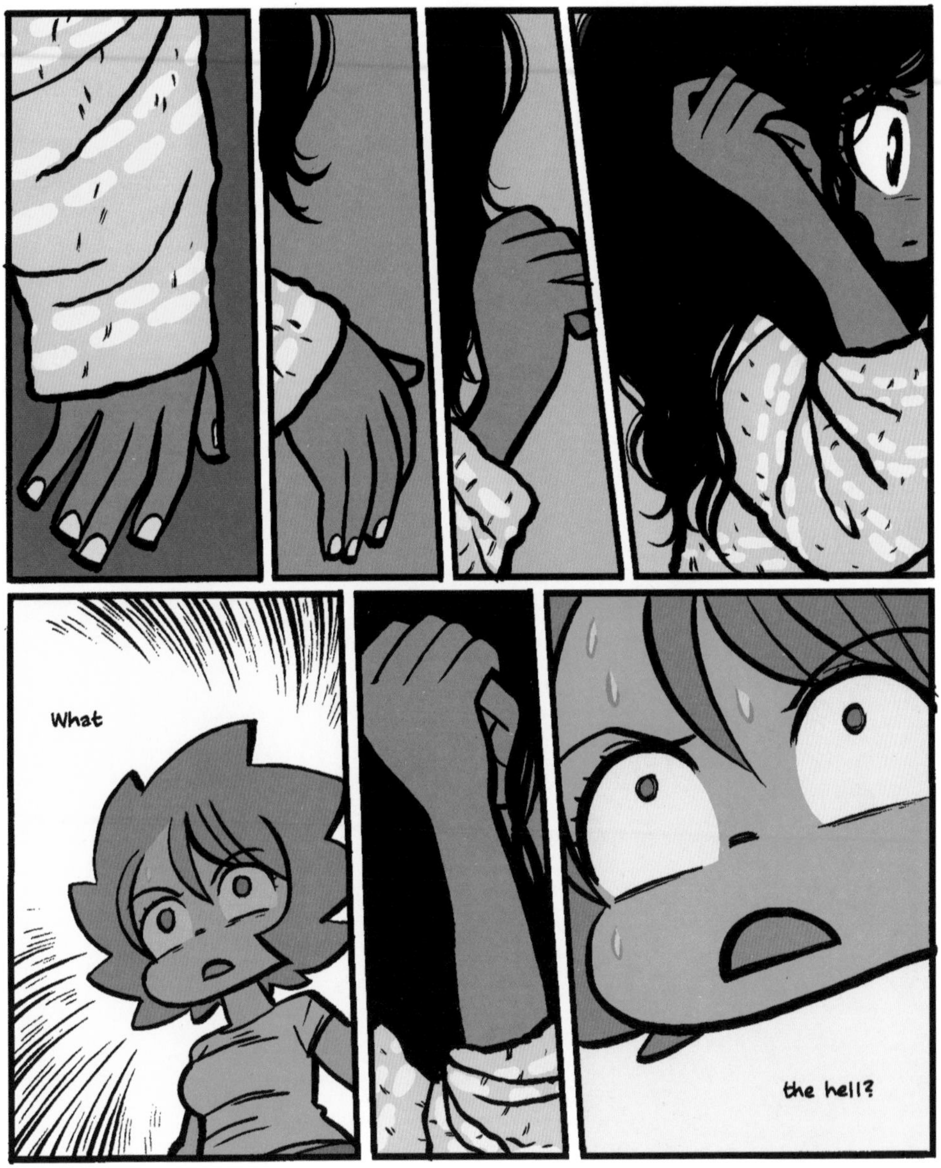
What
the hell?

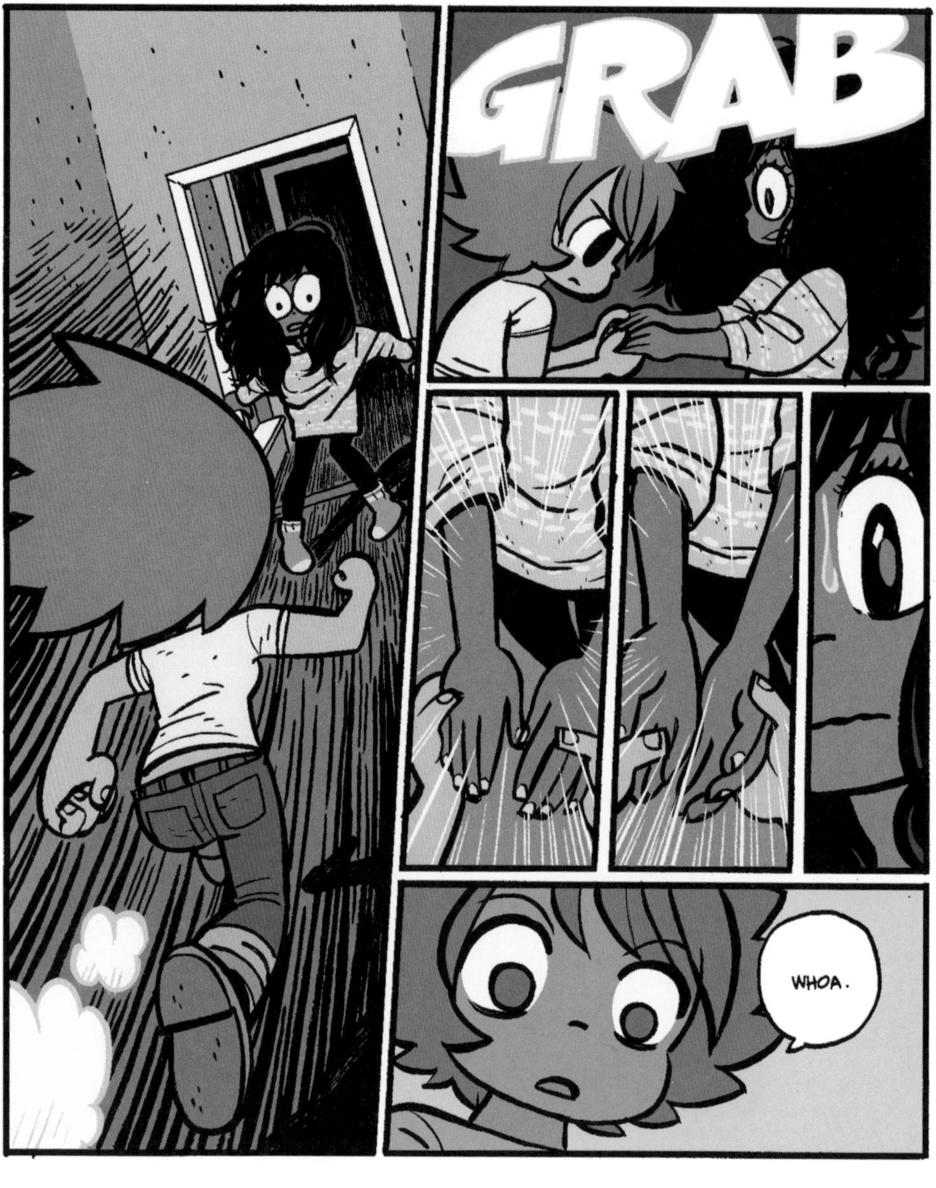
GRAB
WHOA.

57

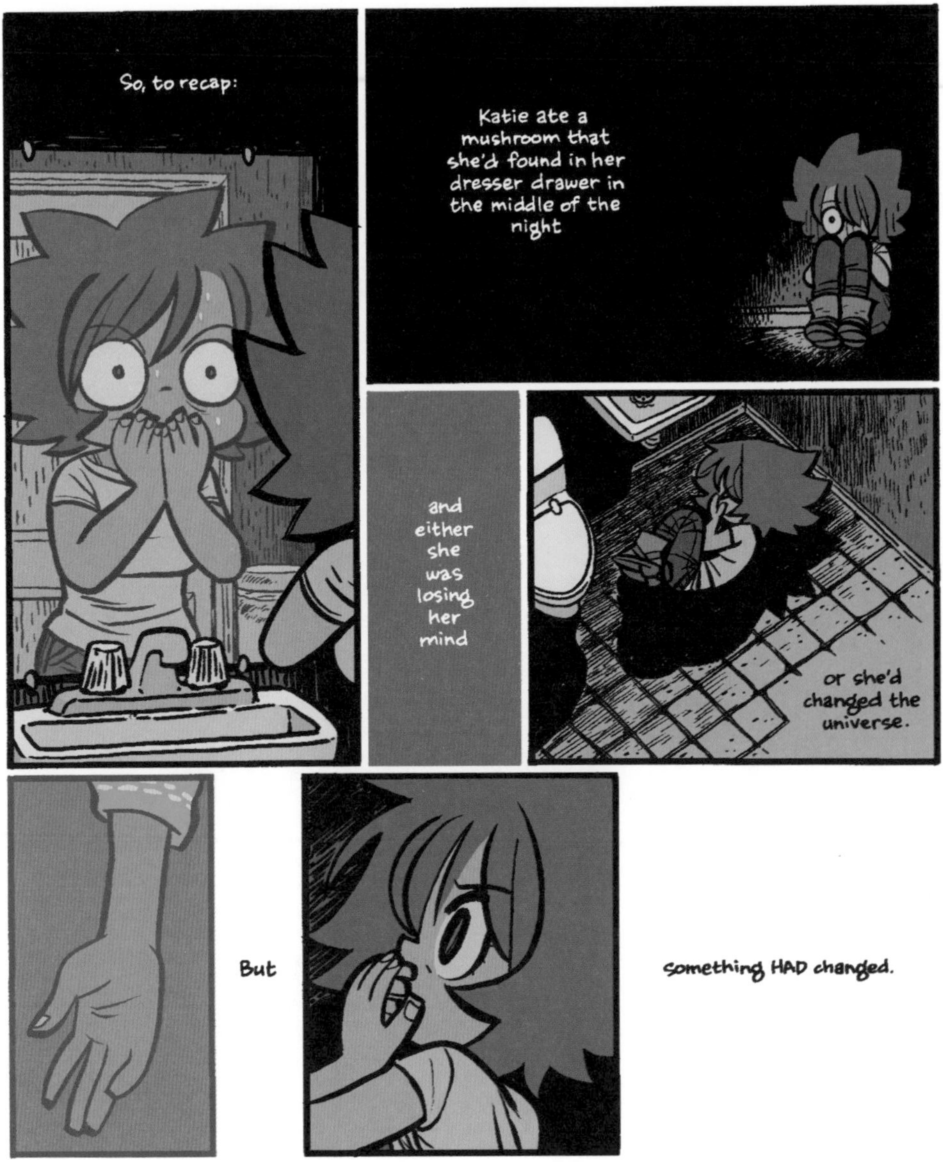
So, to recap:
Katie ate a mushroom that she'd found in her dresser drawer in the middle of the night
and either she was losing her mind
or she'd changed the universe.
But
something HAD changed.

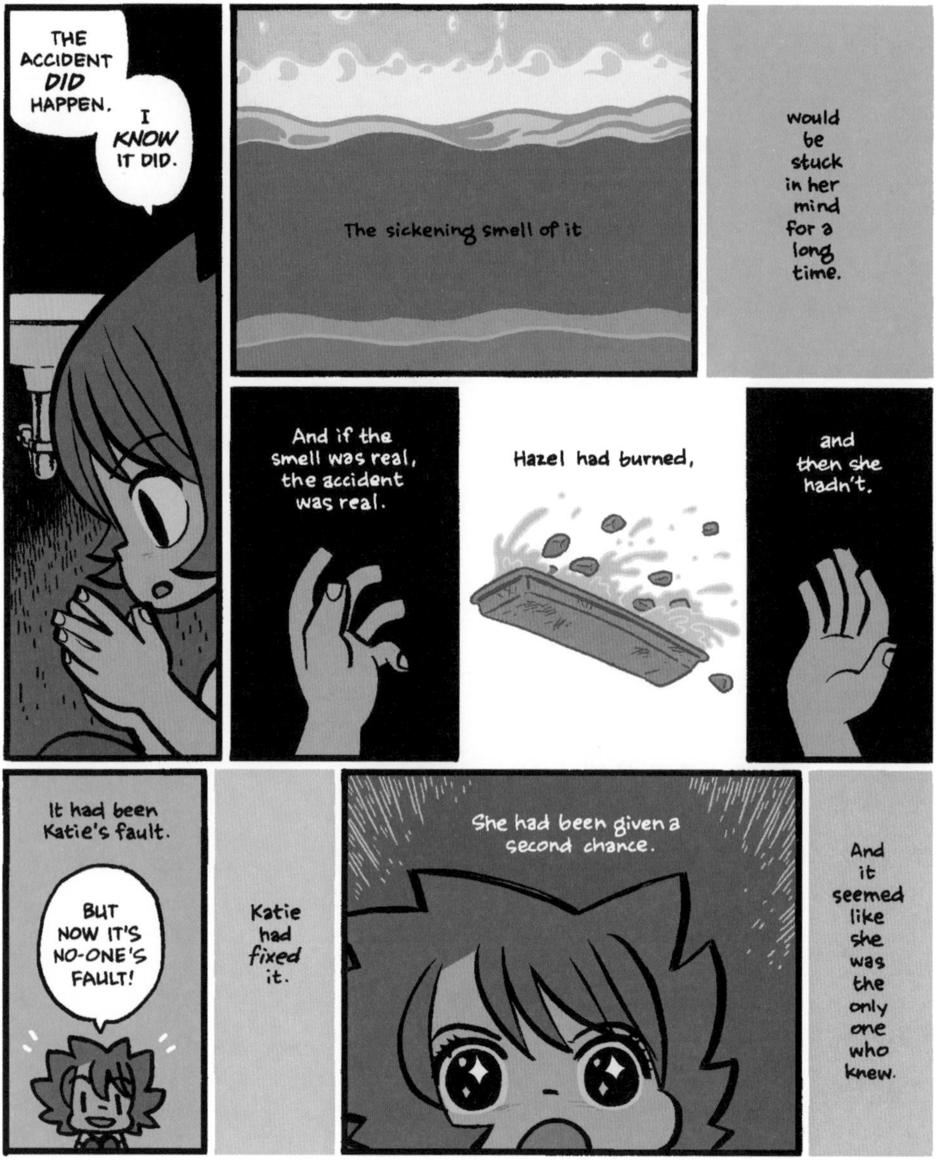
THE ACCIDENT *DID* HAPPEN.
I *KNOW* IT DID.
The sickening smell of it
would be stuck in her mind for a long time.
And if the smell was real, the accident was real.
Hazel had burned,
and then she hadn't.
It had been Katie's fault.
BUT NOW IT'S NO-ONE'S FAULT!
Katie had *fixed* it.
She had been given a second chance.
And it seemed like she was the only one who knew.

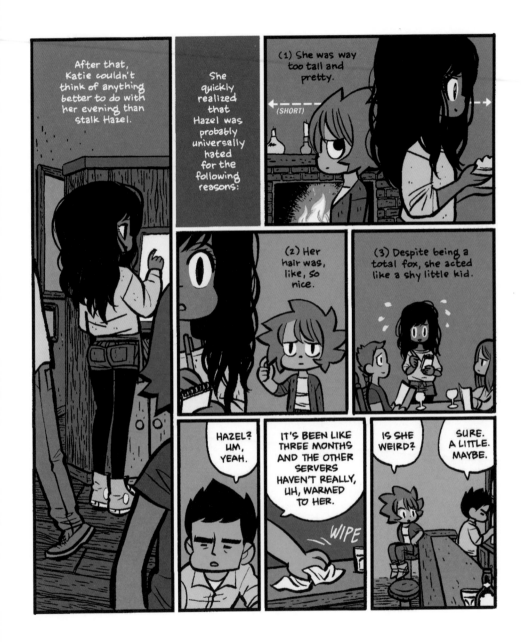

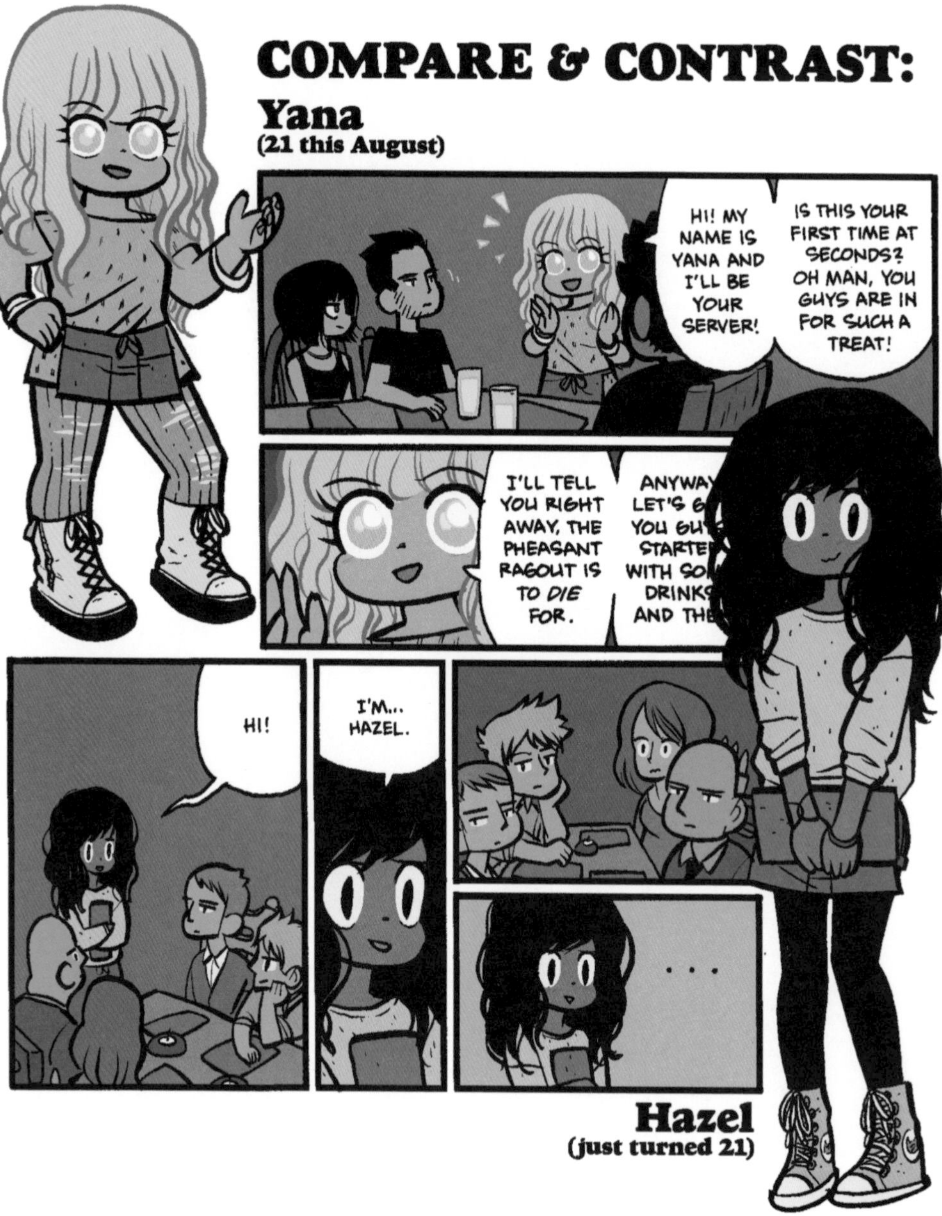
COMPARE & CONTRAST:
Yana
(21 this August)
HI! MY NAME IS YANA AND I'LL BE YOUR SERVER!
IS THIS YOUR FIRST TIME AT SECONDS? OH MAN, YOU GUYS ARE IN FOR SUCH A TREAT!
I'LL TELL YOU RIGHT AWAY, THE PHEASANT RAGOUT IS TO *DIE* FOR.
ANYWA LET'S G YOU GU STARTE WITH SO DRINK AND TH
HI!
I'M... HAZEL.
. . .
Hazel
(just turned 21)

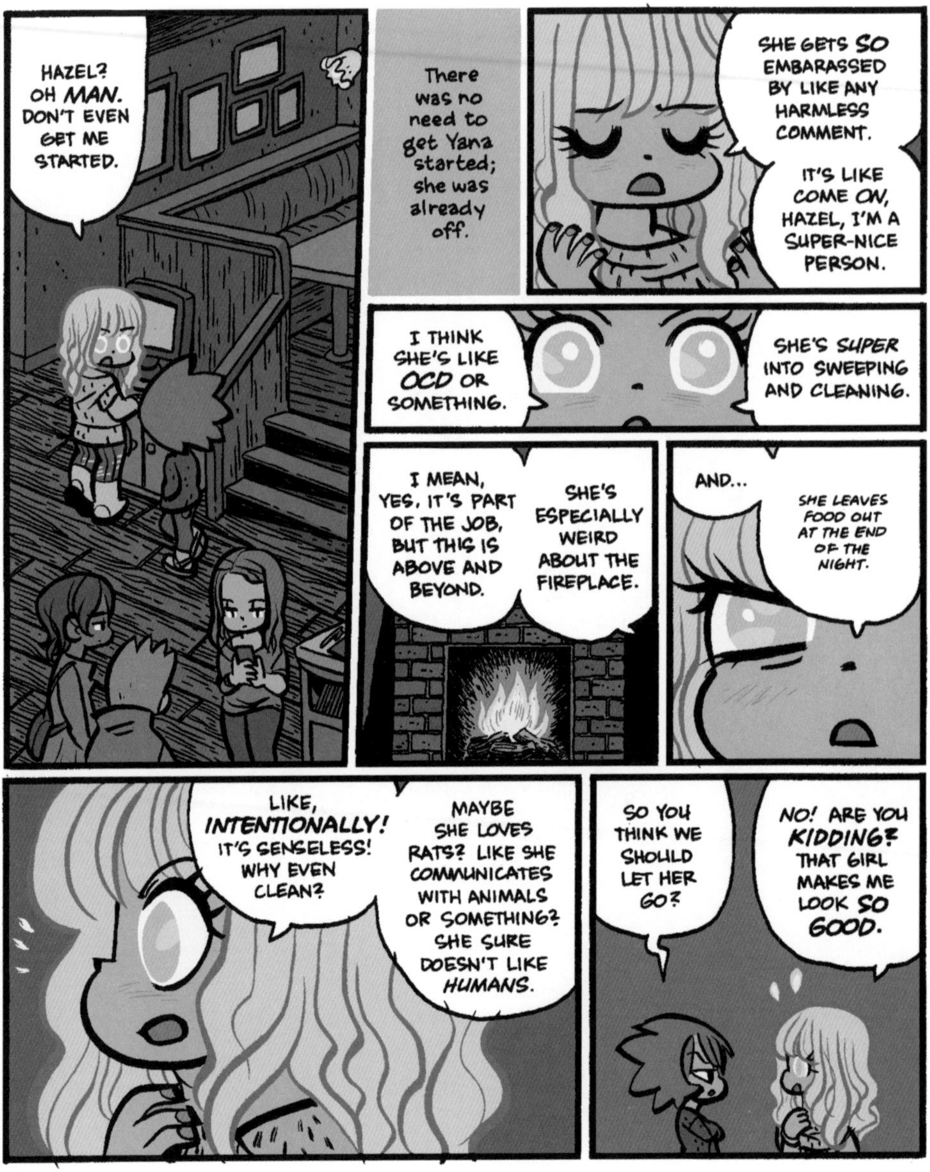
HAZEL? OH MAN. DON'T EVEN GET ME STARTED.
There was no need to get Yana started; she was already off.
SHE GETS SO EMBARASSED BY LIKE ANY HARMLESS COMMENT.
IT'S LIKE COME ON, HAZEL, I'M A SUPER-NICE PERSON.
I THINK SHE'S LIKE OCD OR SOMETHING.
SHE'S SUPER INTO SWEEPING AND CLEANING.
I MEAN, YES, IT'S PART OF THE JOB, BUT THIS IS ABOVE AND BEYOND.
SHE'S ESPECIALLY WEIRD ABOUT THE FIREPLACE.
AND...
SHE LEAVES FOOD OUT AT THE END OF THE NIGHT.
LIKE, INTENTIONALLY! IT'S SENSELESS! WHY EVEN CLEAN?
MAYBE SHE LOVES RATS? LIKE SHE COMMUNICATES WITH ANIMALS OR SOMETHING? SHE SURE DOESN'T LIKE HUMANS.
SO YOU THINK WE SHOULD LET HER GO?
NO! ARE YOU KIDDING? THAT GIRL MAKES ME LOOK SO GOOD.

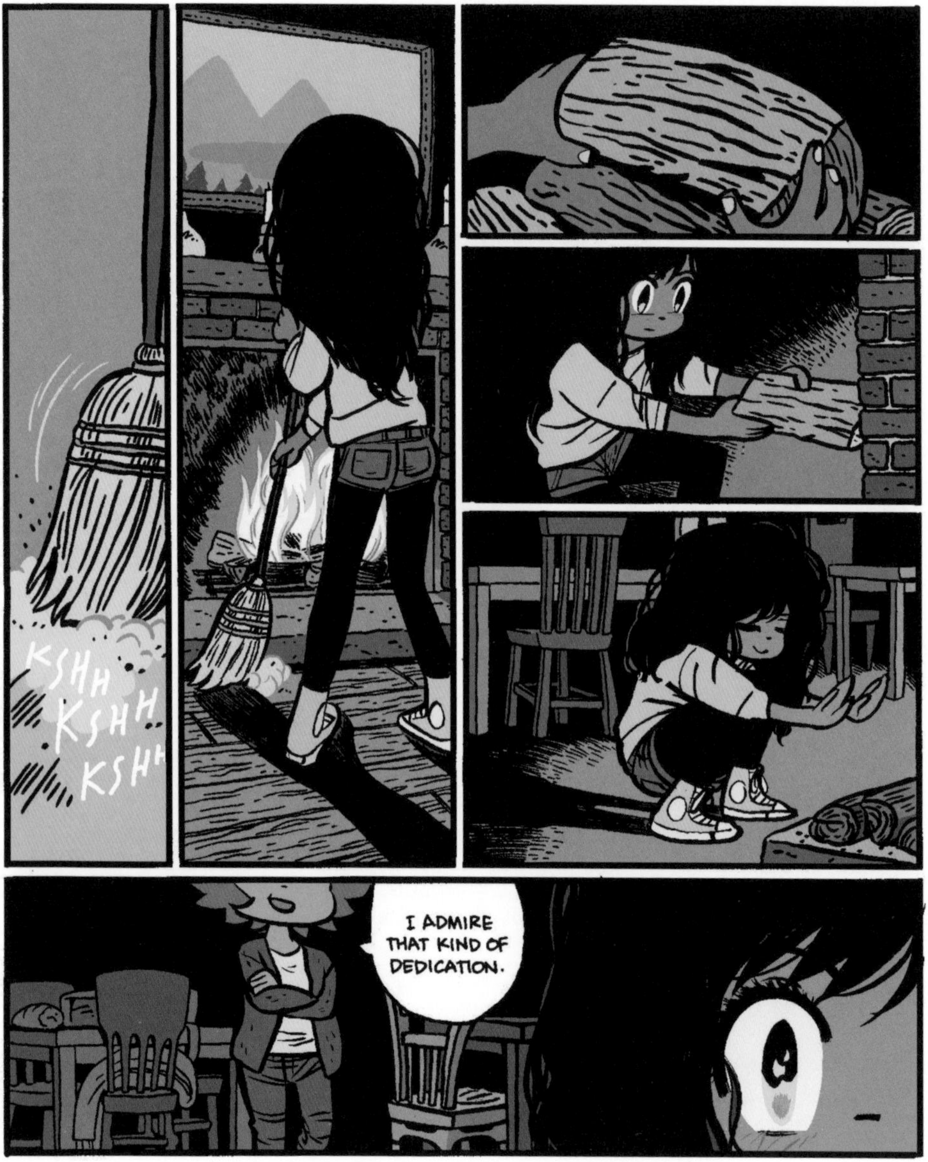
KSHH
KSHH
KSHH
I ADMIRE THAT KIND OF DEDICATION.

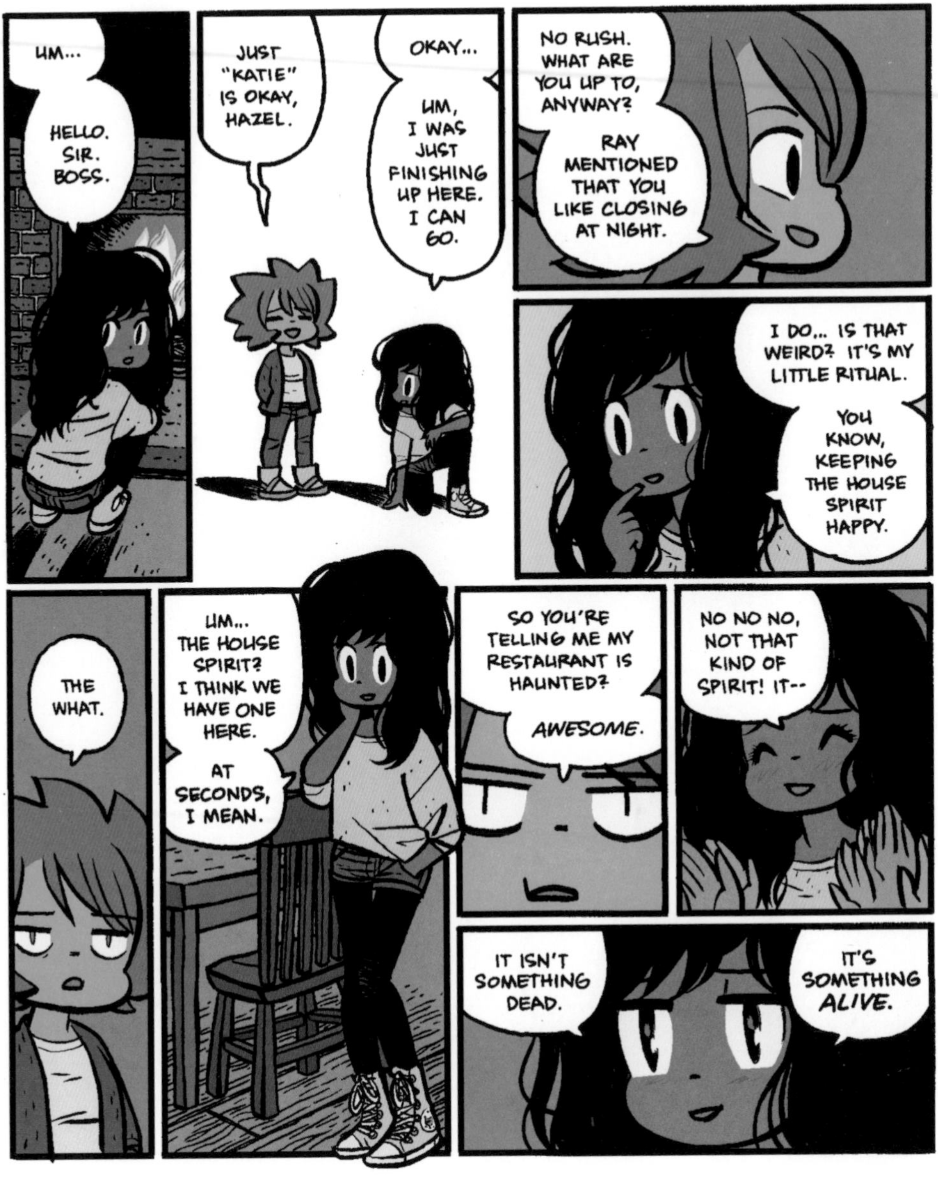
UM...
HELLO. SIR. BOSS.
JUST "KATIE" IS OKAY, HAZEL.
OKAY...
UM, I WAS JUST FINISHING UP HERE. I CAN GO.
NO RUSH. WHAT ARE YOU UP TO, ANYWAY?
RAY MENTIONED THAT YOU LIKE CLOSING AT NIGHT.
I DO... IS THAT WEIRD? IT'S MY LITTLE RITUAL.
YOU KNOW, KEEPING THE HOUSE SPIRIT HAPPY.
THE WHAT.
UM... THE HOUSE SPIRIT? I THINK WE HAVE ONE HERE.
AT SECONDS, I MEAN.
SO YOU'RE TELLING ME MY RESTAURANT IS HAUNTED?
AWESOME.
NO NO NO, NOT THAT KIND OF SPIRIT! IT--
IT ISN'T SOMETHING DEAD.
IT'S SOMETHING ALIVE.

67

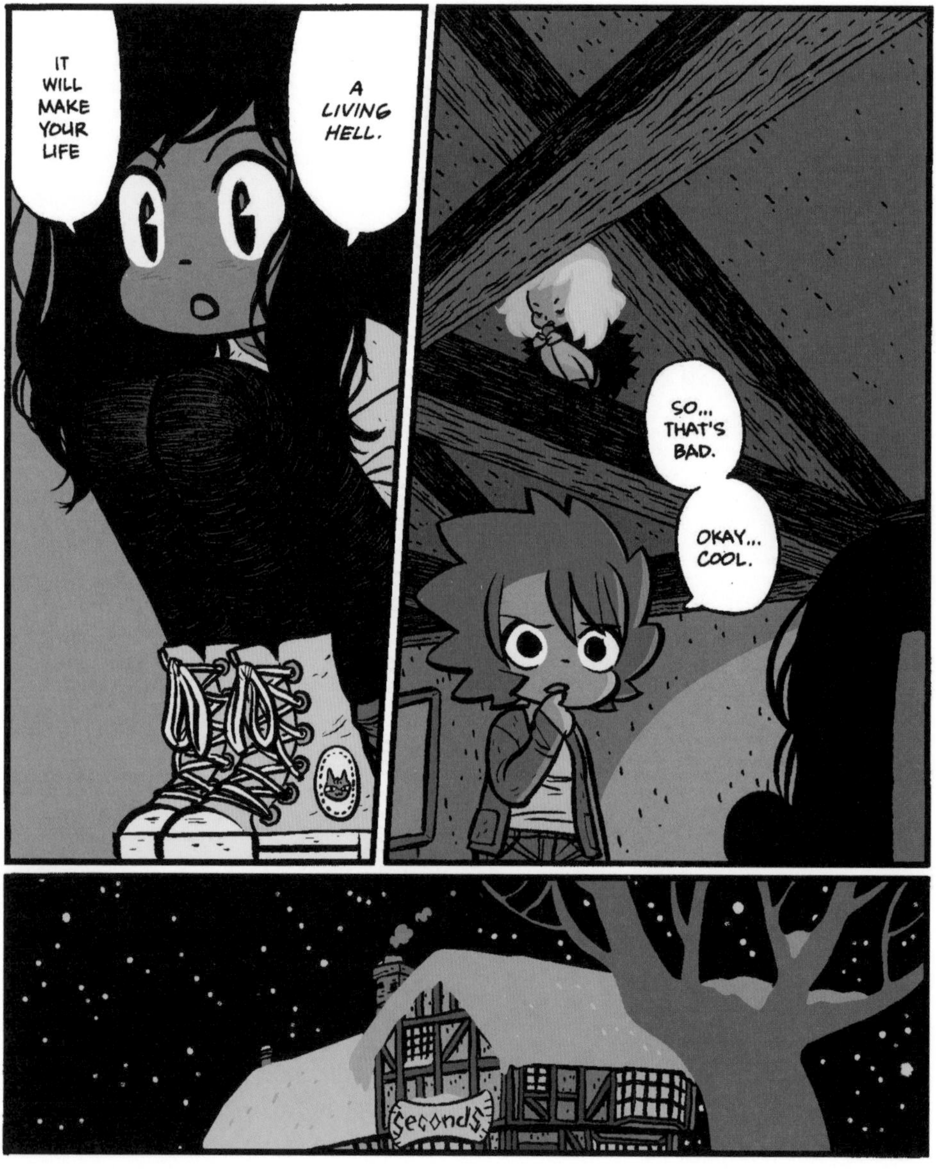
IT WILL MAKE YOUR LIFE
A LIVING HELL.
SO... THAT'S BAD.
OKAY... COOL.
seconds

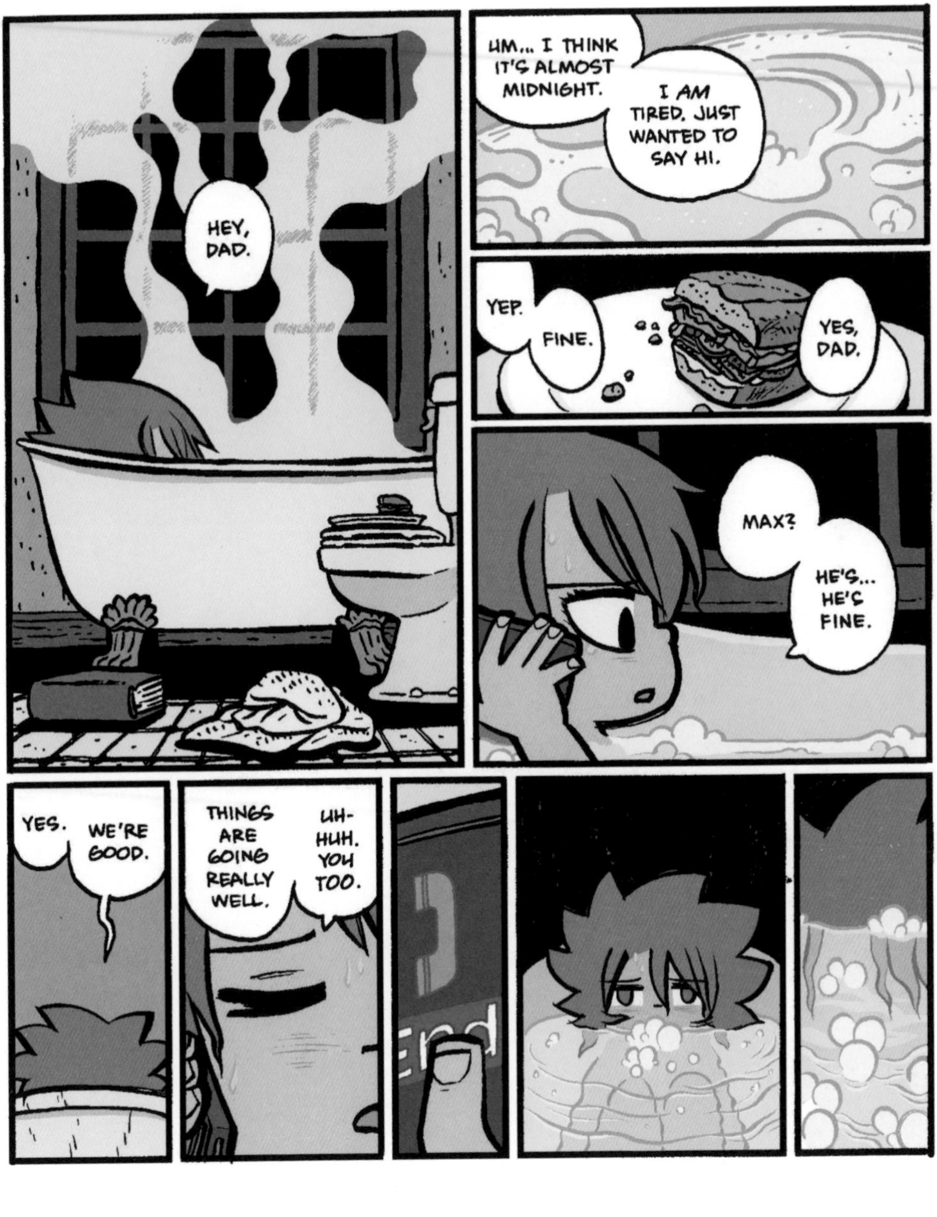
HEY, DAD.
UM... I THINK IT'S ALMOST MIDNIGHT.
I AM TIRED. JUST WANTED TO SAY HI.
YEP.
FINE.
YES, DAD.
MAX?
HE'S... HE'S FINE.
YES.
WE'RE GOOD.
THINGS ARE GOING REALLY WELL.
UH-HUH. YOU TOO.
End

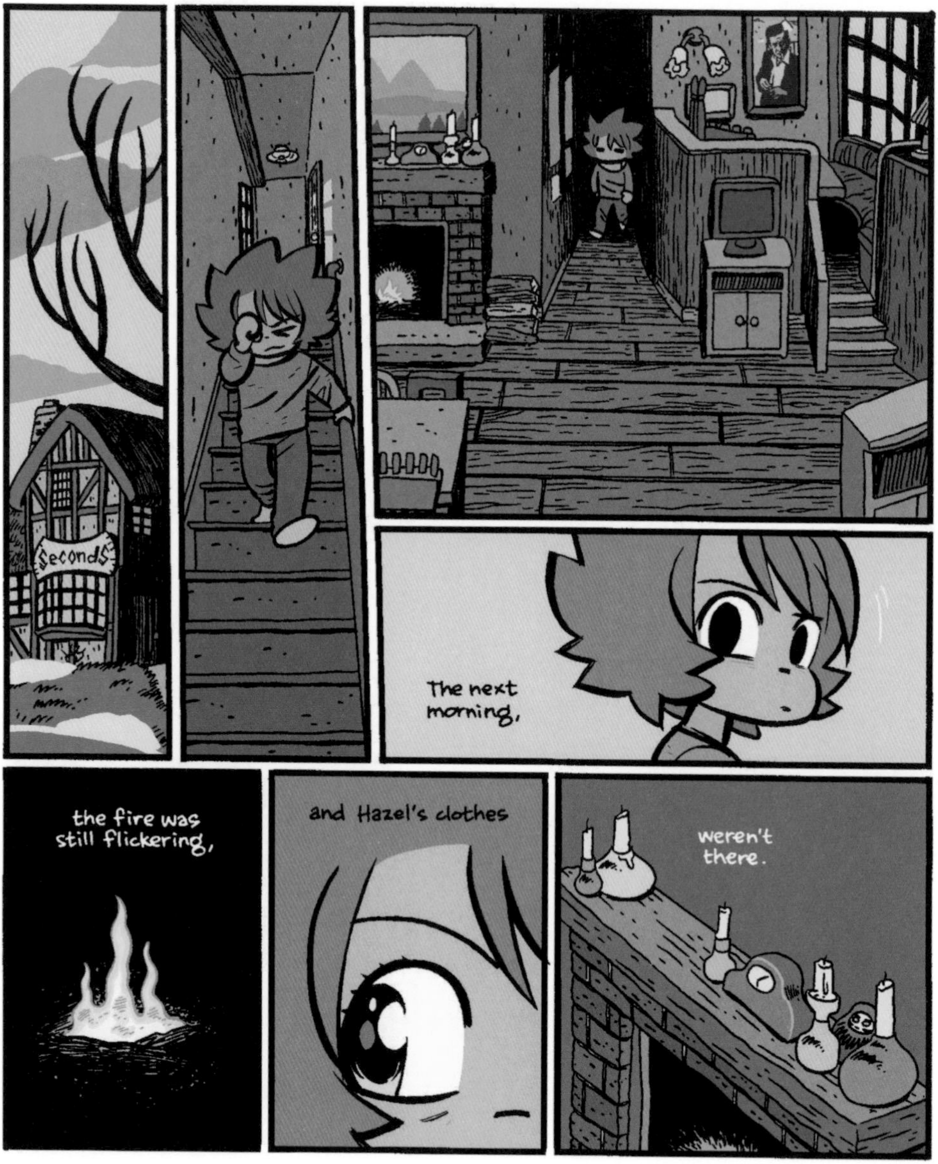
Seconds
The next morning,
the fire was still flickering,
and Hazel's clothes
weren't there.

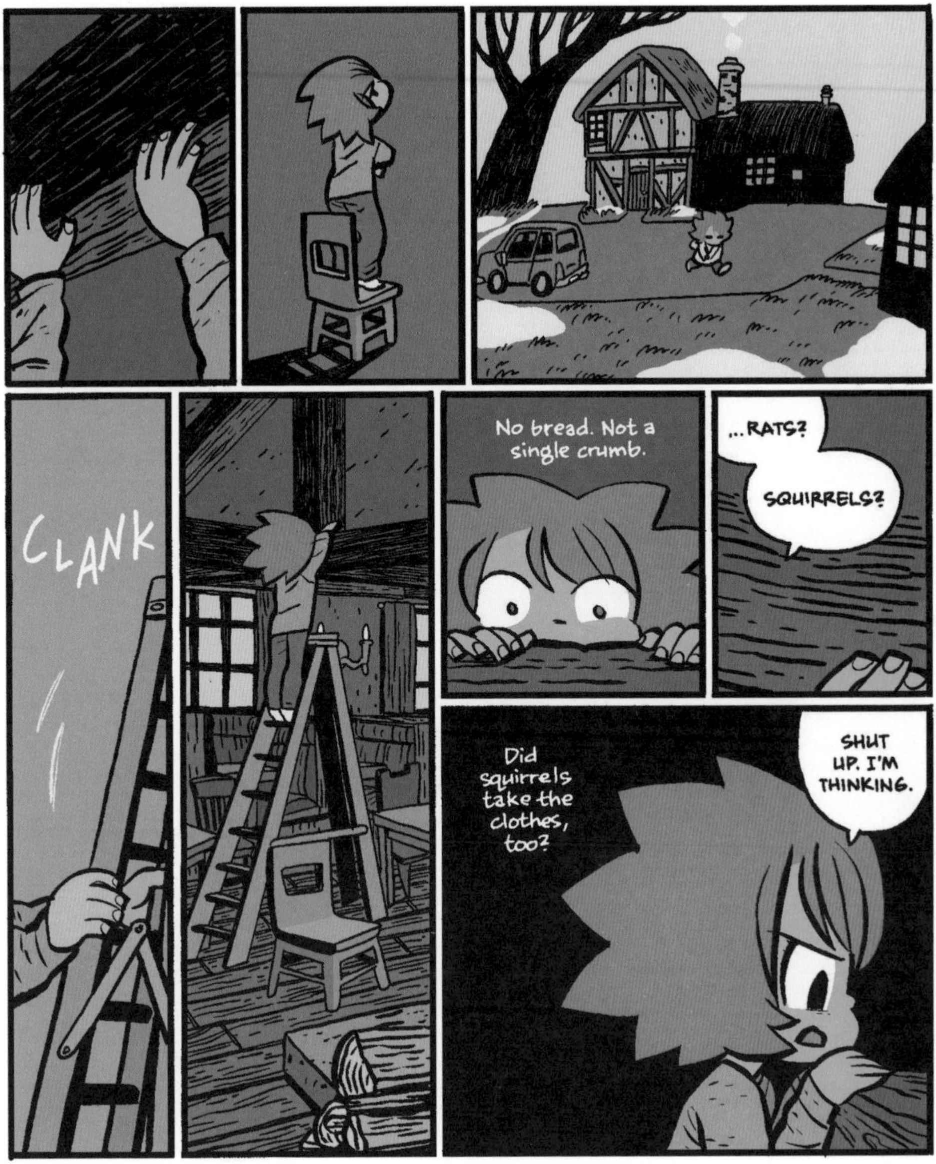
CLANK
No bread. Not a single crumb.
...RATS?
SQUIRRELS?
Did squirrels take the clothes, too?
SHUT UP. I'M THINKING.

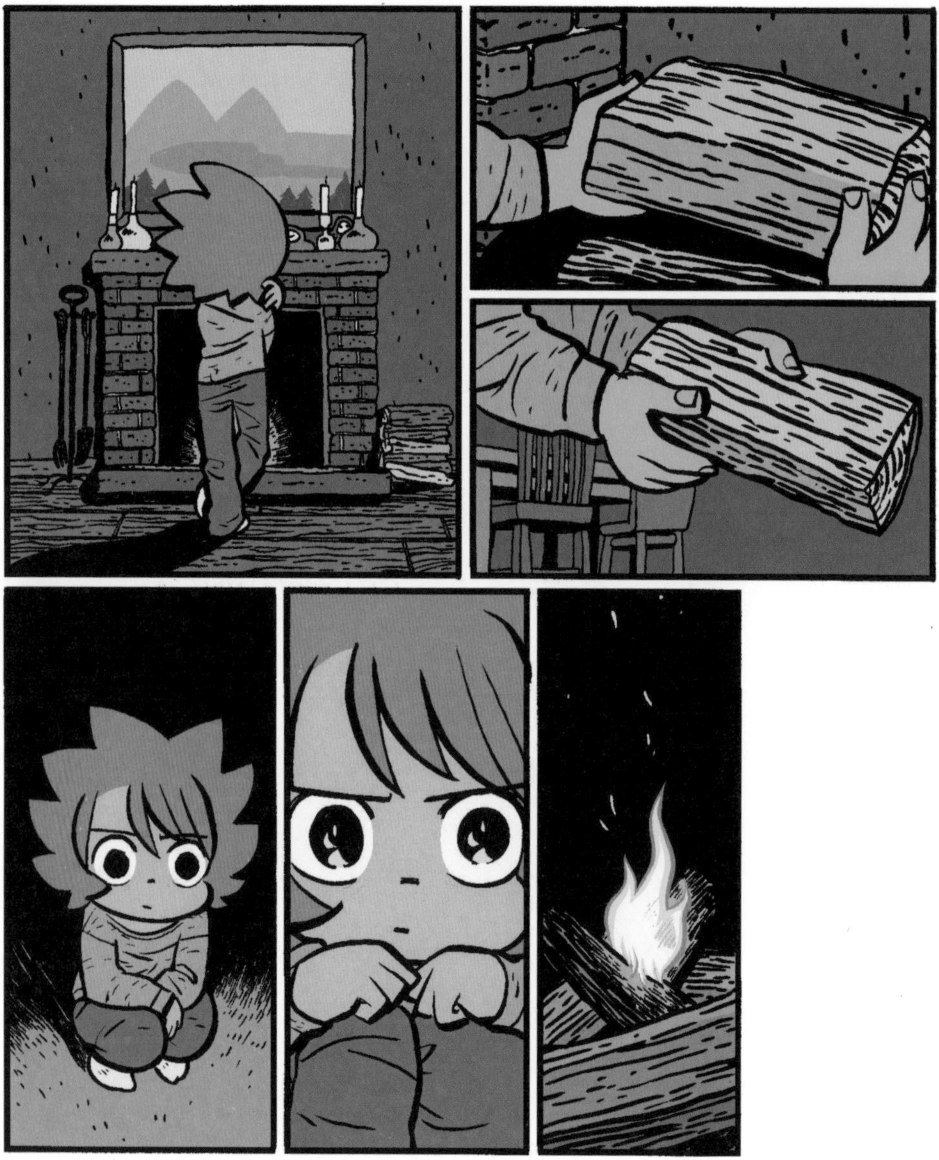

3

Lis

It felt like she hadn't seen Arthur in a week, which was unusual.

HEY.

WHERE AAARE YOU, DUDE?

I TOLD YOU LIKE FIFTY TIMES.

I KNOW. SORRY. BRAIN BAD.

She suddenly remembered, but only after it was too late.

...FUNERAL.

I... UM... I'M SORRY FOR YOUR... I MEAN... YOU KNOW...

IT IS WHAT IT IS, KATIE. ENOUGH ABOUT ME. I'M FINE. ARE YOU ALRIGHT?

OH... SURE... YEAH. THINGS ARE OKAY...

GREAT. LISTEN, JUST LEAVE THE SITE TO ME, KATIE. EVERYTHING'S FINE. THERE'S NOTHING TO GET ALARMED ABOUT. I'M TAKING CARE OF IT.

771 Talmadge Street

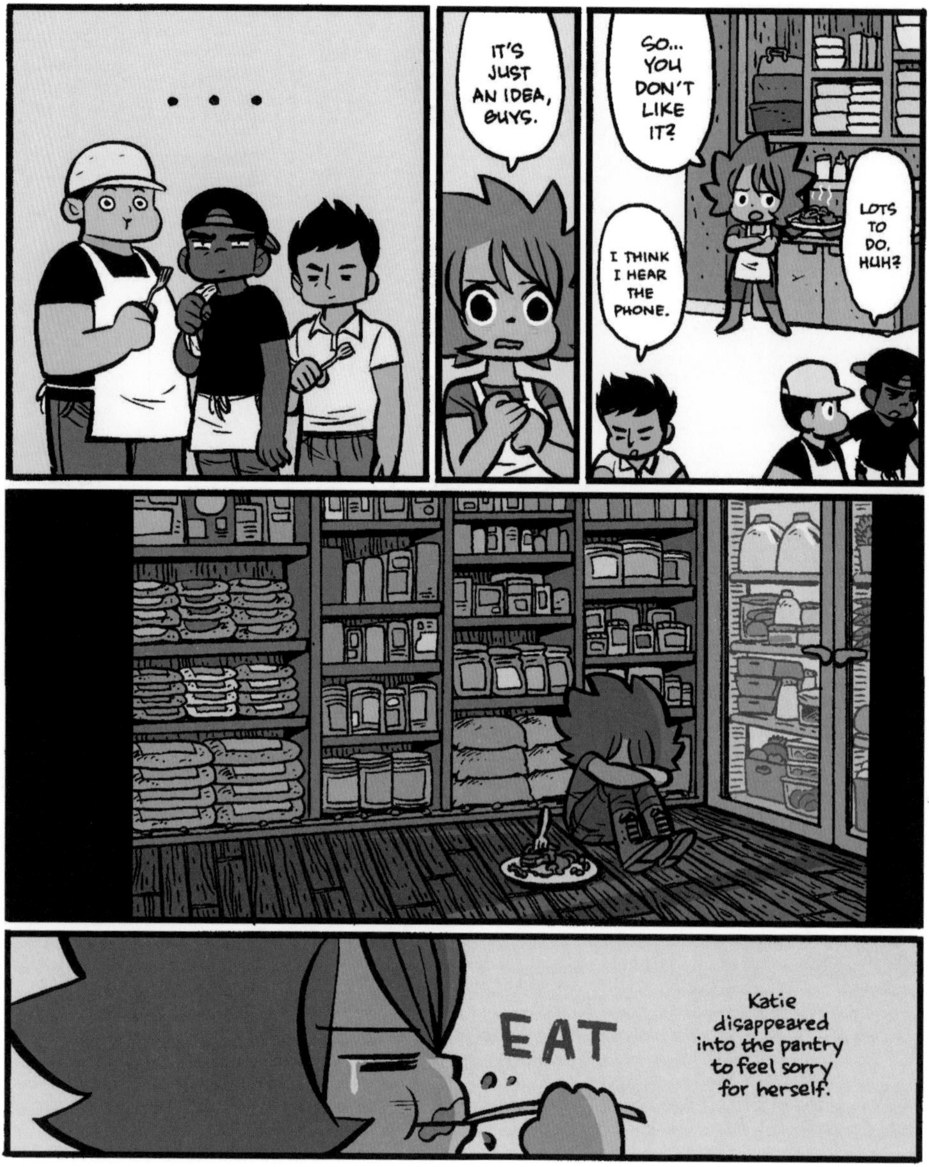
. . .
IT'S JUST AN IDEA, GUYS.
SO... YOU DON'T LIKE IT?
I THINK I HEAR THE PHONE.
LOTS TO DO, HUH?
EAT
Katie disappeared into the pantry to feel sorry for herself.

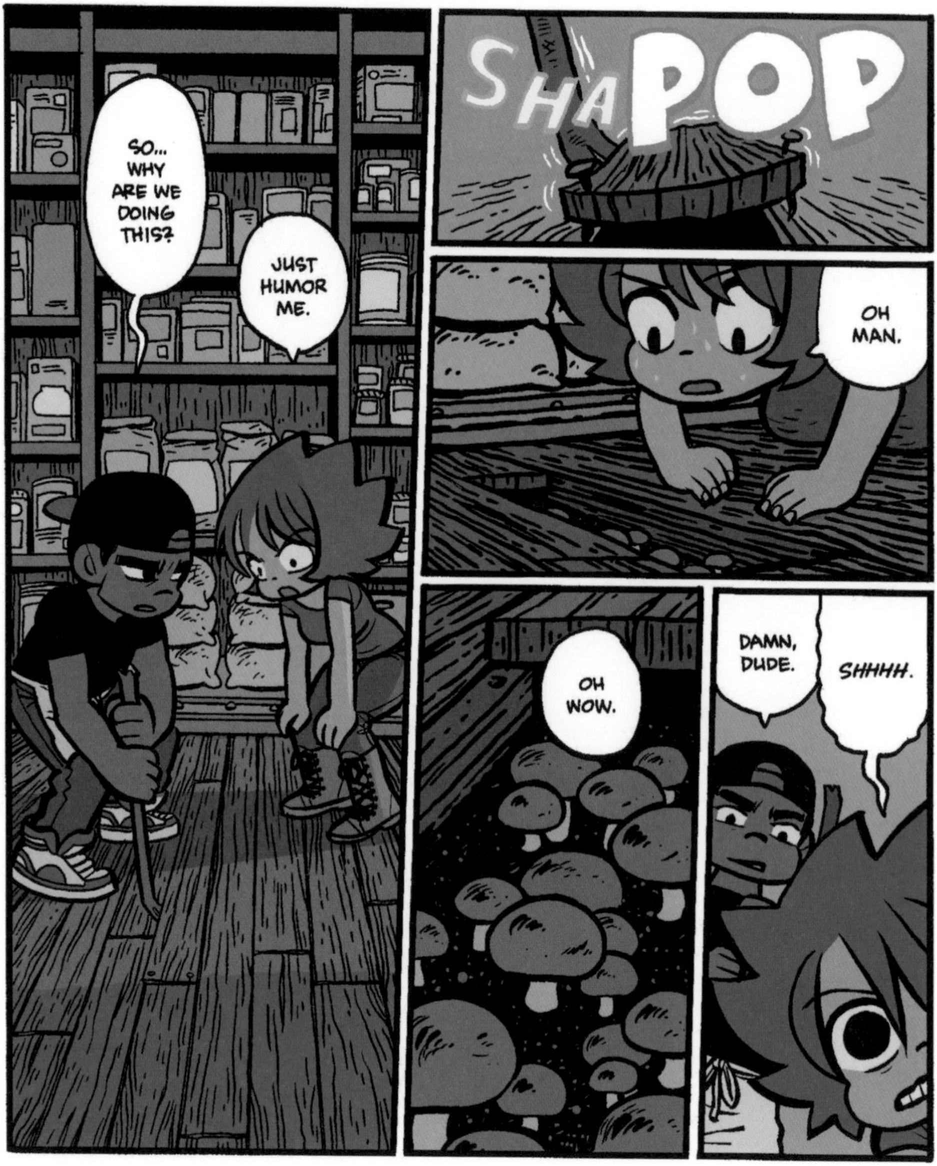
SO... WHY ARE WE DOING THIS?
JUST HUMOR ME.
SHAPOP
OH MAN.
OH WOW.
DAMN, DUDE.
SHHHH.

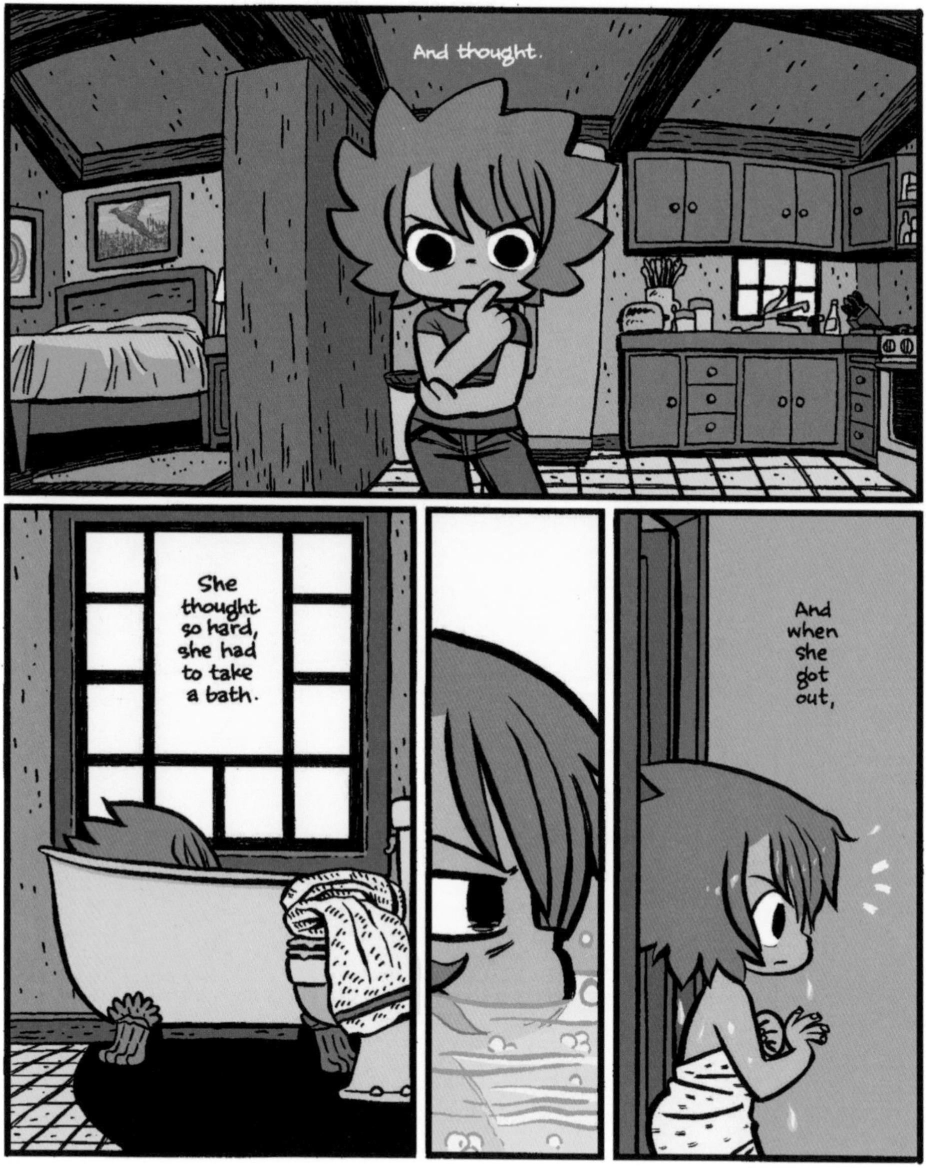

And thought.
She thought so hard, she had to take a bath.
And when she got out,

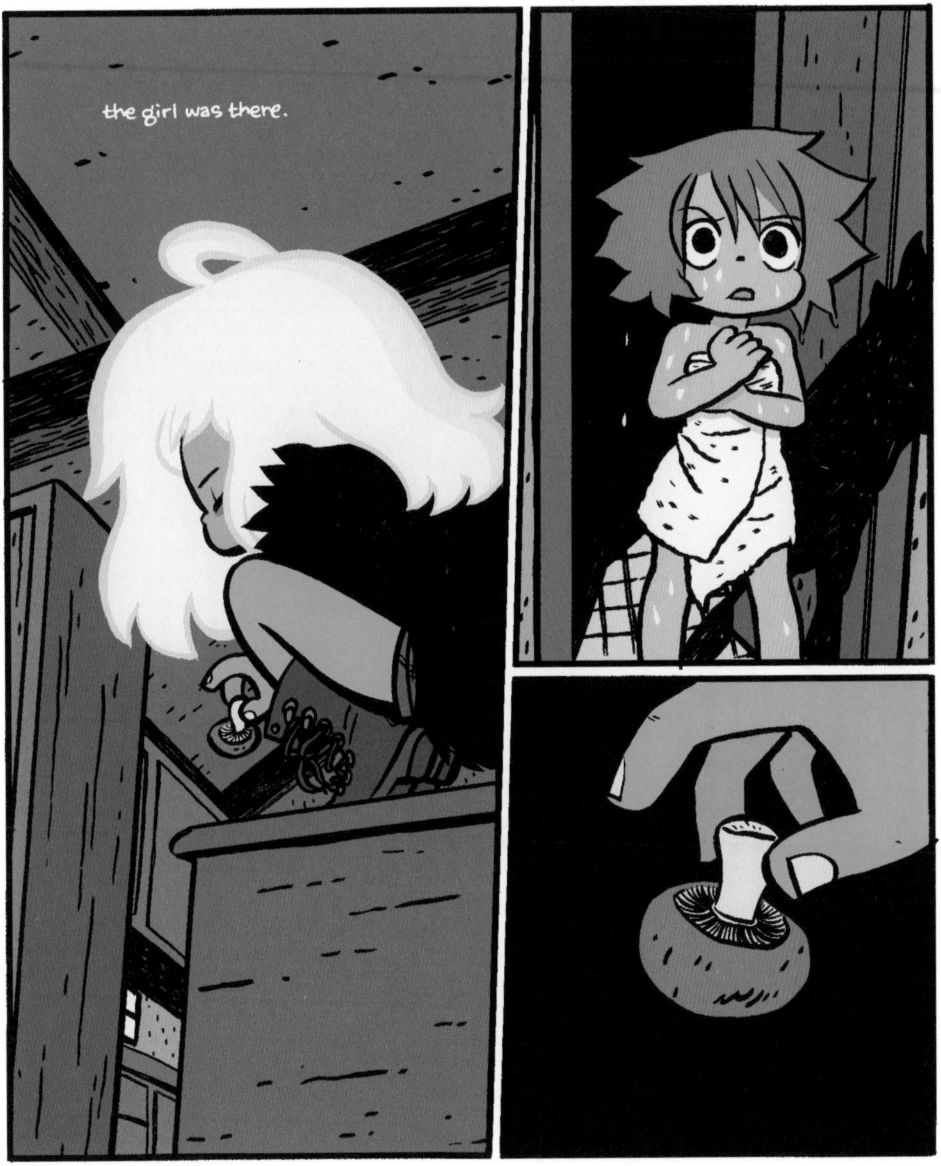
the girl was there.

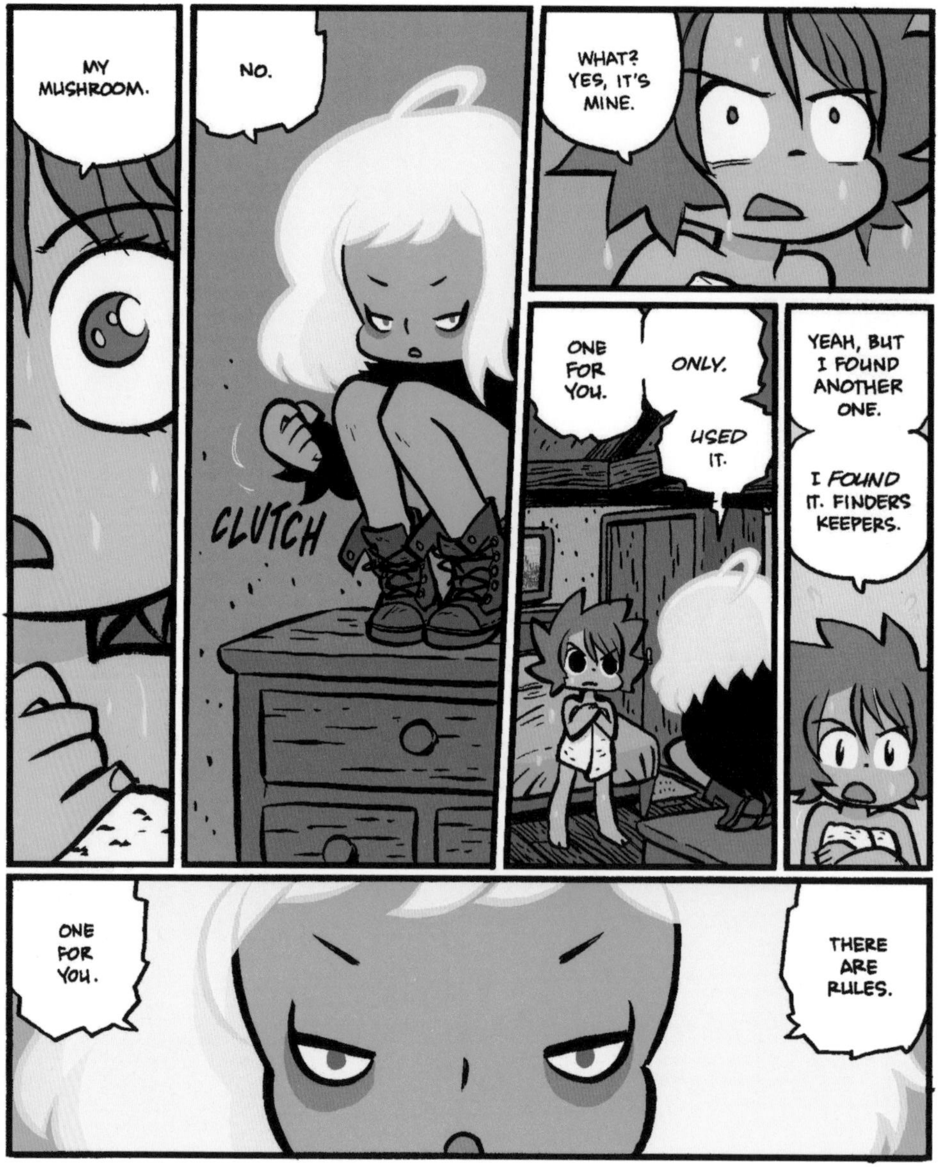
MY MUSHROOM.
NO.
CLUTCH
WHAT? YES, IT'S MINE.
ONE FOR YOU.
ONLY.
USED IT.
YEAH, BUT I FOUND ANOTHER ONE.
I *FOUND* IT. FINDERS KEEPERS.
ONE FOR YOU.
THERE ARE RULES.

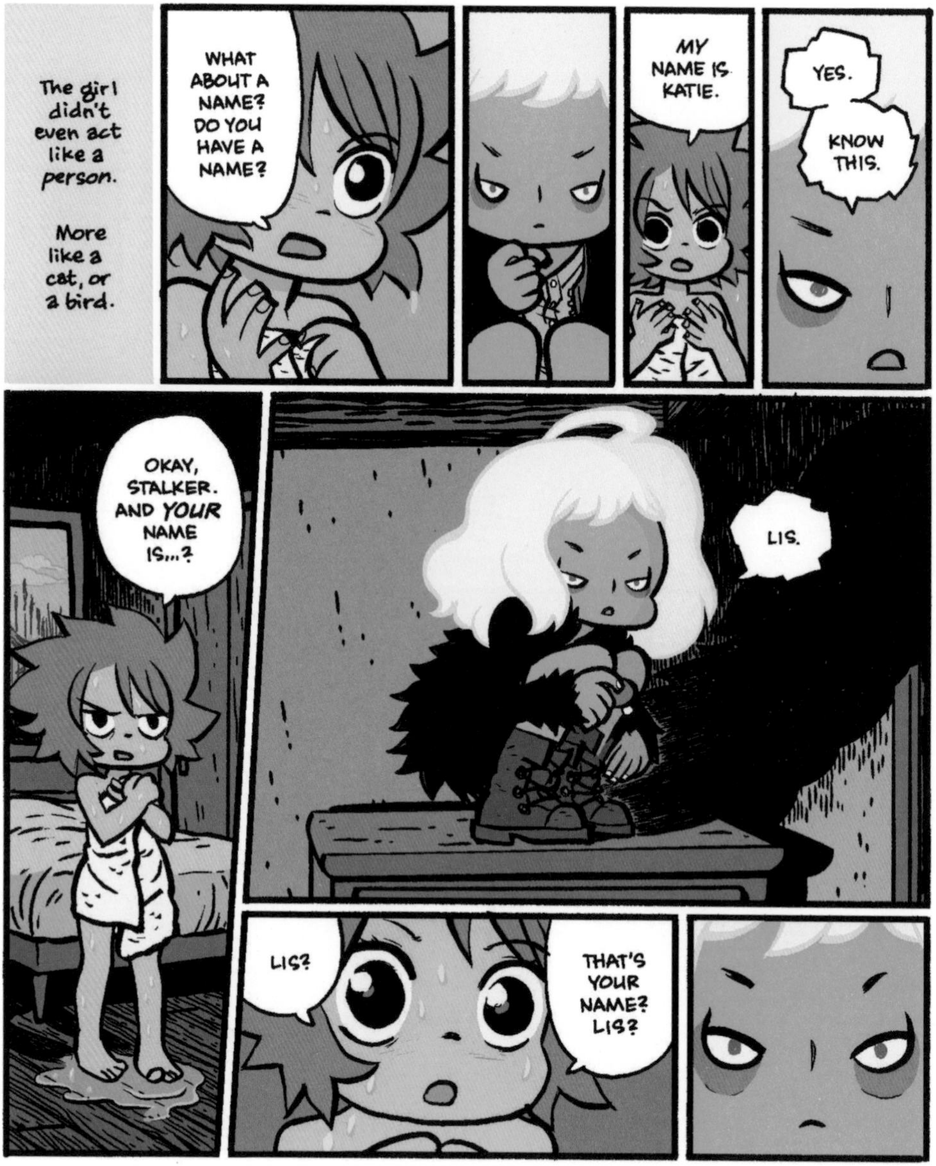
The girl didn't even act like a *person*.
More like a cat, or a bird.
WHAT ABOUT A NAME? DO YOU HAVE A NAME?
MY NAME IS KATIE.
YES.
KNOW THIS.
OKAY, STALKER. AND *YOUR* NAME IS...?
LIS.
LIS?
THAT'S YOUR NAME? LIS?

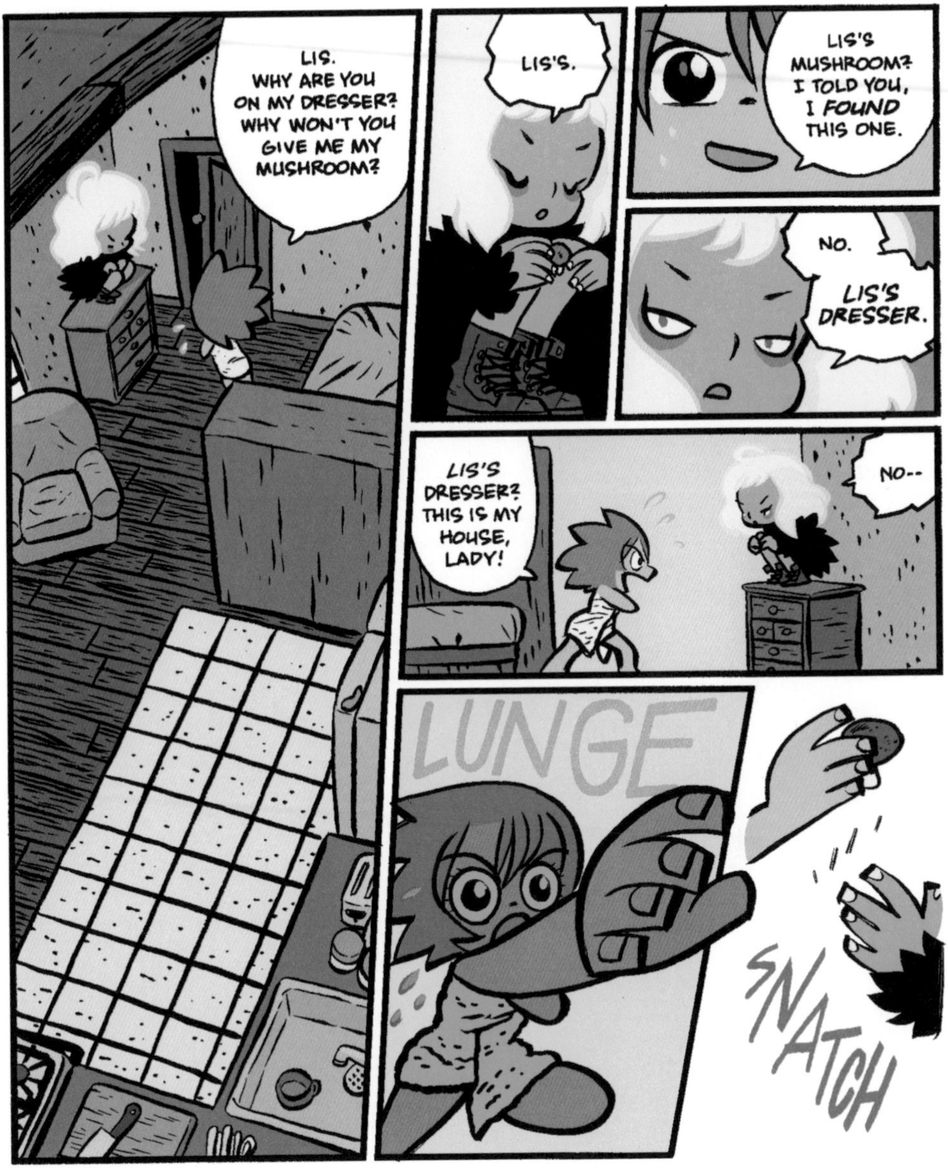
LIS.
WHY ARE YOU ON MY DRESSER? WHY WON'T YOU GIVE ME MY MUSHROOM?
LIS'S.
LIS'S MUSHROOM? I TOLD YOU, I *FOUND* THIS ONE.
NO.
LIS'S DRESSER.
LIS'S DRESSER? THIS IS MY HOUSE, LADY!
NO--
LUNGE
SNATCH

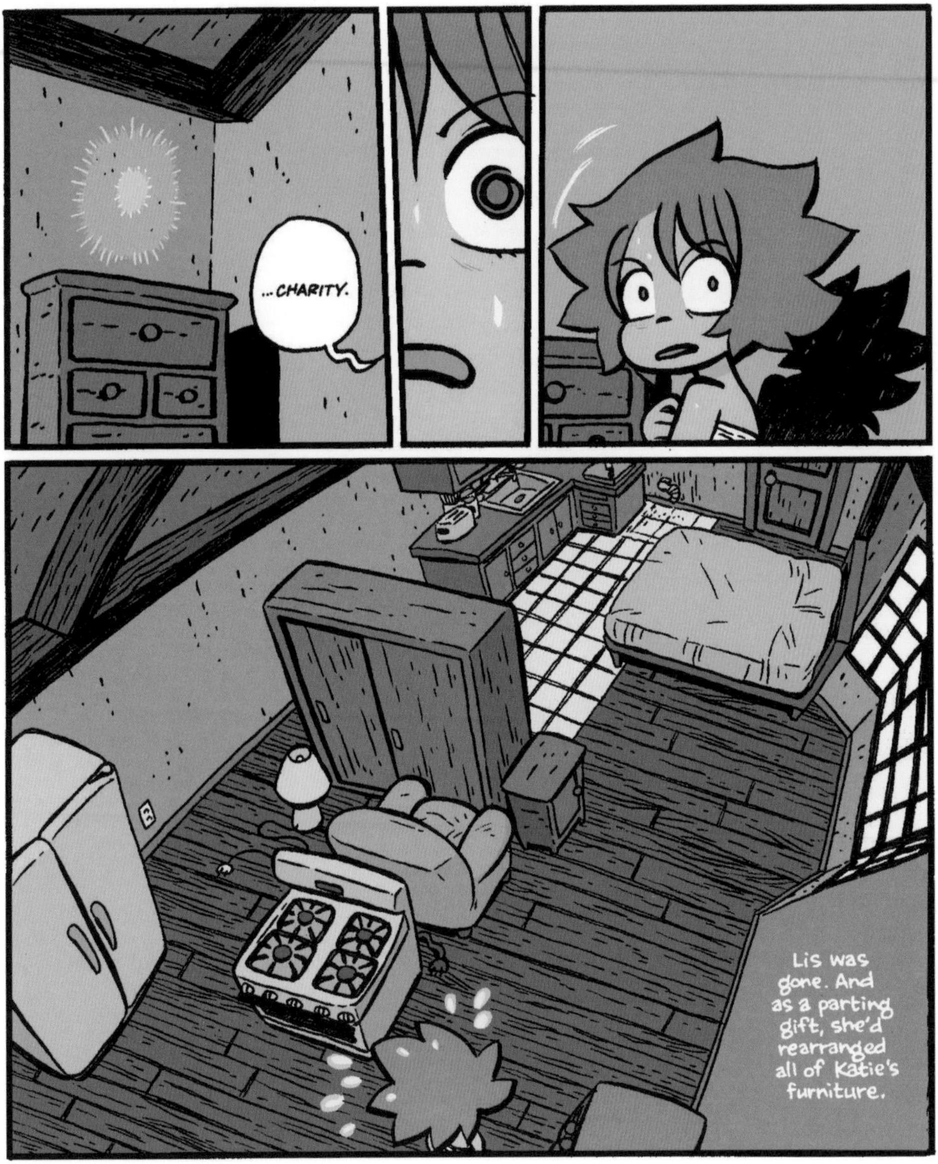
...CHARITY.
Lis was gone. And as a parting gift, she'd rearranged all of Katie's furniture.

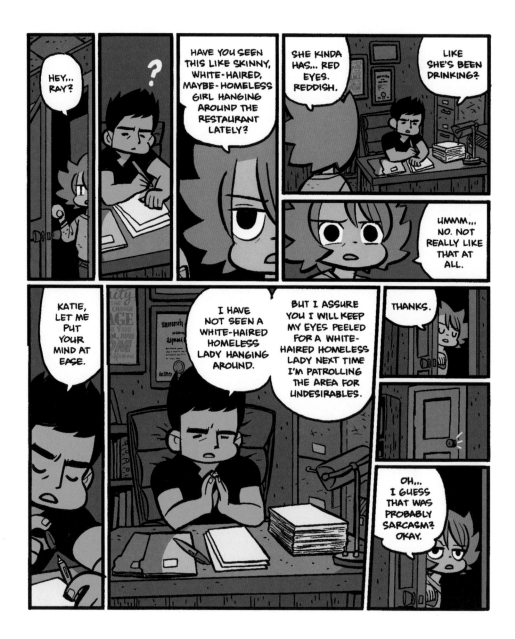

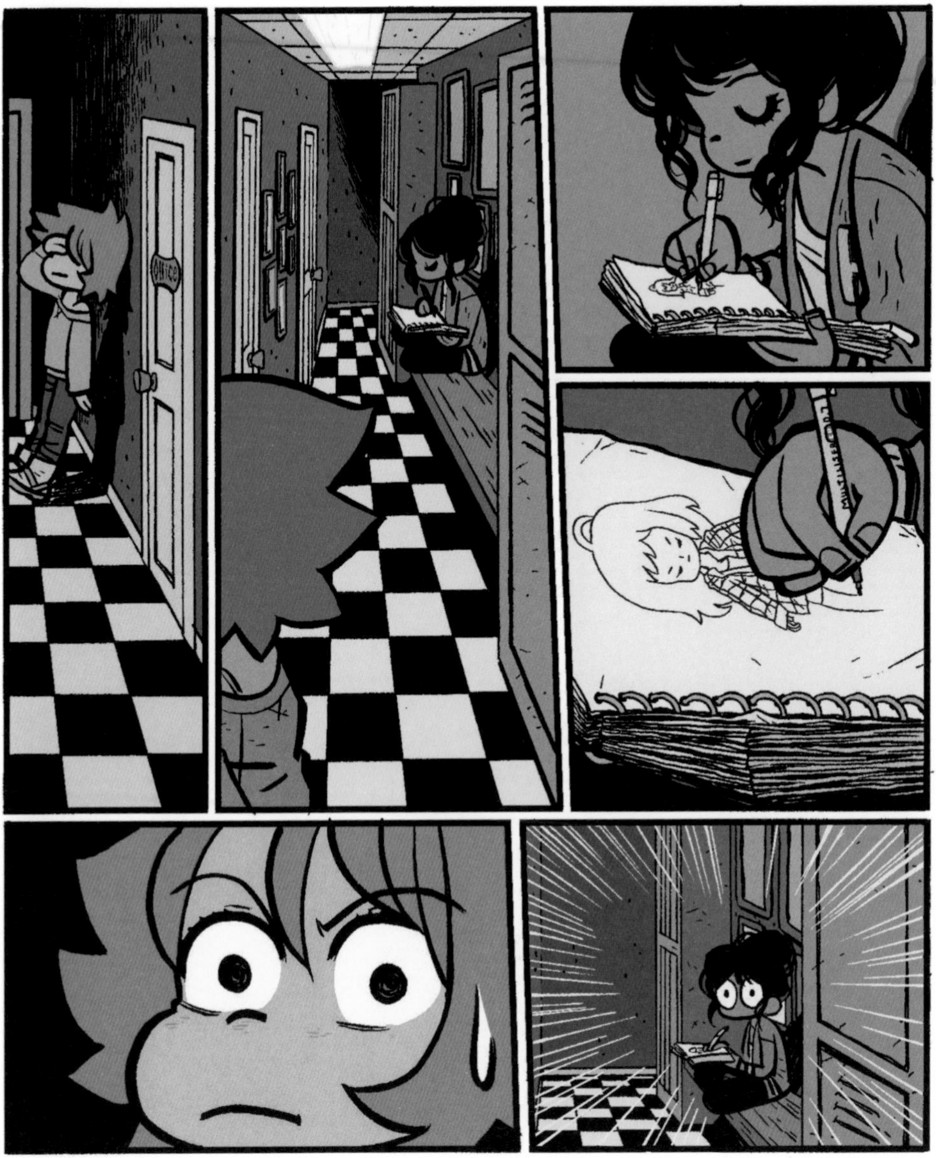

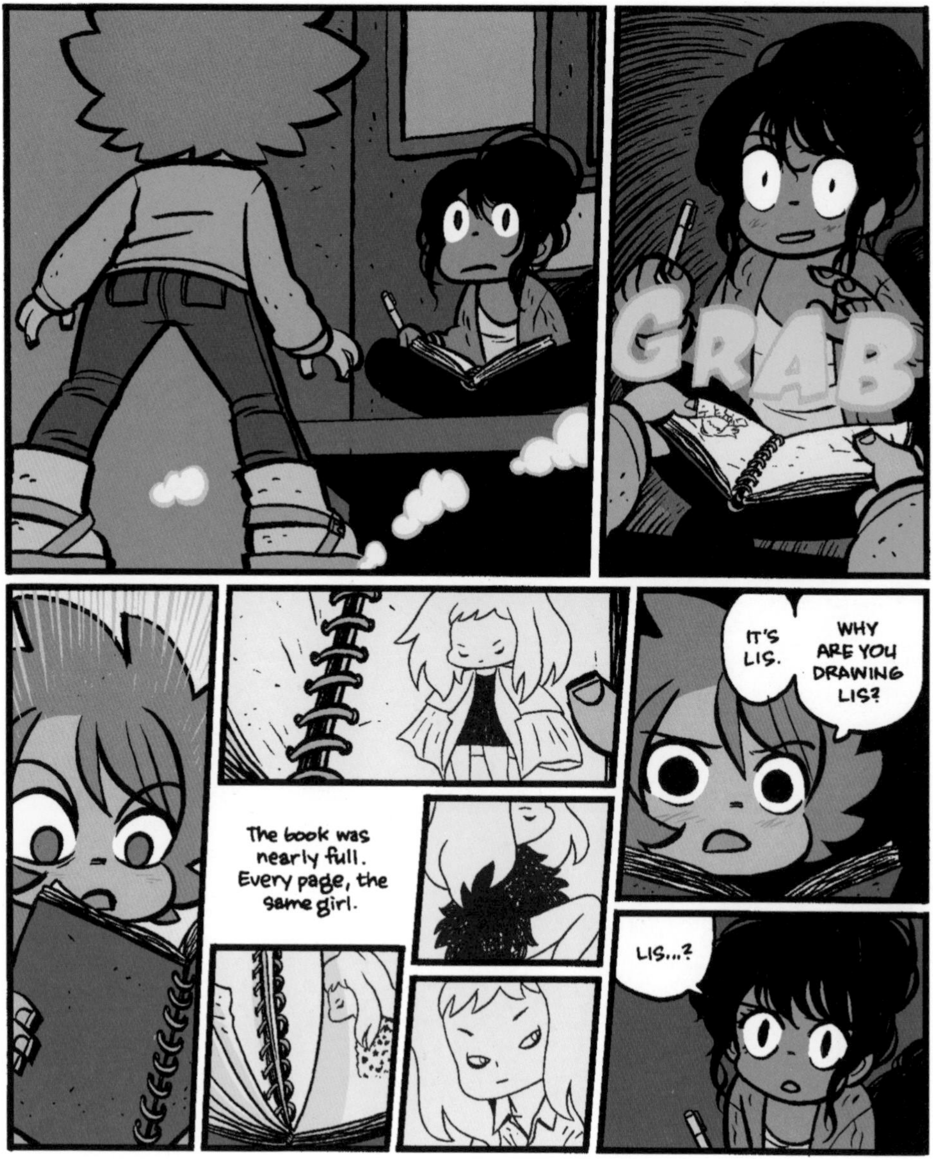
GRAB
IT'S LIS.
WHY ARE YOU DRAWING LIS?
The book was nearly full. Every page, the same girl.
LIS...?

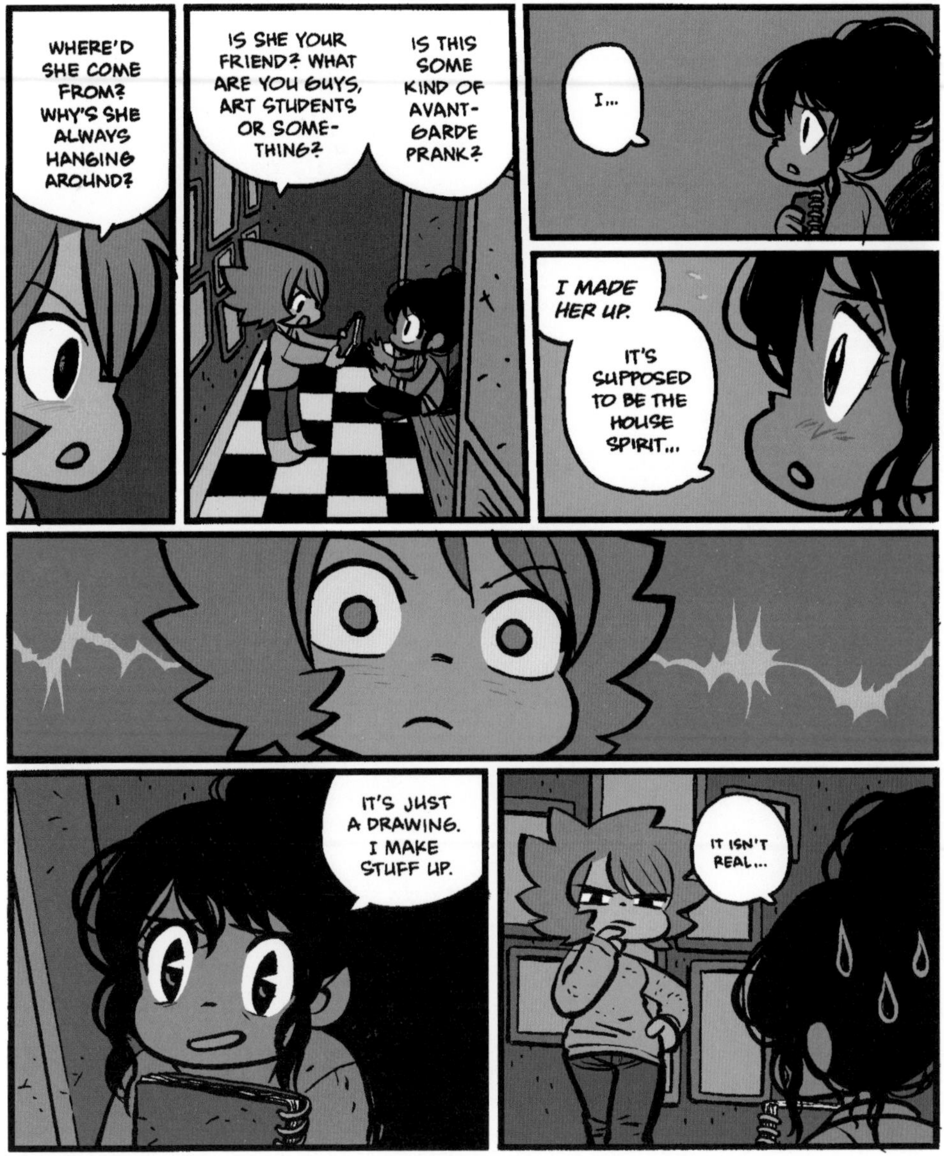
WHERE'D SHE COME FROM? WHY'S SHE ALWAYS HANGING AROUND?
IS SHE YOUR FRIEND? WHAT ARE YOU GUYS, ART STUDENTS OR SOME-THING?
IS THIS SOME KIND OF AVANT-GARDE PRANK?
I...
I MADE HER UP.
IT'S SUPPOSED TO BE THE HOUSE SPIRIT...
IT'S JUST A DRAWING. I MAKE STUFF UP.
IT ISN'T REAL...

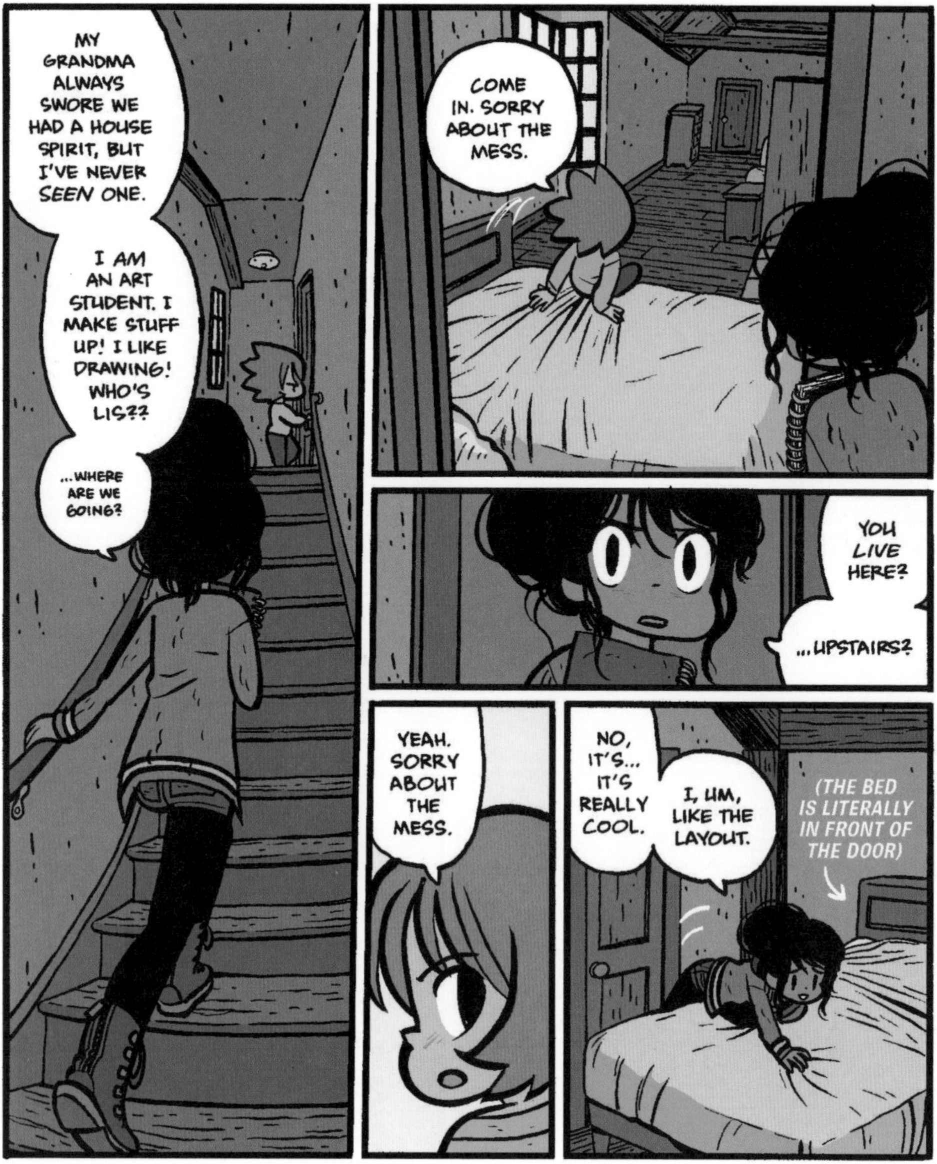
MY GRANDMA ALWAYS SWORE WE HAD A HOUSE SPIRIT, BUT I'VE NEVER SEEN ONE.
I AM AN ART STUDENT. I MAKE STUFF UP! I LIKE DRAWING! WHO'S LIS??
...WHERE ARE WE GOING?
COME IN. SORRY ABOUT THE MESS.
YOU LIVE HERE?
...UPSTAIRS?
YEAH. SORRY ABOUT THE MESS.
NO, IT'S... IT'S REALLY COOL.
I, UM, LIKE THE LAYOUT.
(THE BED IS LITERALLY IN FRONT OF THE DOOR)

93

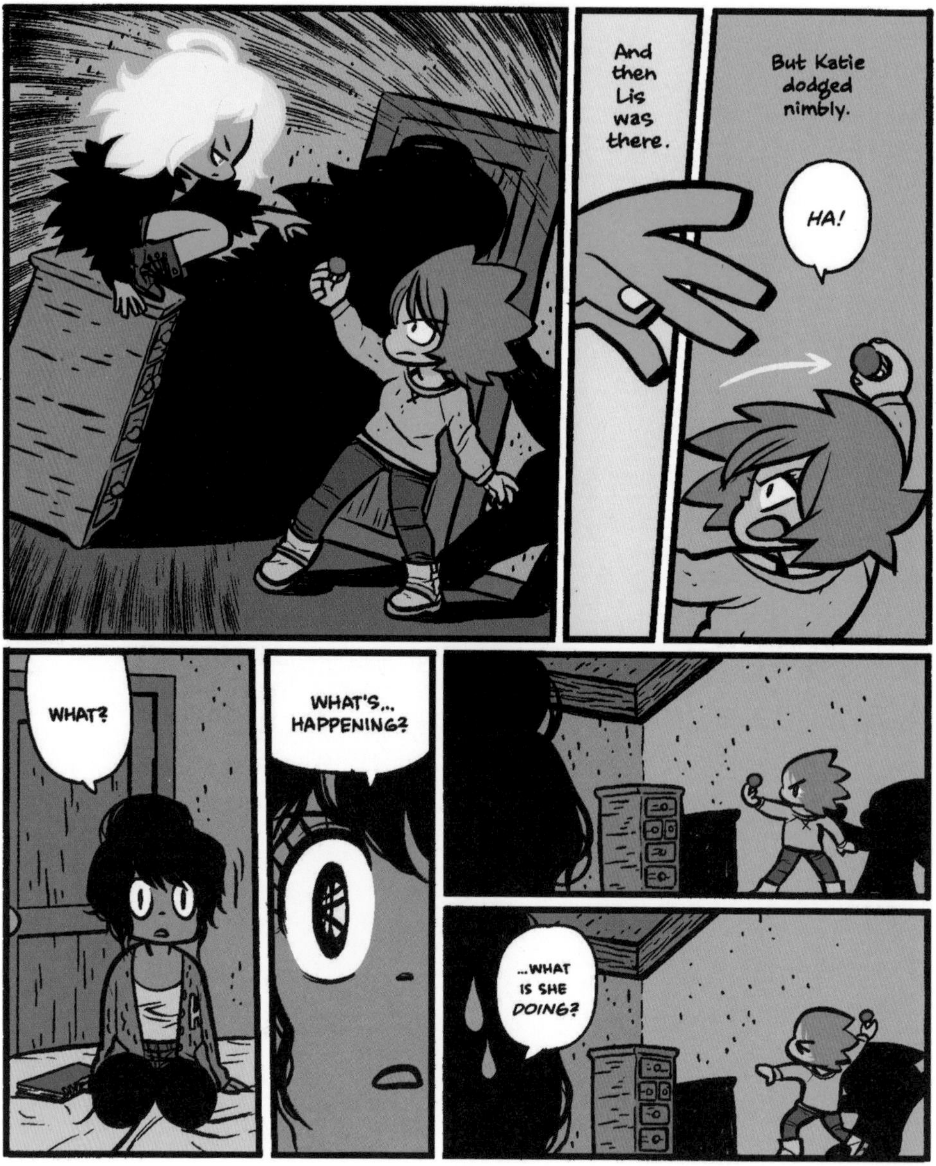
And then Lis was there.
But Katie dodged nimbly.
HA!
WHAT?
WHAT'S... HAPPENING?
...WHAT IS SHE DOING?

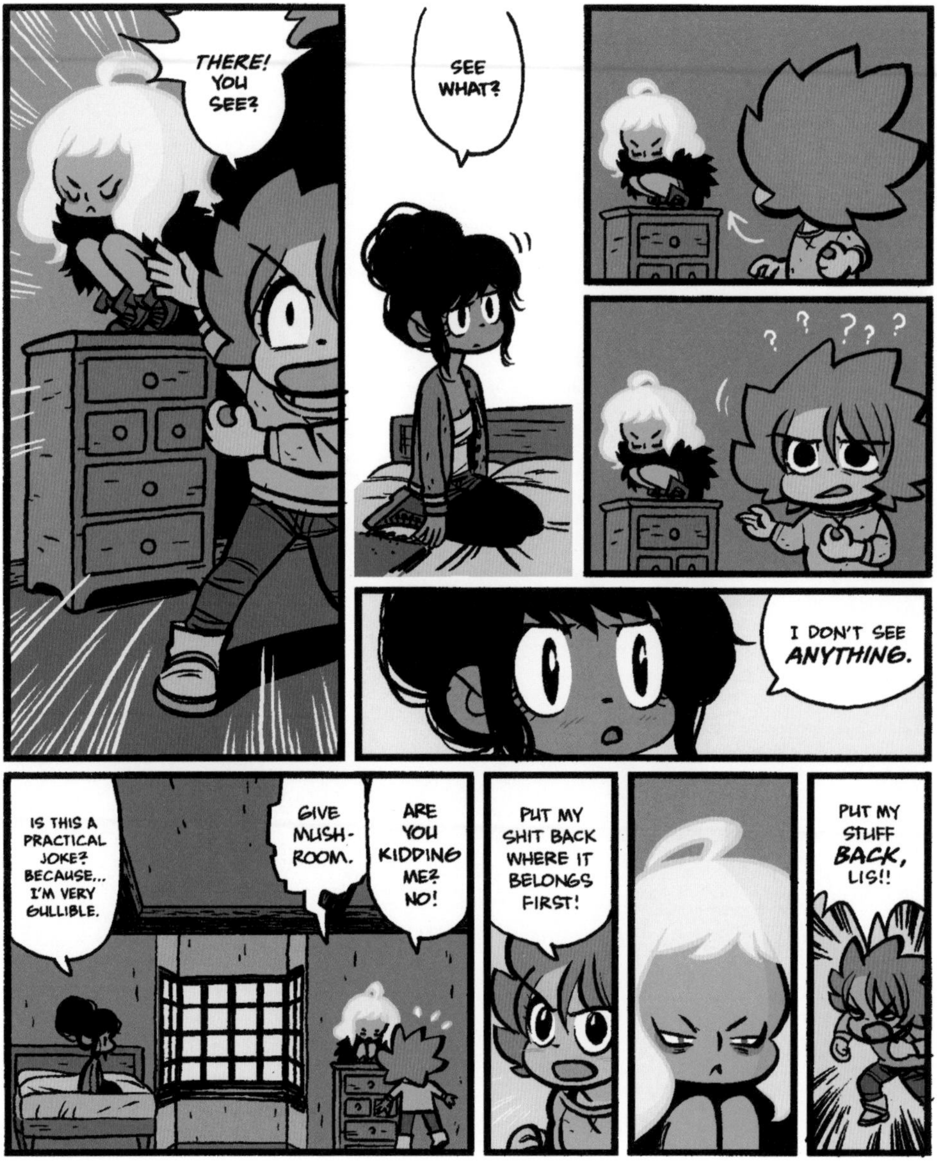
THERE! YOU SEE?
SEE WHAT?
I DON'T SEE ANYTHING.
IS THIS A PRACTICAL JOKE? BECAUSE... I'M VERY GULLIBLE.
GIVE MUSH-ROOM.
ARE YOU KIDDING ME? NO!
PUT MY SHIT BACK WHERE IT BELONGS FIRST!
PUT MY STUFF BACK, LIS!!

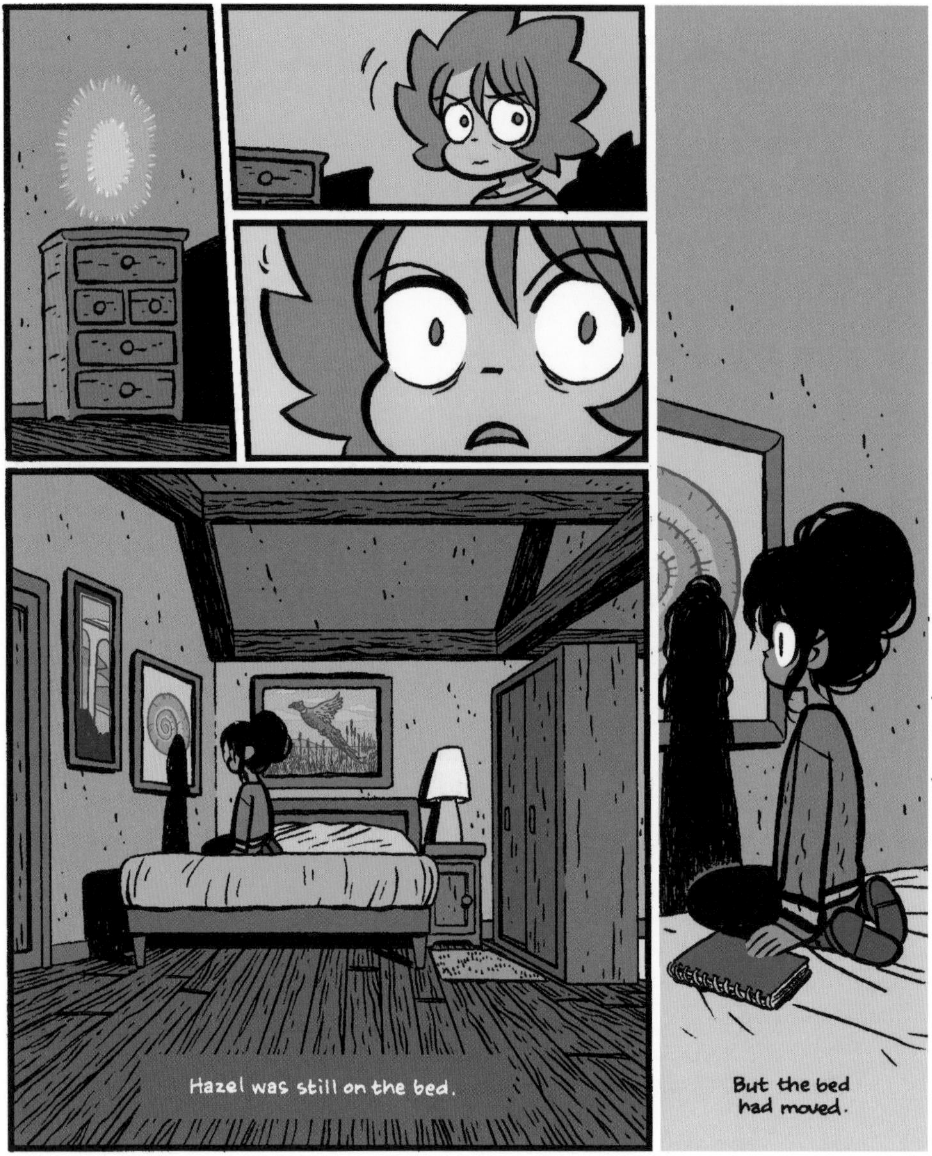
Hazel was still on the bed.
But the bed had moved.

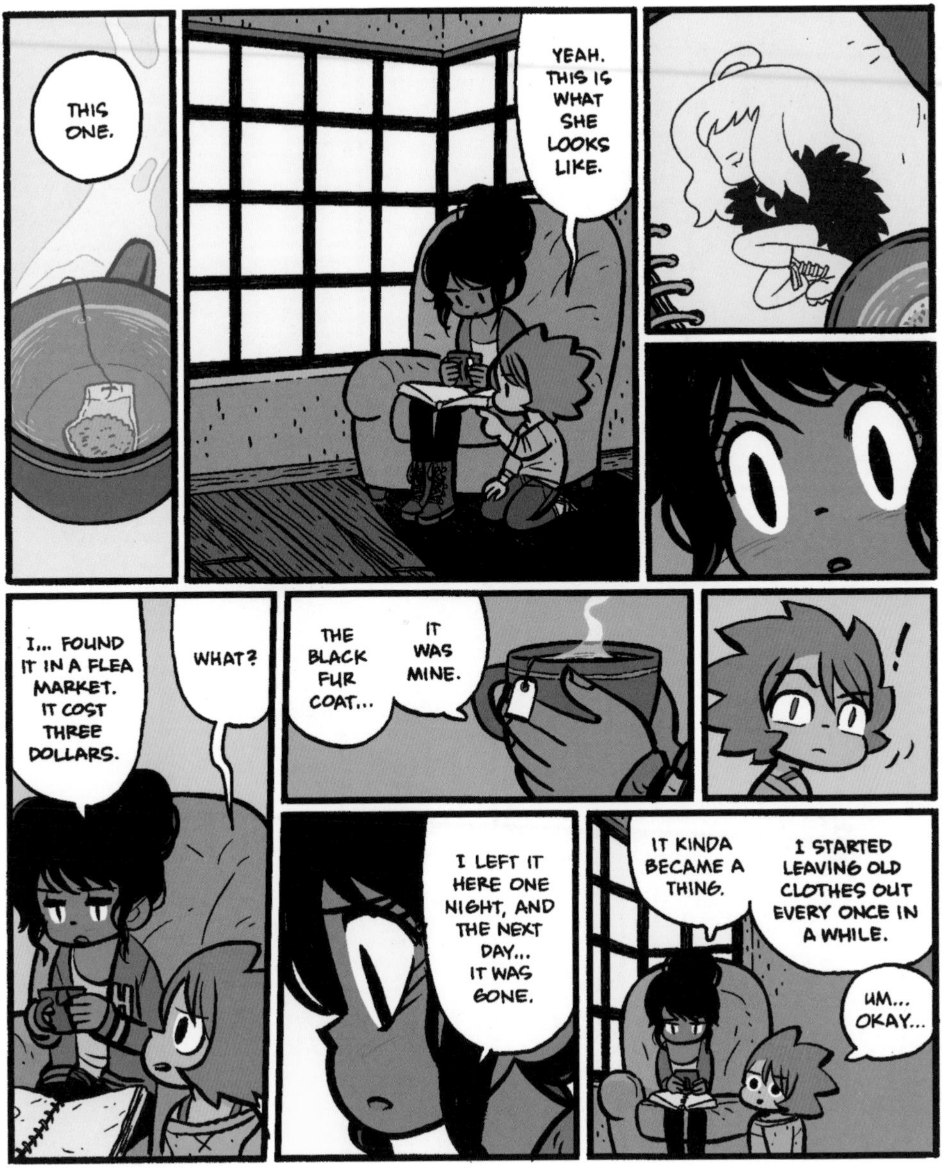

THIS ONE.
YEAH. THIS IS WHAT SHE LOOKS LIKE.
I... FOUND IT IN A FLEA MARKET. IT COST THREE DOLLARS.
WHAT?
THE BLACK FUR COAT...
IT WAS MINE.
!
I LEFT IT HERE ONE NIGHT, AND THE NEXT DAY... IT WAS GONE.
IT KINDA BECAME A THING.
I STARTED LEAVING OLD CLOTHES OUT EVERY ONCE IN A WHILE.
UM... OKAY...

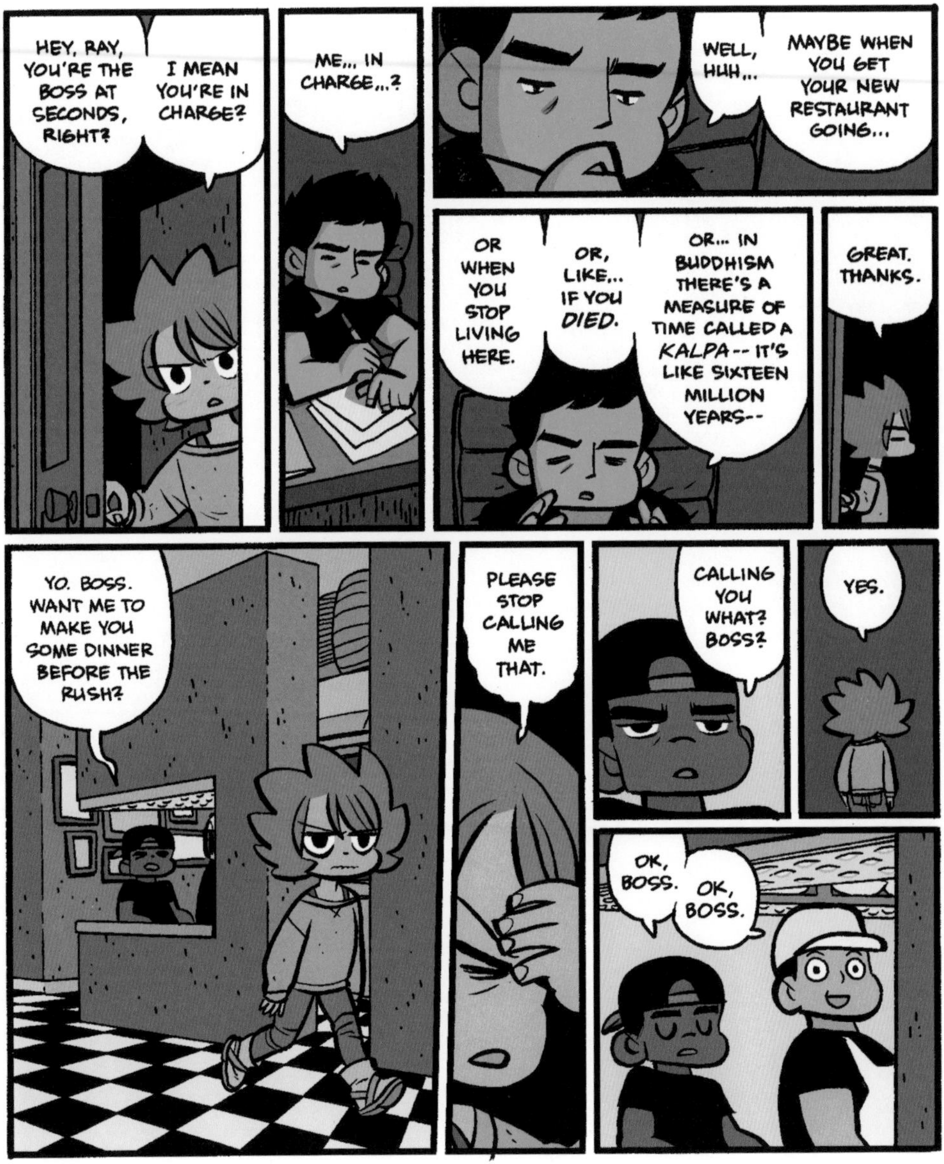
HEY, RAY, YOU'RE THE BOSS AT SECONDS, RIGHT?
I MEAN YOU'RE IN CHARGE?
ME... IN CHARGE...?
WELL, HUH...
MAYBE WHEN YOU GET YOUR NEW RESTAURANT GOING...
OR WHEN YOU STOP LIVING HERE.
OR, LIKE... IF YOU *DIED*.
OR... IN BUDDHISM THERE'S A MEASURE OF TIME CALLED A *KALPA*-- IT'S LIKE SIXTEEN MILLION YEARS--
GREAT. THANKS.
YO. BOSS. WANT ME TO MAKE YOU SOME DINNER BEFORE THE RUSH?
PLEASE STOP CALLING ME THAT.
CALLING YOU WHAT? BOSS?
YES.
OK, BOSS.
OK, BOSS.

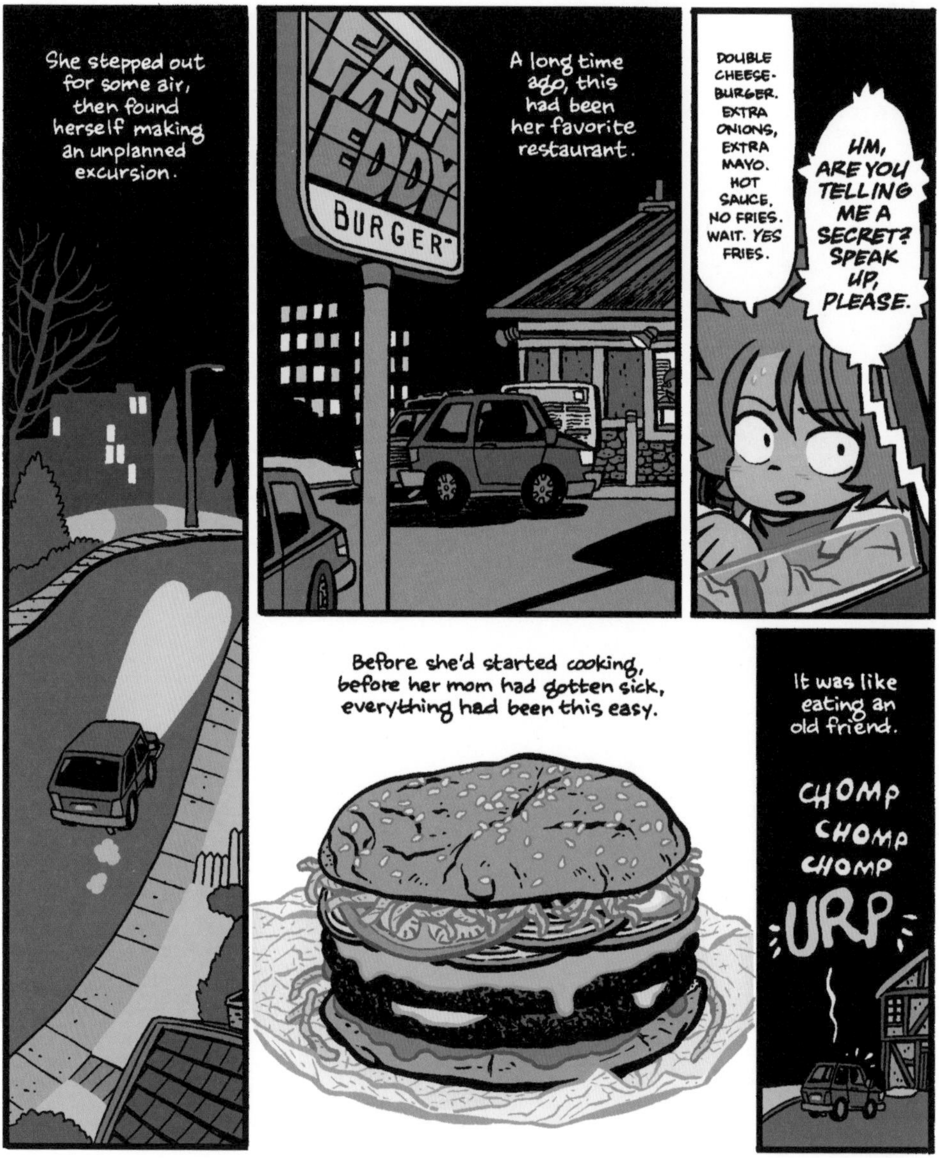

She stepped out for some air, then found herself making an unplanned excursion.
FAST EDDY BURGER
A long time ago, this had been her favorite restaurant.
DOUBLE CHEESE-BURGER. EXTRA ONIONS, EXTRA MAYO. HOT SAUCE. NO FRIES. WAIT. YES FRIES.
UM, ARE YOU TELLING ME A SECRET? SPEAK UP, PLEASE.
Before she'd started cooking, before her mom had gotten sick, everything had been this easy.
It was like eating an old friend.
CHOMP
CHOMP
CHOMP
URP

101

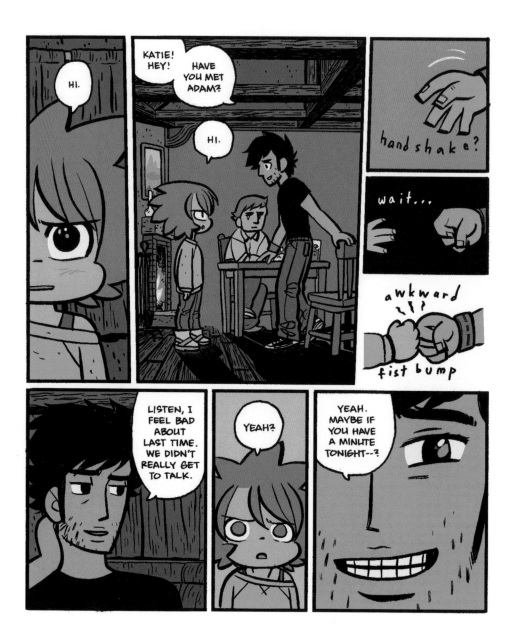

REVISION #2

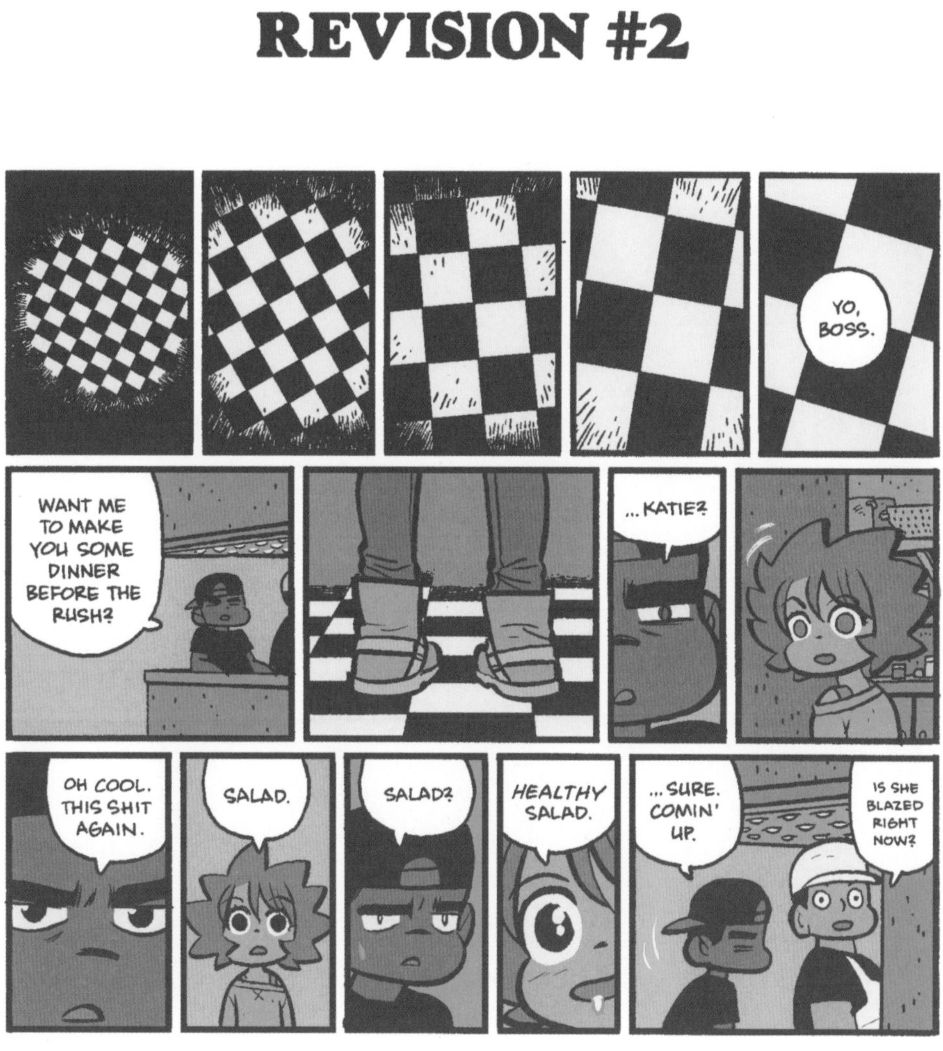
YO, BOSS.
WANT ME TO MAKE YOU SOME DINNER BEFORE THE RUSH?
...KATIE?
OH COOL. THIS SHIT AGAIN.
SALAD.
SALAD?
HEALTHY SALAD.
...SURE. COMIN' UP.
IS SHE BLAZED RIGHT NOW?

His smile   faltered.

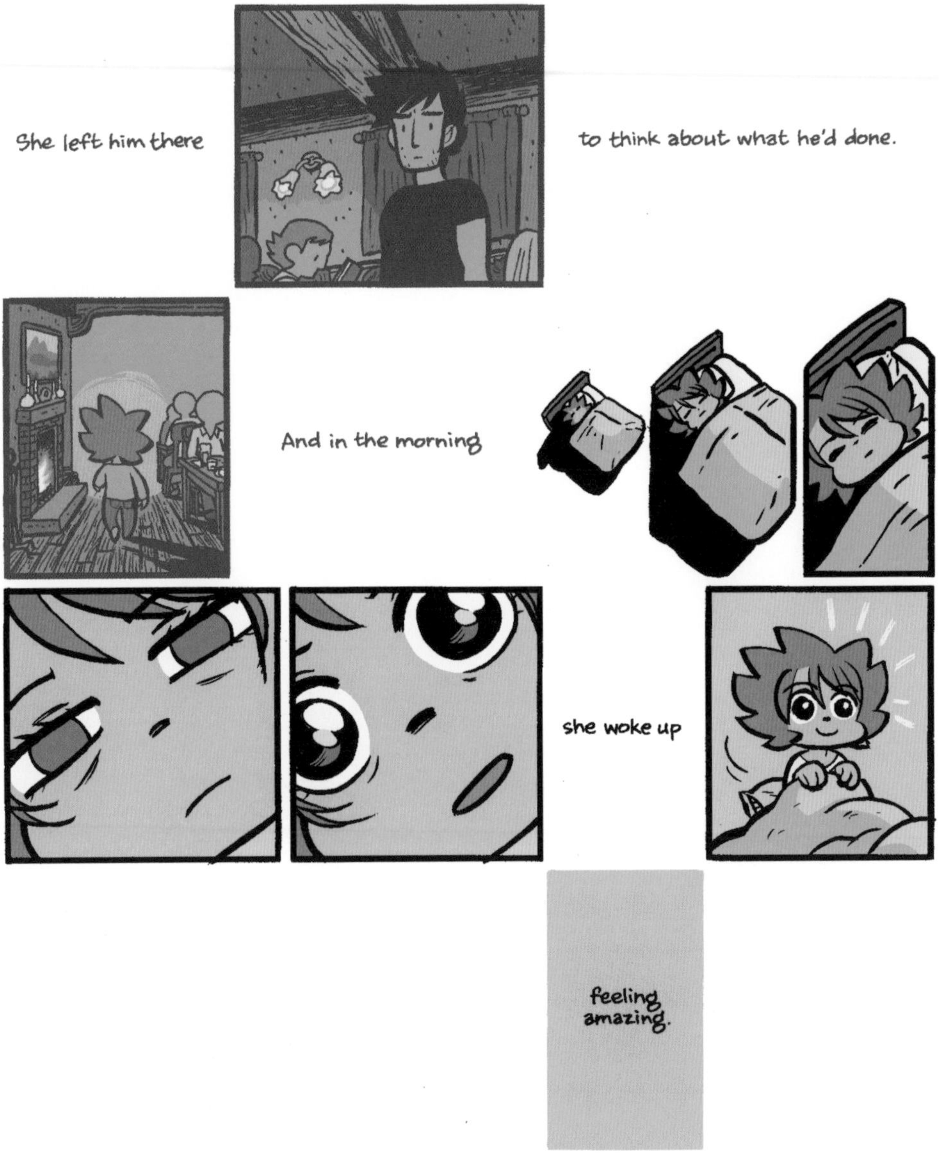
She left him there
to think about what he'd done.
And in the morning
she woke up
feeling amazing.

4
Rules

Arthur called as Katie was getting dressed.

HOW ARE THINGS?

THINGS ARE GREAT! AND WEIRD. ...THEY'RE WEIRD.

EXCELLENT. SO, YES, PERMITS HAVE BEEN DELAYED, THE CONTRACTOR IS BEING A PETULANT CHILD...

...BUT WHEN YOU GO IN THERE, PLEASE DON'T FREAK OUT ON HIM.

NOT YET, HA HA.

ARTHUR, I KNOW YOU JUST DID A FUNERAL AND YOU'RE PROBABLY MEGA BUMMED RIGHT NOW.

BUT THIS IS ALL GONNA WORK OUT. I HAVE A STRONG FEELING.

YEAH. YOU'RE RIGHT.

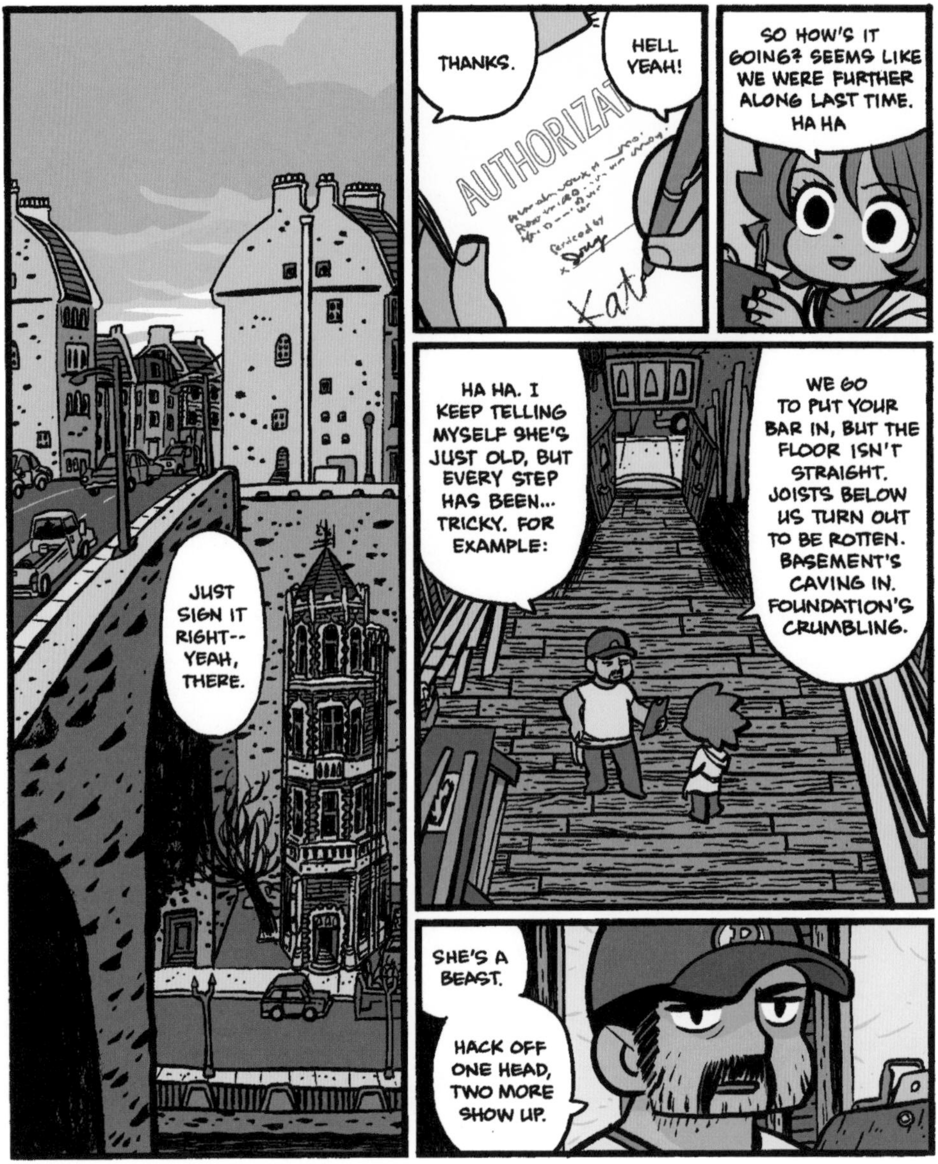
JUST SIGN IT RIGHT-- YEAH, THERE.
THANKS.
HELL YEAH!
AUTHORIZAT
SO HOW'S IT GOING? SEEMS LIKE WE WERE FURTHER ALONG LAST TIME. HA HA
HA HA. I KEEP TELLING MYSELF SHE'S JUST OLD, BUT EVERY STEP HAS BEEN... TRICKY. FOR EXAMPLE:
WE GO TO PUT YOUR BAR IN, BUT THE FLOOR ISN'T STRAIGHT. JOISTS BELOW US TURN OUT TO BE ROTTEN. BASEMENT'S CAVING IN. FOUNDATION'S CRUMBLING.
SHE'S A BEAST.
HACK OFF ONE HEAD, TWO MORE SHOW UP.

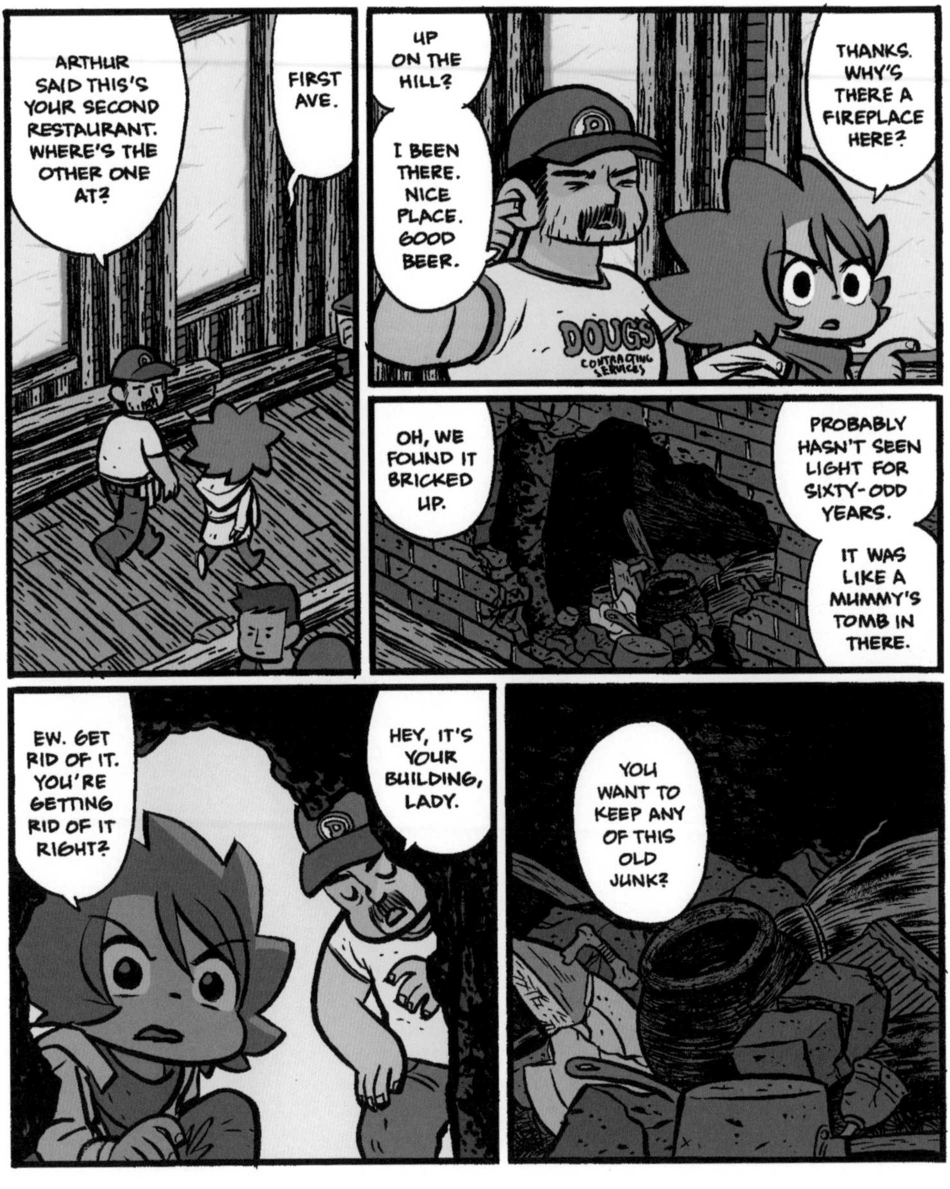
ARTHUR SAID THIS'S YOUR SECOND RESTAURANT. WHERE'S THE OTHER ONE AT?
FIRST AVE.
UP ON THE HILL?
I BEEN THERE. NICE PLACE. GOOD BEER.
THANKS. WHY'S THERE A FIREPLACE HERE?
DOUGS CONTRACTING SERVICES
OH, WE FOUND IT BRICKED UP.
PROBABLY HASN'T SEEN LIGHT FOR SIXTY-ODD YEARS.
IT WAS LIKE A MUMMY'S TOMB IN THERE.
EW. GET RID OF IT. YOU'RE GETTING RID OF IT RIGHT?
HEY, IT'S YOUR BUILDING, LADY.
YOU WANT TO KEEP ANY OF THIS OLD JUNK?

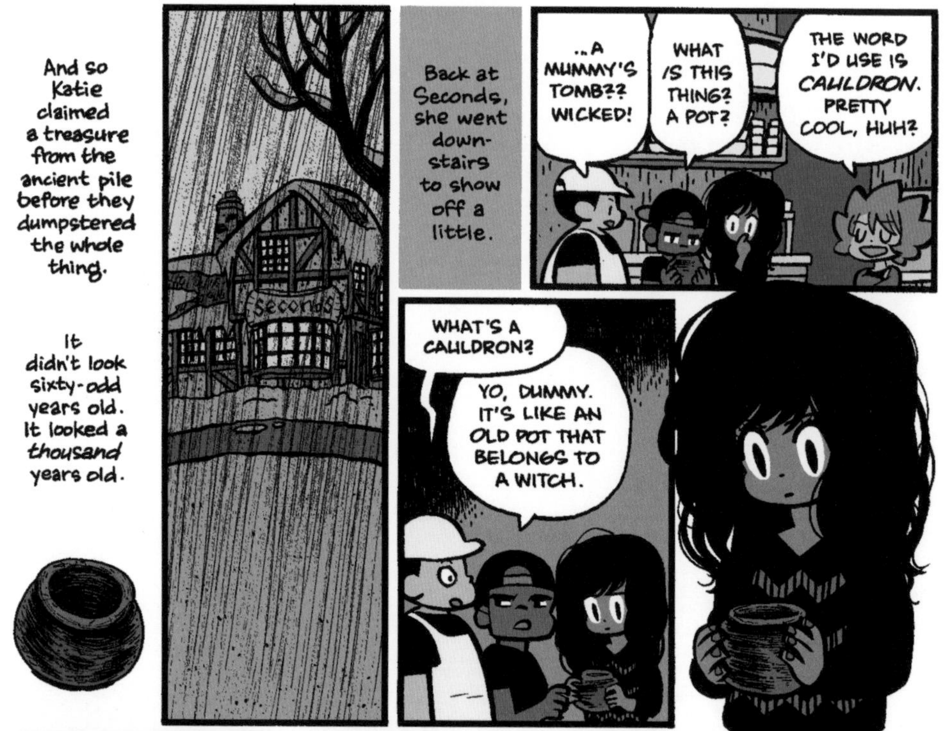
And so Katie claimed a treasure from the ancient pile before they dumpstered the whole thing.
It didn't look sixty-odd years old. It looked a *thousand* years old.
Seconds
Back at Seconds, she went down-stairs to show off a little.
..A MUMMY'S TOMB?? WICKED!
WHAT *IS* THIS THING? A POT?
THE WORD I'D USE IS *CAULDRON*. PRETTY COOL, HUH?
WHAT'S A CAULDRON?
YO, DUMMY. IT'S LIKE AN OLD POT THAT BELONGS TO A WITCH.
• • •
...WHAT?

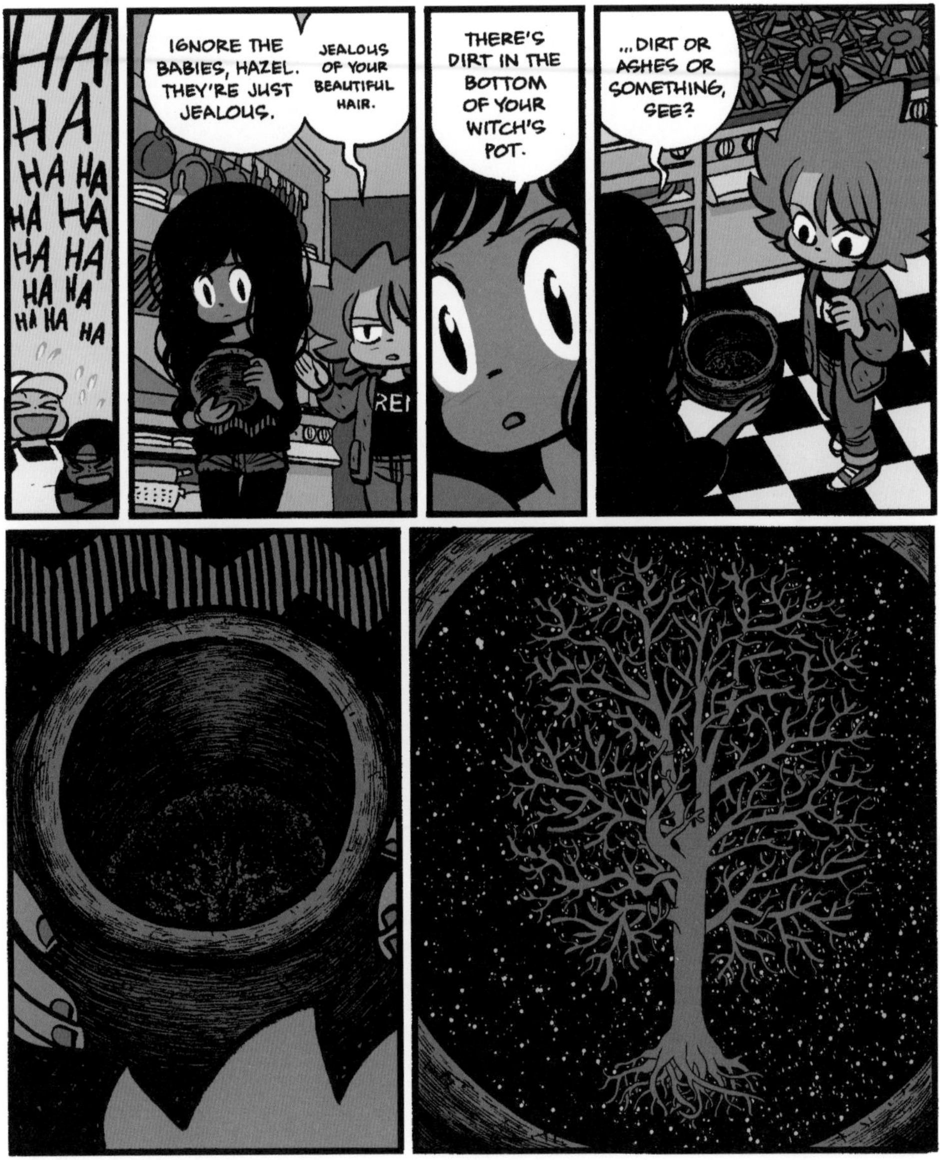
HA HA HA HA HA HA HA HA HA HA HA HA HA HA HA
IGNORE THE BABIES, HAZEL. THEY'RE JUST JEALOUS.
JEALOUS OF YOUR BEAUTIFUL HAIR.
THERE'S DIRT IN THE BOTTOM OF YOUR WITCH'S POT.
...DIRT OR ASHES OR SOMETHING, SEE?

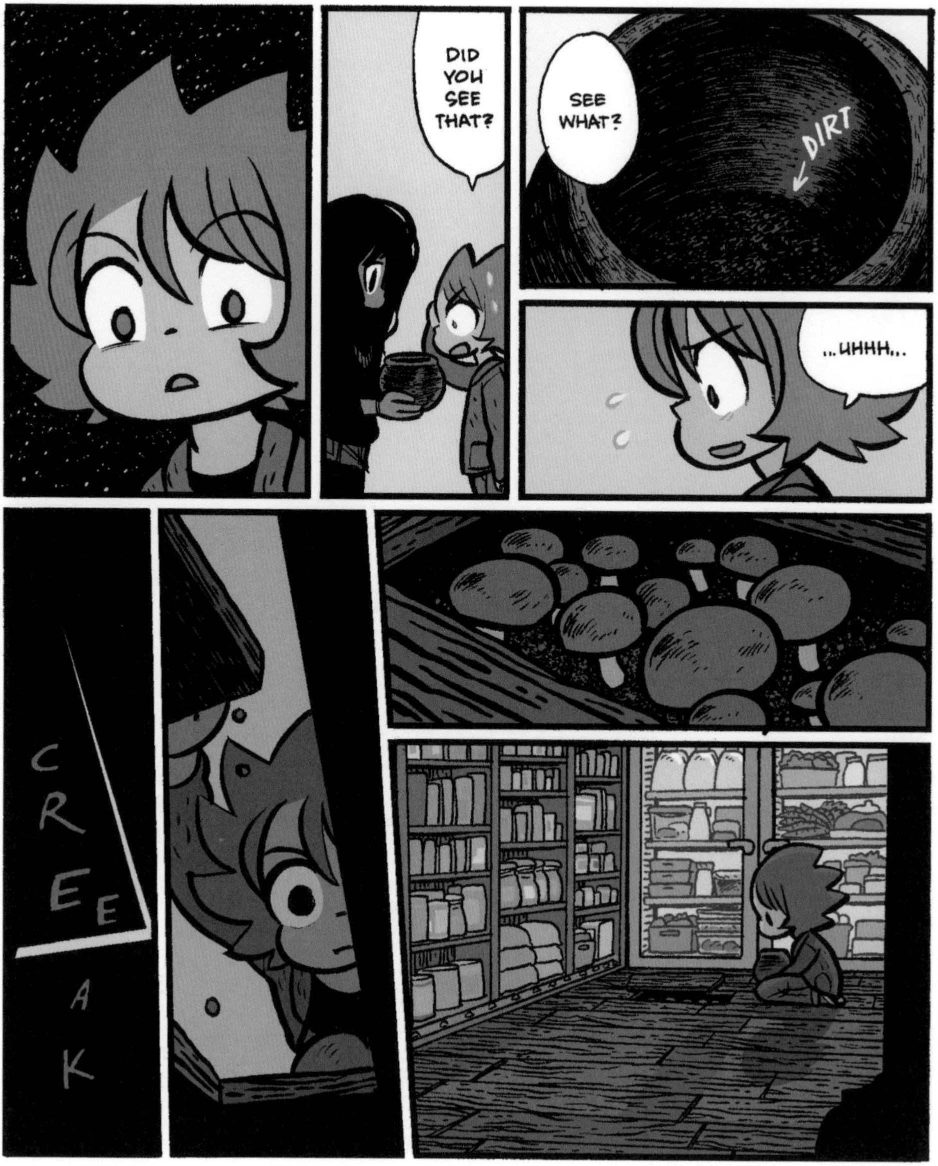

DID YOU SEE THAT?
SEE WHAT?
DIRT
...UHHH...
CREEAK

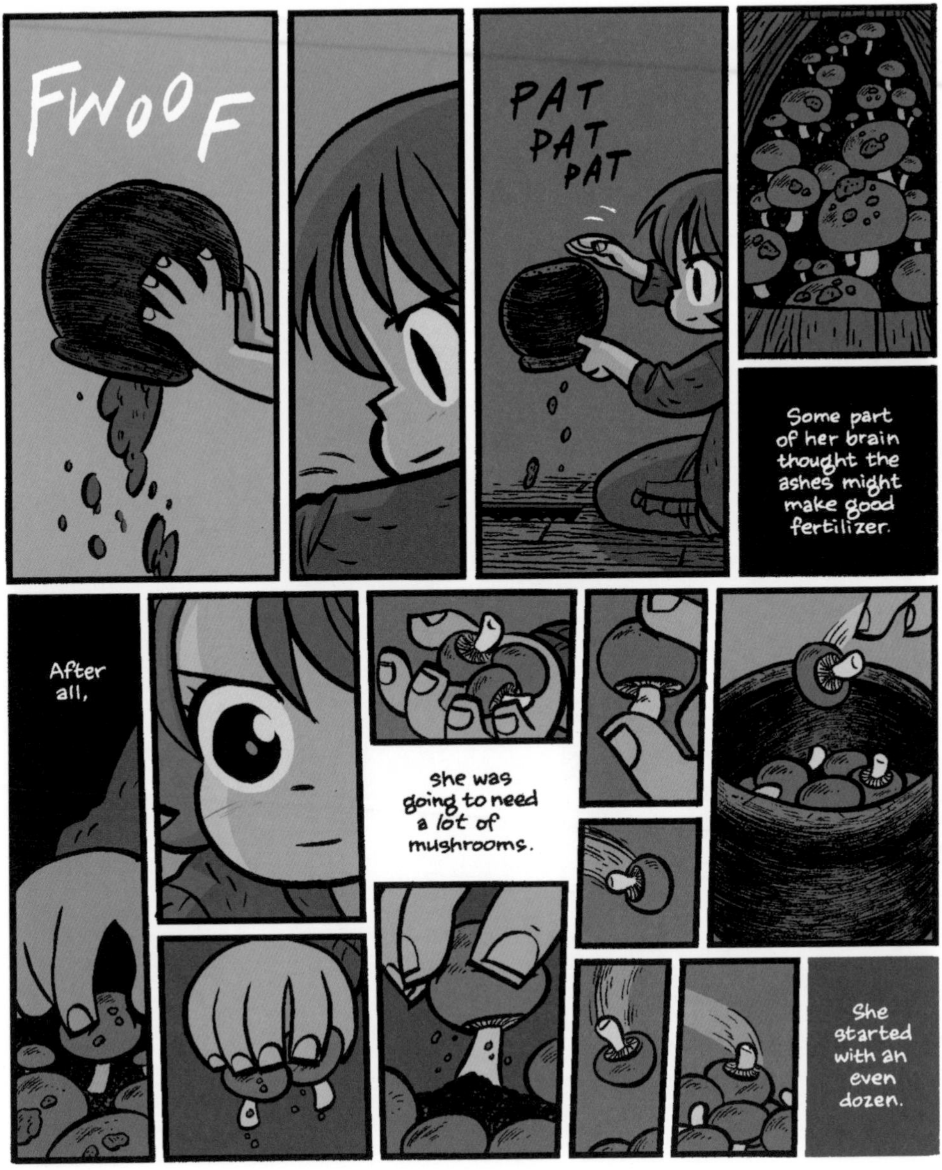
FWOOF
PAT PAT PAT
Some part of her brain thought the ashes might make good fertilizer.
After all,
she was going to need a *lot* of mushrooms.
She started with an even dozen.

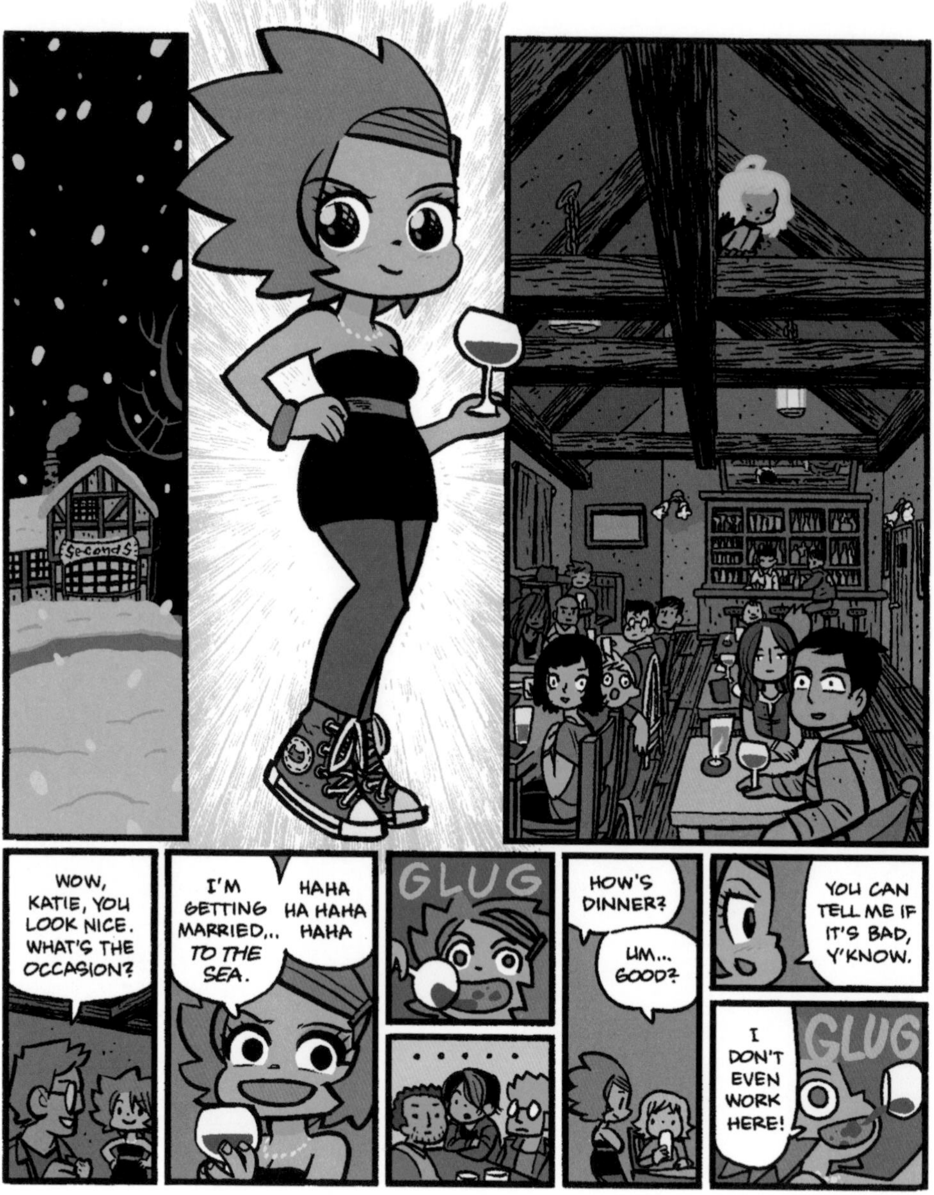
SECONDS
WOW, KATIE, YOU LOOK NICE. WHAT'S THE OCCASION?
I'M GETTING MARRIED... *TO THE SEA.*
HAHA HA HAHA HAHA
GLUG
• • • • •
HOW'S DINNER?
UM... GOOD?
YOU CAN TELL ME IF IT'S BAD, Y'KNOW.
I DON'T EVEN WORK HERE!
GLUG

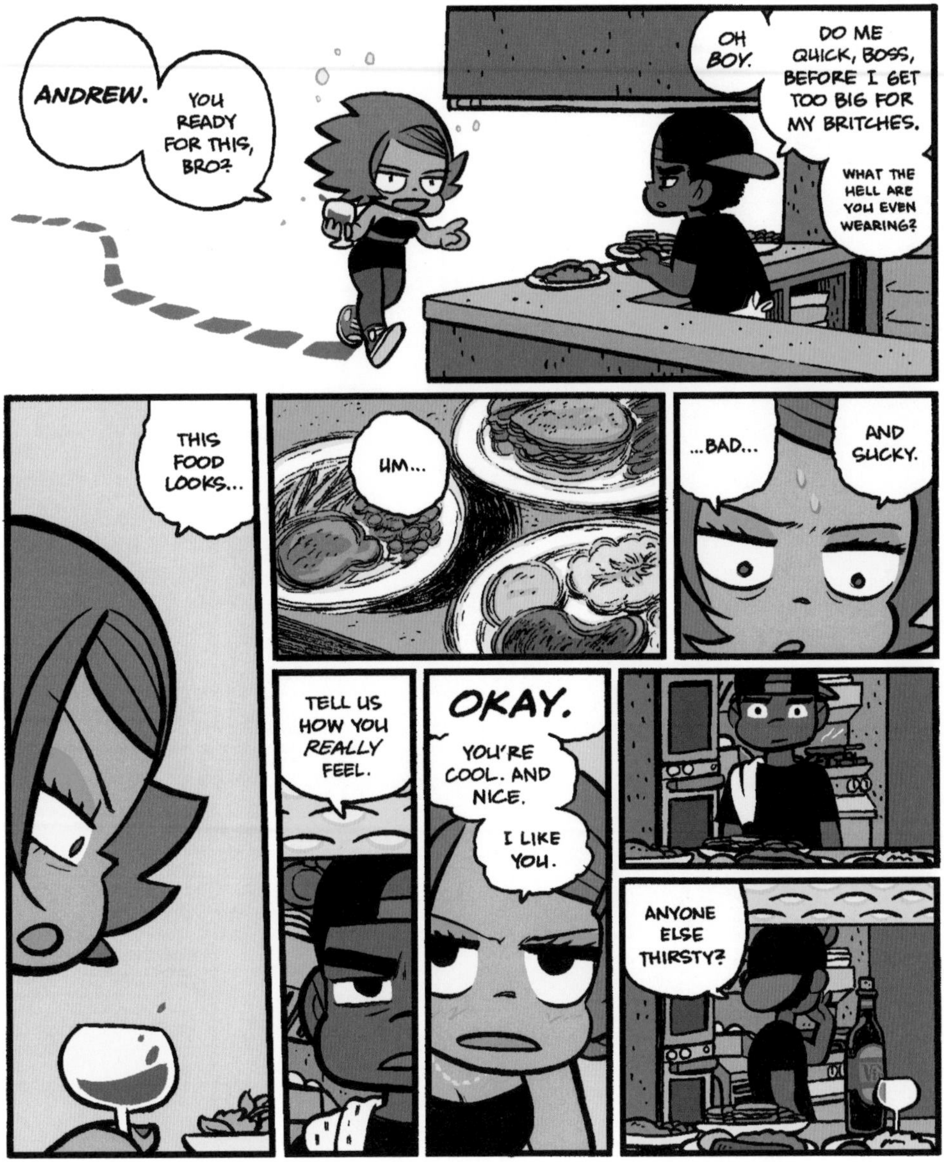

ANDREW.
YOU READY FOR THIS, BRO?
OH BOY.
DO ME QUICK, BOSS, BEFORE I GET TOO BIG FOR MY BRITCHES.
WHAT THE HELL ARE YOU EVEN WEARING?
THIS FOOD LOOKS...
UM...
...BAD...
AND SUCKY.
TELL US HOW YOU *REALLY* FEEL.
OKAY.
YOU'RE COOL. AND NICE.
I LIKE YOU.
ANYONE ELSE THIRSTY?

REVISION #3

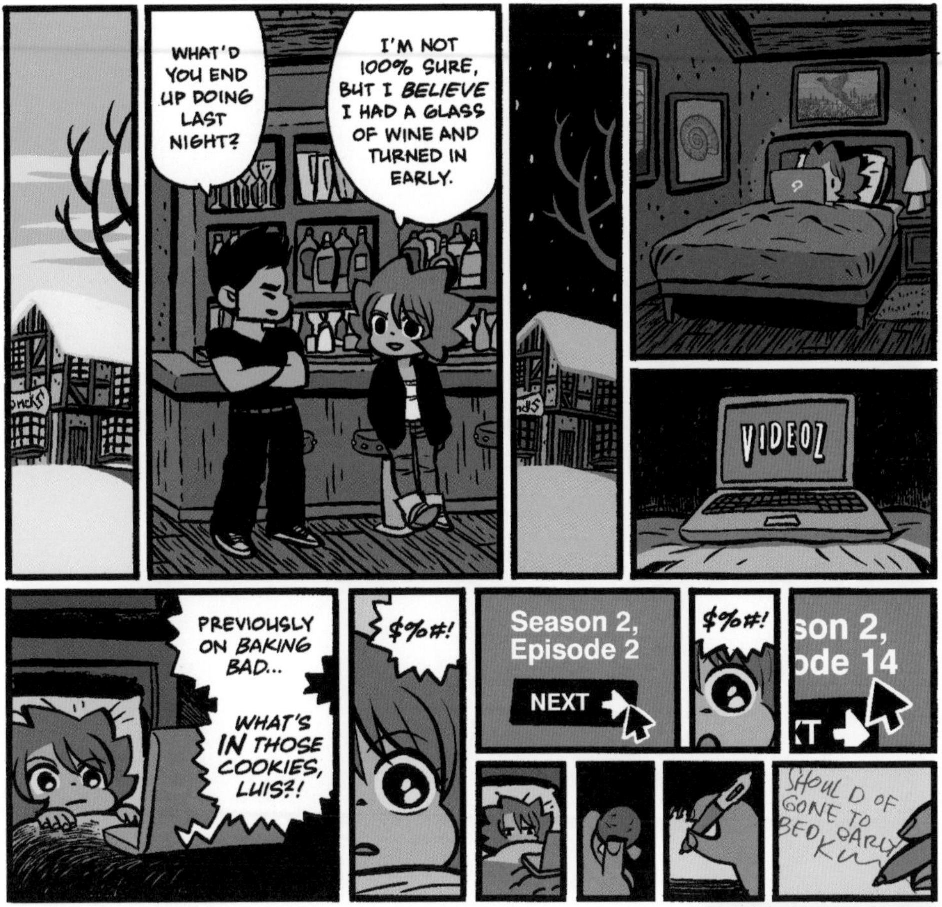
WHAT'D YOU END UP DOING LAST NIGHT?
I'M NOT 100% SURE, BUT I *BELIEVE* I HAD A GLASS OF WINE AND TURNED IN EARLY.
VIDEOZ
PREVIOUSLY ON *BAKING BAD*...
WHAT'S **IN** THOSE COOKIES, LUIS?!
$%#!
Season 2, Episode 2
NEXT
$%#!
son 2, ode 14
XT
SHOULD OF GONE TO BED EARLY

REVISION #4

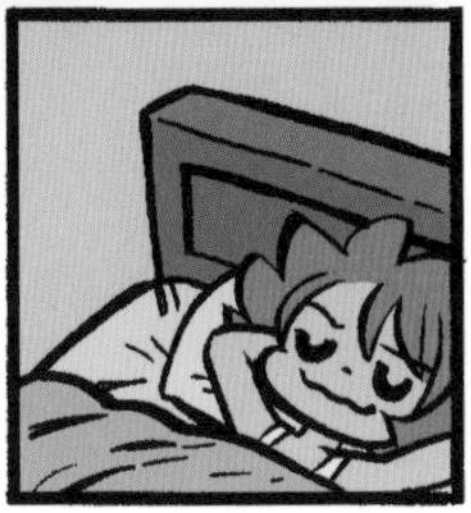

REVISION #5

122

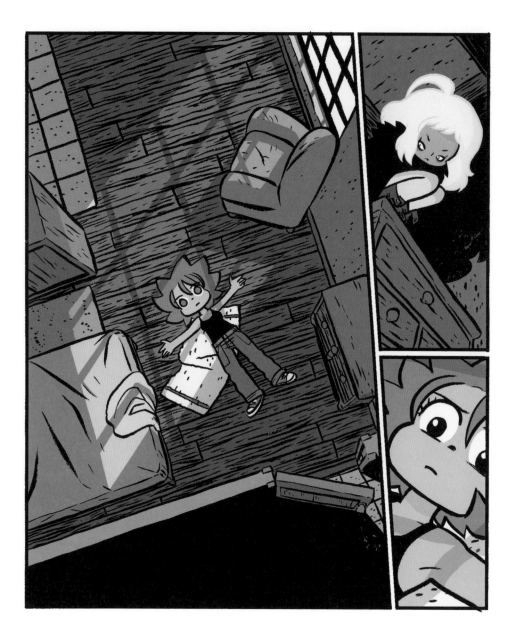

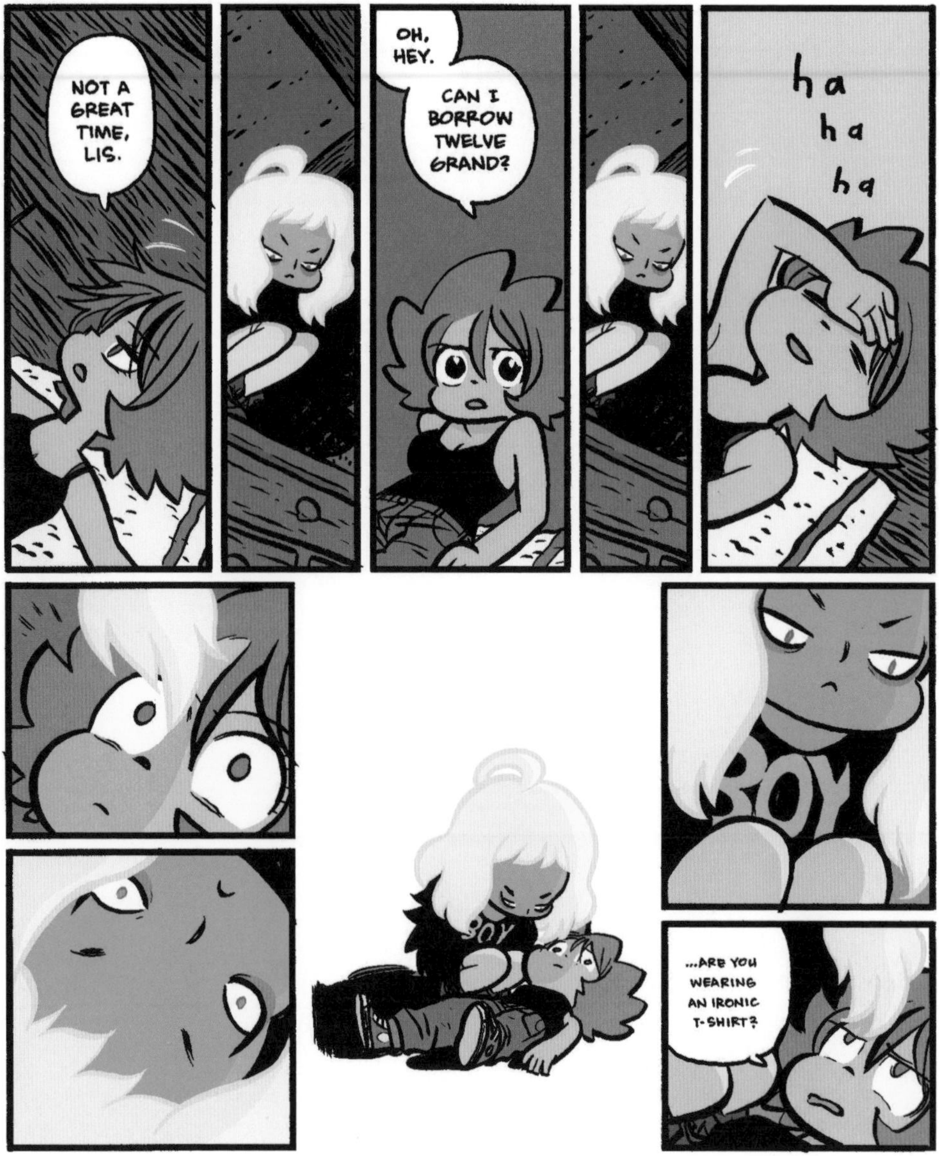
NOT A GREAT TIME, LIS.
OH, HEY.
CAN I BORROW TWELVE GRAND?
ha ha ha
...ARE YOU WEARING AN IRONIC T-SHIRT?
BOY

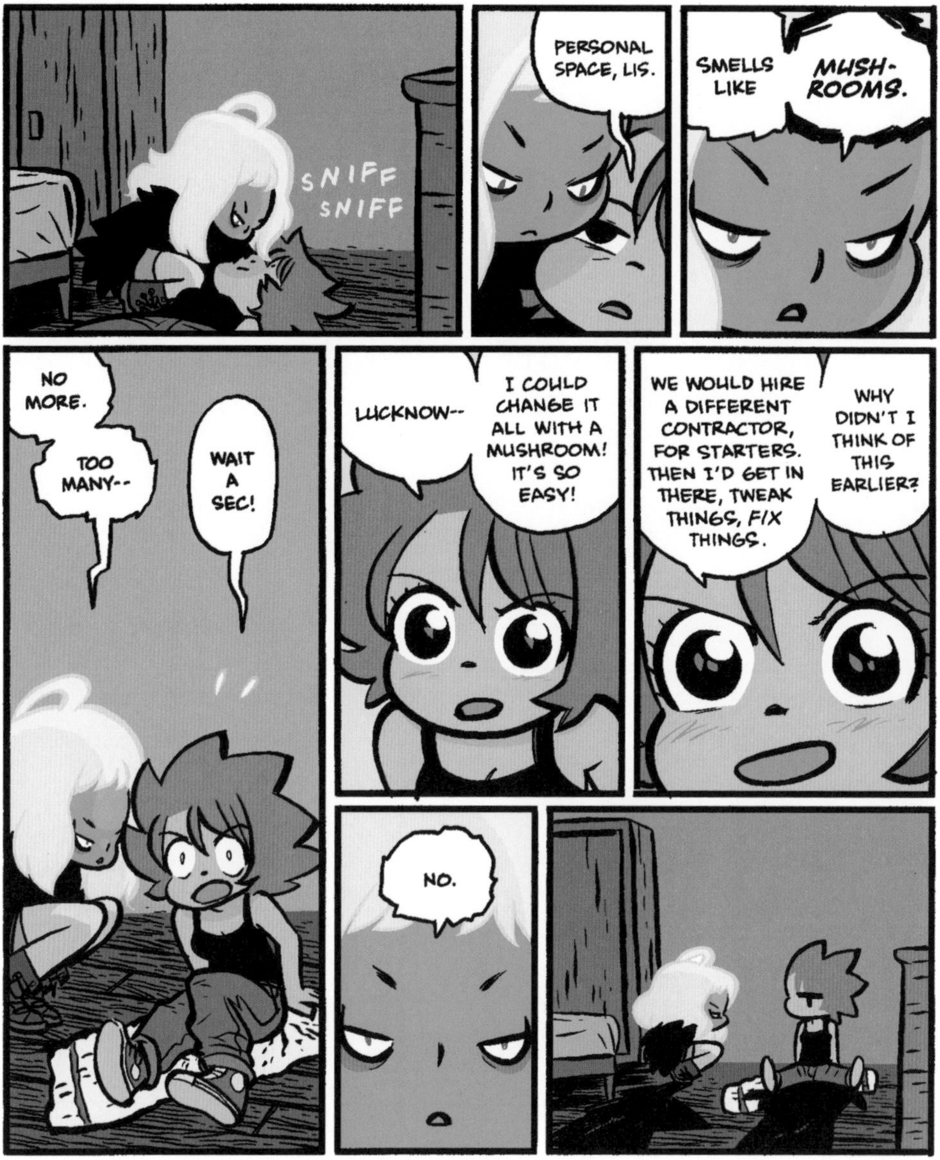
SNIFF SNIFF
PERSONAL SPACE, LIS.
SMELLS LIKE
MUSH-ROOMS.
NO MORE.
TOO MANY--
WAIT A SEC!
LUCKNOW--
I COULD CHANGE IT ALL WITH A MUSHROOM! IT'S SO EASY!
WE WOULD HIRE A DIFFERENT CONTRACTOR, FOR STARTERS. THEN I'D GET IN THERE, TWEAK THINGS, FIX THINGS.
WHY DIDN'T I THINK OF THIS EARLIER?
NO.

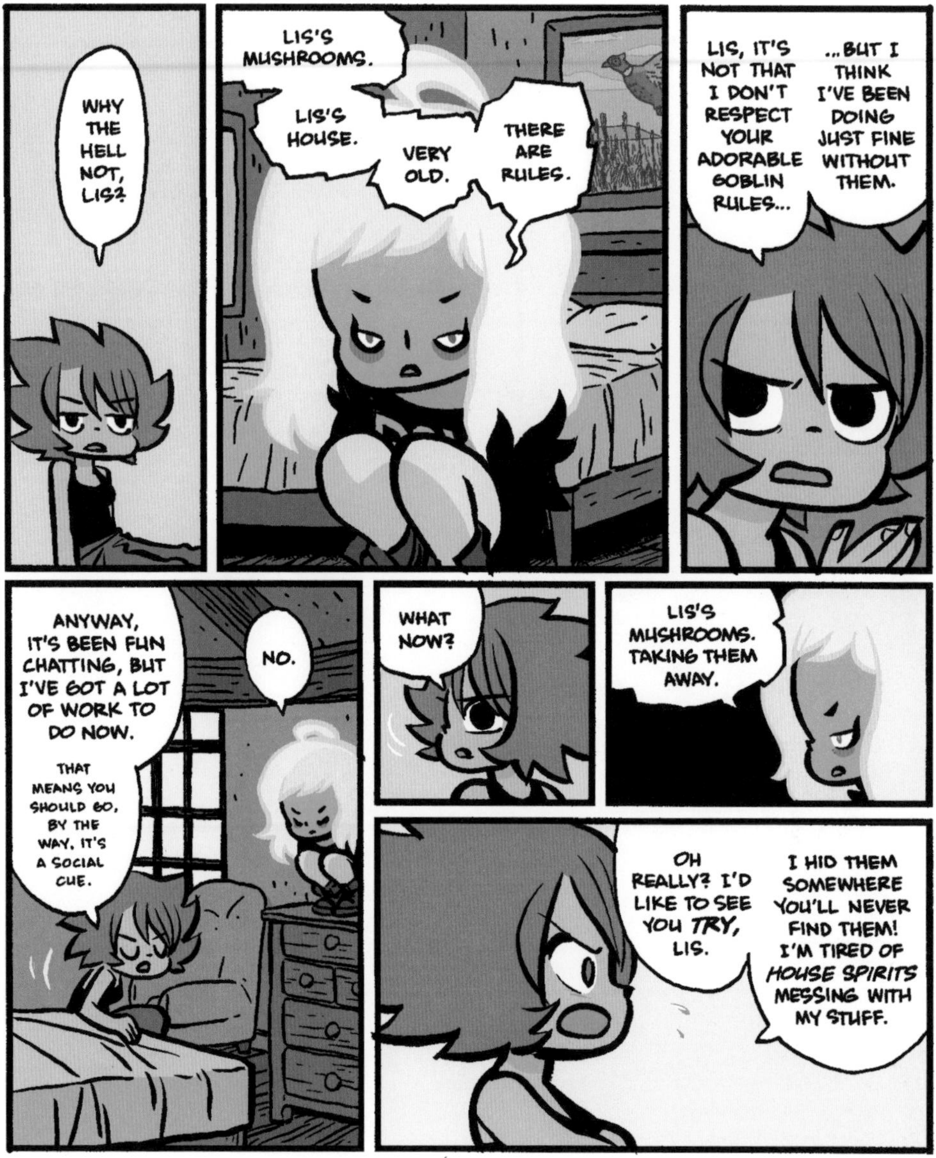
WHY THE HELL NOT, LIS?
LIS'S MUSHROOMS.
LIS'S HOUSE.
VERY OLD.
THERE ARE RULES.
LIS, IT'S NOT THAT I DON'T RESPECT YOUR ADORABLE GOBLIN RULES...
...BUT I THINK I'VE BEEN DOING JUST FINE WITHOUT THEM.
ANYWAY, IT'S BEEN FUN CHATTING, BUT I'VE GOT A LOT OF WORK TO DO NOW.
THAT MEANS YOU SHOULD GO, BY THE WAY. IT'S A SOCIAL CUE.
NO.
WHAT NOW?
LIS'S MUSHROOMS. TAKING THEM AWAY.
OH REALLY? I'D LIKE TO SEE YOU *TRY*, LIS.
I HID THEM SOMEWHERE YOU'LL NEVER FIND THEM! I'M TIRED OF *HOUSE SPIRITS* MESSING WITH MY STUFF.

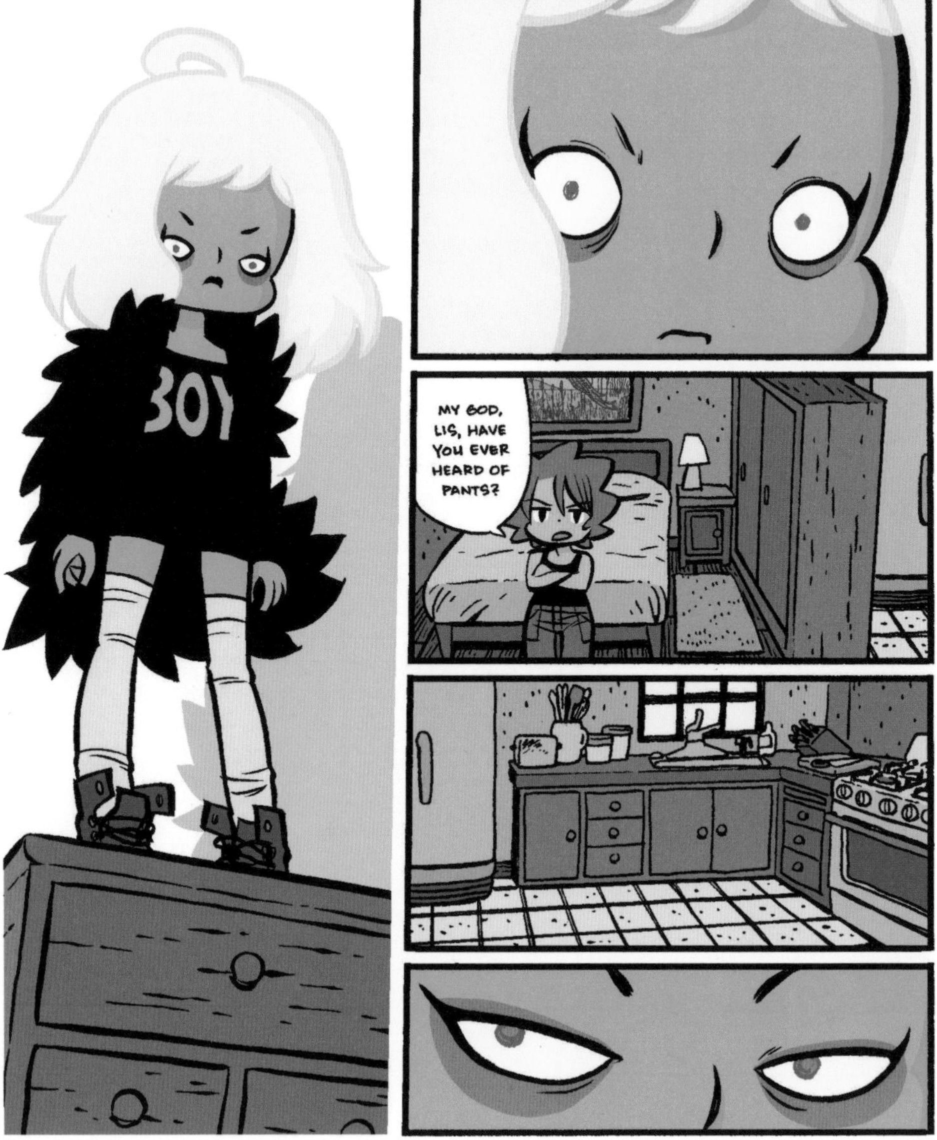

BOY
MY GOD, LIS, HAVE YOU EVER HEARD OF PANTS?

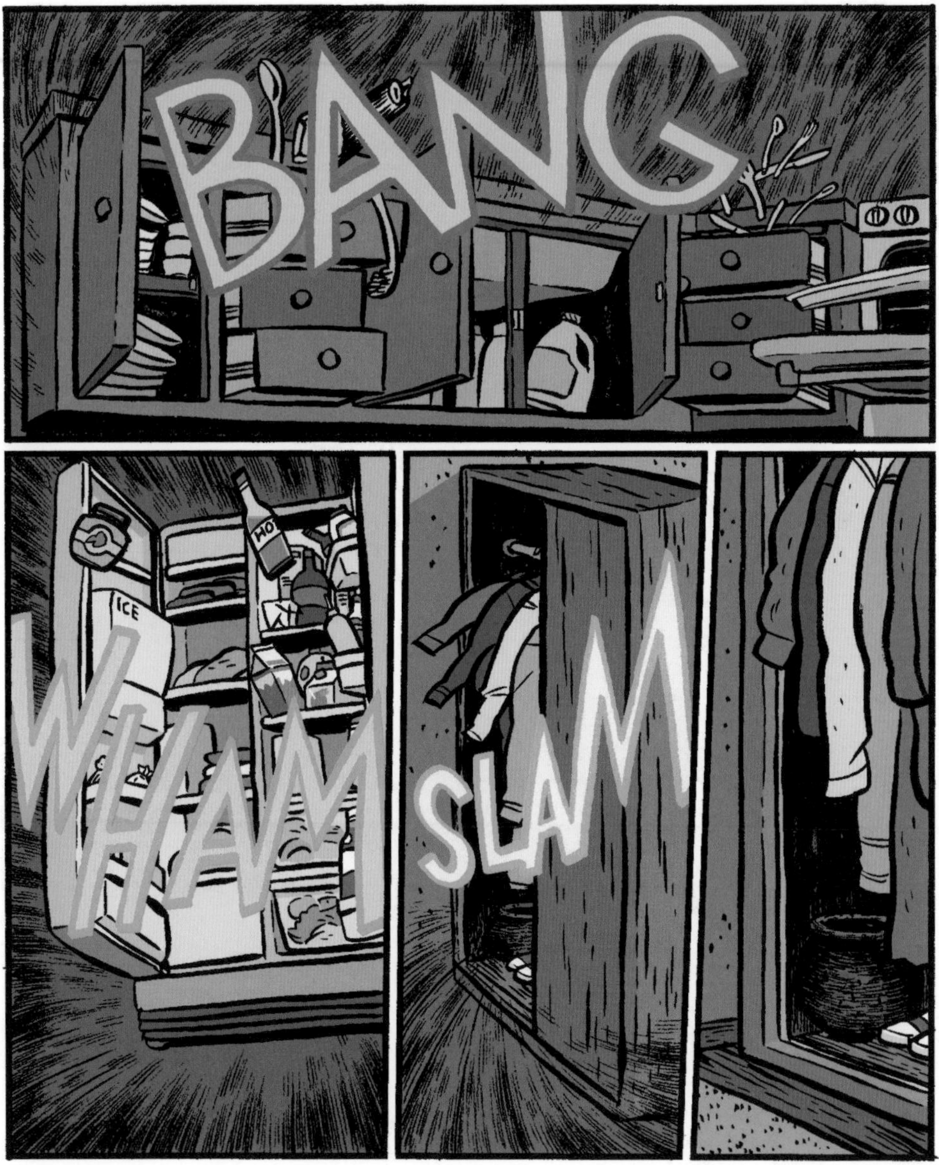
BANG
ICE
HOT
WHAM
SLAM

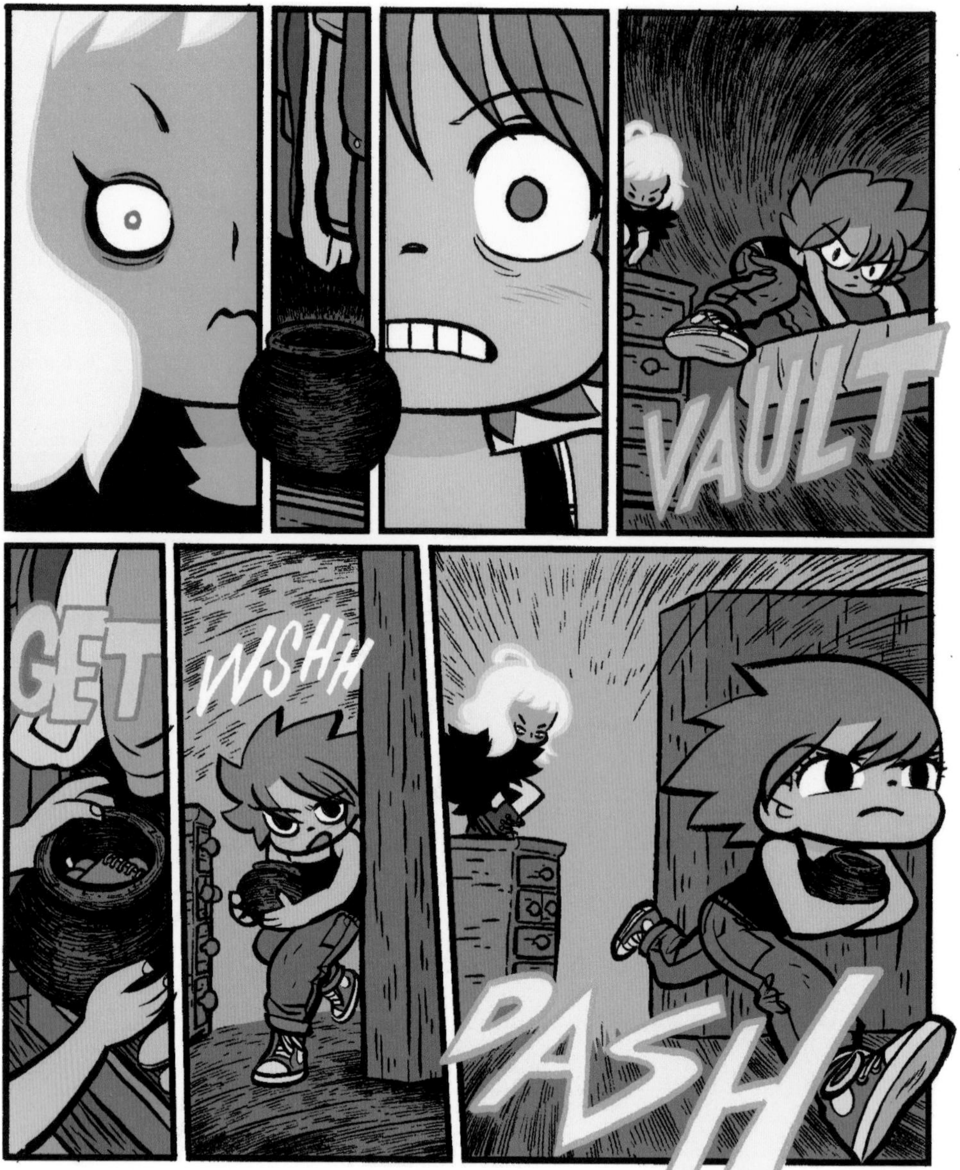
VAULT
GET
WSHH
DASH

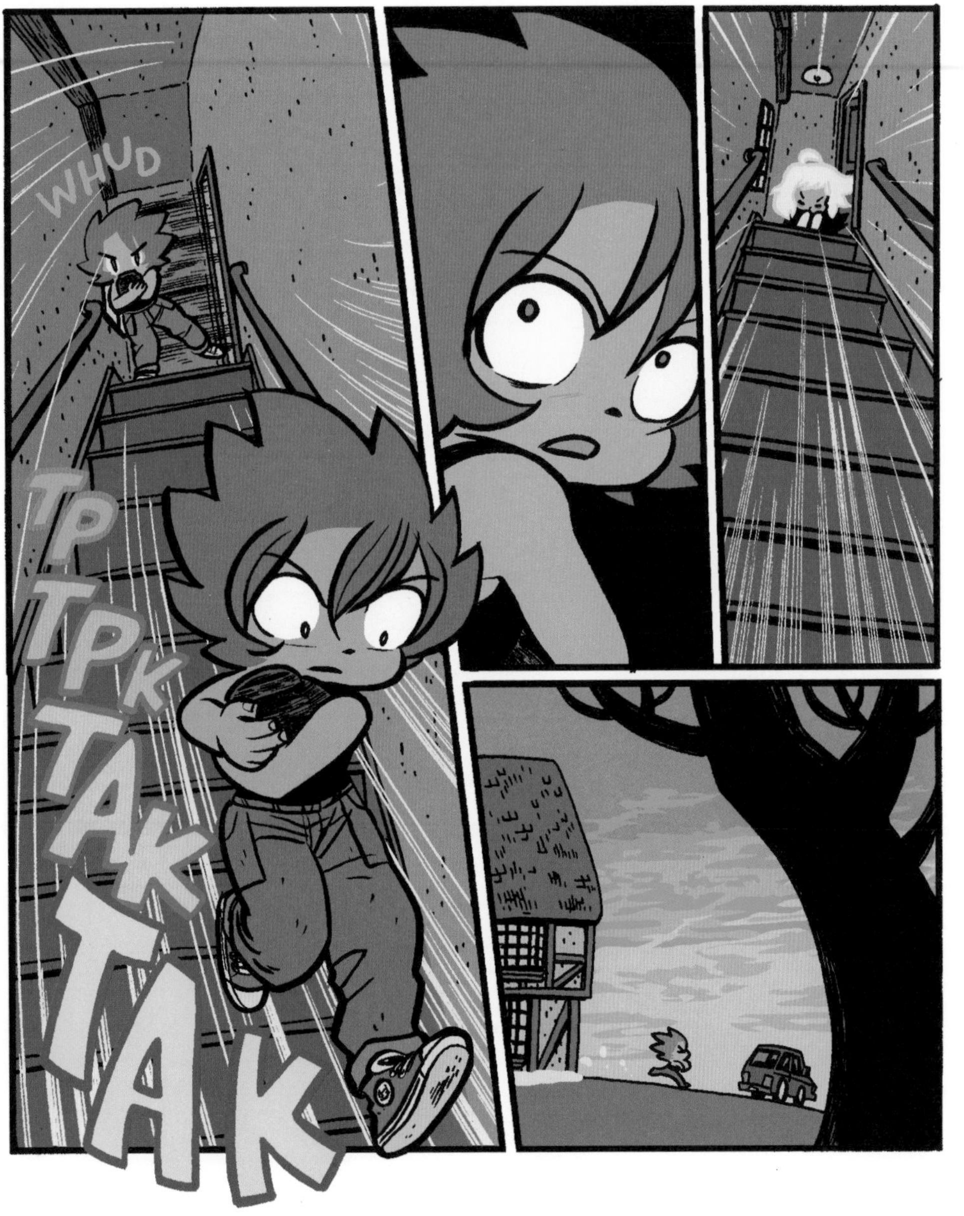
WHUD
TP
TPK
TAK
TAK

132

The mushroom, somehow, remained unchewed.

BLEAH

1. Write you
2. Ingest one m
3. Go to s
4. Wake c

EVENTS MUST OCCUR C

EVENTS MUST OCCUR ON THESE PREMISES

Things had to have happened AT Seconds?

Lis hadn't followed her outside. Maybe Lis couldn't follow her outside.

If Lis was the house spirit of Seconds, and the mushrooms were some kind of extension of Lis, it *almost* made sense.

Katie wiped off the uneaten mushroom, threw it back in the witch's pot, and hid the whole thing in the back seat of her car.

At the very least she knew Lis wouldn't steal her stash.

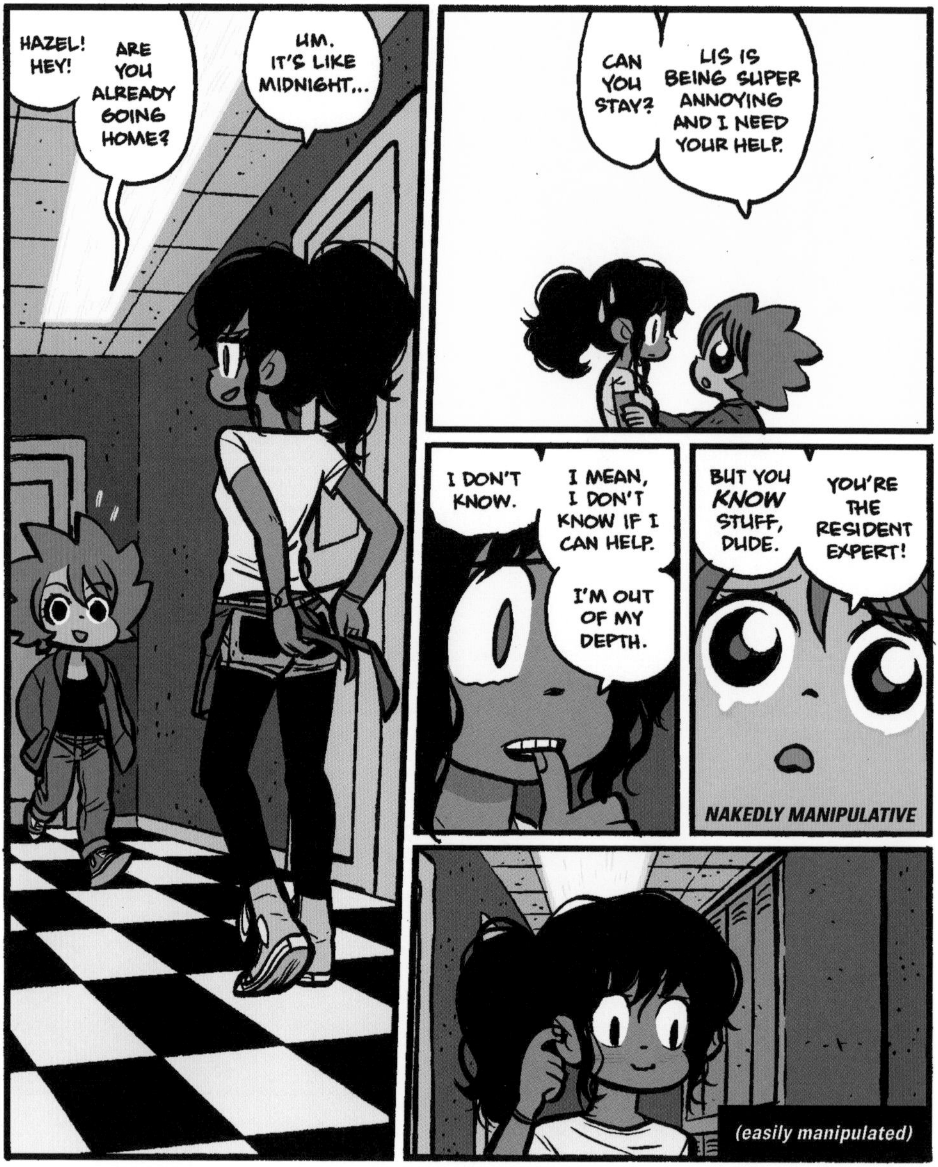

HAZEL! HEY!
ARE YOU ALREADY GOING HOME?
UM. IT'S LIKE MIDNIGHT...
CAN YOU STAY?
LIS IS BEING SUPER ANNOYING AND I NEED YOUR HELP.
I DON'T KNOW.
I MEAN, I DON'T KNOW IF I CAN HELP.
I'M OUT OF MY DEPTH.
BUT YOU KNOW STUFF, DUDE.
YOU'RE THE RESIDENT EXPERT!
NAKEDLY MANIPULATIVE
(easily manipulated)

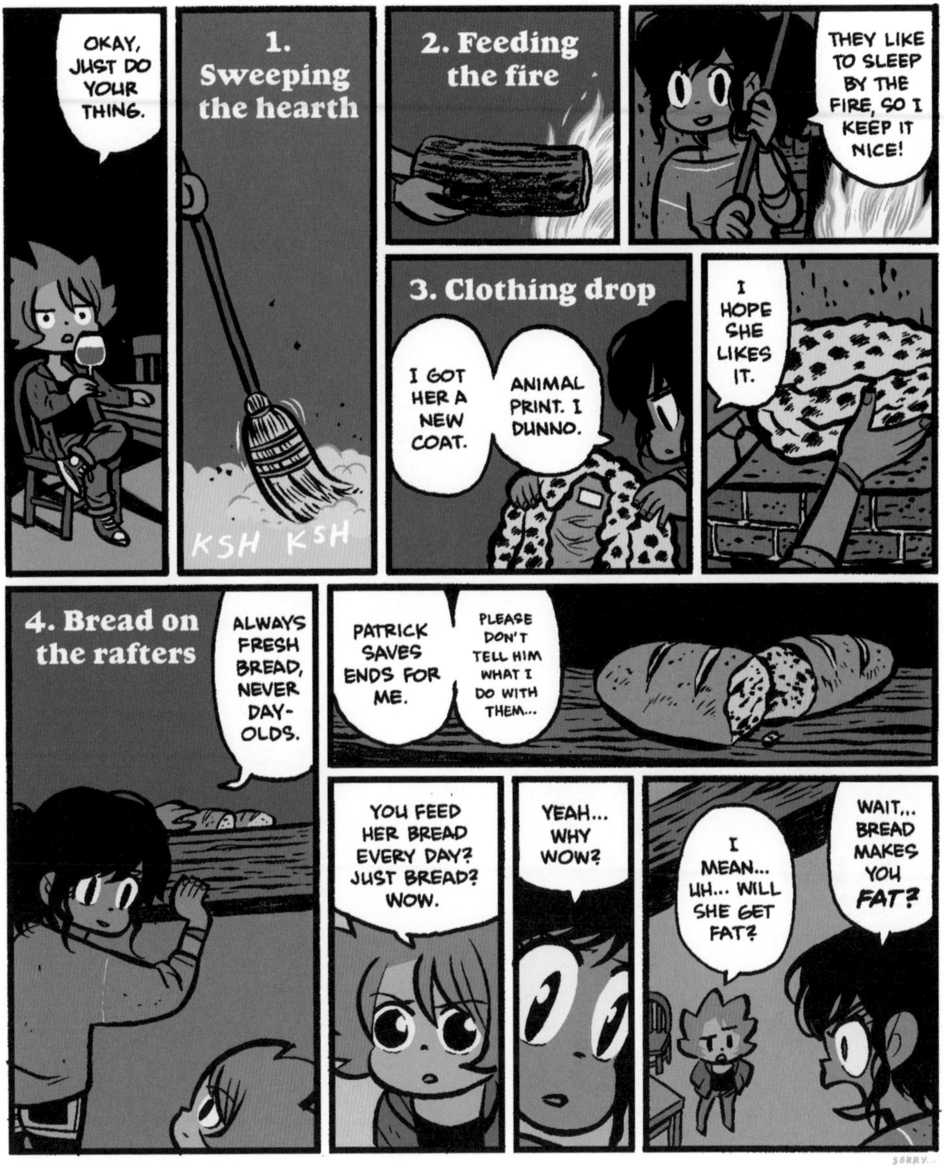
OKAY, JUST DO YOUR THING.
1. Sweeping the hearth
KSH KSH
2. Feeding the fire
THEY LIKE TO SLEEP BY THE FIRE, SO I KEEP IT NICE!
3. Clothing drop
I GOT HER A NEW COAT.
ANIMAL PRINT. I DUNNO.
I HOPE SHE LIKES IT.
4. Bread on the rafters
ALWAYS FRESH BREAD, NEVER DAY-OLDS.
PATRICK SAVES ENDS FOR ME.
PLEASE DON'T TELL HIM WHAT I DO WITH THEM...
YOU FEED HER BREAD EVERY DAY? JUST BREAD? WOW.
YEAH... WHY WOW?
I MEAN... UH... WILL SHE GET FAT?
WAIT... BREAD MAKES YOU FAT?
SORRY...

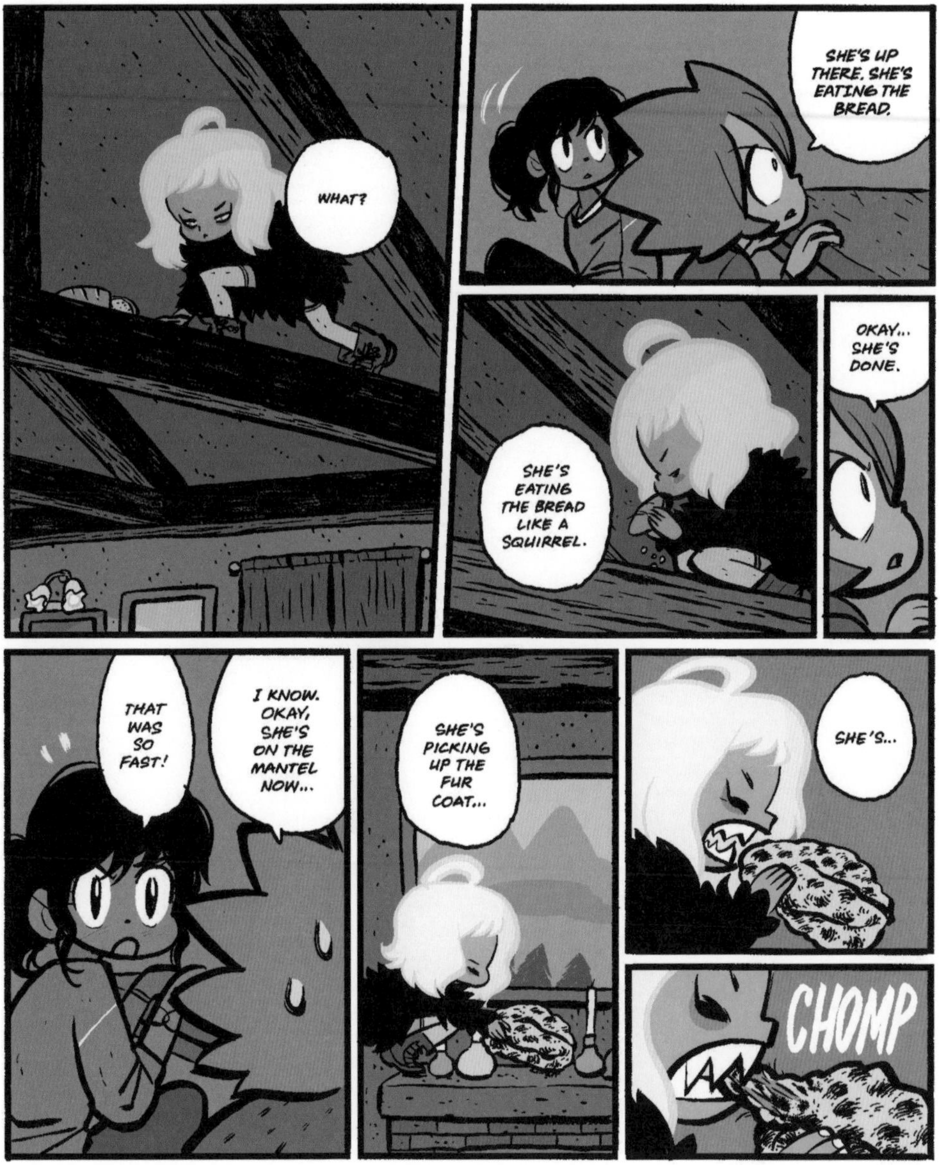
WHAT?
SHE'S UP THERE. SHE'S EATING THE BREAD.
SHE'S EATING THE BREAD LIKE A SQUIRREL.
OKAY... SHE'S DONE.
THAT WAS SO FAST!
I KNOW. OKAY, SHE'S ON THE MANTEL NOW...
SHE'S PICKING UP THE FUR COAT...
SHE'S...
CHOMP

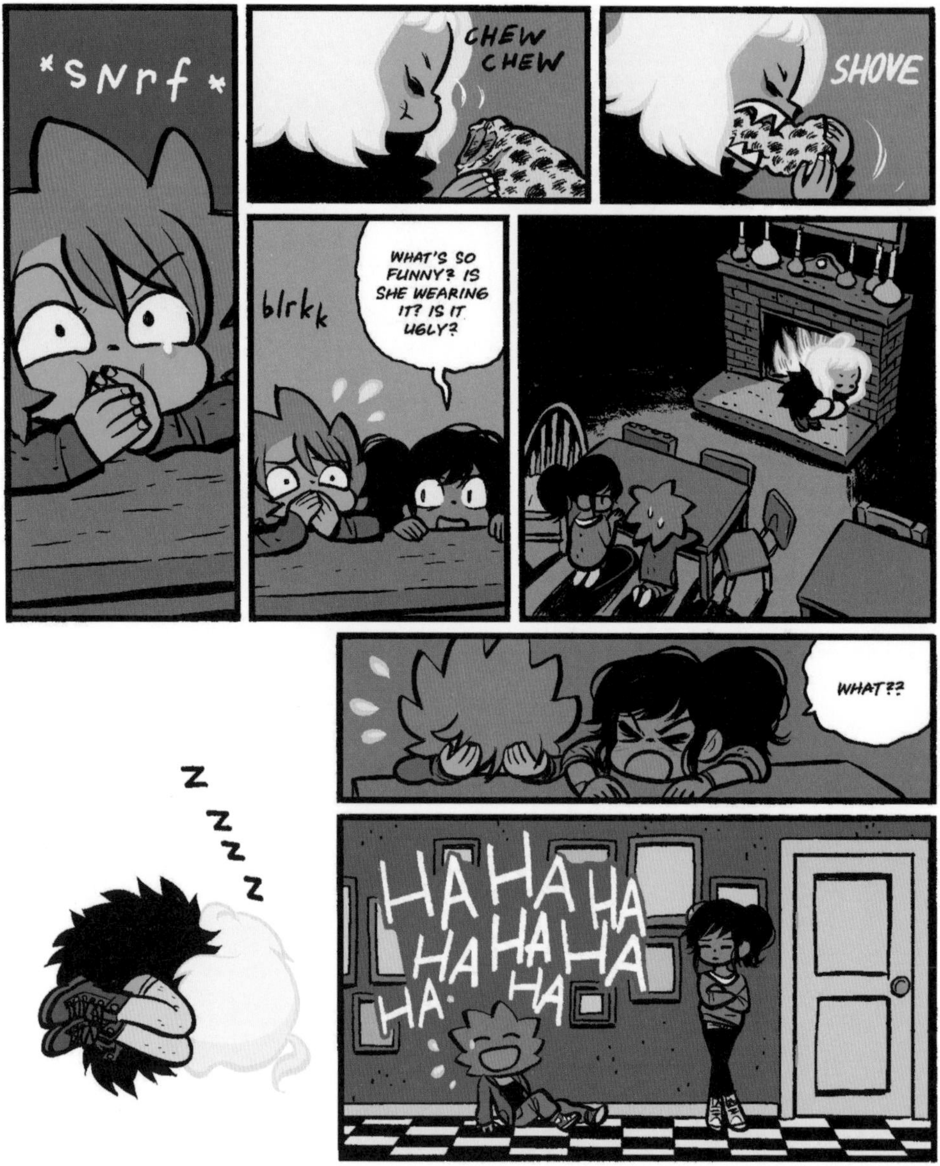
SNrf
CHEW CHEW
SHOVE
blrkk
WHAT'S SO FUNNY? IS SHE WEARING IT? IS IT UGLY?
WHAT??
Z Z Z Z
HA HA HA HA HA HA HA HA HA HA

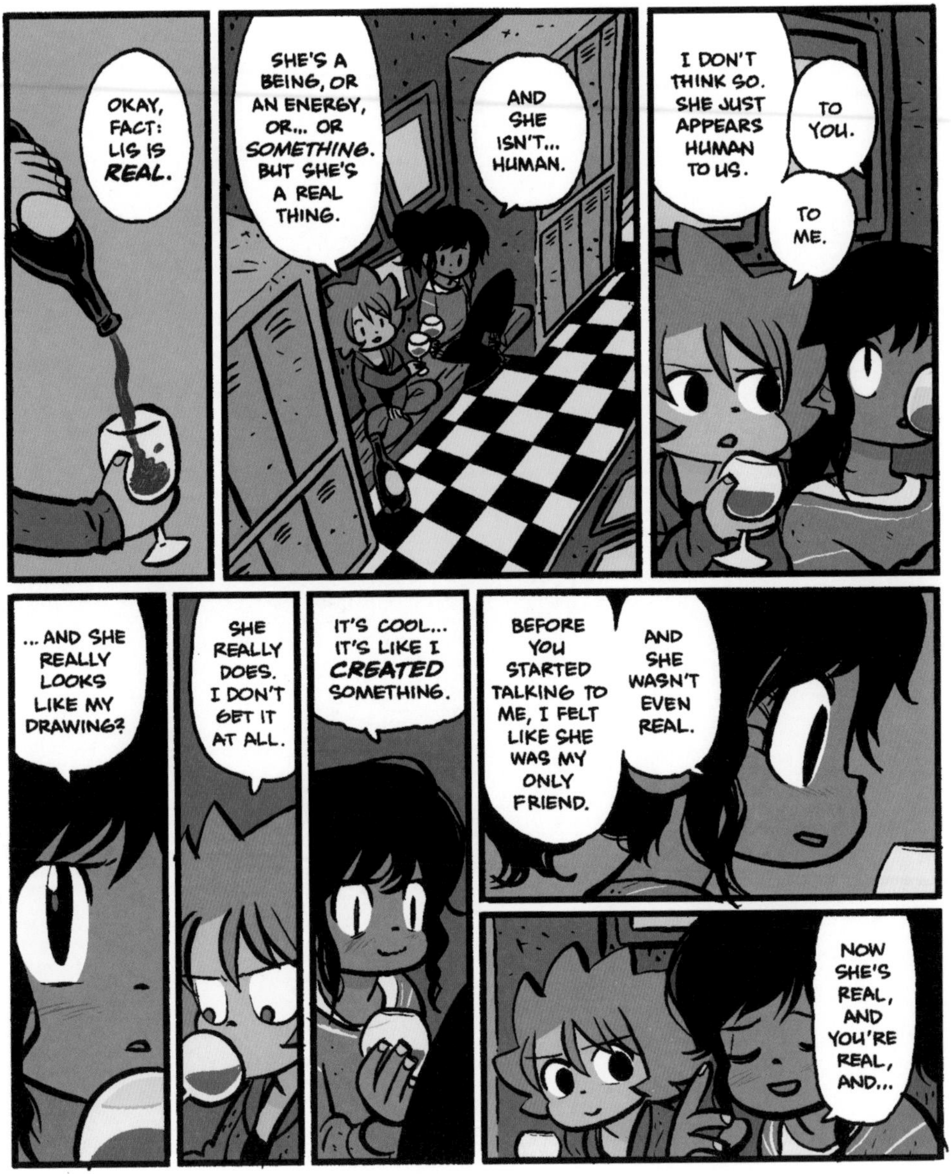
OKAY, FACT: LIS IS REAL.
SHE'S A BEING, OR AN ENERGY, OR... OR SOMETHING. BUT SHE'S A REAL THING.
AND SHE ISN'T... HUMAN.
I DON'T THINK SO. SHE JUST APPEARS HUMAN TO US.
TO YOU.
TO ME.
...AND SHE REALLY LOOKS LIKE MY DRAWING?
SHE REALLY DOES. I DON'T GET IT AT ALL.
IT'S COOL... IT'S LIKE I CREATED SOMETHING.
BEFORE YOU STARTED TALKING TO ME, I FELT LIKE SHE WAS MY ONLY FRIEND.
AND SHE WASN'T EVEN REAL.
NOW SHE'S REAL, AND YOU'RE REAL, AND...

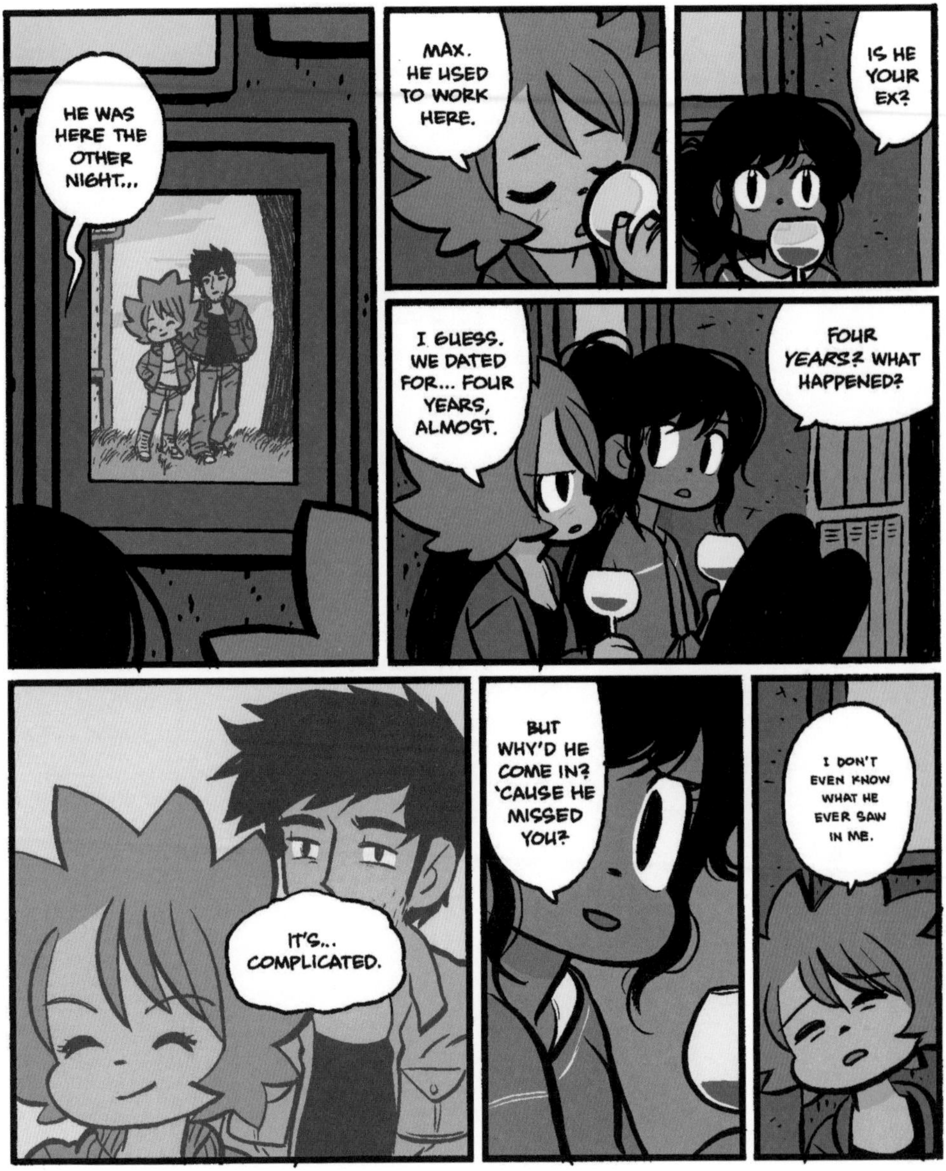
HE WAS HERE THE OTHER NIGHT...
MAX. HE USED TO WORK HERE.
IS HE YOUR EX?
I GUESS. WE DATED FOR... FOUR YEARS, ALMOST.
FOUR *YEARS?* WHAT HAPPENED?
IT'S... COMPLICATED.
BUT WHY'D HE COME IN? 'CAUSE HE MISSED YOU?
I DON'T EVEN KNOW WHAT HE EVER SAW IN ME.

HE WAS A FRIEND OF RAY'S, AND I JUST NEEDED GENERAL KITCHEN HELP, SO HE WAS IT.

(Max, five minutes before his first shift)

I HATED HIM AT FIRST. HE WAS LIKE ANDREW TIMES A BILLION. SUCH HOT SHIT. LEATHER JACKET, BLONDE ON HIS ARM. AND HE COULD BARELY COOK.

SELFIE!

BUT WE COULD *TALK.* WE WORKED TOGETHER EVERY NIGHT AND THE CONVERSATION NEVER ENDED.

SO YEAH, ME AND MAX HOOKING UP WAS INEVITABLE.

HE GOT BETTER IN THE KITCHEN. WE MADE EACH OTHER STRONGER.

WHEN SECONDS GOT POPULAR WE HAD TO HIRE NEW LINE *COOKS* AND START SPLITTING THE WEEK.

Andrew (TRAINEE)

WE NEVER SAW EACH OTHER ANYMORE. THAT GOT HARD.

AND I GUESS WHAT WE HAD WASN'T THAT STRONG.

142

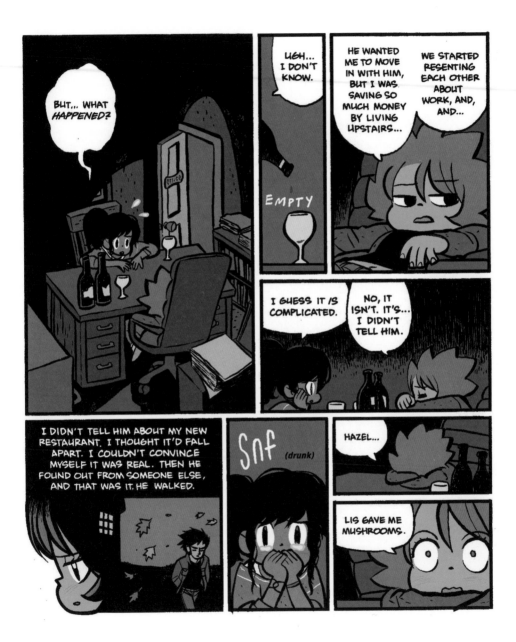

BUT... WHAT HAPPENED?

UGH... I DON'T KNOW.

EMPTY

HE WANTED ME TO MOVE IN WITH HIM, BUT I WAS SAVING SO MUCH MONEY BY LIVING UPSTAIRS...

WE STARTED RESENTING EACH OTHER ABOUT WORK, AND, AND...

I GUESS IT IS COMPLICATED.

NO, IT ISN'T. IT'S... I DIDN'T TELL HIM.

I DIDN'T TELL HIM ABOUT MY NEW RESTAURANT. I THOUGHT IT'D FALL APART. I COULDN'T CONVINCE MYSELF IT WAS REAL. THEN HE FOUND OUT FROM SOMEONE ELSE, AND THAT WAS IT. HE WALKED.

Snf (drunk)

HAZEL...

LIS GAVE ME MUSHROOMS.

143

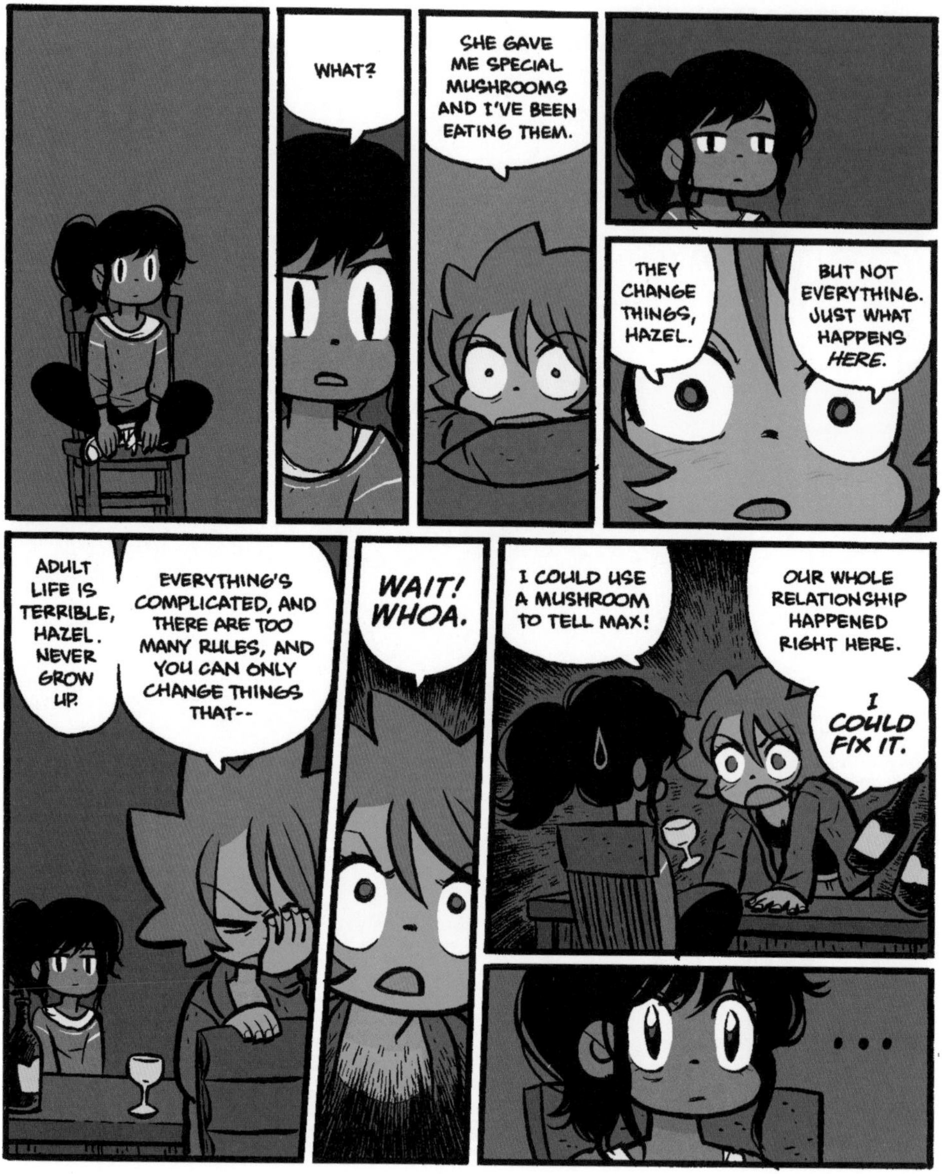
WHAT?
SHE GAVE ME SPECIAL MUSHROOMS AND I'VE BEEN EATING THEM.
THEY CHANGE THINGS, HAZEL.
BUT NOT EVERYTHING. JUST WHAT HAPPENS *HERE.*
ADULT LIFE IS TERRIBLE, HAZEL. NEVER GROW UP.
EVERYTHING'S COMPLICATED, AND THERE ARE TOO MANY RULES, AND YOU CAN ONLY CHANGE THINGS THAT--
WAIT! WHOA.
I COULD USE A MUSHROOM TO TELL MAX!
OUR WHOLE RELATIONSHIP HAPPENED RIGHT HERE.
I COULD FIX IT.
...

 The next thing she knew, she was writing.

Writing about Max.

REVISION #6

146

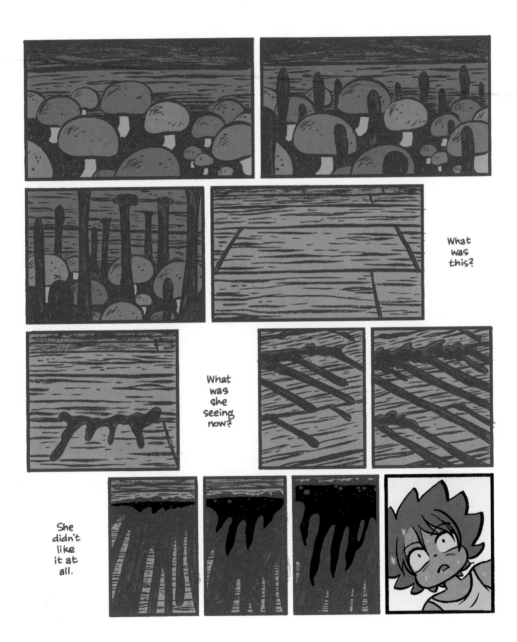

What was this?

What was she seeing now?

She didn't like it at all.

147

And when she woke up,

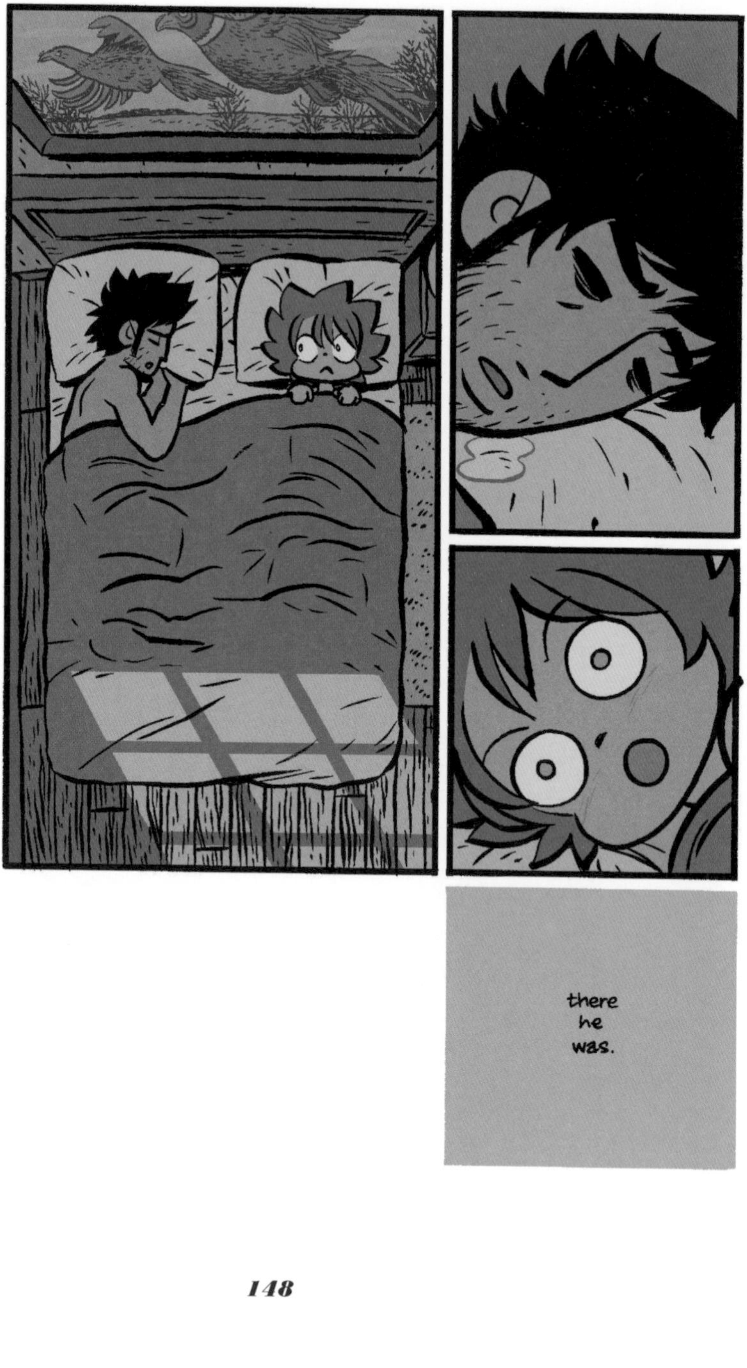
there he was.

5
Max

Max was here.
Z Z Z
Max was real.
POKE
MUHH... STOP
This was real life.
STOP
WHYYY

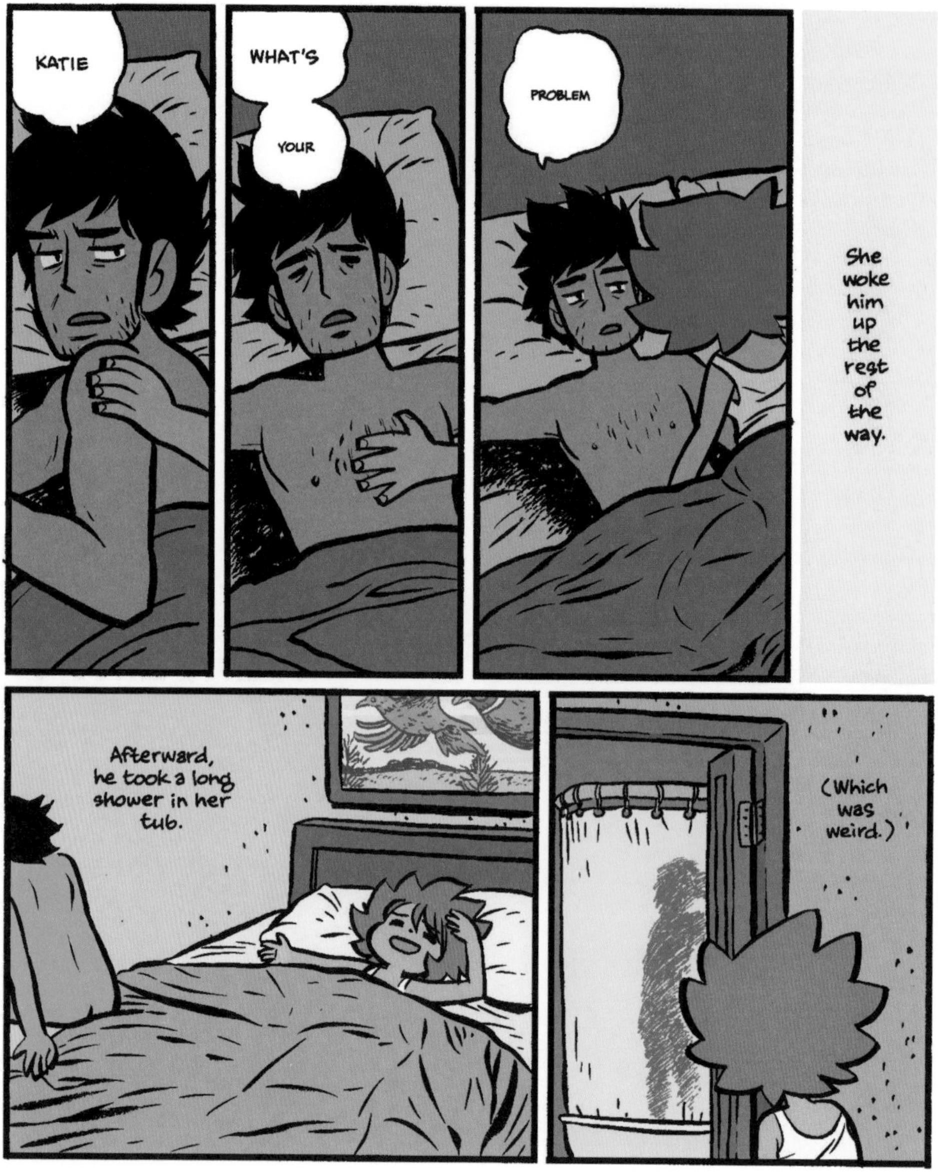
KATIE
WHAT'S
YOUR
PROBLEM
She woke him up the rest of the way.
Afterward, he took a long shower in her tub.
(Which was weird.)

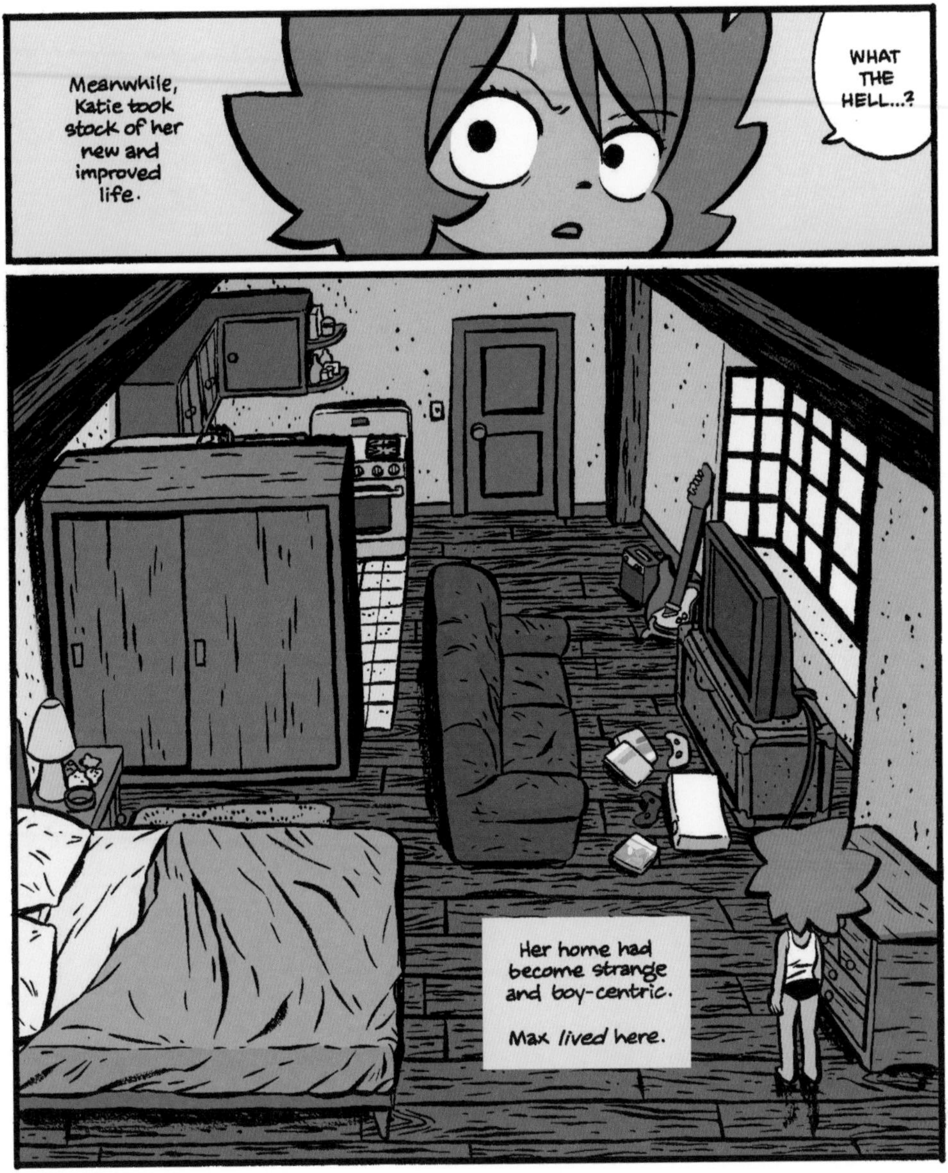
Meanwhile, Katie took stock of her new and improved life.
WHAT THE HELL...?
Her home had become strange and boy-centric.
Max *lived* here.

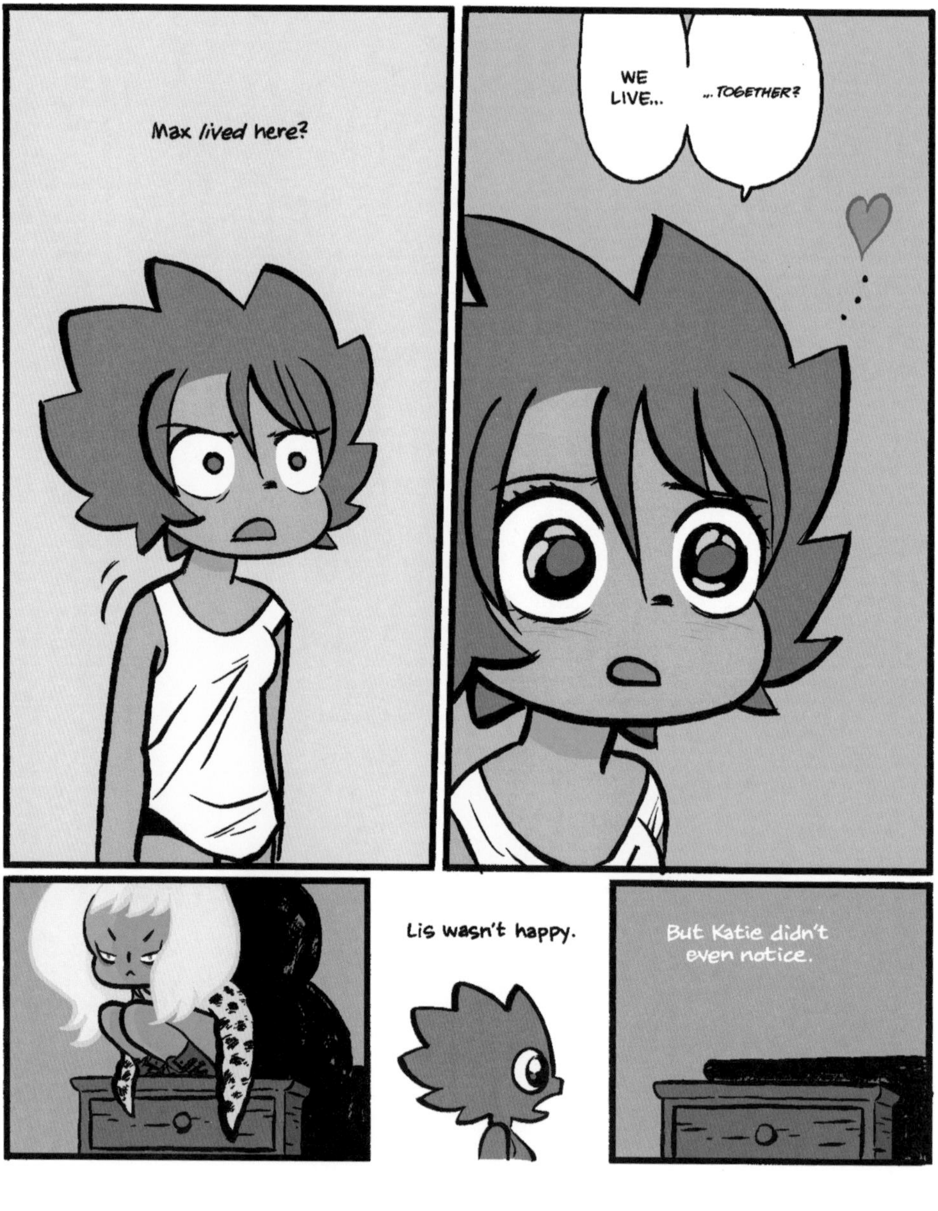
Max *lived* here?
WE LIVE...
...TOGETHER?
Lis wasn't happy.
But Katie didn't even notice.

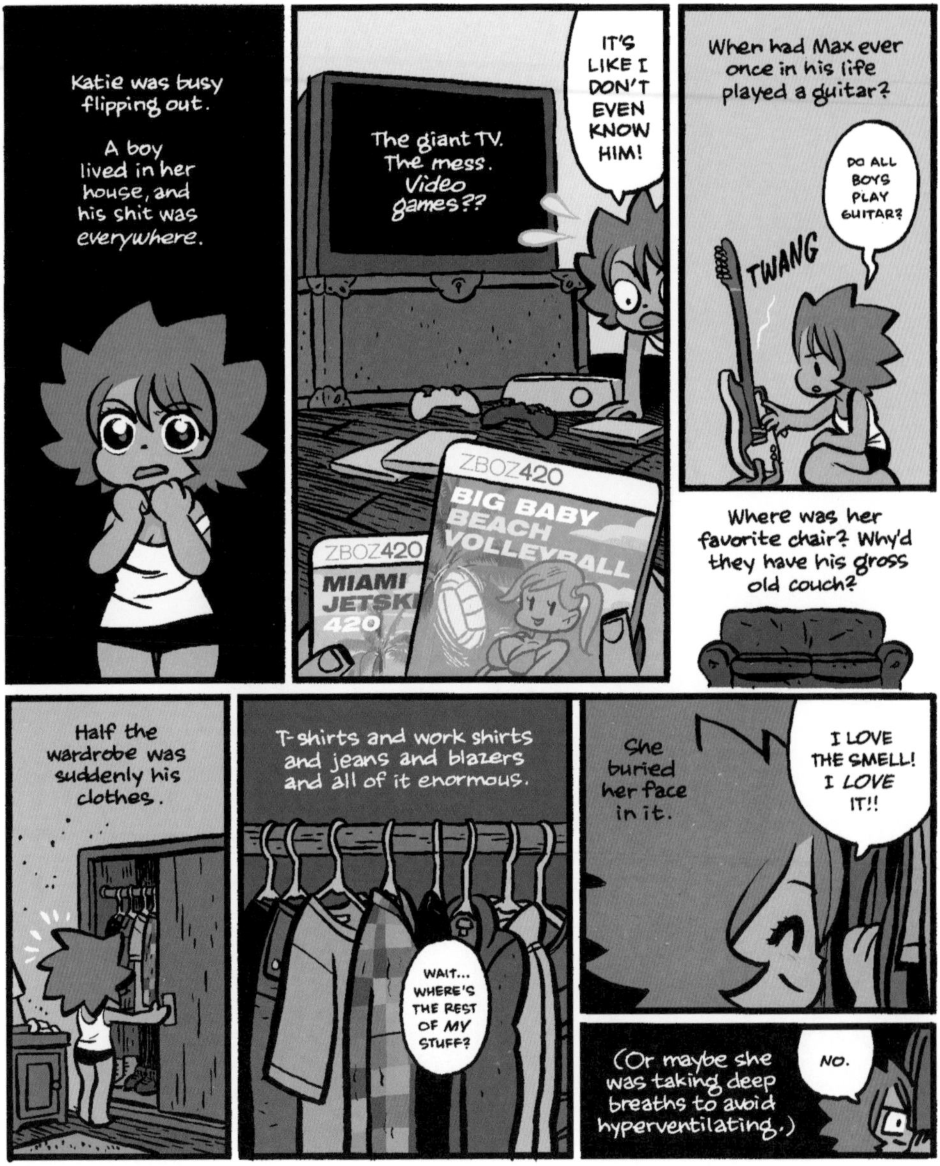
Katie was busy flipping out.
A boy lived in her house, and his shit was *everywhere*.
The giant TV. The mess. Video games??
IT'S LIKE I DON'T EVEN KNOW HIM!
ZBOZ420
MIAMI JETSKI 420
ZBOZ420
BIG BABY BEACH VOLLEYBALL
When had Max ever once in his life played a guitar?
DO ALL BOYS PLAY GUITAR?
TWANG
Where was her favorite chair? Why'd they have his gross old couch?
Half the wardrobe was suddenly his clothes.
T-shirts and work shirts and jeans and blazers and all of it enormous.
WAIT... WHERE'S THE REST OF *MY* STUFF?
She buried her face in it.
I LOVE THE SMELL! I *LOVE* IT!!
(Or maybe she was taking deep breaths to avoid hyperventilating.)
NO.

She dressed cute.

She felt newly confident.

She felt cool.

She pushed away her questions and confusion.

This was good. It was just good.

HI.

HI...

KATIE. REALLY?

MMM. MMMAX. MAX MAX MAX MAX MAX.

WE HAVE WORK, KATIE.

BUT *MAAAX!!!*

154

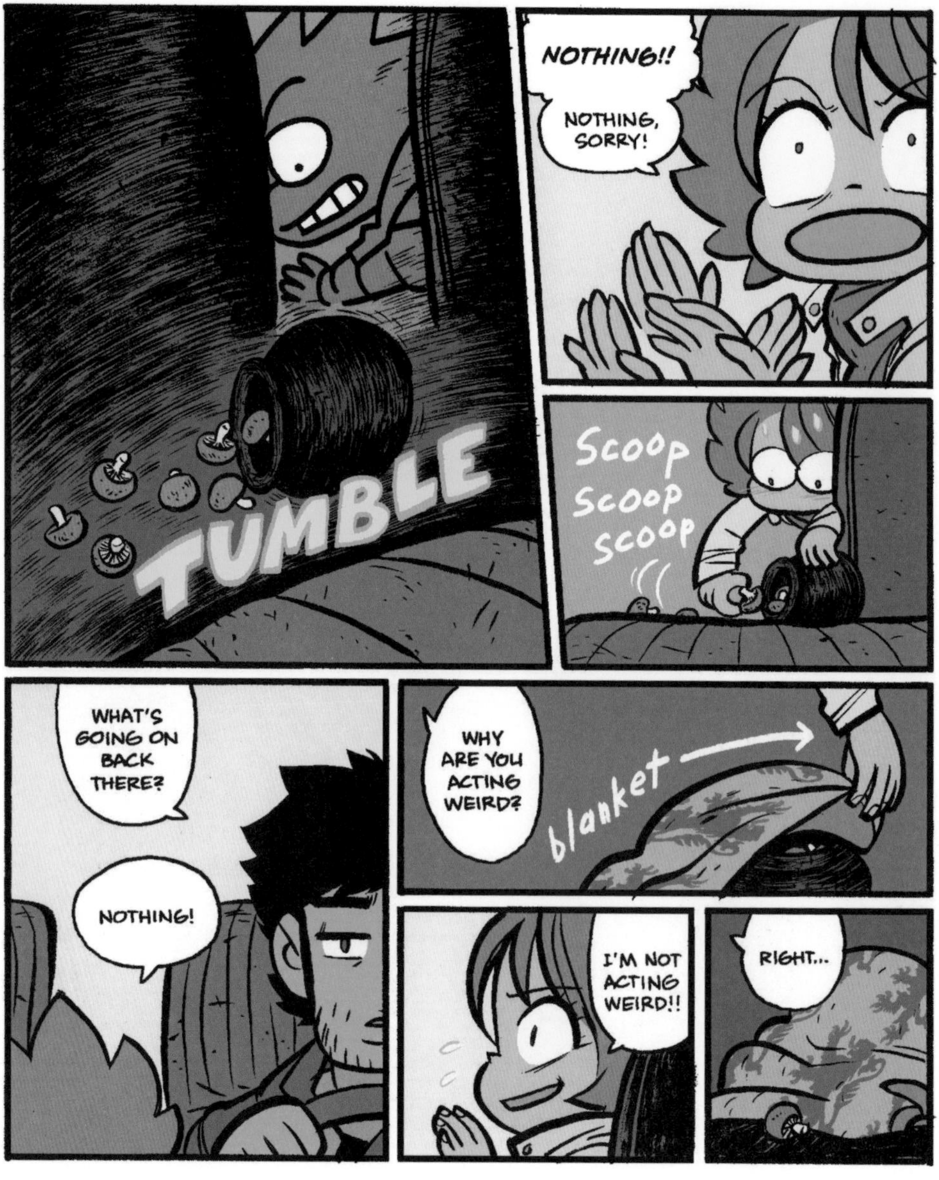
TUMBLE
NOTHING!!
NOTHING, SORRY!
Scoop
Scoop
scoop
WHAT'S GOING ON BACK THERE?
NOTHING!
WHY ARE YOU ACTING WEIRD?
blanket
I'M NOT ACTING WEIRD!!
RIGHT...

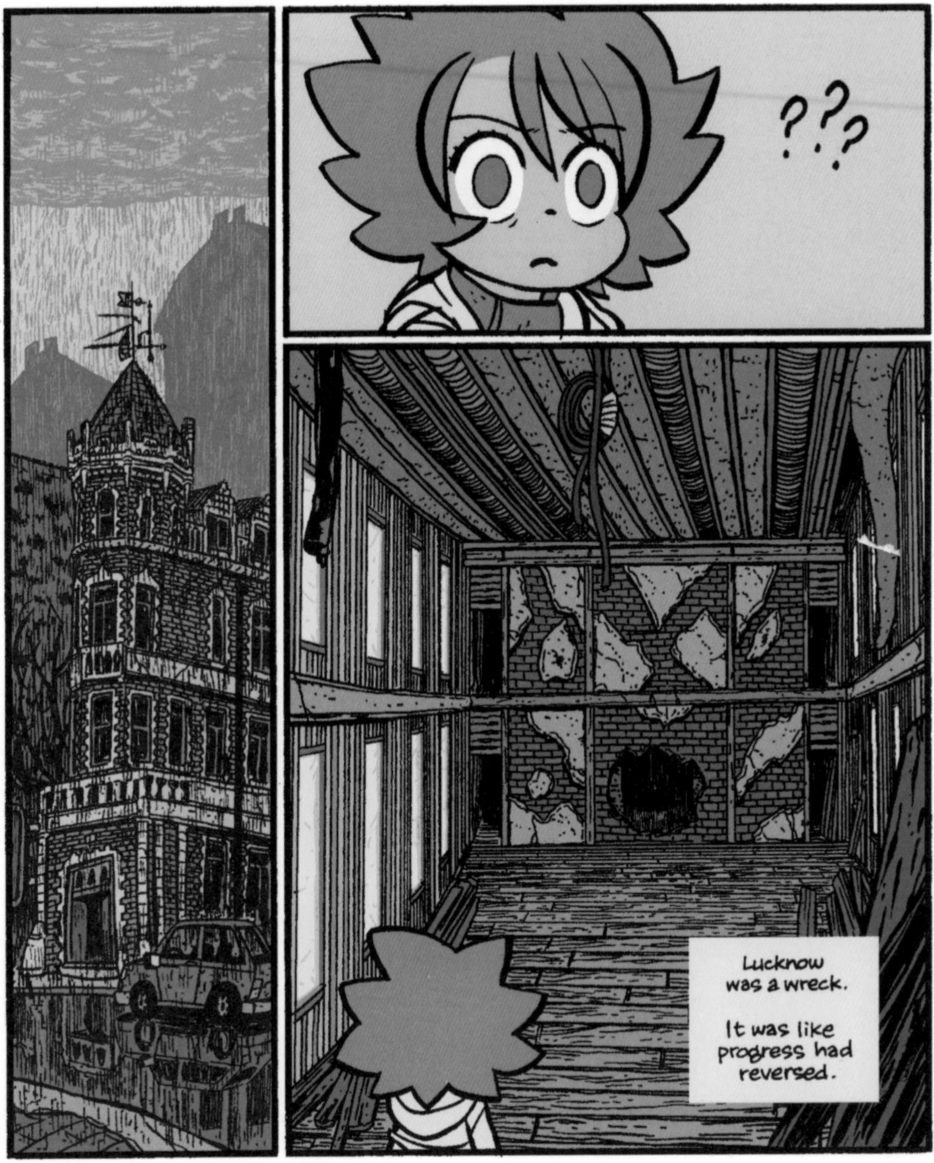
???
Lucknow was a wreck.
It was like progress had reversed.

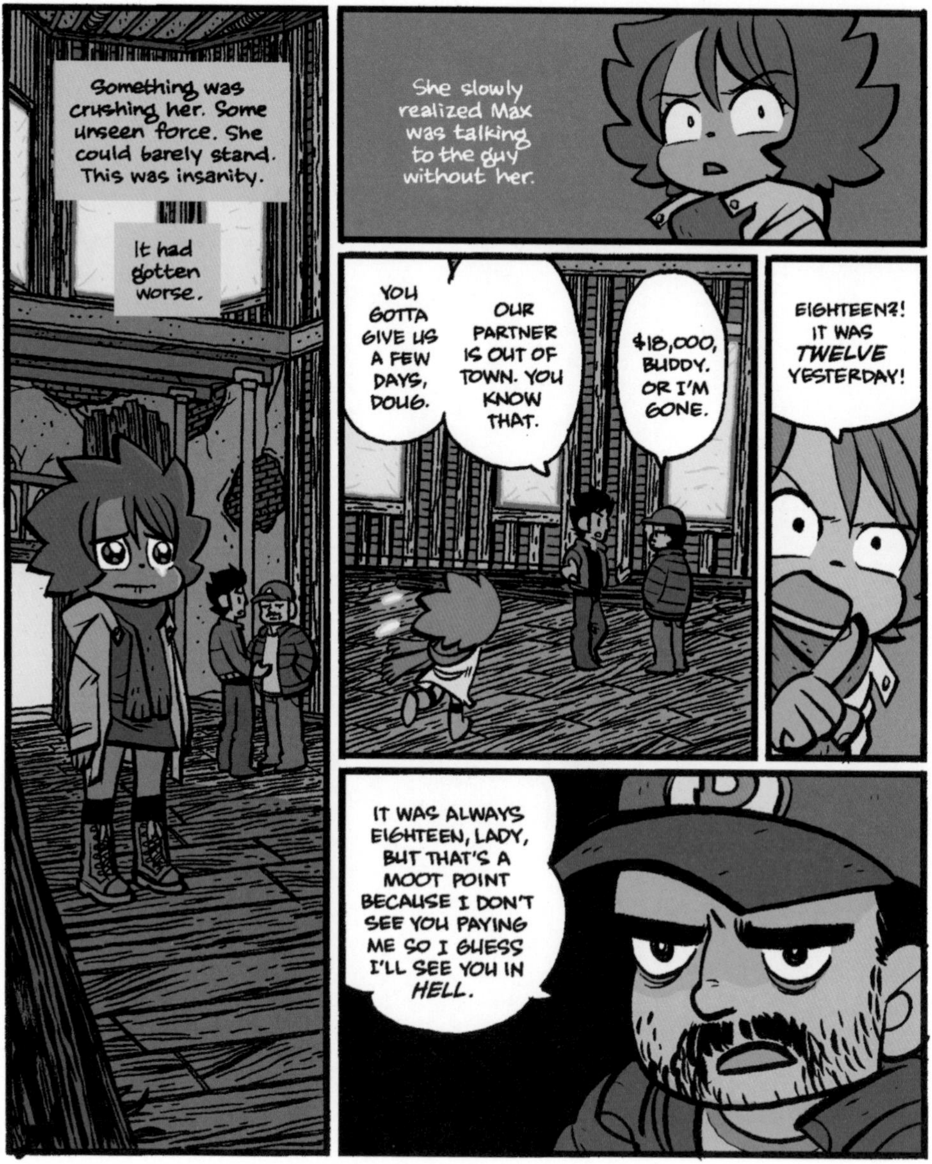
Something was crushing her. Some unseen force. She could barely stand. This was insanity.
It had gotten worse.
She slowly realized Max was talking to the guy without her.
YOU GOTTA GIVE US A FEW DAYS, DOUG.
OUR PARTNER IS OUT OF TOWN. YOU KNOW THAT.
$18,000, BUDDY. OR I'M GONE.
EIGHTEEN?! IT WAS *TWELVE* YESTERDAY!
IT WAS ALWAYS EIGHTEEN, LADY, BUT THAT'S A MOOT POINT BECAUSE I DON'T SEE YOU PAYING ME SO I GUESS I'LL SEE YOU IN *HELL*.

159

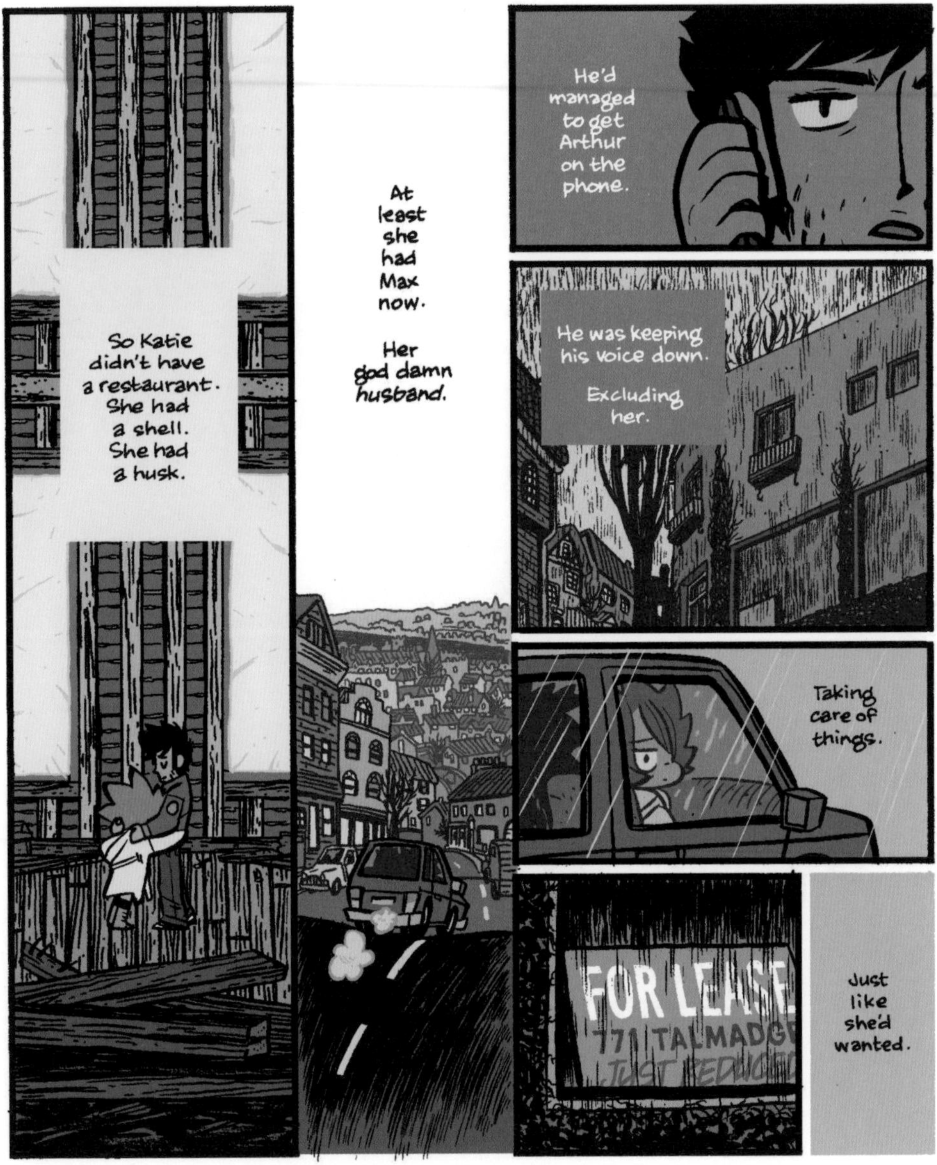
So Katie
didn't have
a restaurant.
She had
a shell.
She had
a husk.
At
least
she
had
Max
now.
Her
god damn
husband.
He'd
managed
to get
Arthur
on the
phone.
He was keeping
his voice down.
Excluding
her.
Taking
care of
things.
FOR LEASE
771 TALMADGE
JUST REDUCED
Just
like
she'd
wanted.

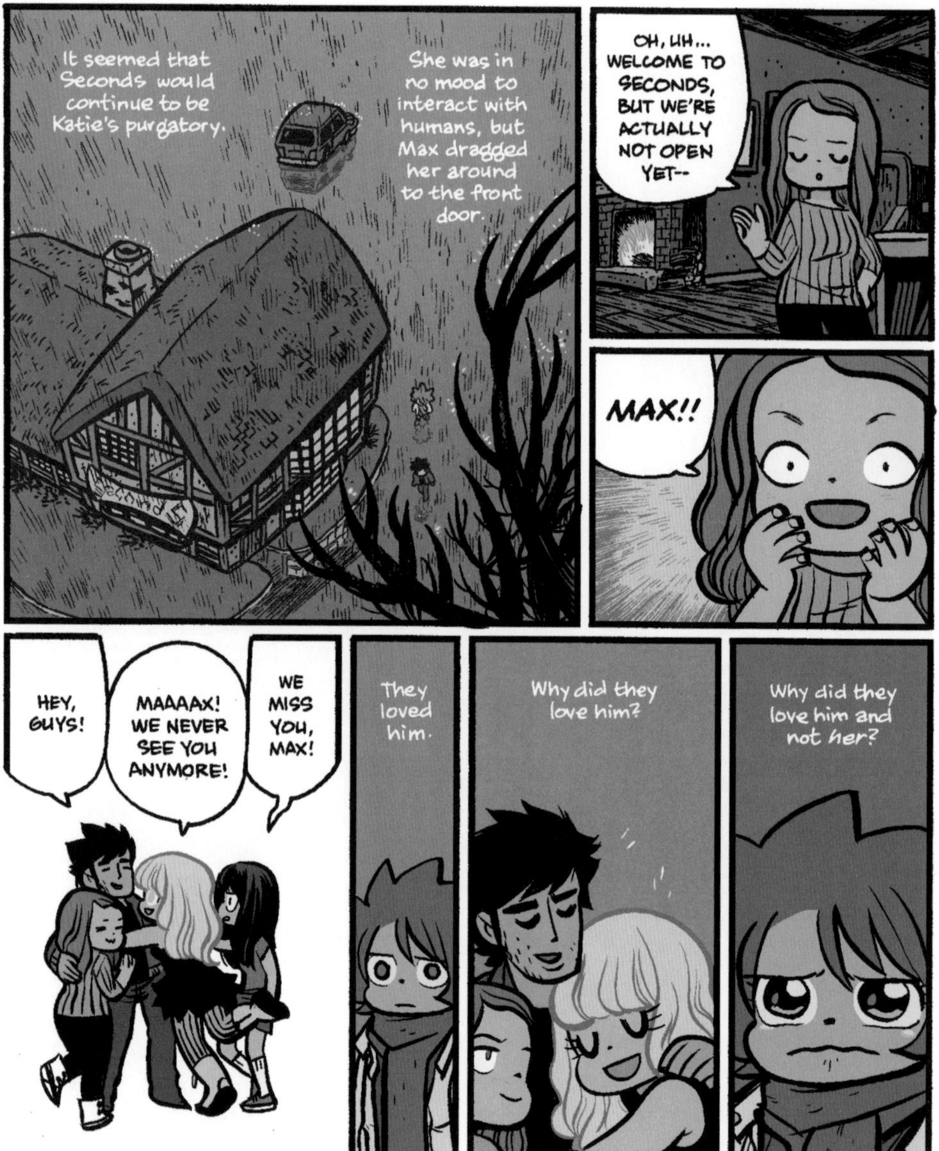
It seemed that Seconds would continue to be Katie's purgatory.
She was in no mood to interact with humans, but Max dragged her around to the front door.
OH, UH... WELCOME TO SECONDS, BUT WE'RE ACTUALLY NOT OPEN YET--
MAX!!
HEY, GUYS!
MAAAAX! WE NEVER SEE YOU ANYMORE!
WE MISS YOU, MAX!
They loved him.
Why did they love him?
Why did they love him and not *her*?

163

164

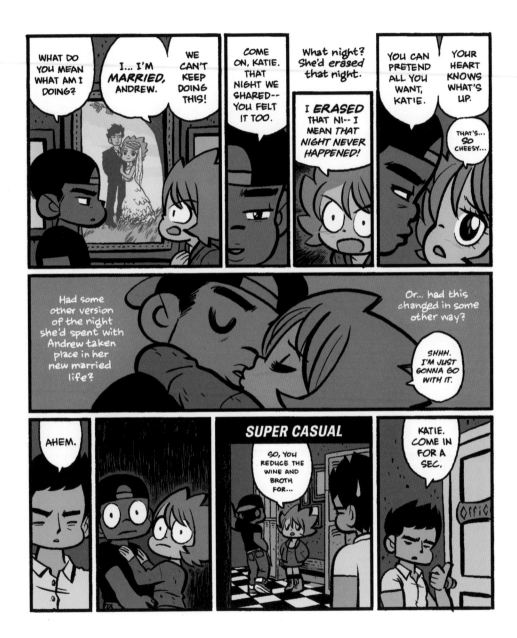

165

168

169

I WANT TO SEE THE MAGIC MUSHROOM PATCH! IS IT LIKE A FAIRY RING?

UMM...

I THINK IT'S SAFEST IF I DON'T-- LIKE, YOU KNOW--

IF THEY FELL INTO THE, UM, WRONG HANDS--

OH GOSH! YOU'RE RIGHT!

I KNOW. I'M SO SORRY.

I GUESS THERE'S ONE QUESTION ON MY MIND.

IF WE ASSUME SHE USES THE MUSHROOMS TO CHANGE LITTLE THINGS FOR US EVERY DAY...

...WHY WOULD SHE START LETTING *YOU* CHANGE *BIG* THINGS?

Katie suddenly remembered the first thing. The accident.

But it didn't seem appropriate to tell Hazel about that.

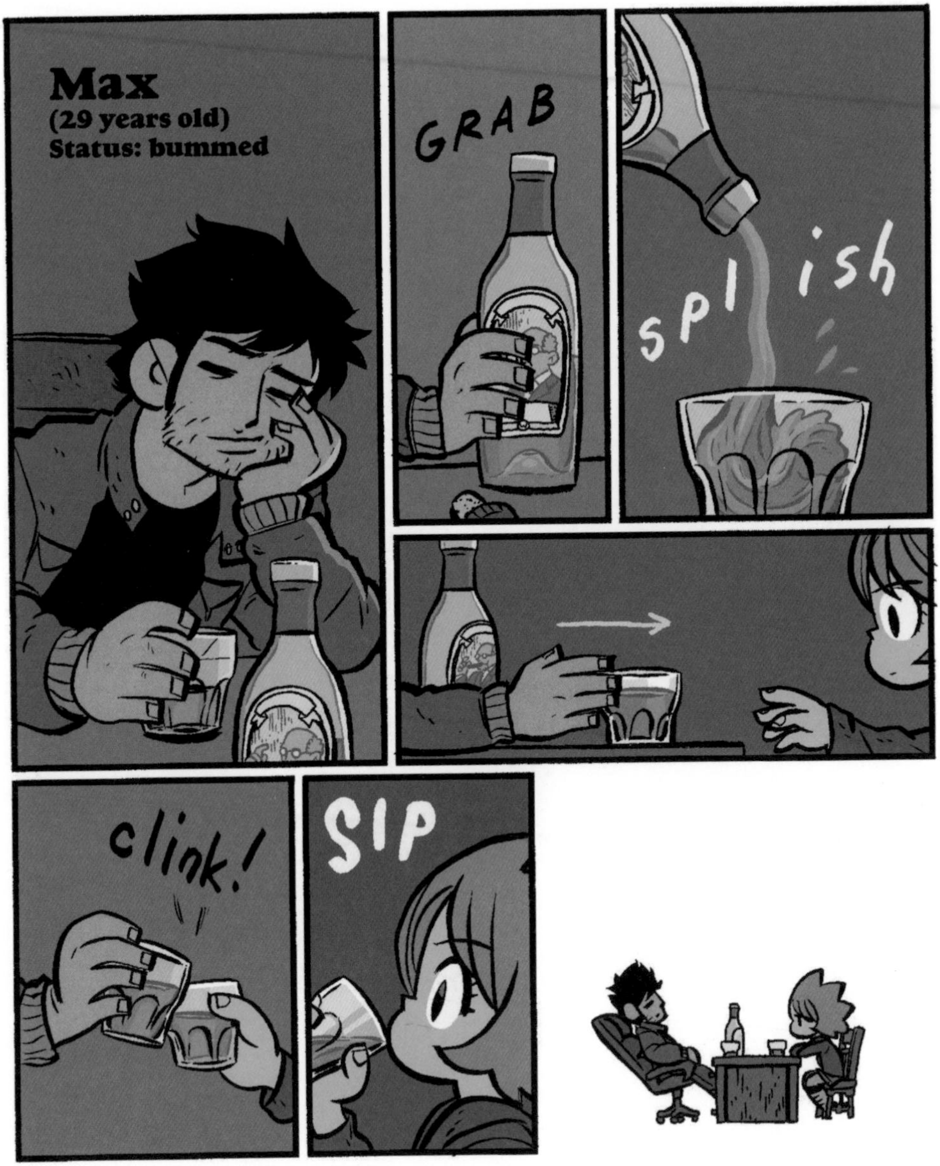
Max
(29 years old)
Status: bummed
GRAB
splish
clink!
SIP

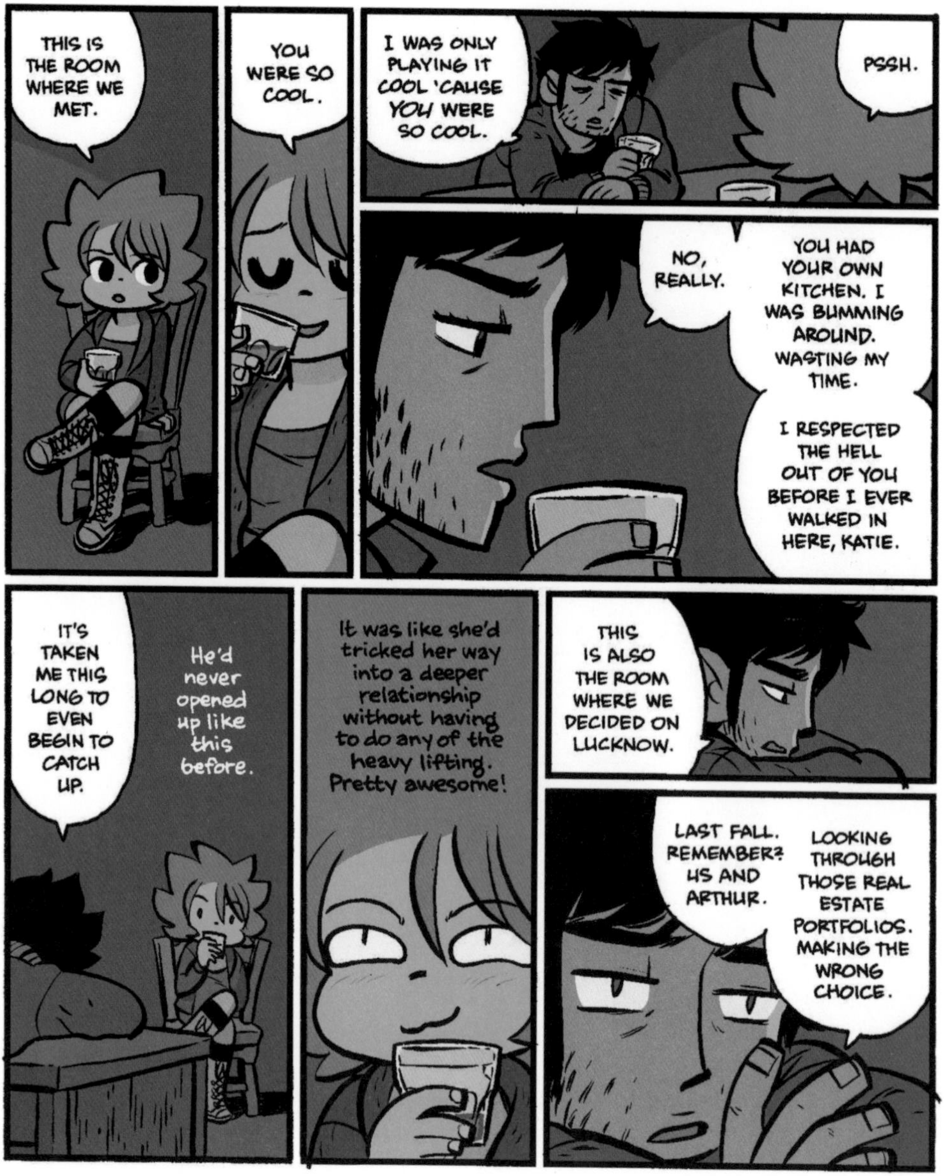
THIS IS THE ROOM WHERE WE MET.
YOU WERE SO COOL.
I WAS ONLY PLAYING IT COOL 'CAUSE YOU WERE SO COOL.
PSSH.
NO, REALLY.
YOU HAD YOUR OWN KITCHEN. I WAS BUMMING AROUND. WASTING MY TIME.
I RESPECTED THE HELL OUT OF YOU BEFORE I EVER WALKED IN HERE, KATIE.
IT'S TAKEN ME THIS LONG TO EVEN BEGIN TO CATCH UP.
He'd never opened up like this before.
It was like she'd tricked her way into a deeper relationship without having to do any of the heavy lifting. Pretty awesome!
THIS IS ALSO THE ROOM WHERE WE DECIDED ON LUCKNOW.
LAST FALL. REMEMBER? US AND ARTHUR.
LOOKING THROUGH THOSE REAL ESTATE PORTFOLIOS. MAKING THE WRONG CHOICE.

175

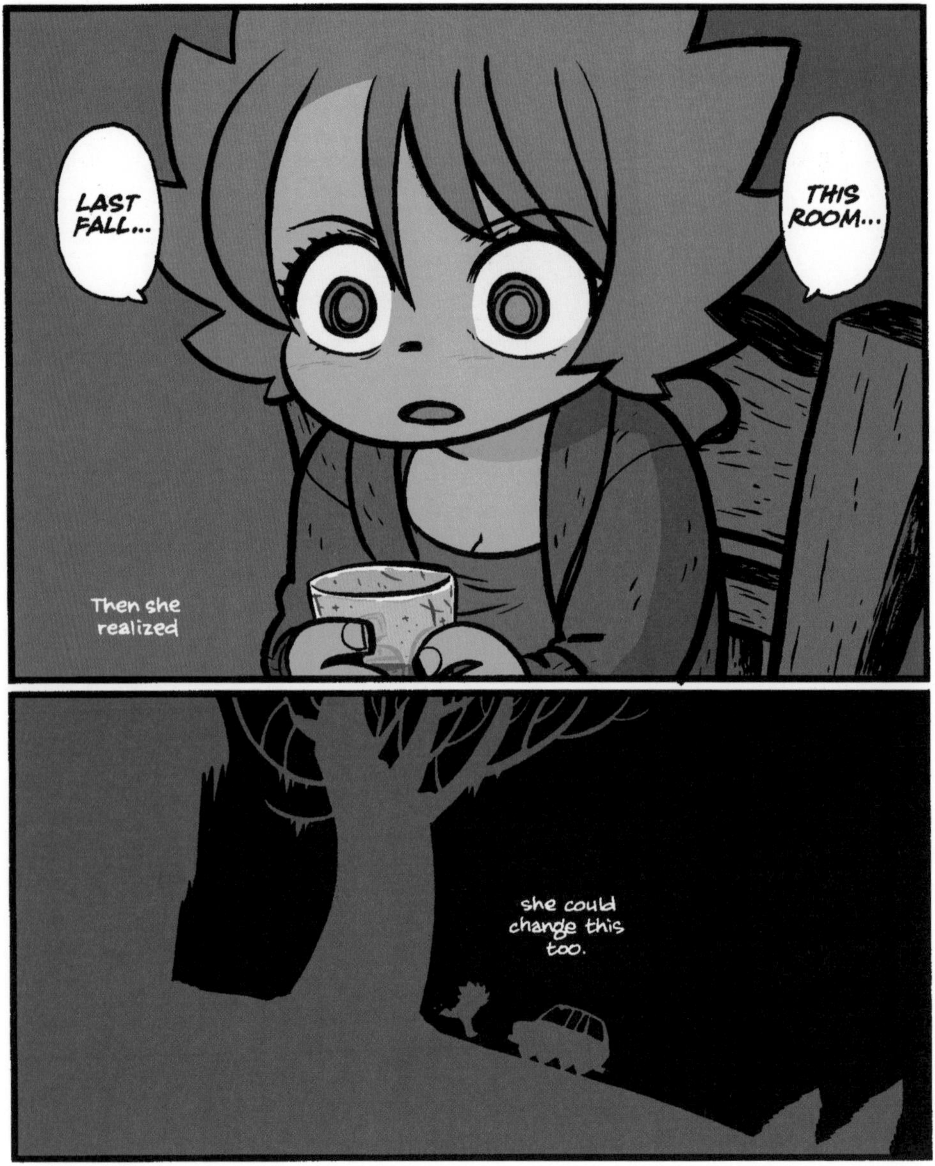
LAST FALL...
THIS ROOM...
Then she realized
she could change this too.

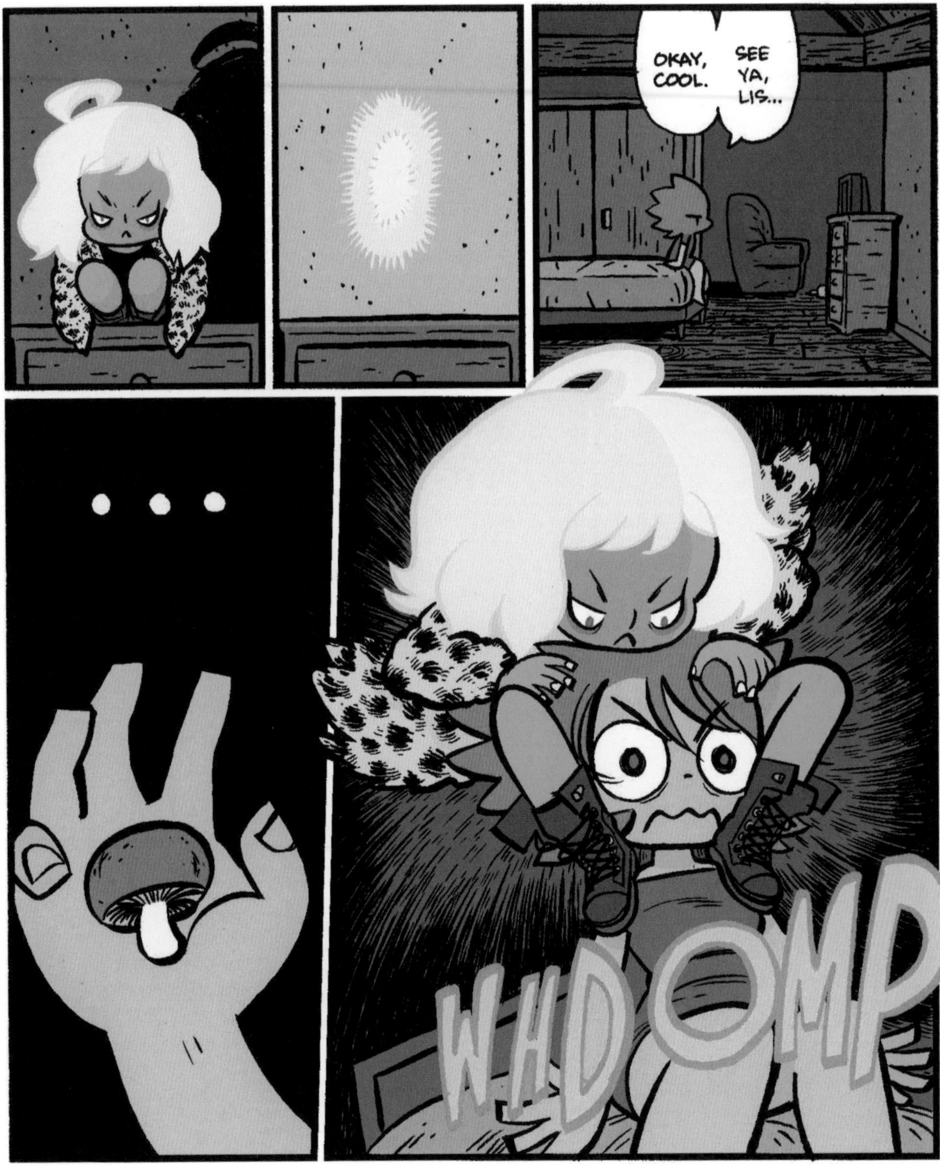
OKAY, COOL.
SEE YA, LIS...
. . .
WHDOMP

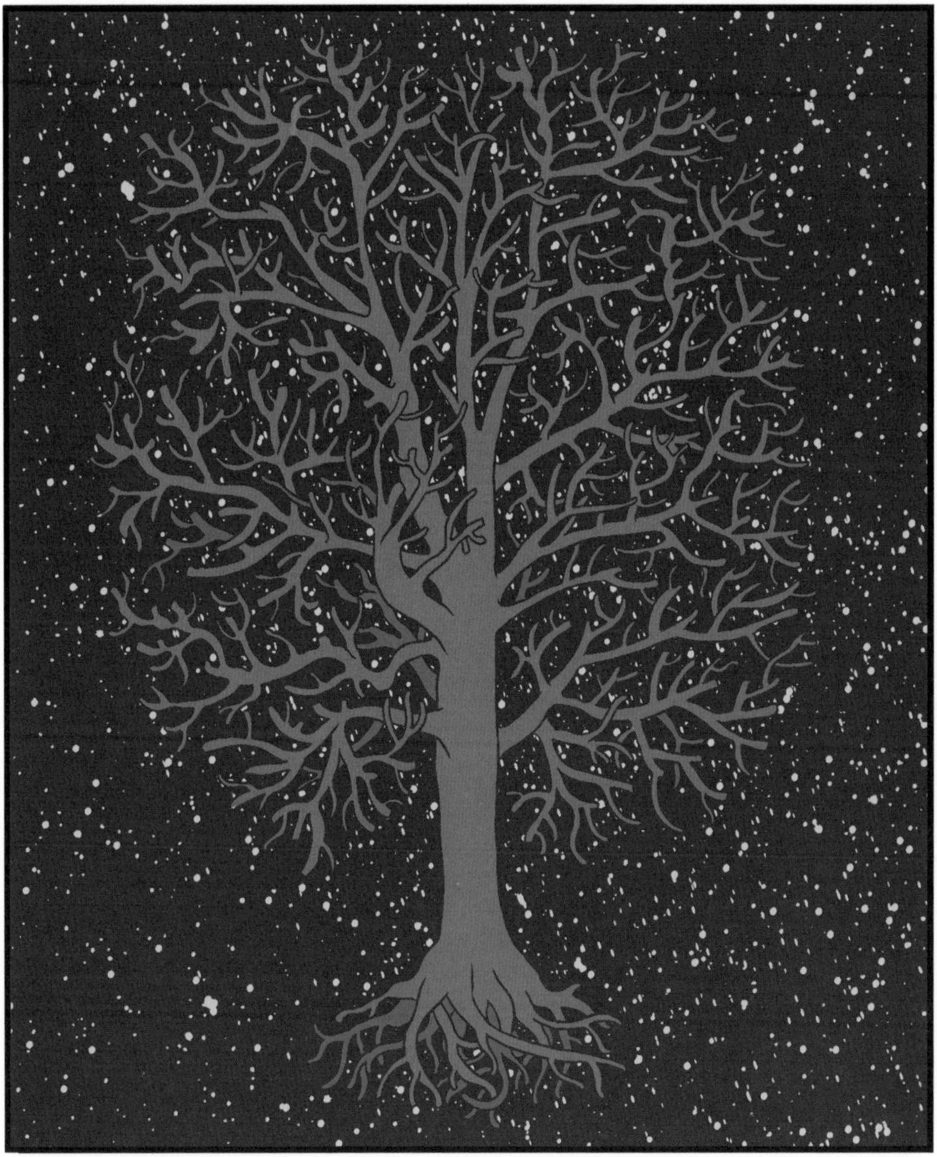

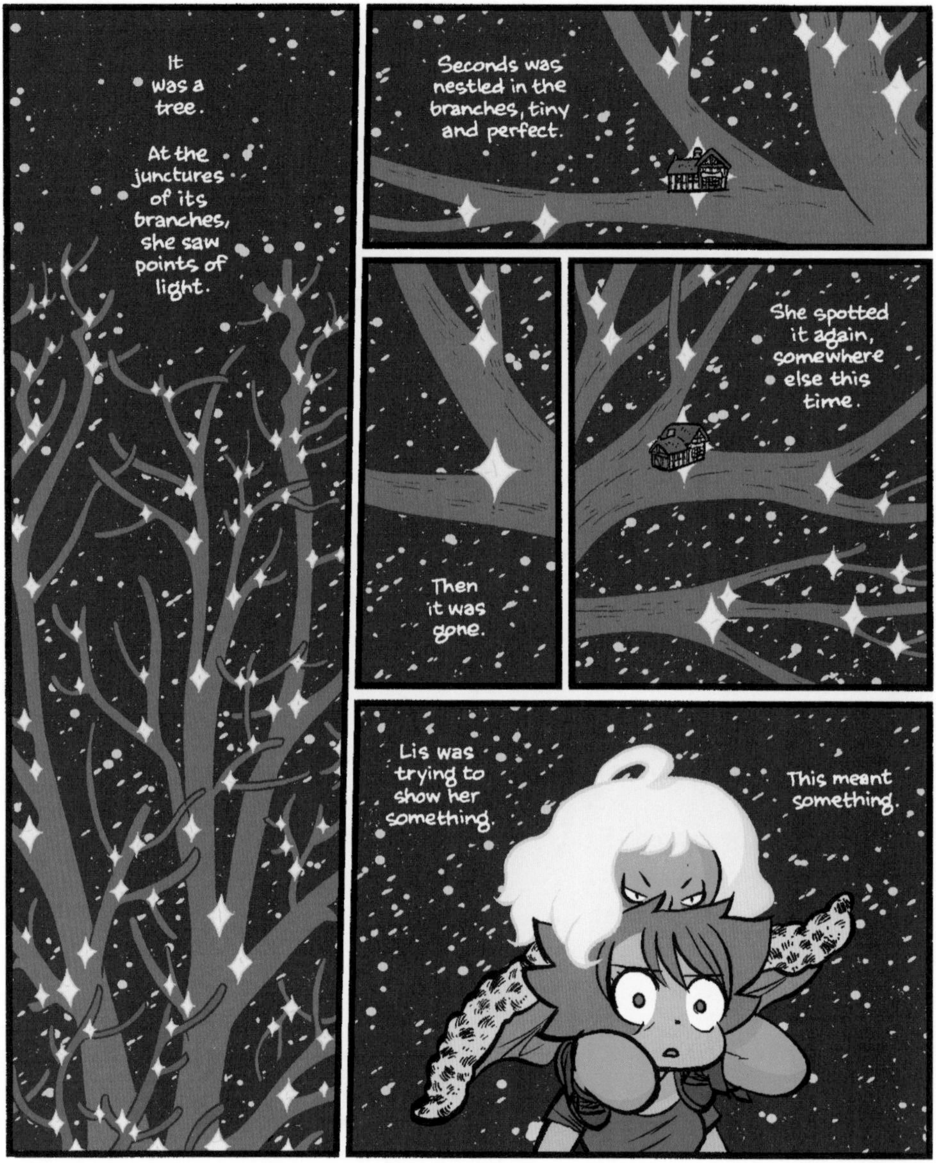
It was a tree.
At the junctures of its branches, she saw points of light.
Seconds was nestled in the branches, tiny and perfect.
Then it was gone.
She spotted it again, somewhere else this time.
Lis was trying to show her something.
This meant something.

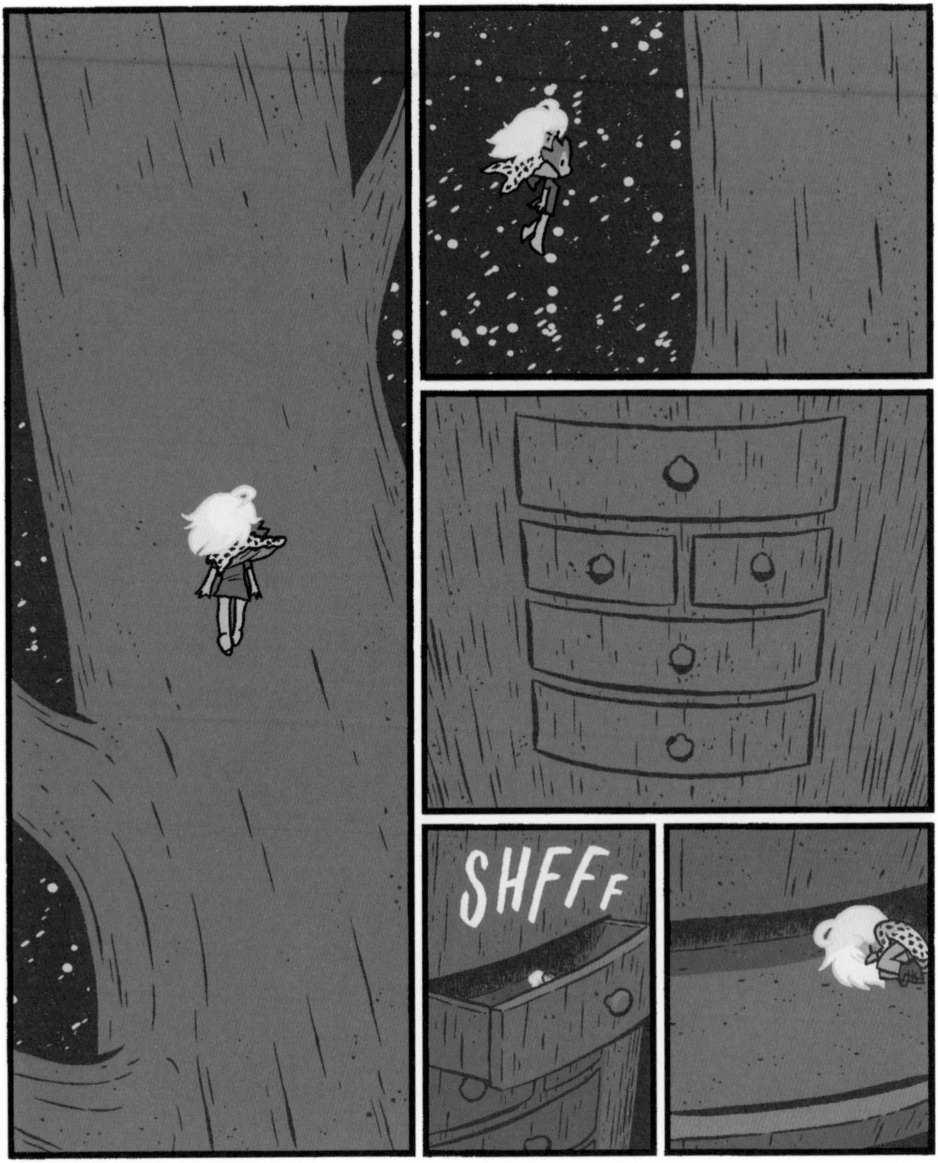
SHFFF

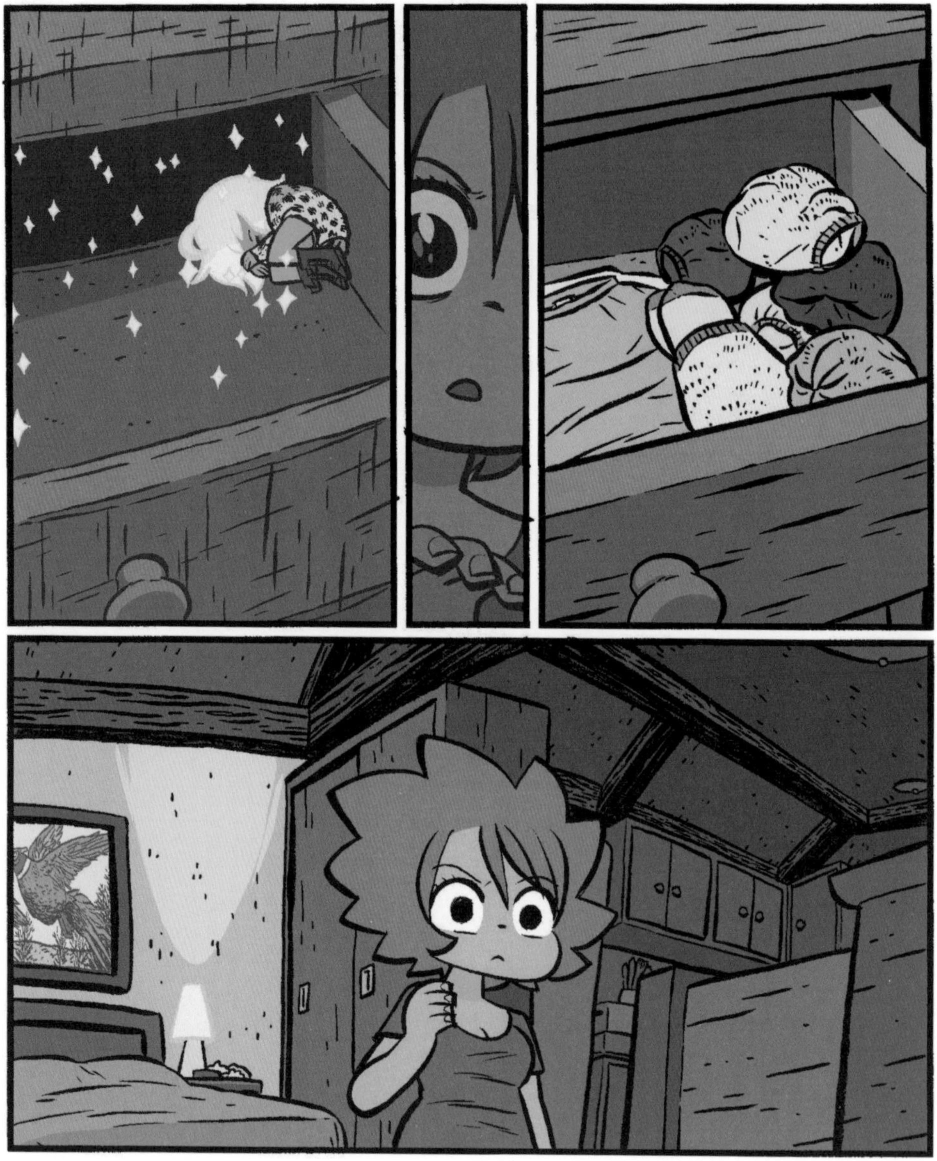

187

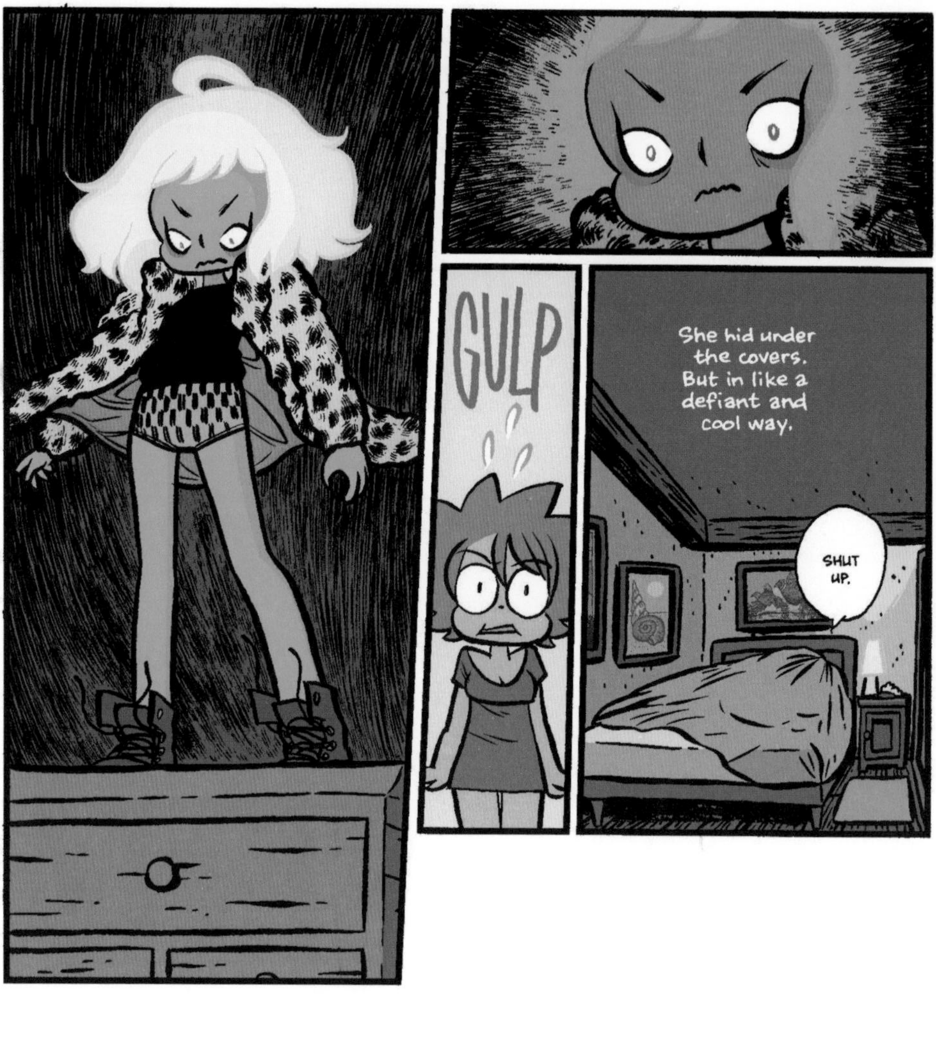
GULP
She hid under the covers. But in like a defiant and cool way.
SHUT UP.

REVISION #7

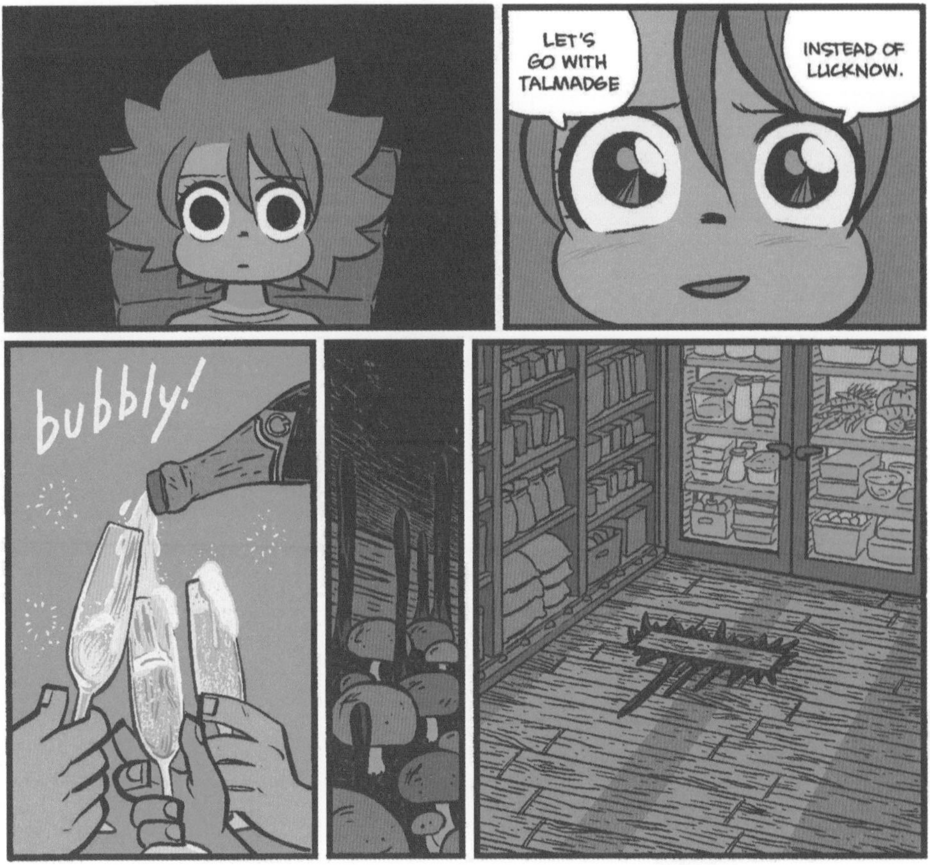
LET'S GO WITH TALMADGE
INSTEAD OF LUCKNOW.
bubbly!

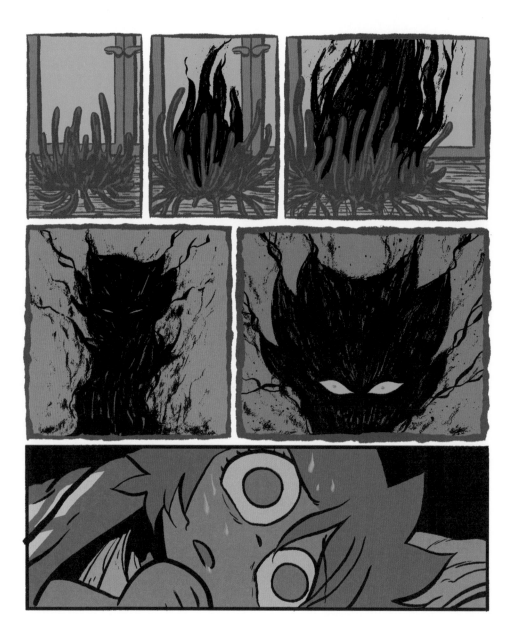

190

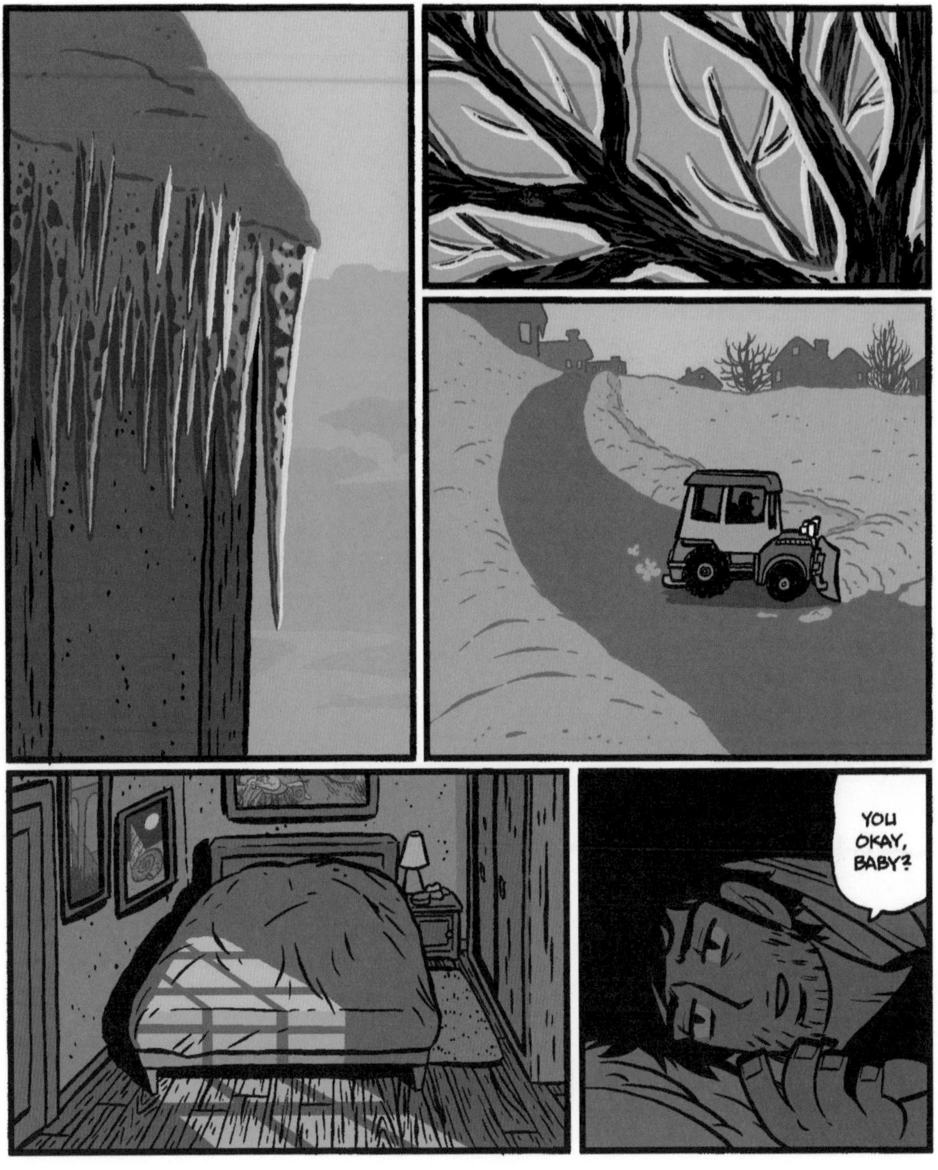
YOU OKAY, BABY?

194

195

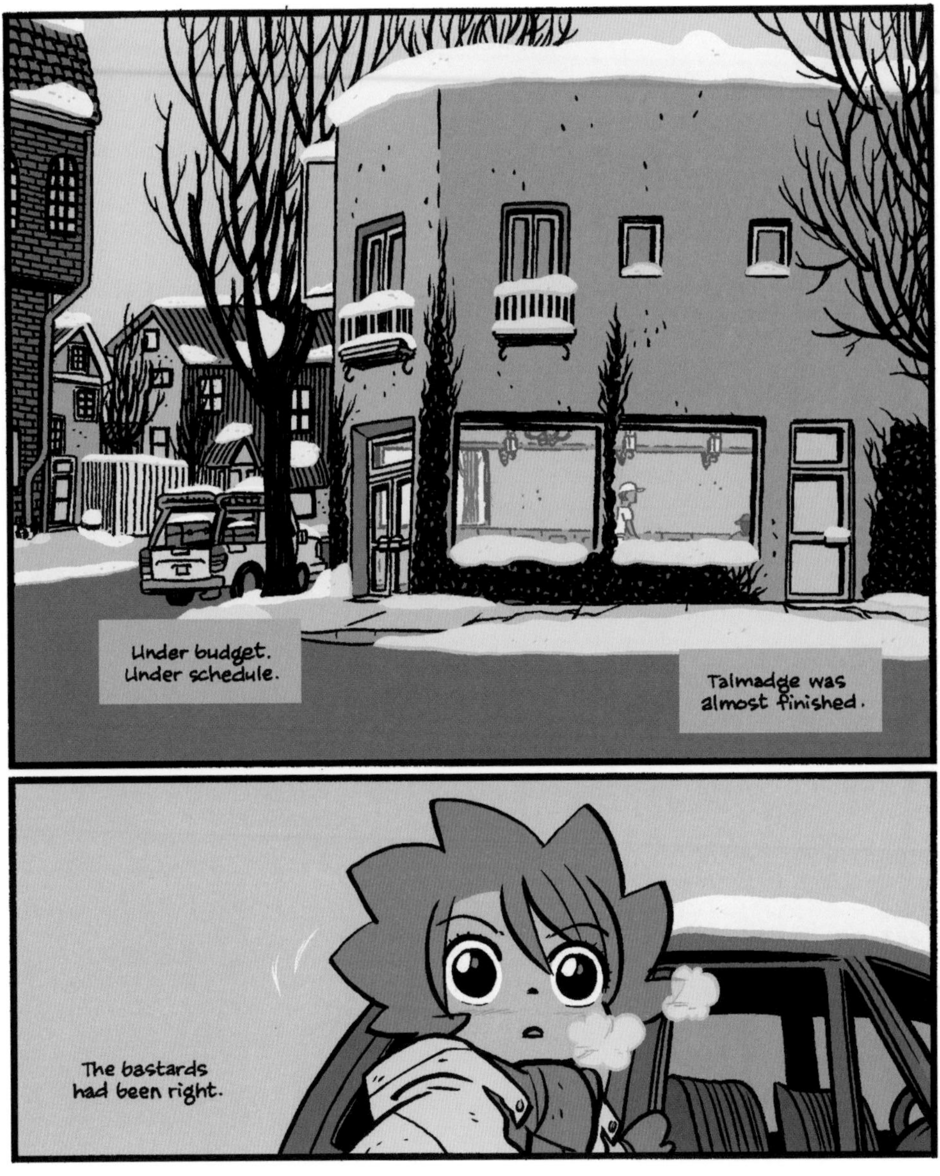
Under budget.
Under schedule.
Talmadge was almost finished.
The bastards had been right.

199

200

I LIKE THE LOGO WE PICKED.

Last fall. Last fall was too far. The farther back she went, the more wide-ranging the ramifications of her changes.

AND MKII IS A GOOD NAME. I THINK IT'S STRONG.

She tried to imagine another Katie, a Katie who thought "MKII" was a good name for a restaurant. Where was she now? When had she given up on life?

MAX AND KATIE'S SECOND RESTAURANT. IT'S CLEVER.

I KNOW IT ISN'T EXACTLY WHAT YOU WANTED.

What was the precise moment at which the two Katies had diverged?

BUT YOU NEED TO COMPROMISE ONCE IN A WHILE, Y'KNOW?

UM, WHERE ARE WE GOING?

They were going to Lucknow. She had to see what was happening at Lucknow.

201

204

Katie stashed the witch's pot in the back of her nightstand.

She couldn't see Lis anywhere.

But Lis was there.

And after, when she went back downstairs,

Katie got turned around between the stairs and the kitchen, which was weird--

--it's not like the hallway was a maze.

206

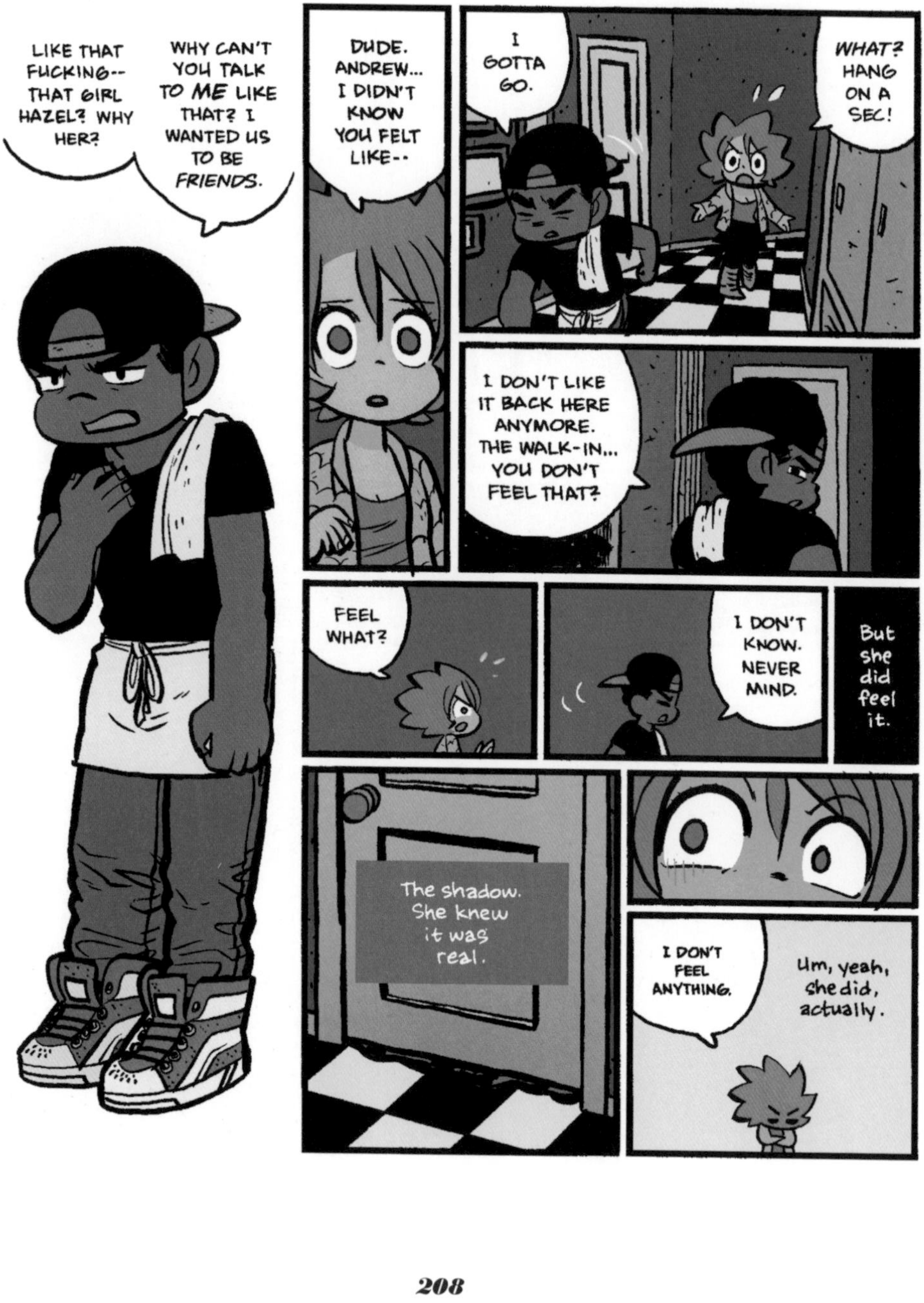
LIKE THAT FUCKING-- THAT GIRL HAZEL? WHY HER?
WHY CAN'T YOU TALK TO ME LIKE THAT? I WANTED US TO BE FRIENDS.
DUDE. ANDREW... I DIDN'T KNOW YOU FELT LIKE--
I GOTTA GO.
WHAT? HANG ON A SEC!
I DON'T LIKE IT BACK HERE ANYMORE. THE WALK-IN... YOU DON'T FEEL THAT?
FEEL WHAT?
I DON'T KNOW. NEVER MIND.
But she did feel it.
The shadow. She knew it was real.
I DON'T FEEL ANYTHING.
Um, yeah, she did, actually.

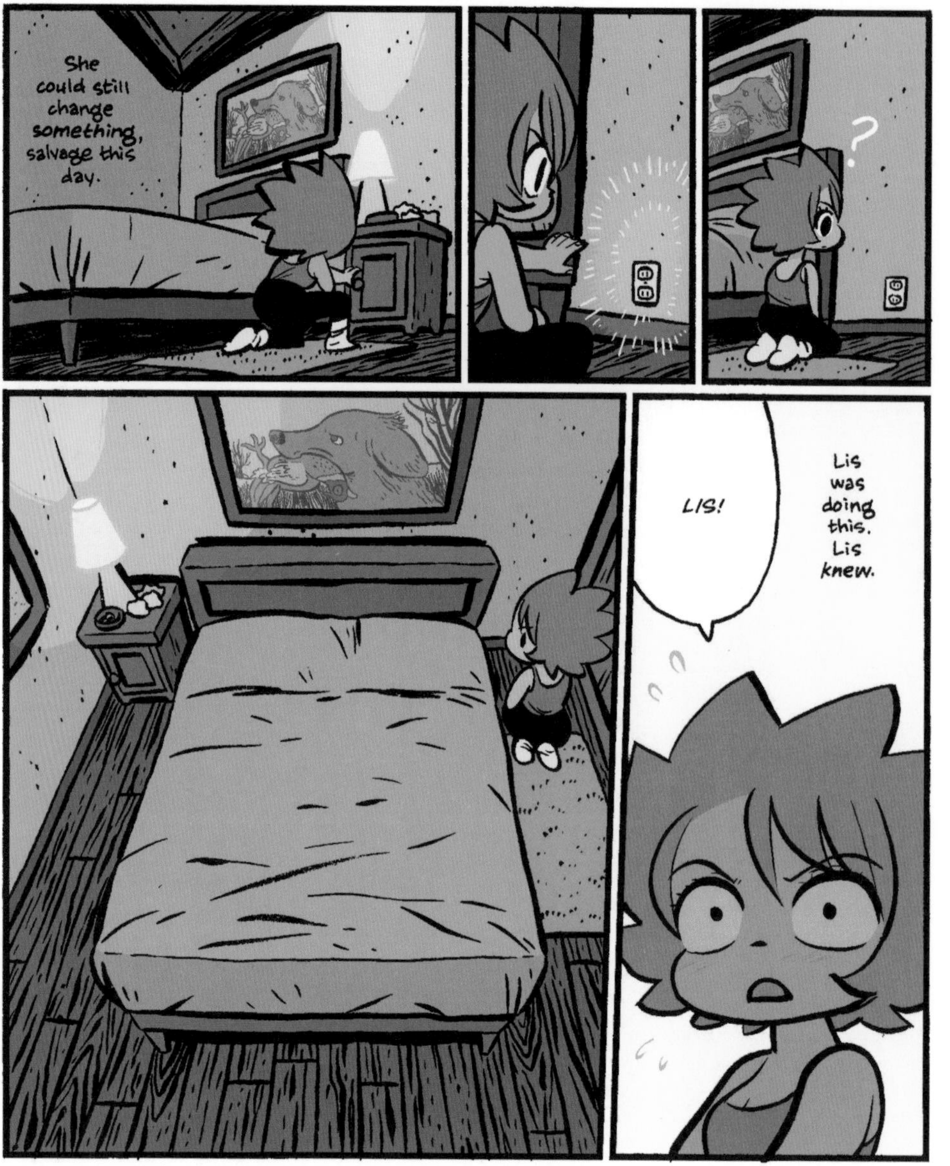
She could still change something, salvage this day.
?
LIS!
Lis was doing this. Lis knew.

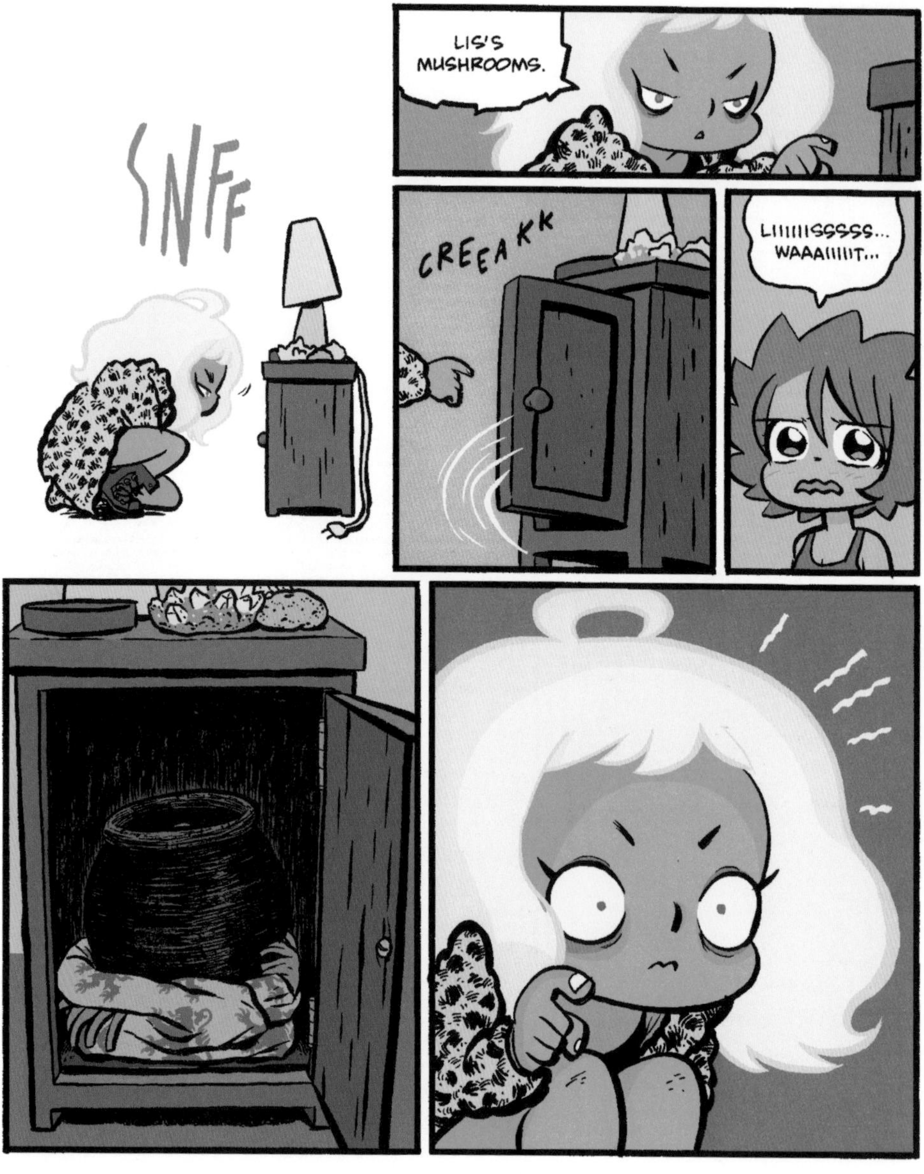
SNFF
LIS'S MUSHROOMS.
CREEAKK
LIIIIISSSSS... WAAAIIIIIT...

REVISION #8

215

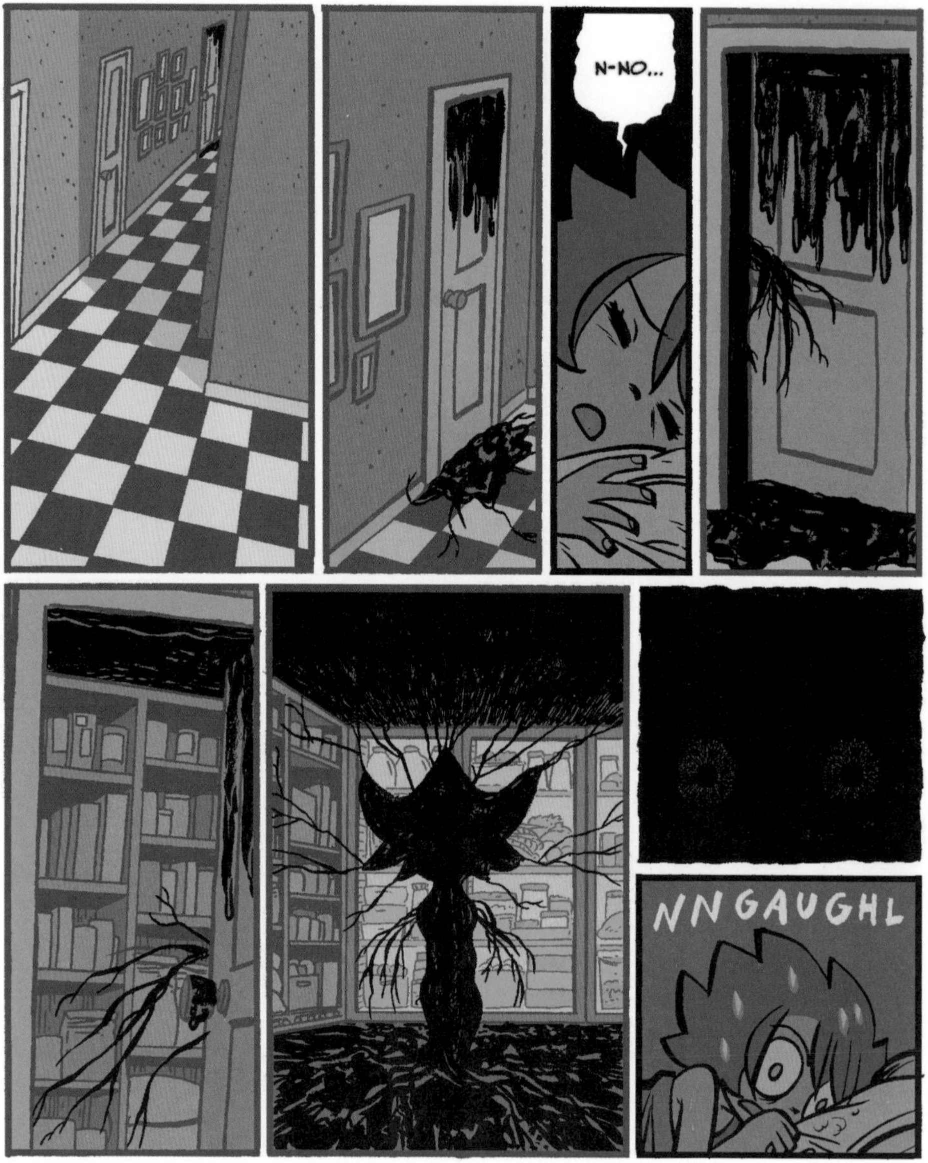
N-NO...
NNGAUGHL

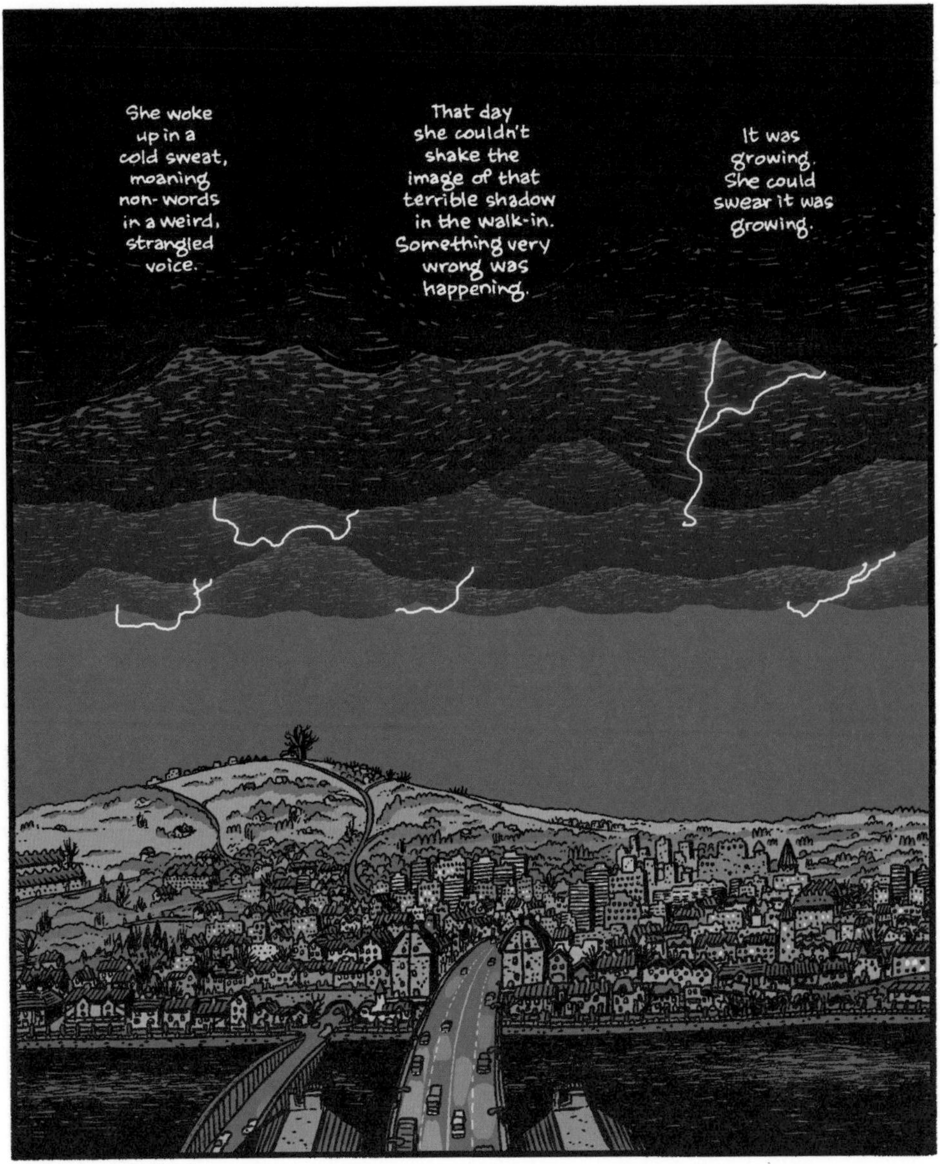
She woke up in a cold sweat, moaning non-words in a weird, strangled voice.
That day she couldn't shake the image of that terrible shadow in the walk-in. Something very wrong was happening.
It was growing. She could swear it was growing.

REVISION #9

And like that, the day was over, and she could barely remember what she needed to change for tomorrow.

They had started cooking, hammering out the details of their new menu. Every moment should have been a delight, but somehow none of them were.

Max was always disappointed in her, as if she'd been perfect once. As if he was now.

Four left.

She could get it right with four more. No problem.

REVISION #10

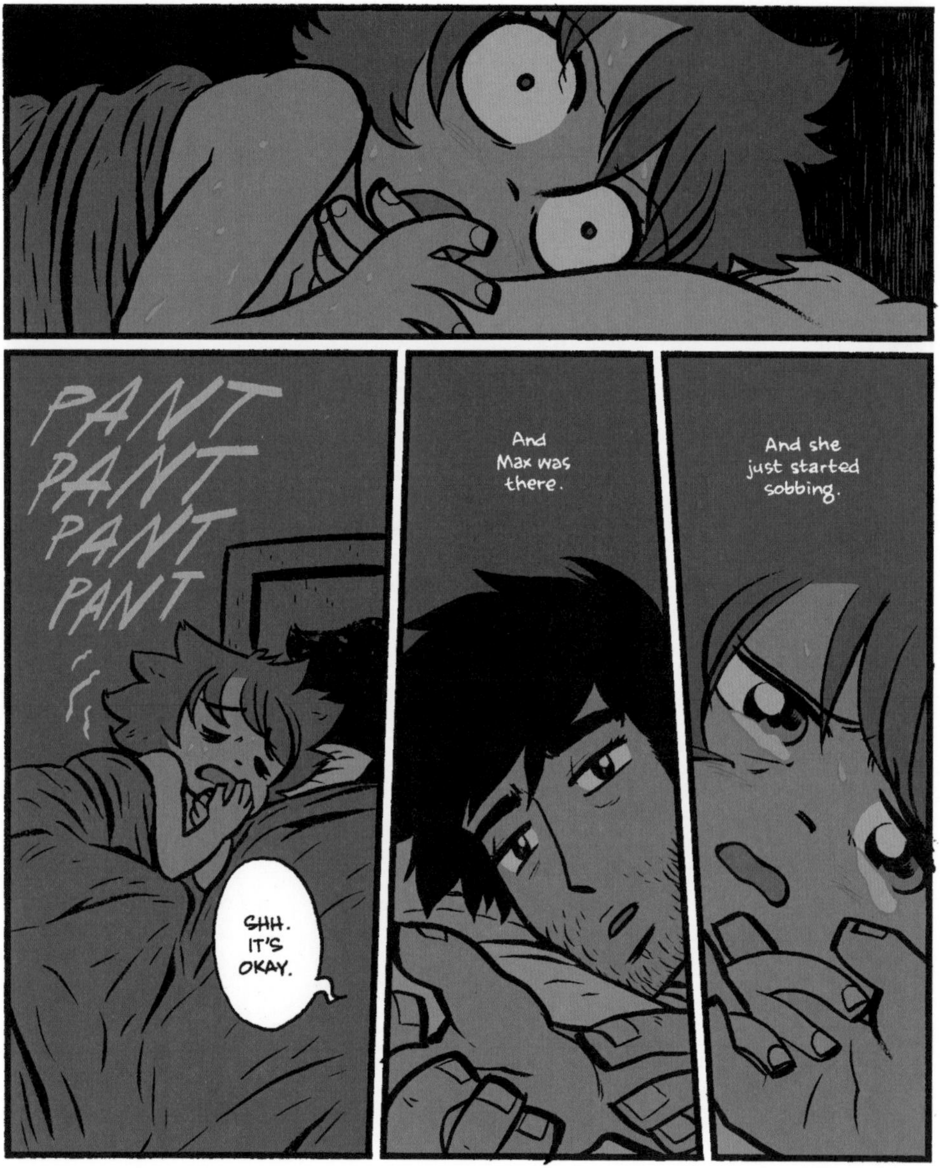
PANT
PANT
PANT
PANT
SHH. IT'S OKAY.
And Max was there.
And she just started sobbing.

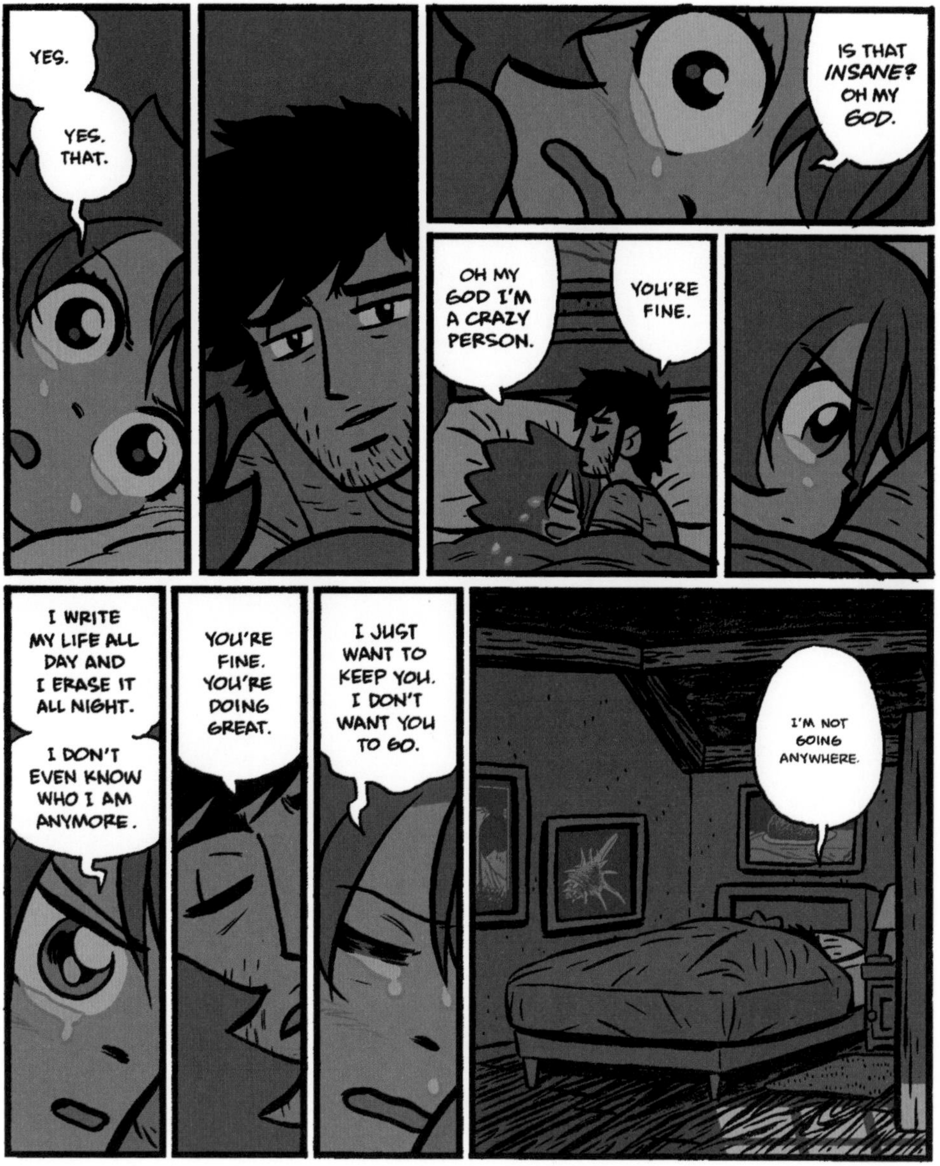
YES.
YES. THAT.
IS THAT INSANE? OH MY GOD.
OH MY GOD I'M A CRAZY PERSON.
YOU'RE FINE.
I WRITE MY LIFE ALL DAY AND I ERASE IT ALL NIGHT.
I DON'T EVEN KNOW WHO I AM ANYMORE.
YOU'RE FINE. YOU'RE DOING GREAT.
I JUST WANT TO KEEP YOU. I DON'T WANT YOU TO GO.
I'M NOT GOING ANYWHERE.

Katie
fell
asleep
again.

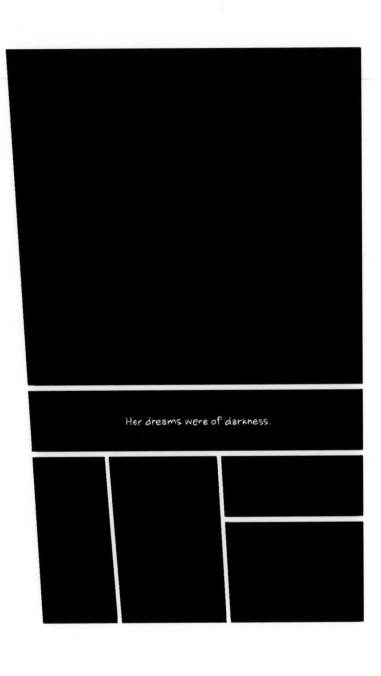

Her dreams were of darkness.

She woke up,

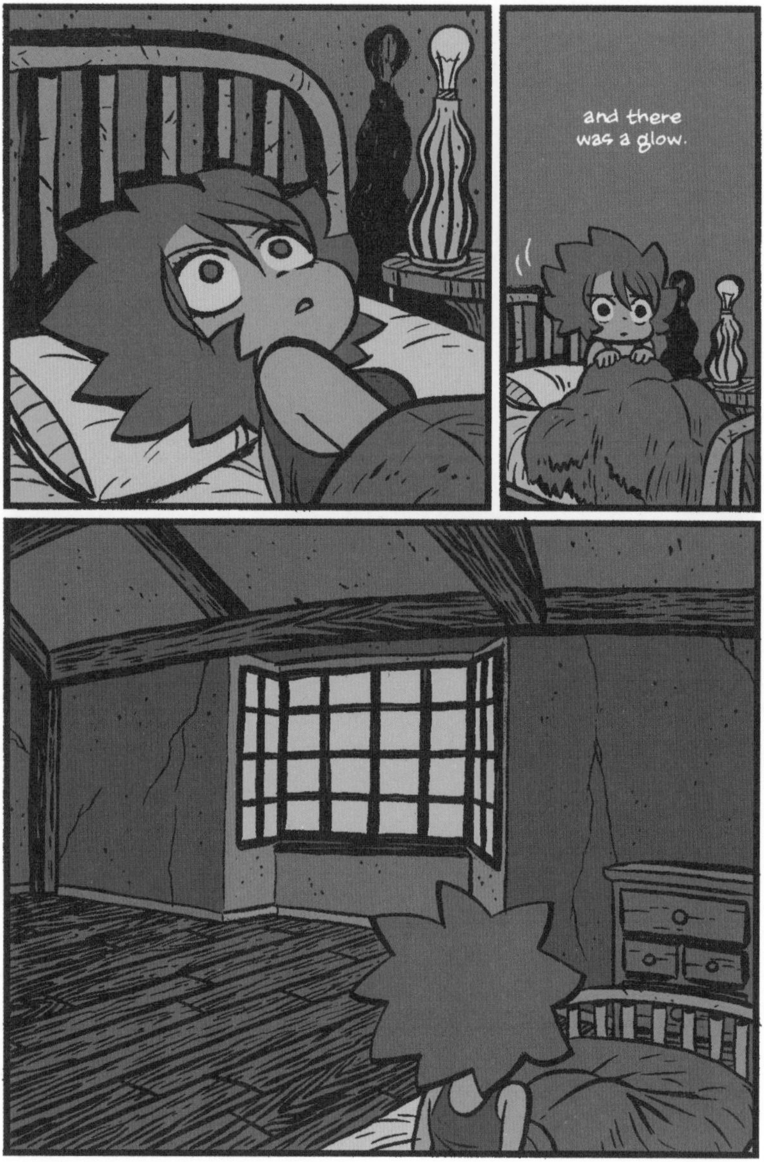
and there was a glow.

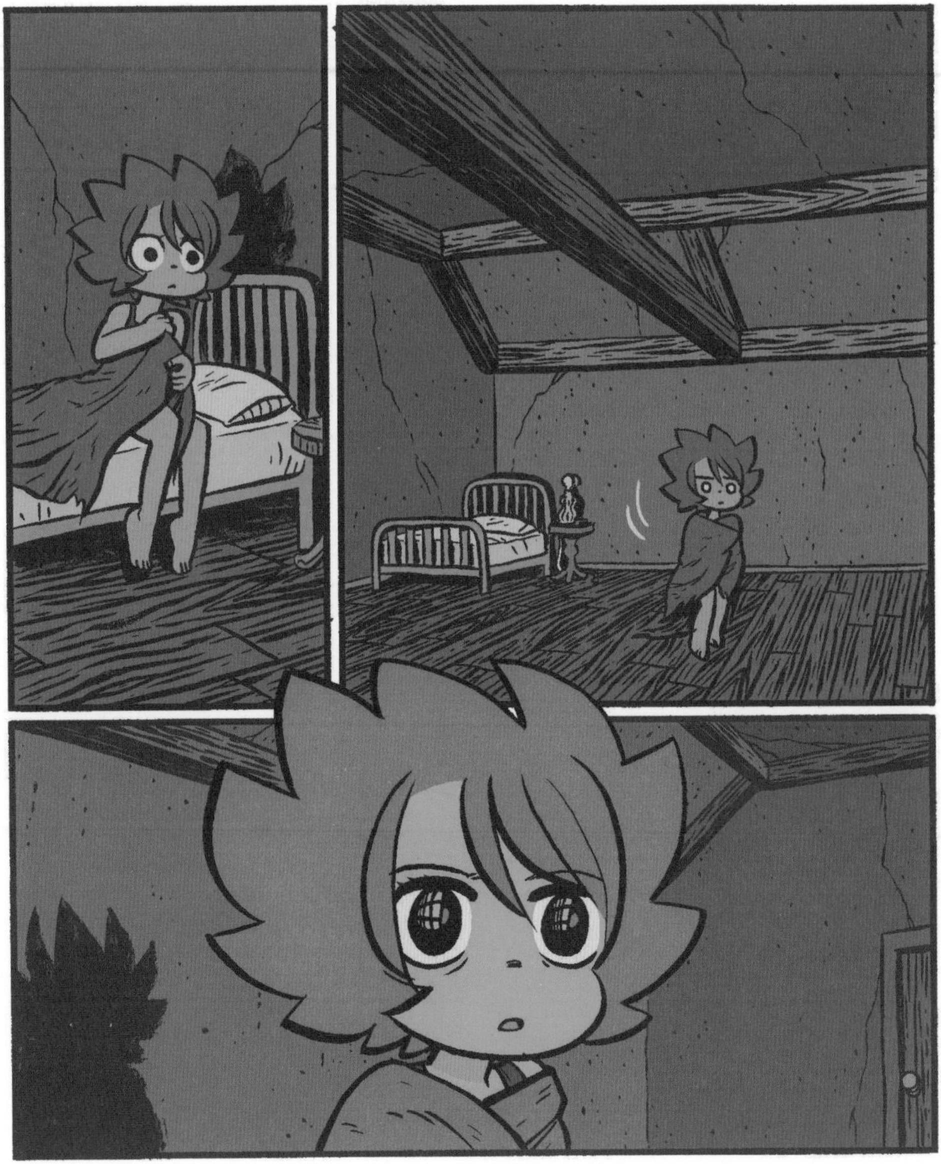

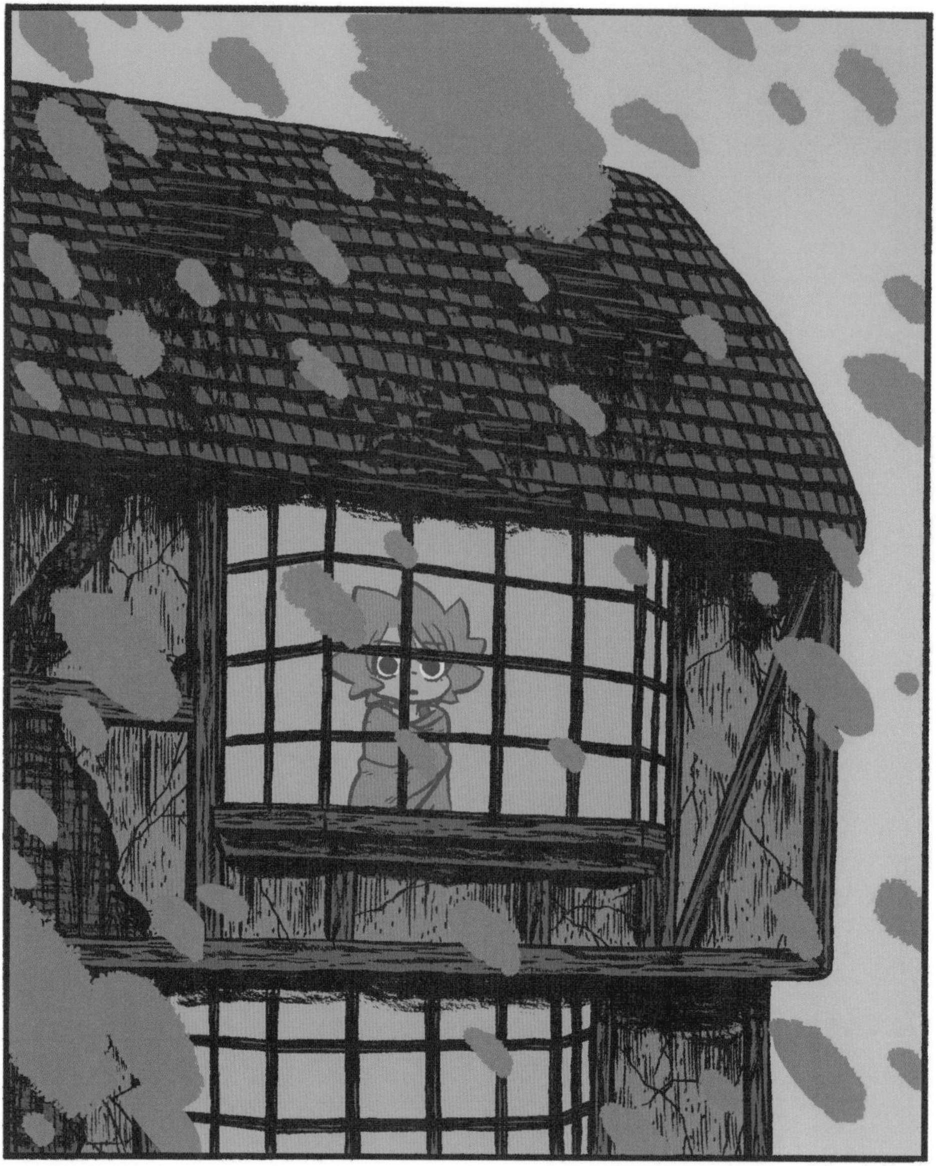

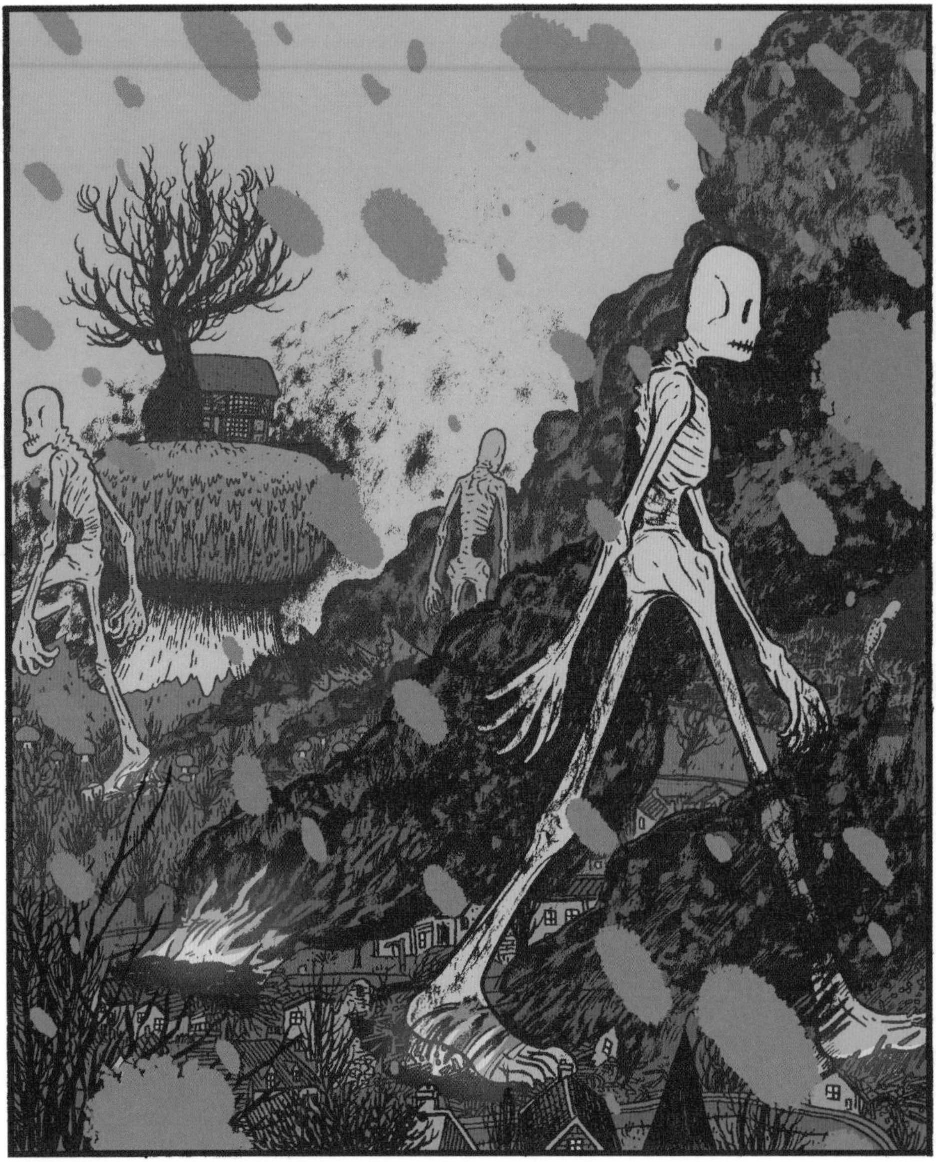

6

Control

When Katie woke up, she was back in her normal bedroom with Max asleep beside her.

She decided to take an early-morning drive. Away from here.

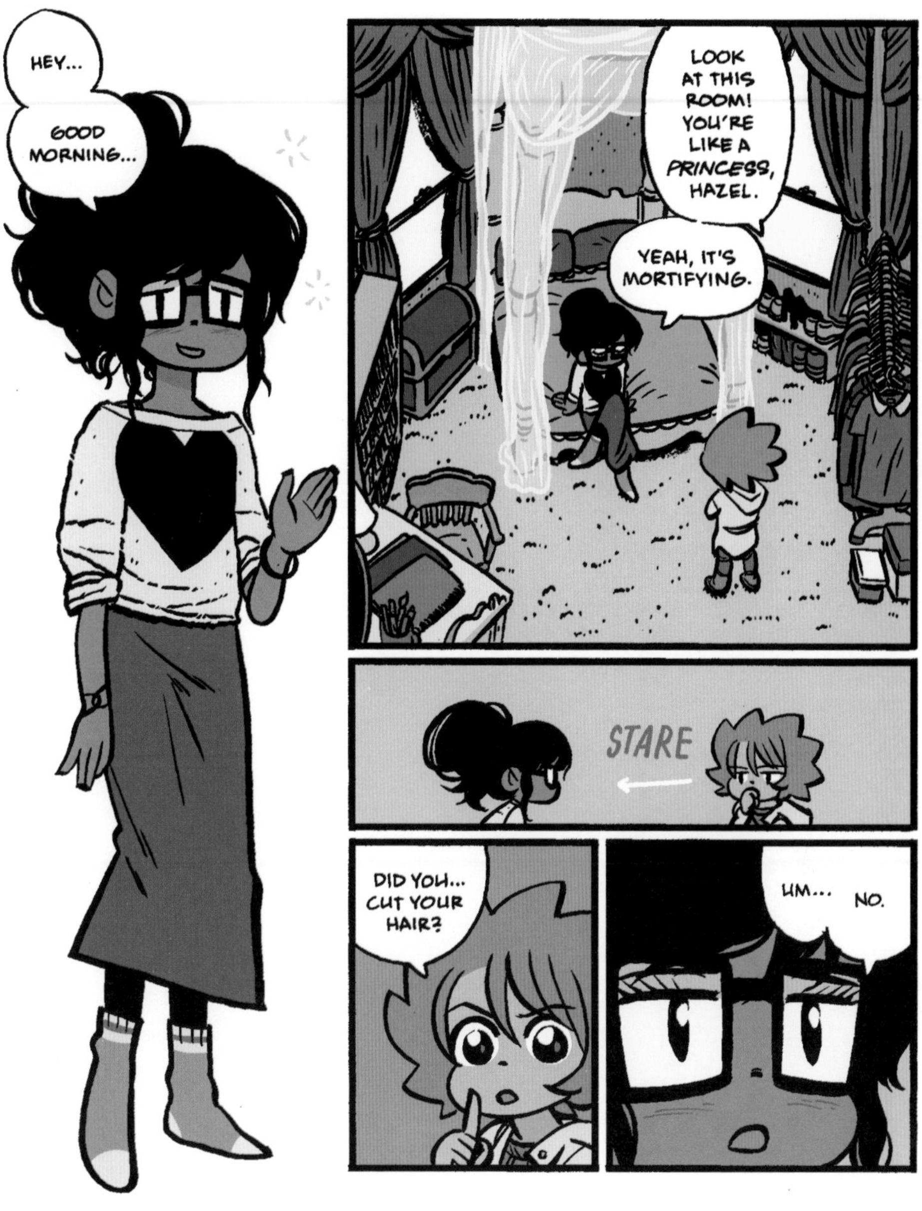
HEY...
GOOD MORNING...
LOOK AT THIS ROOM! YOU'RE LIKE A *PRINCESS*, HAZEL.
YEAH, IT'S MORTIFYING.
STARE
DID YOU... CUT YOUR HAIR?
UM...
NO.

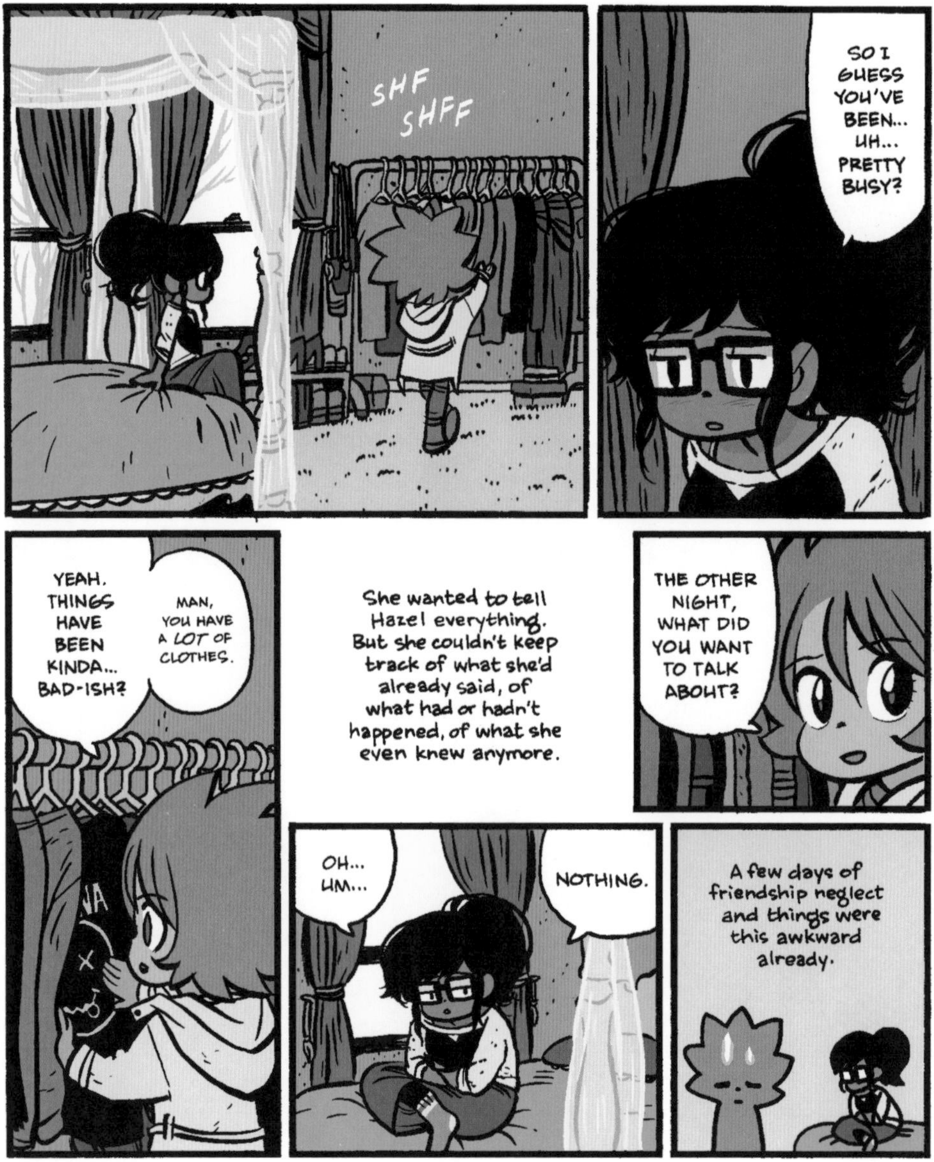
SHF
SHFF
SO I GUESS YOU'VE BEEN... UH... PRETTY BUSY?
YEAH. THINGS HAVE BEEN KINDA... BAD-ISH?
MAN, YOU HAVE A LOT OF CLOTHES.
She wanted to tell Hazel everything. But she couldn't keep track of what she'd already said, of what had or hadn't happened, of what she even knew anymore.
THE OTHER NIGHT, WHAT DID YOU WANT TO TALK ABOUT?
OH... UM...
NOTHING.
A few days of friendship neglect and things were this awkward already.

233

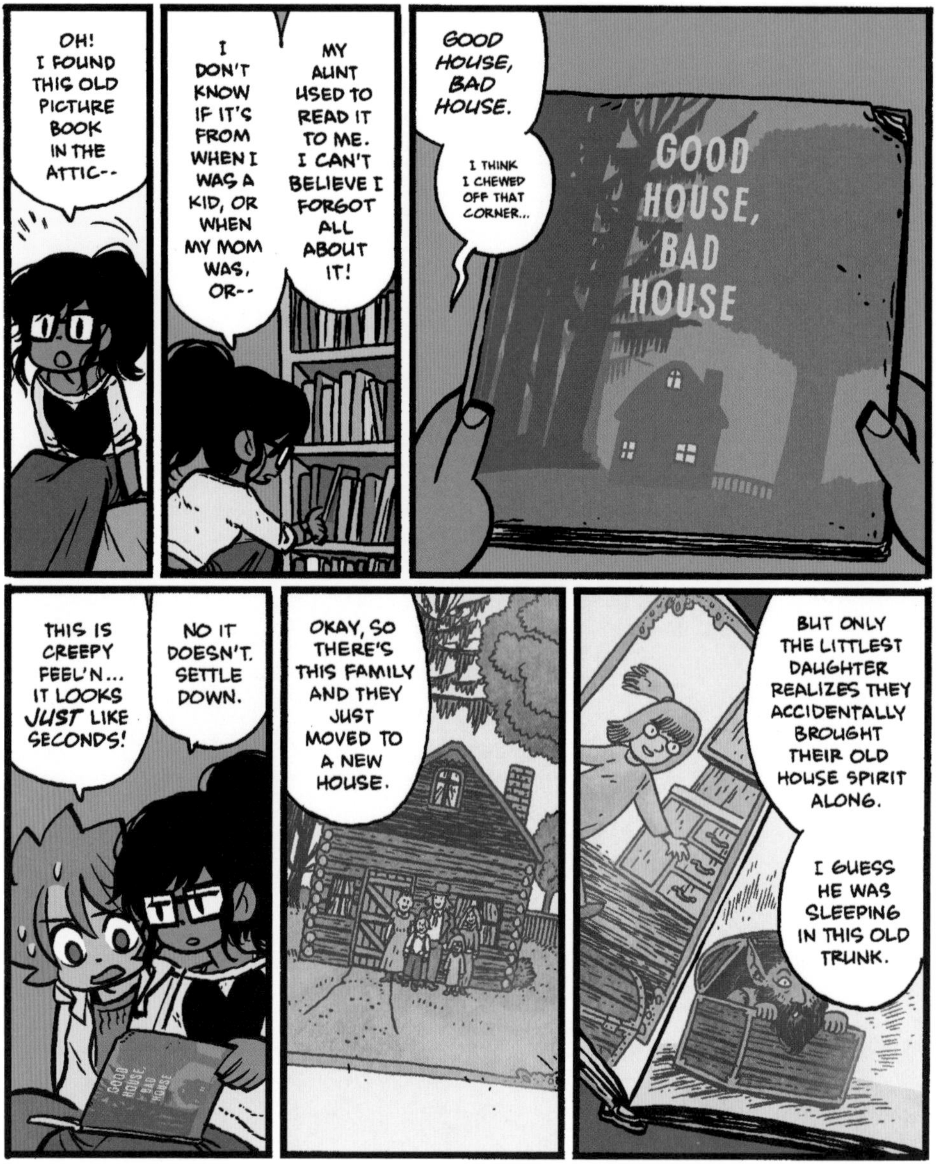
OH! I FOUND THIS OLD PICTURE BOOK IN THE ATTIC--
I DON'T KNOW IF IT'S FROM WHEN I WAS A KID, OR WHEN MY MOM WAS, OR--
MY AUNT USED TO READ IT TO ME. I CAN'T BELIEVE I FORGOT ALL ABOUT IT!
GOOD HOUSE, BAD HOUSE.
GOOD HOUSE, BAD HOUSE
I THINK I CHEWED OFF THAT CORNER...
THIS IS CREEPY FEEL'N... IT LOOKS JUST LIKE SECONDS!
NO IT DOESN'T. SETTLE DOWN.
GOOD HOUSE, BAD HOUSE
OKAY, SO THERE'S THIS FAMILY AND THEY JUST MOVED TO A NEW HOUSE.
BUT ONLY THE LITTLEST DAUGHTER REALIZES THEY ACCIDENTALLY BROUGHT THEIR OLD HOUSE SPIRIT ALONG.
I GUESS HE WAS SLEEPING IN THIS OLD TRUNK.

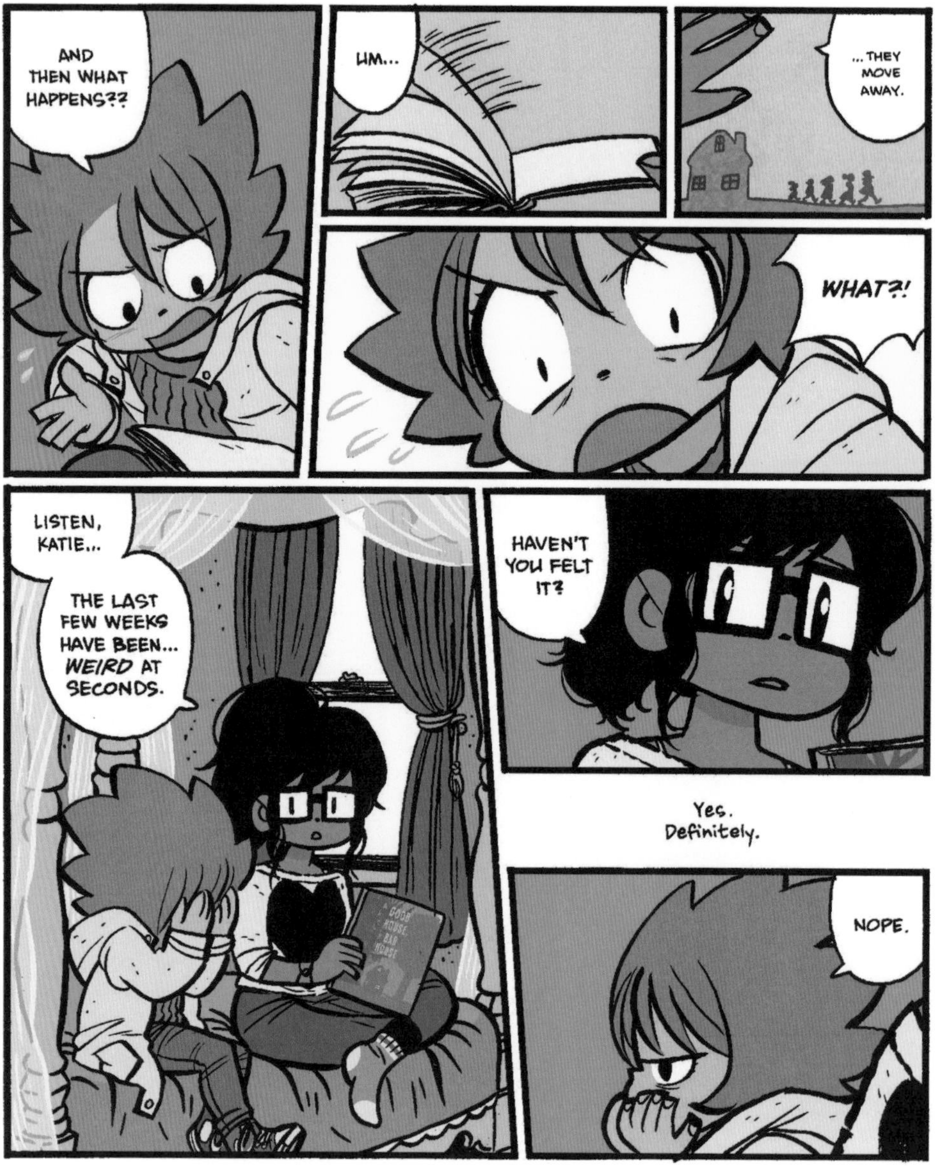
AND THEN WHAT HAPPENS??
UM...
...THEY MOVE AWAY.
WHAT?!
LISTEN, KATIE...
THE LAST FEW WEEKS HAVE BEEN... *WEIRD* AT SECONDS.
HAVEN'T YOU FELT IT?
Yes. Definitely.
NOPE.

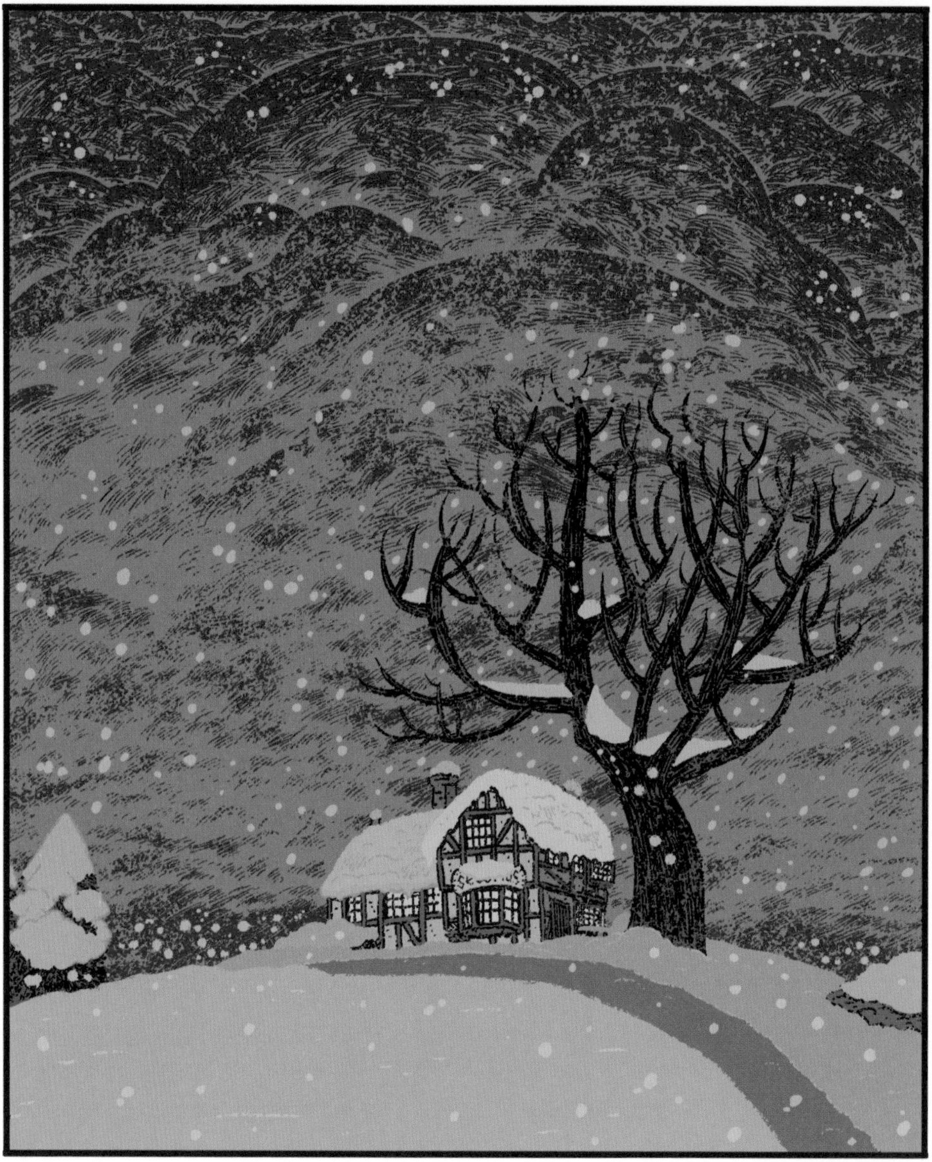

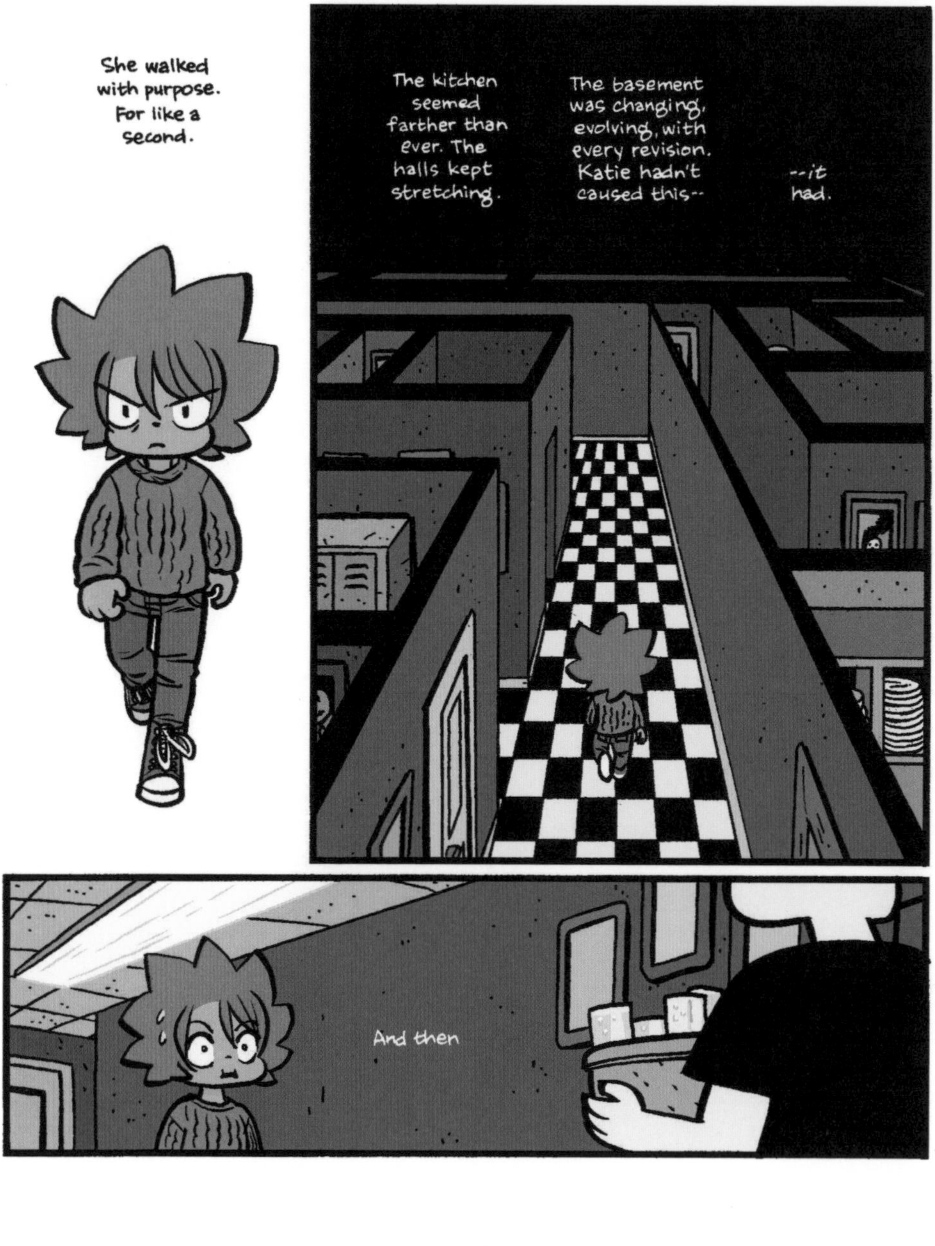
She walked with purpose. For like a second.
The kitchen seemed farther than ever. The halls kept stretching.
The basement was changing, evolving, with every revision. Katie hadn't caused this--
--it had.
And then

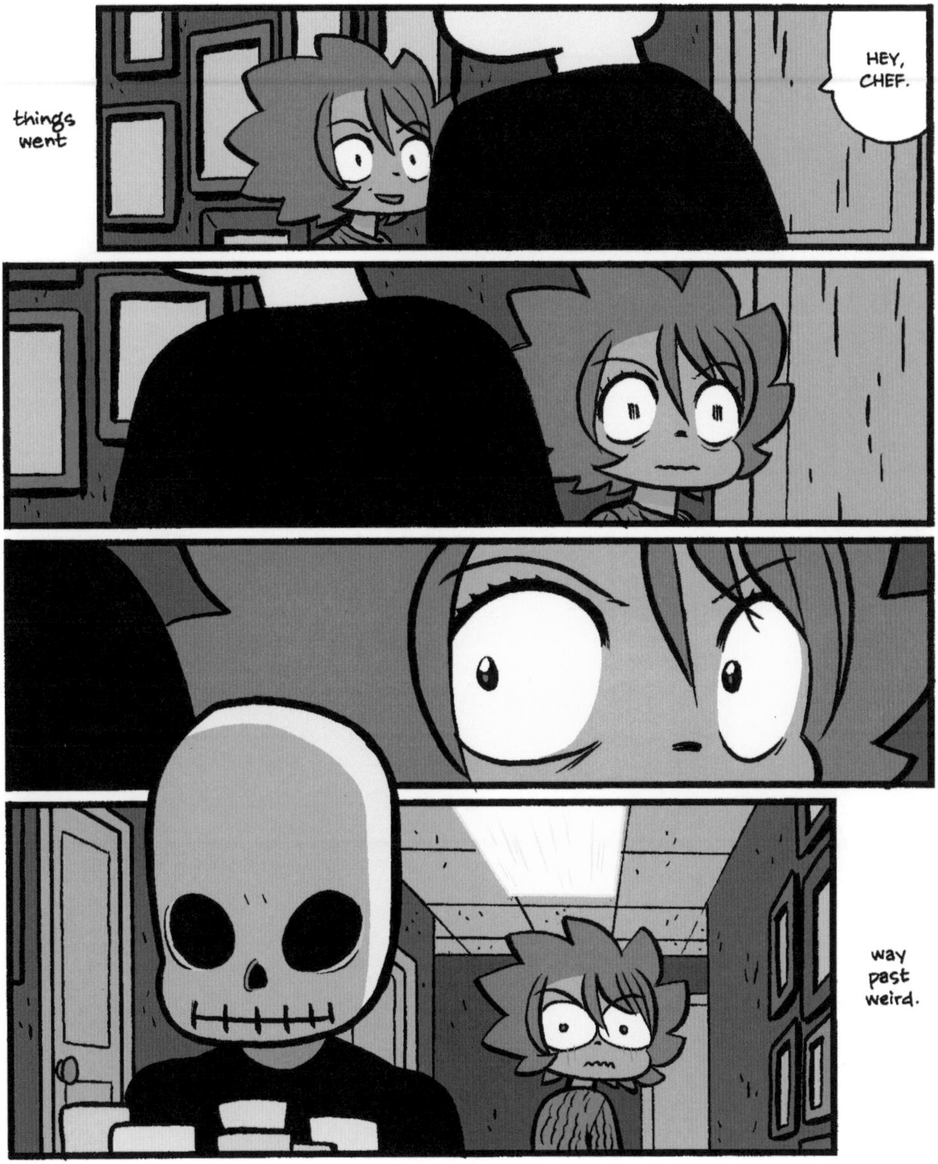
things went
HEY, CHEF.
way past weird.

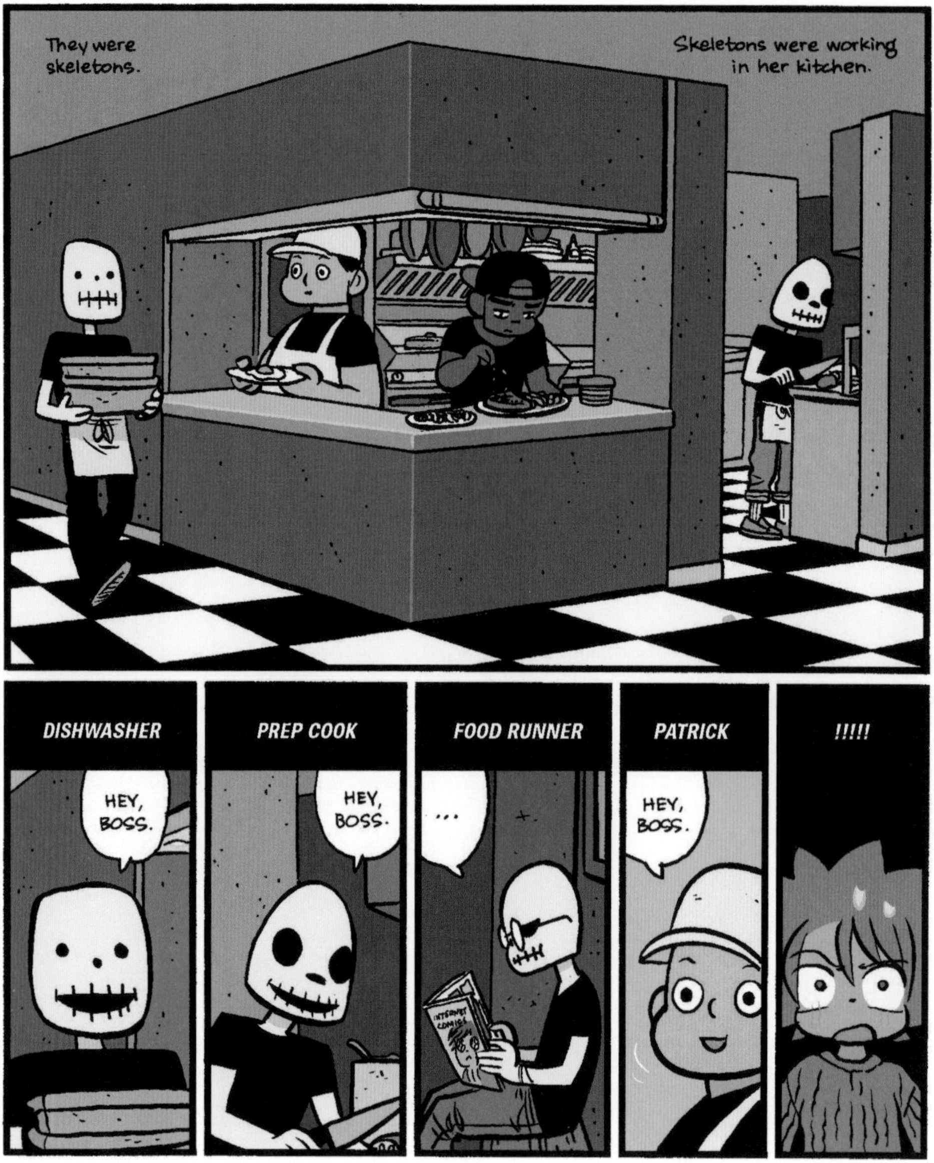
They were skeletons.
Skeletons were working in her kitchen.
DISHWASHER
HEY, BOSS.
PREP COOK
HEY, BOSS.
FOOD RUNNER
...
PATRICK
HEY, BOSS.
!!!!!

243

245

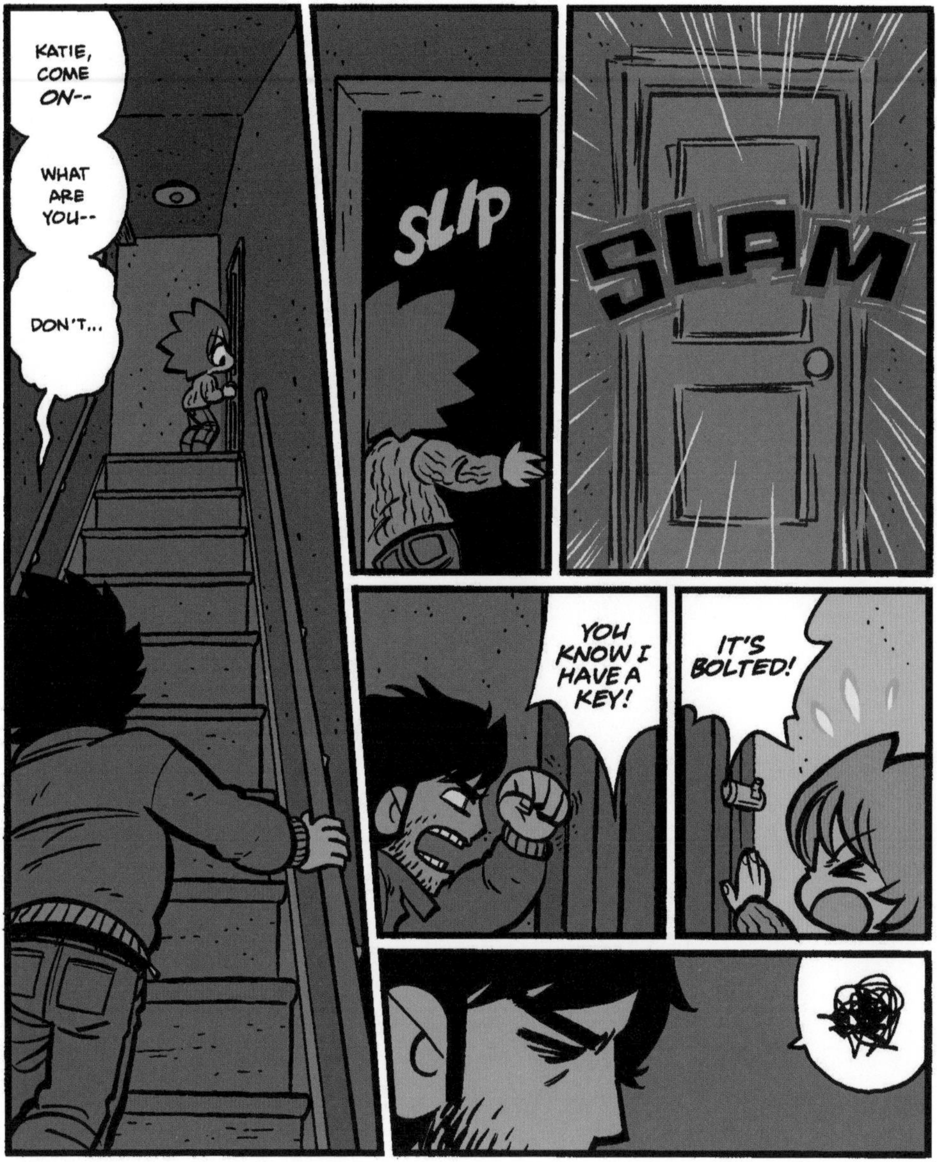

KATIE, COME ON--
WHAT ARE YOU--
DON'T...
SLIP
SLAM
YOU KNOW I HAVE A KEY!
IT'S BOLTED!

250

REVISION #11

She
felt it.

The
world
shuddered
and
changed.

She
felt
it.

She
half fell
into the
dresser.

The
pounding
on the
door had
stopped.

Max
was
gone.

Katie changed her sweater,

just so she could take the last two mushrooms.

and keep them with her.

She couldn't let them out of her sight. The stakes were too high now.

1
2

Then she headed

???????

Things shifted again.

She practically fell down the stairs.

Something else had changed.

She hadn't caused this one.

Who'd caused this one?

And then she knew. She knew, for sure, deep in her bones, that she wasn't in control anymore.

The state of the dining room did not dispel this notion.

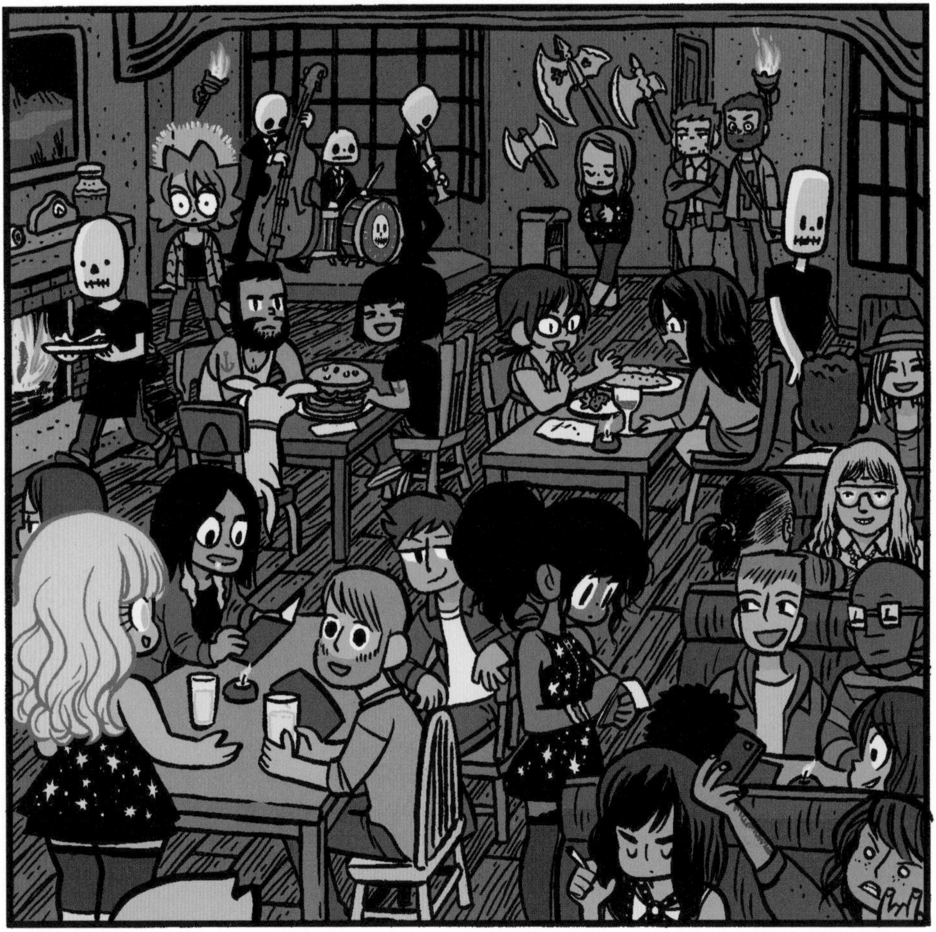

258

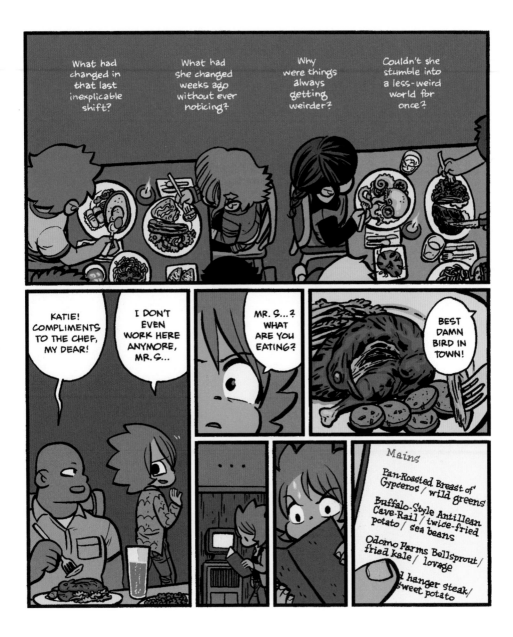

259

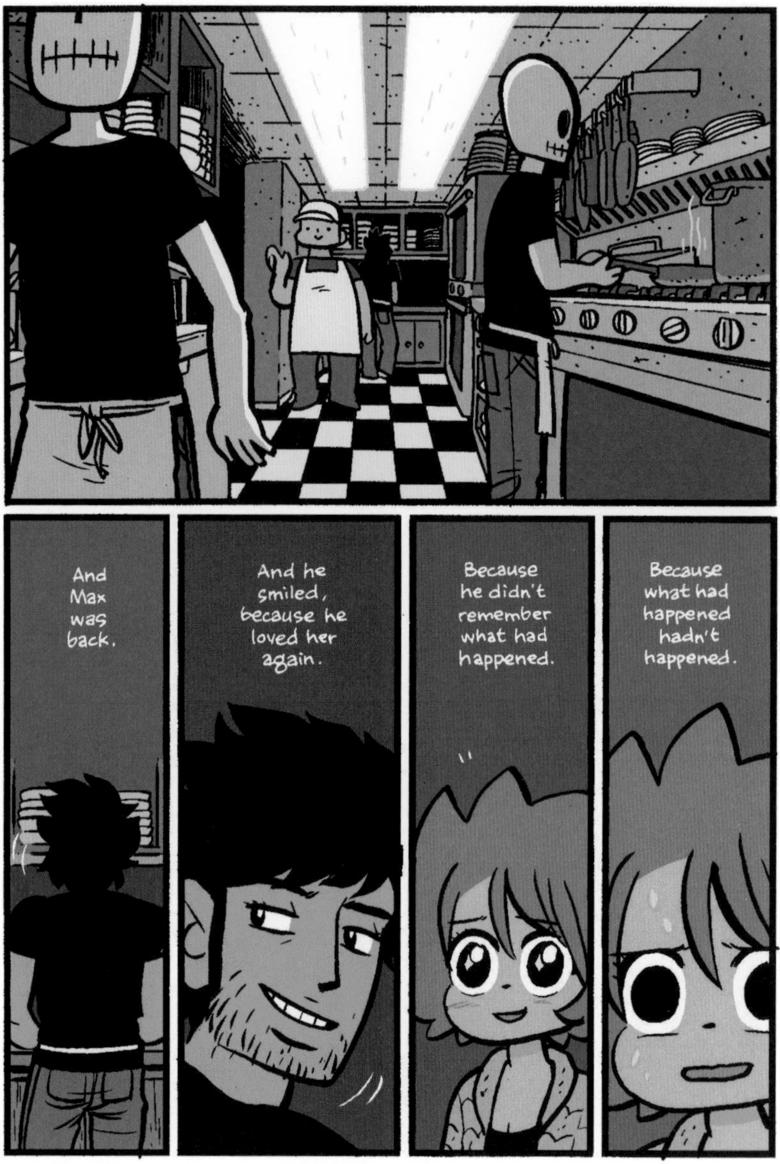
The kitchen was hot and dark and impossibly far from the stairs.
And Max was back.
And he smiled, because he loved her again.
Because he didn't remember what had happened.
Because what had happened hadn't happened.

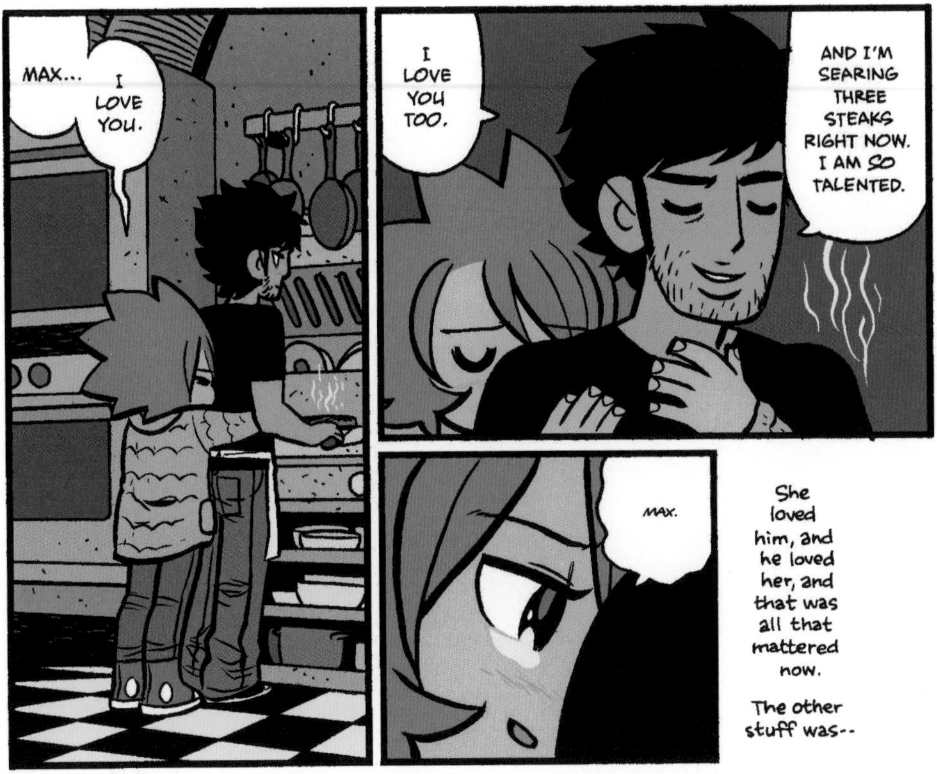
MAX...
I LOVE YOU.
I LOVE YOU TOO.
AND I'M SEARING THREE STEAKS RIGHT NOW. I AM SO TALENTED.
MAX.
She loved him, and he loved her, and that was all that mattered now.
The other stuff was--

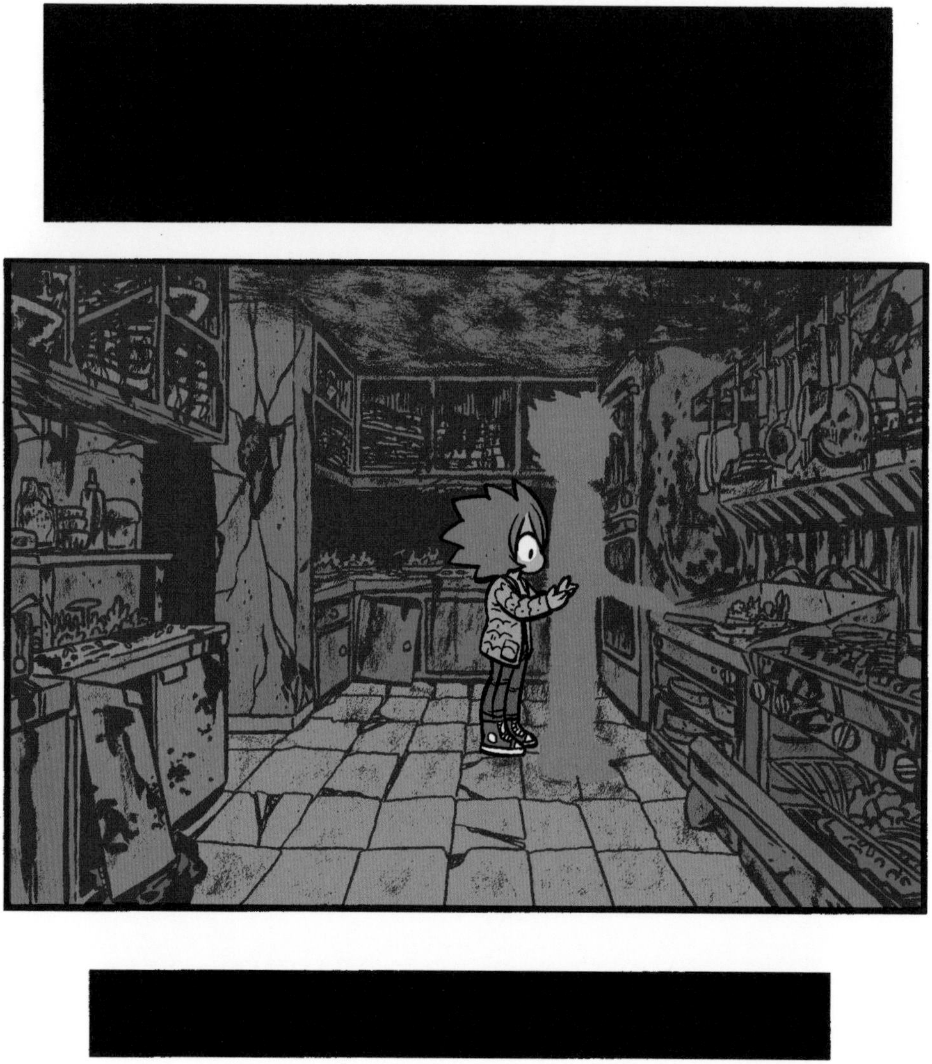

263

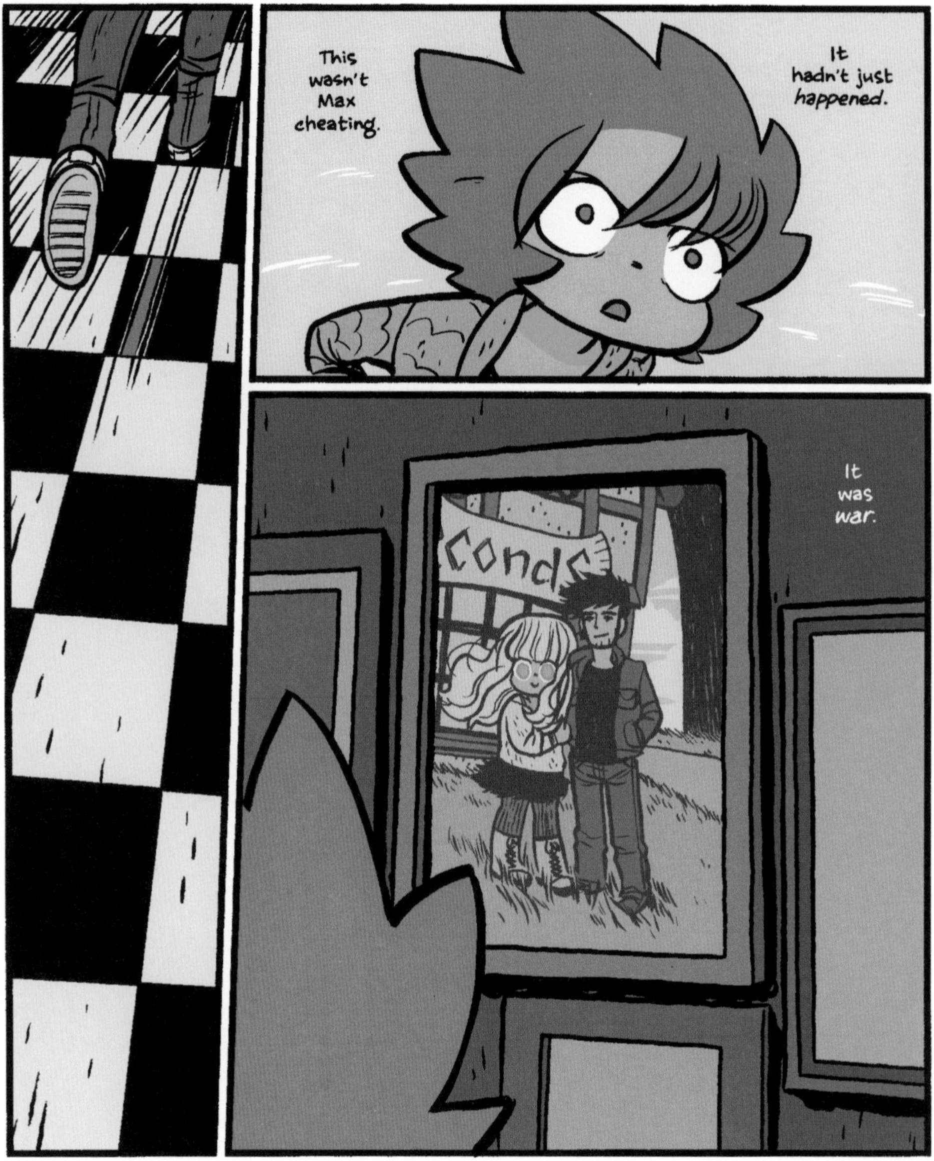
This wasn't Max cheating.
It hadn't just *happened*.
conds
It was *war*.

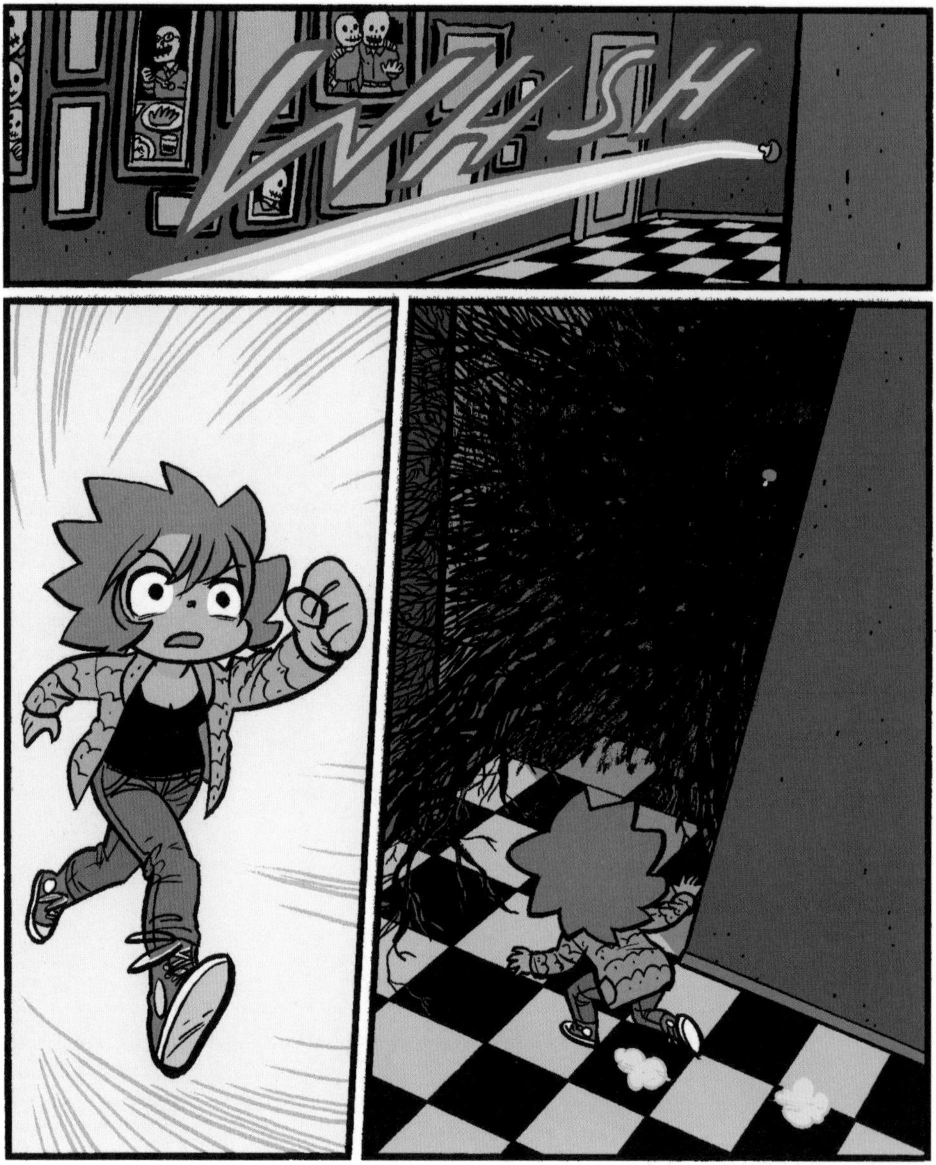
WHSH

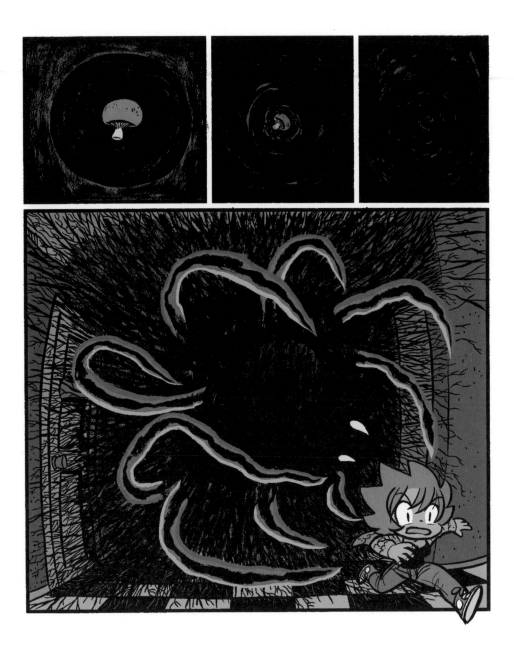

THE LAST
MUSHROOM

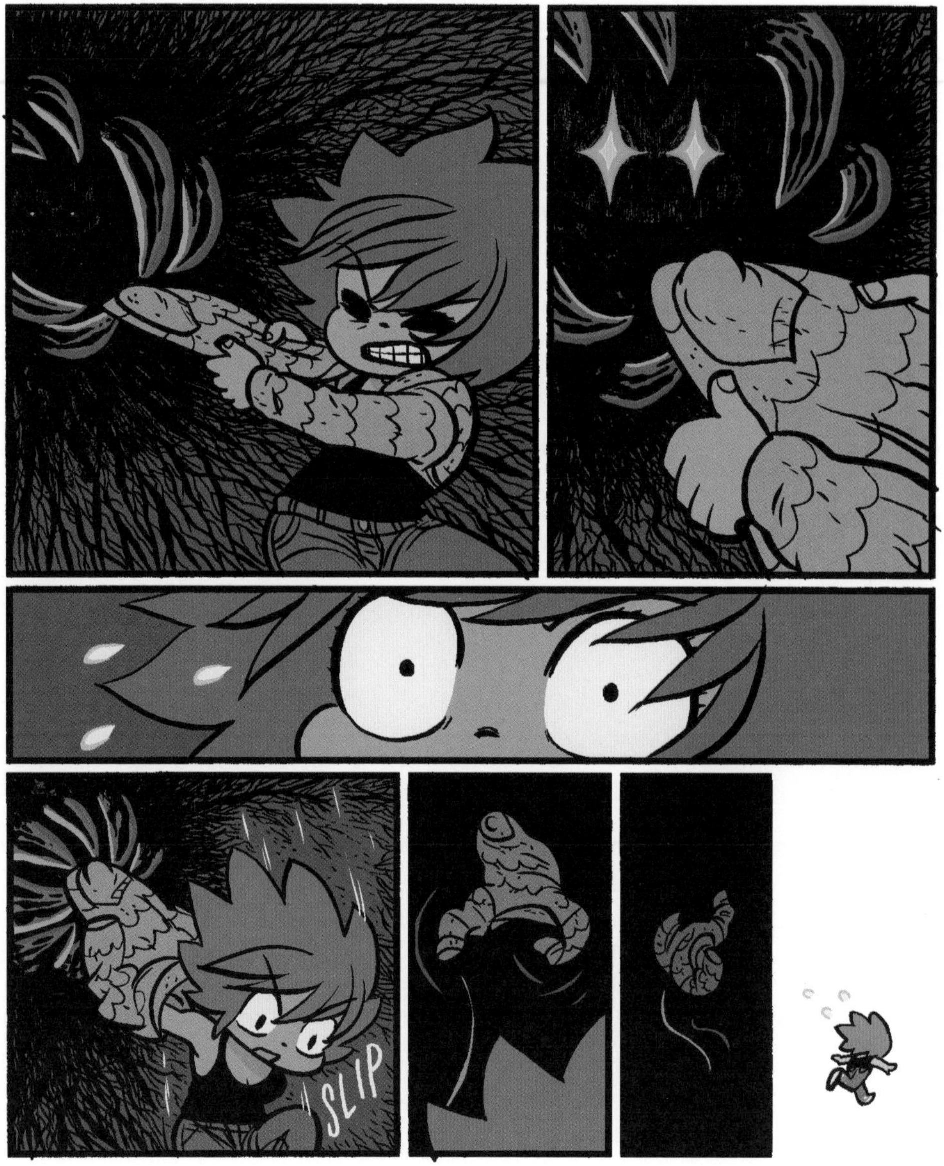
SLIP

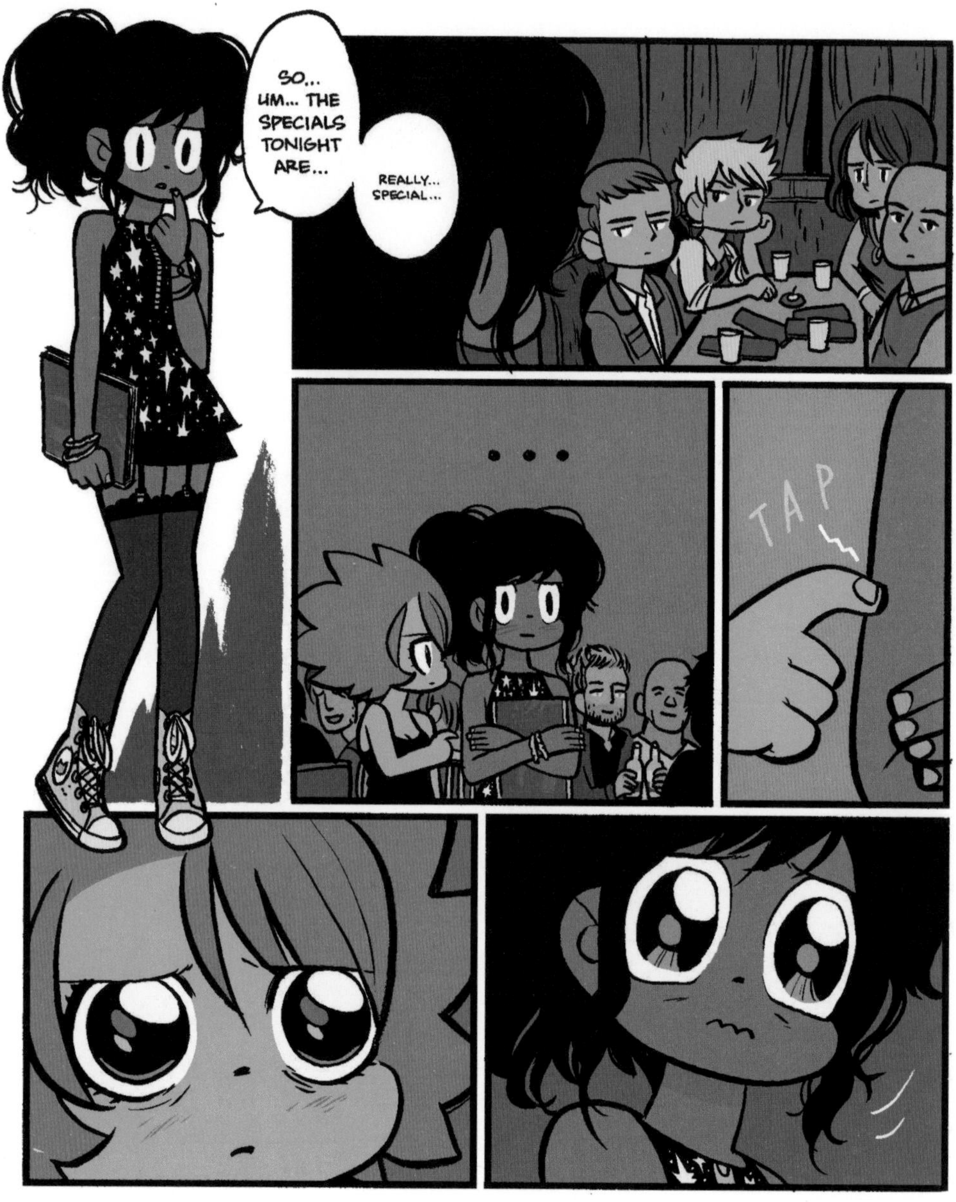
SO... UM... THE SPECIALS TONIGHT ARE...
REALLY... SPECIAL...
• • •
TAP

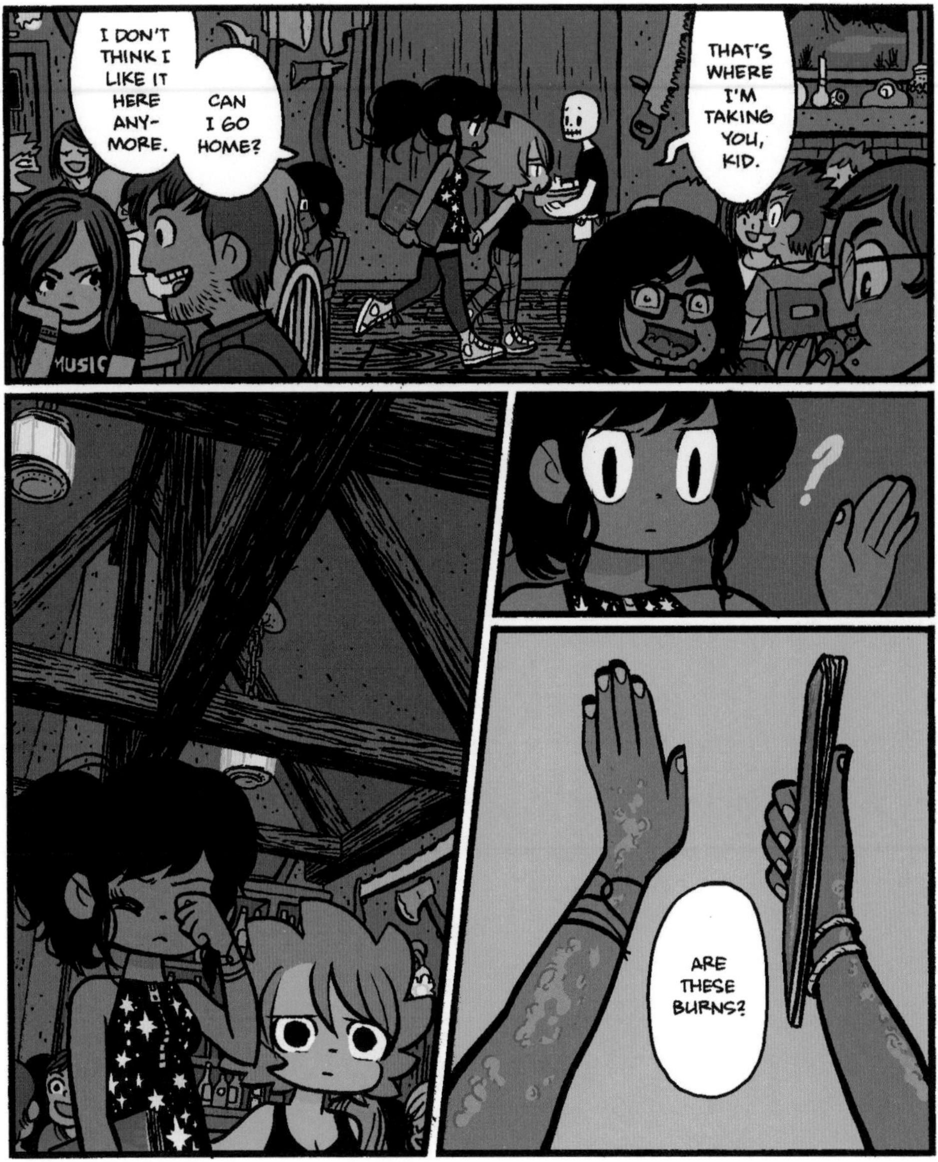
I DON'T THINK I LIKE IT HERE ANYMORE.
CAN I GO HOME?
THAT'S WHERE I'M TAKING YOU, KID.
?
ARE THESE BURNS?

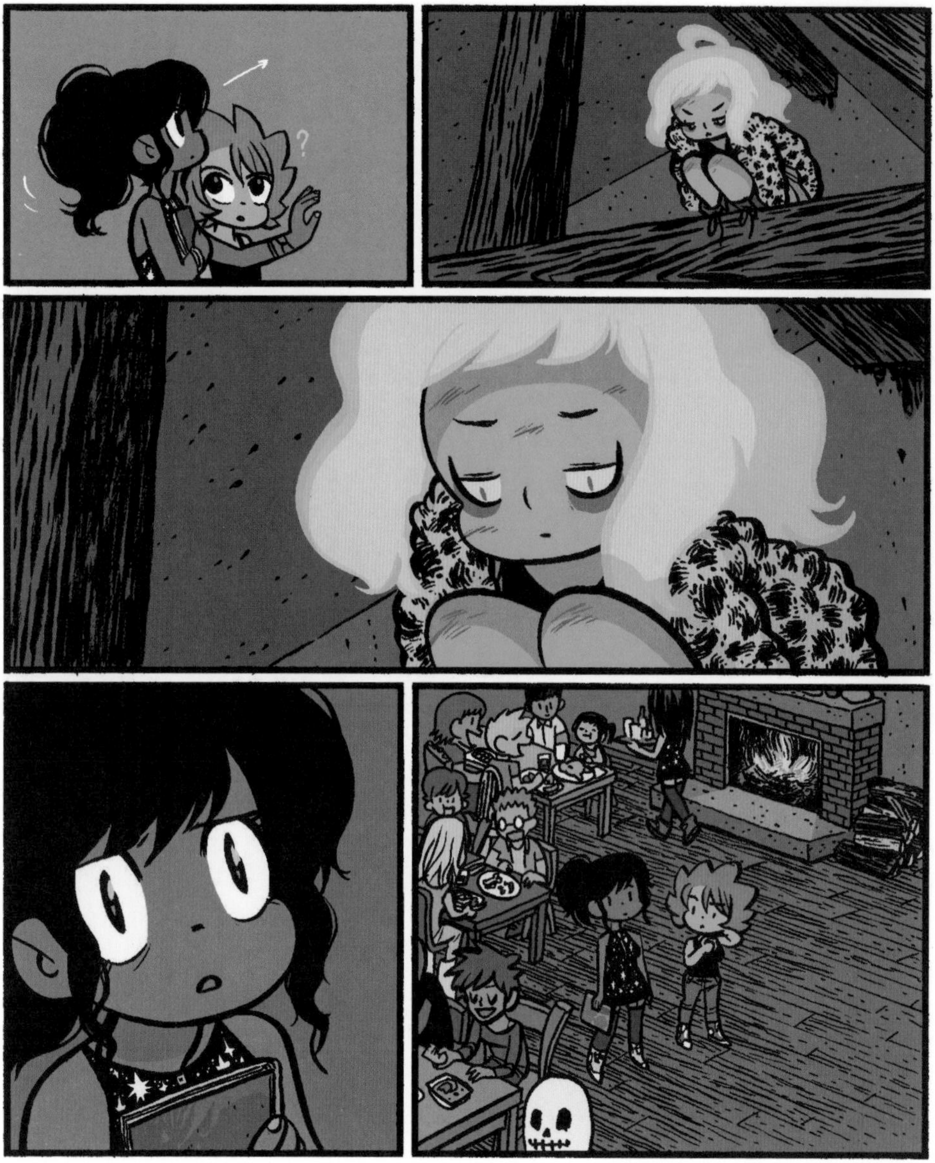
?

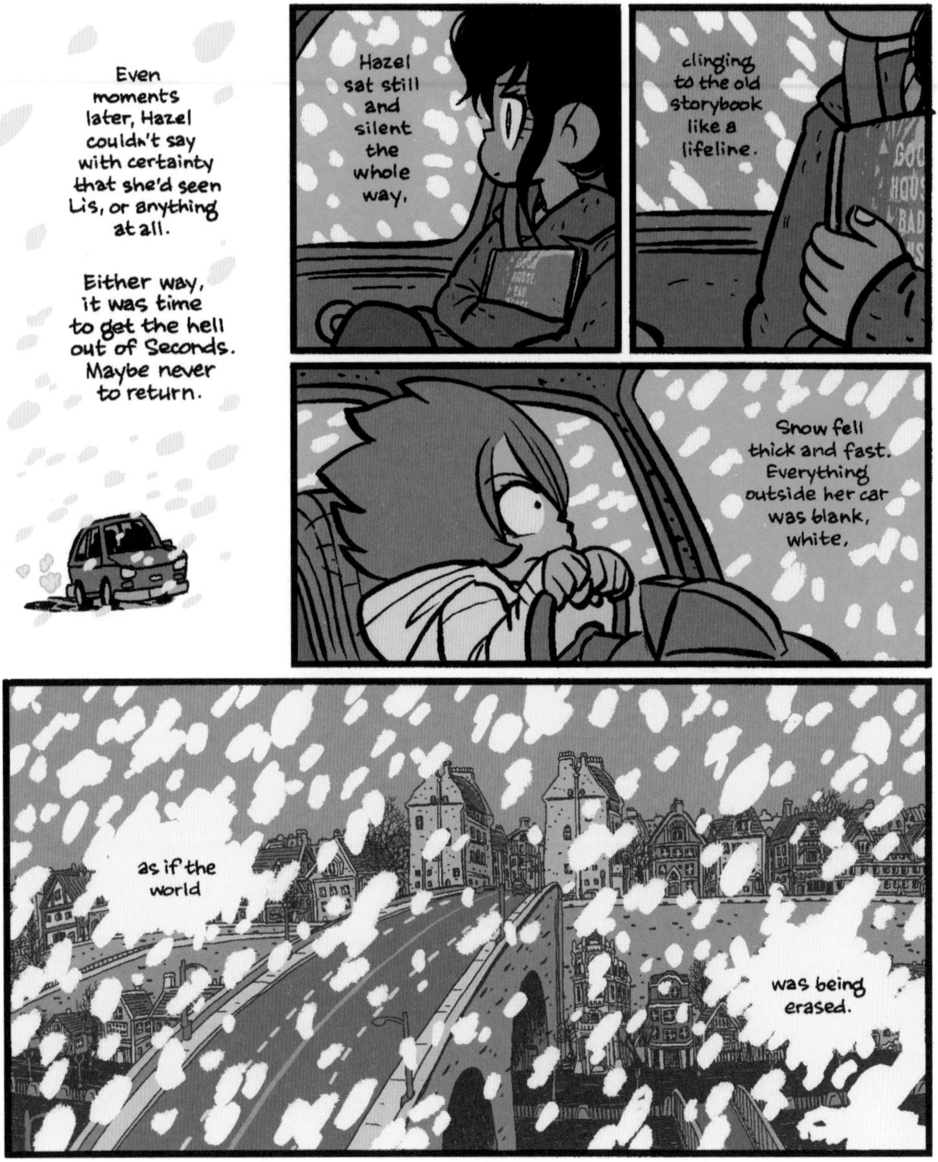
Even moments later, Hazel couldn't say with certainty that she'd seen Lis, or anything at all.
Either way, it was time to get the hell out of Seconds. Maybe never to return.
Hazel sat still and silent the whole way,
clinging to the old storybook like a lifeline.
Snow fell thick and fast. Everything outside her car was blank, white,
as if the world
was being erased.

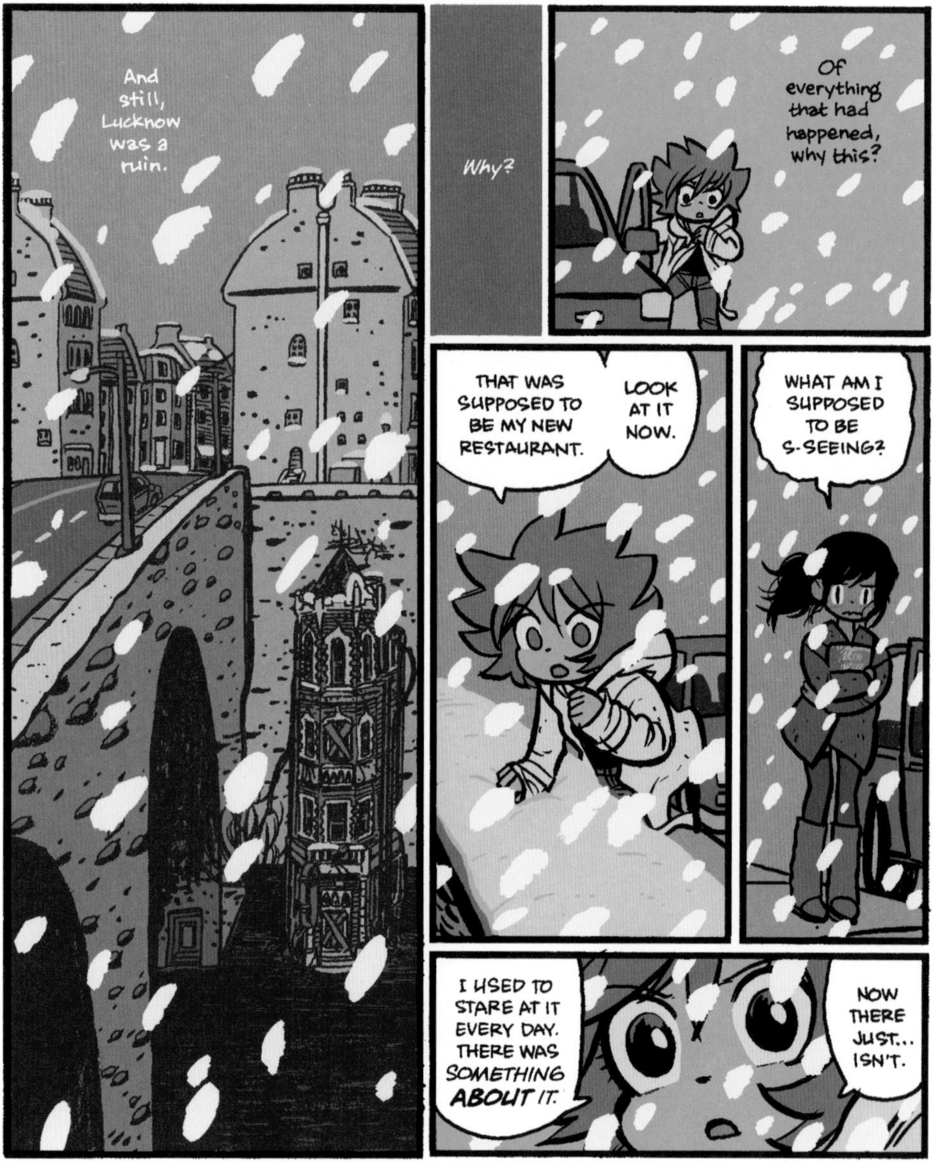

And still, Lucknow was a ruin.
Why?
Of everything that had happened, why this?
THAT WAS SUPPOSED TO BE MY NEW RESTAURANT.
LOOK AT IT NOW.
WHAT AM I SUPPOSED TO BE S-SEEING?
I USED TO STARE AT IT EVERY DAY. THERE WAS SOMETHING ABOUT IT.
NOW THERE JUST... ISN'T.

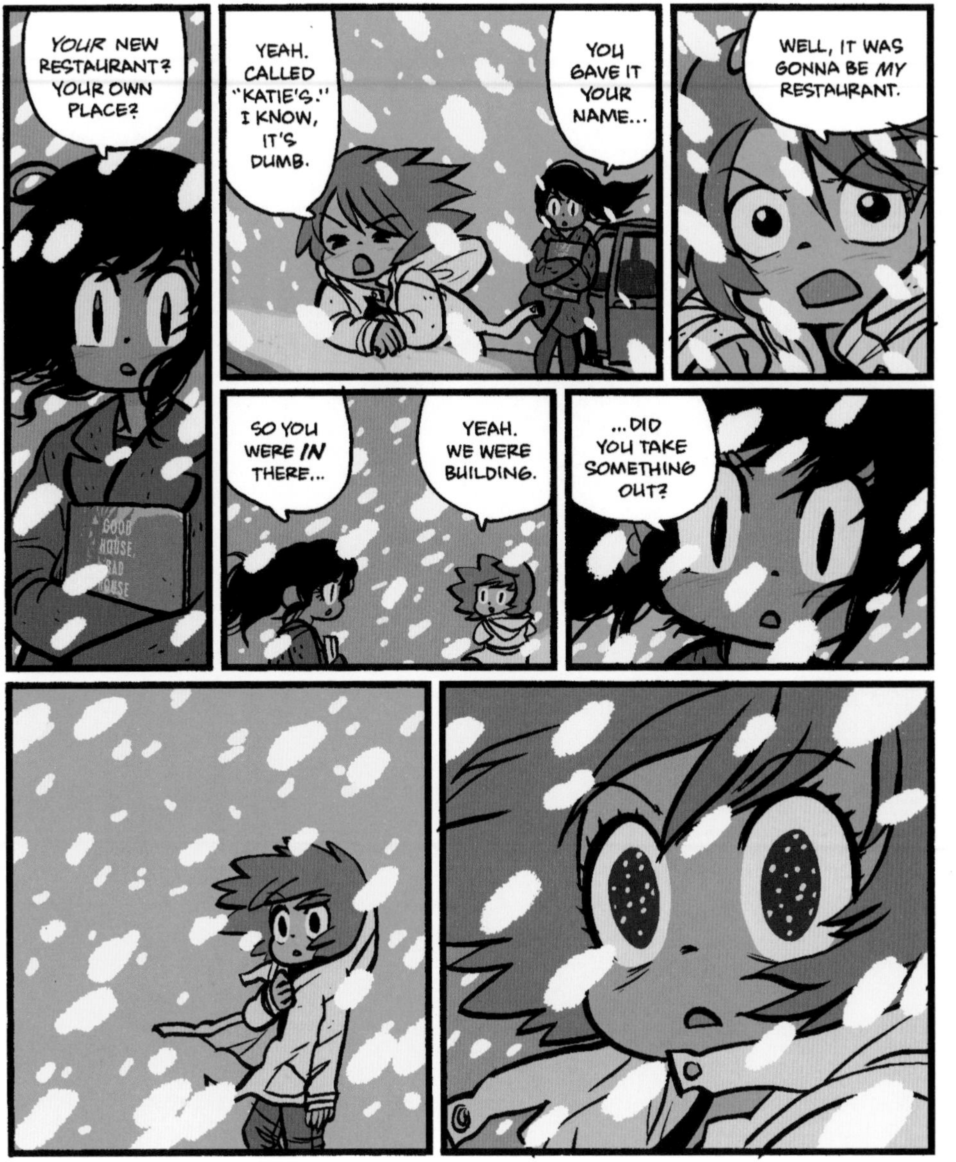

YOUR NEW RESTAURANT? YOUR OWN PLACE?
YEAH. CALLED "KATIE'S." I KNOW, IT'S DUMB.
YOU GAVE IT YOUR NAME...
WELL, IT WAS GONNA BE *MY* RESTAURANT.
GOOD HOUSE, BAD HOUSE
SO YOU WERE *IN* THERE...
YEAH. WE WERE BUILDING.
...DID YOU TAKE SOMETHING OUT?

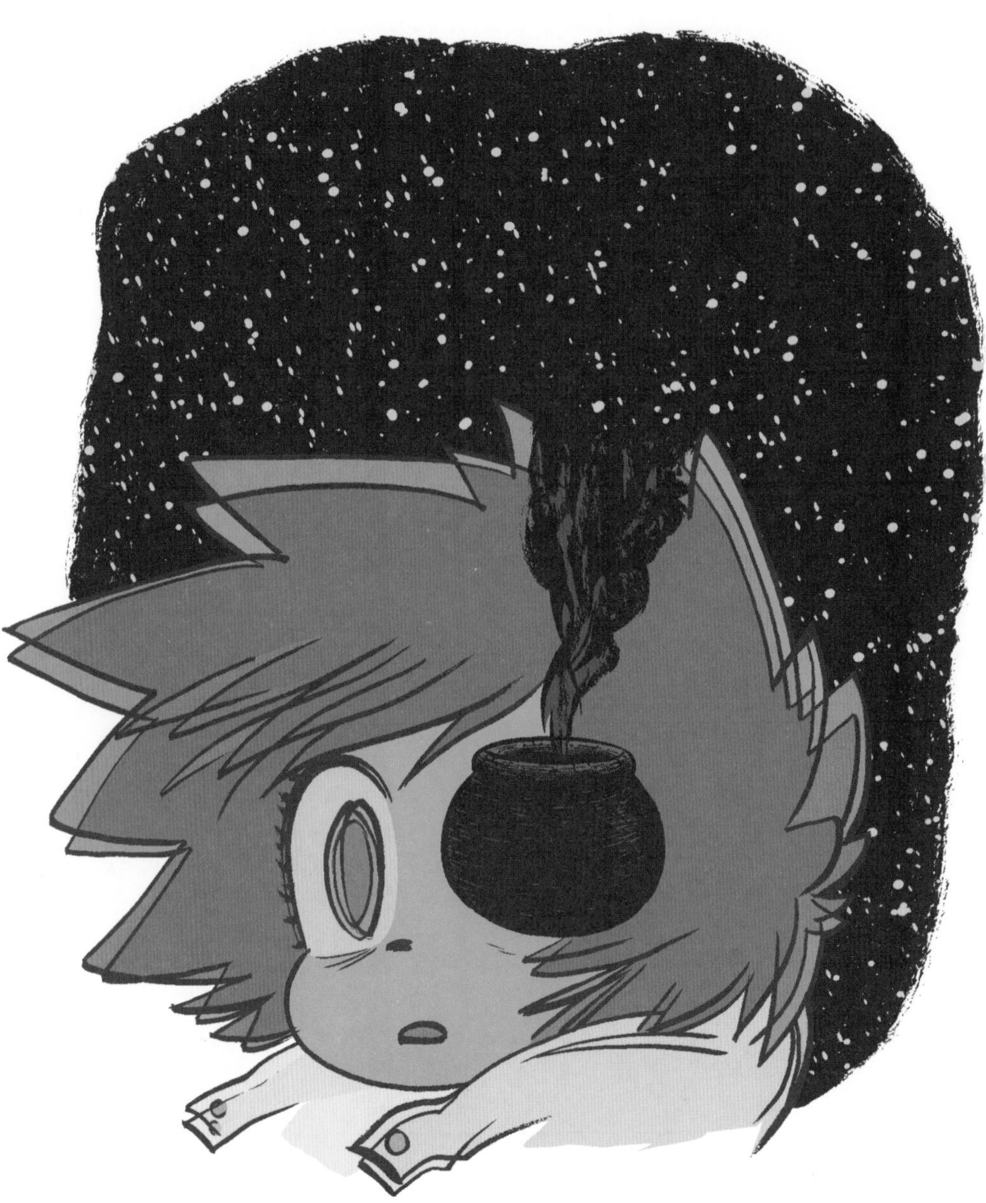

7

Can't Go Back

The witch's pot.

If she could find it, if she could bring it back--

IT'D FIX EVERYTHING!

...well... Maybe it'd help, anyway.

First of all, she had to get Hazel home safely.

280

And like that, she was at the start again,

a little bit closer to the end.

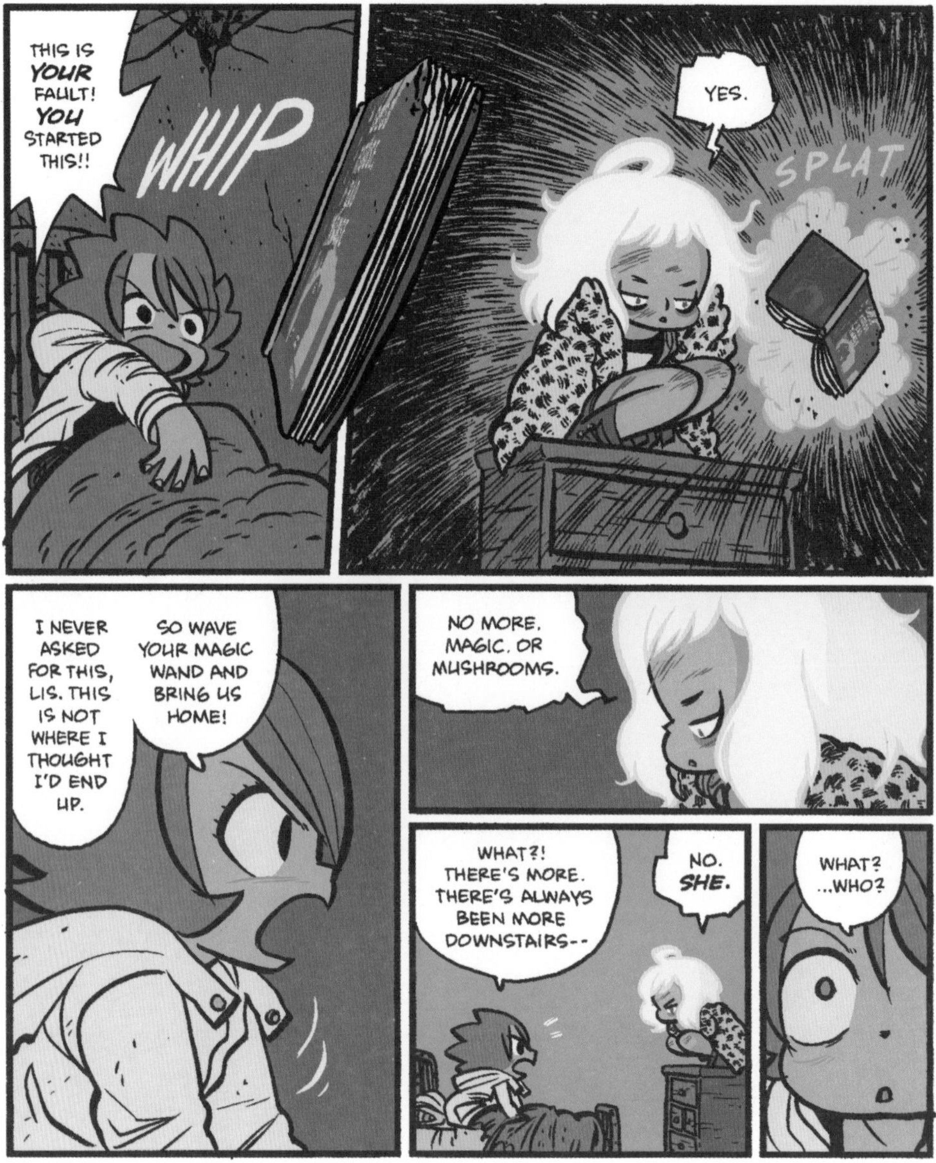
THIS IS YOUR FAULT! YOU STARTED THIS!!
WHIP
YES.
SPLAT
I NEVER ASKED FOR THIS, LIS. THIS IS NOT WHERE I THOUGHT I'D END UP.
SO WAVE YOUR MAGIC WAND AND BRING US HOME!
NO MORE. MAGIC. OR MUSHROOMS.
WHAT?! THERE'S MORE. THERE'S ALWAYS BEEN MORE DOWNSTAIRS--
NO. SHE.
WHAT? ...WHO?

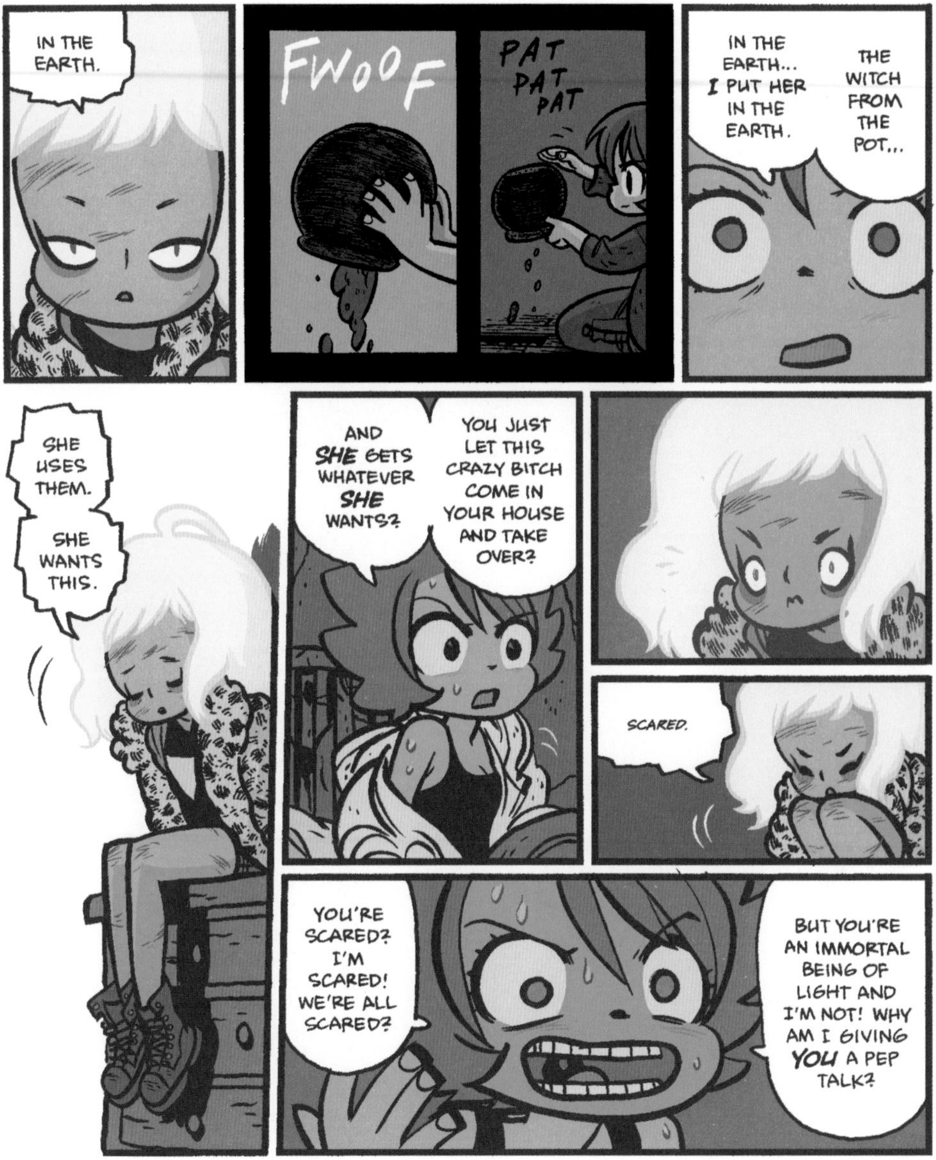
IN THE EARTH.
FWOOF
PAT PAT PAT
IN THE EARTH... I PUT HER IN THE EARTH.
THE WITCH FROM THE POT...
SHE USES THEM.
SHE WANTS THIS.
AND SHE GETS WHATEVER SHE WANTS?
YOU JUST LET THIS CRAZY BITCH COME IN YOUR HOUSE AND TAKE OVER?
SCARED.
YOU'RE SCARED? I'M SCARED! WE'RE ALL SCARED?
BUT YOU'RE AN IMMORTAL BEING OF LIGHT AND I'M NOT! WHY AM I GIVING YOU A PEP TALK?

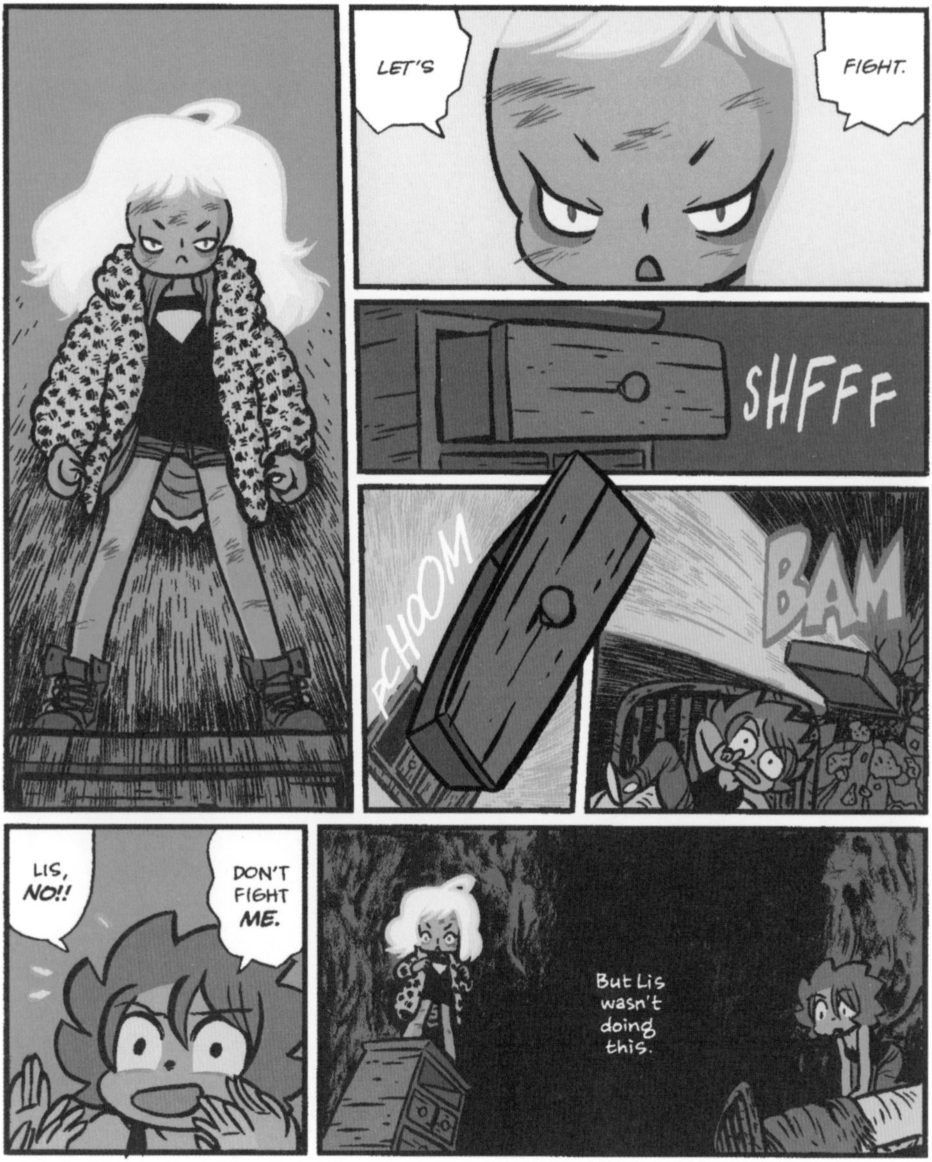
LET'S
FIGHT.
SHFFF
PCHOOM
BAM
LIS, NO!!
DON'T FIGHT ME.
But Lis wasn't doing this.

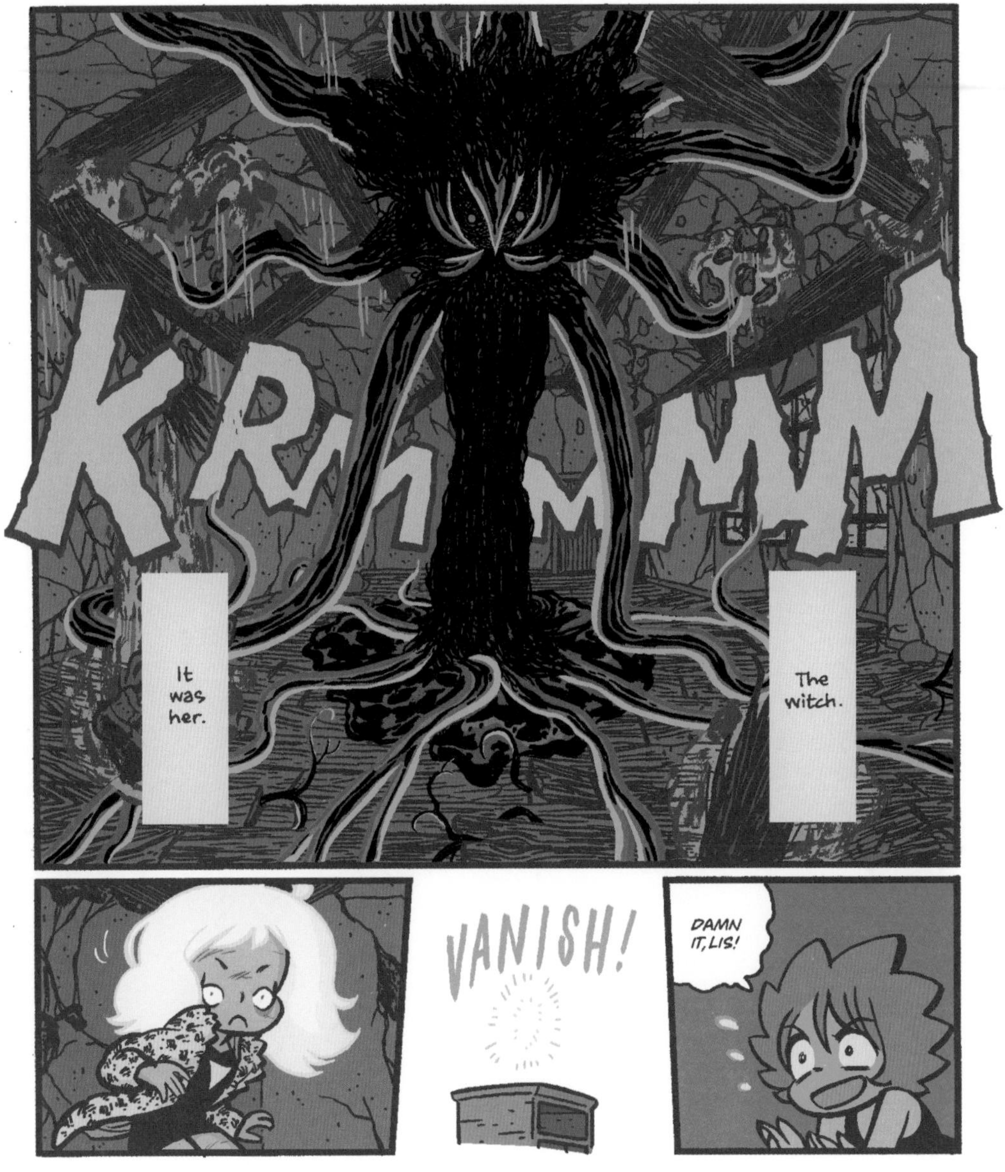
It was her.
The witch.
VANISH!
DAMN IT, LIS!

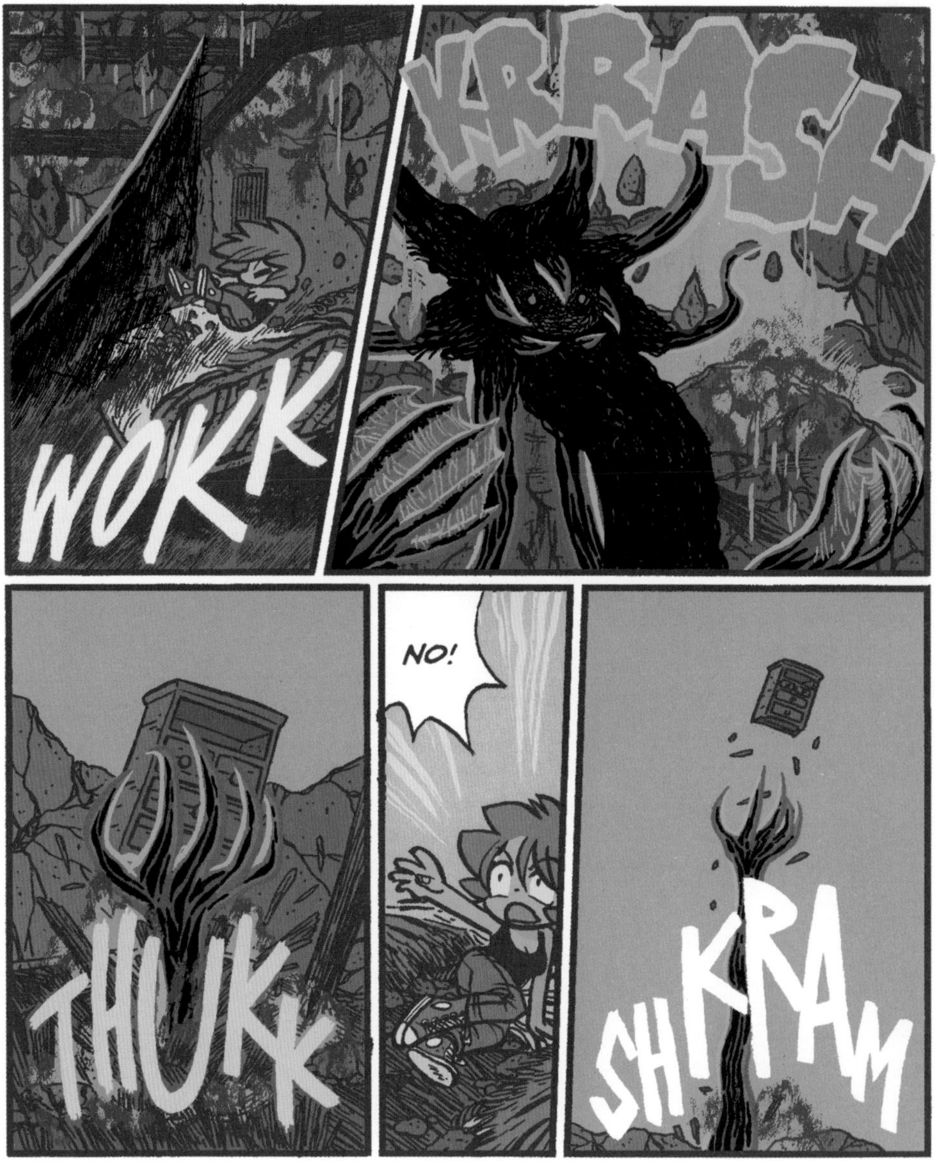
WOKK
KRRASH
THUKK
NO!
SHKRAM

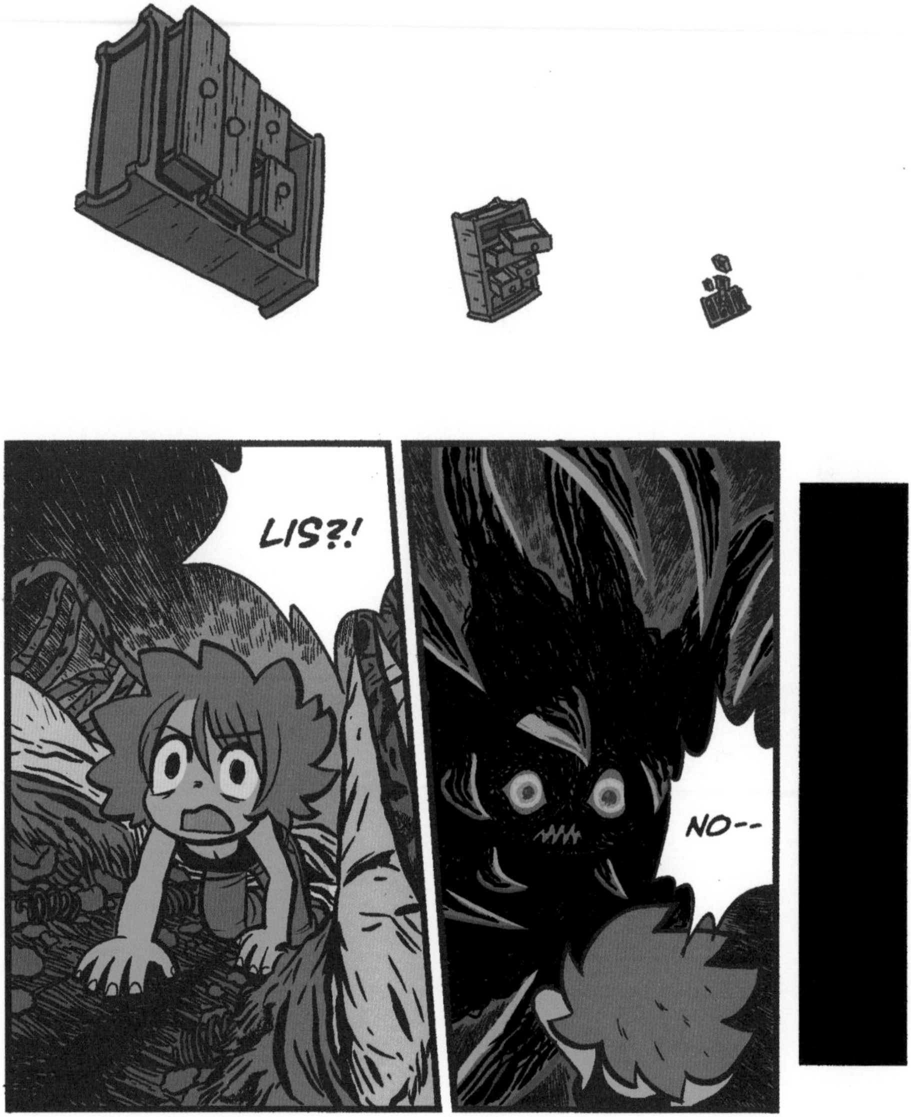
LIS?!
NO--

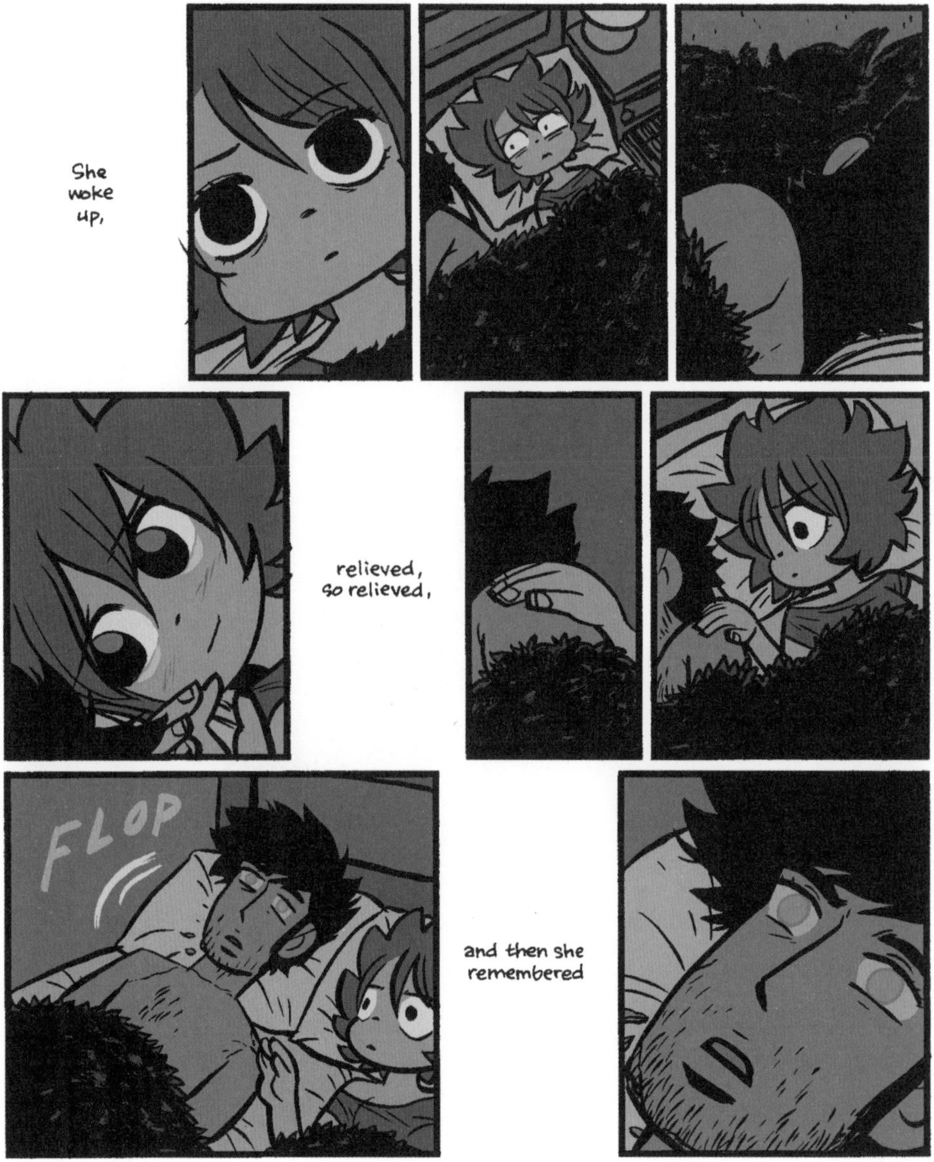
She woke up,
relieved, so relieved,
FLOP
and then she remembered

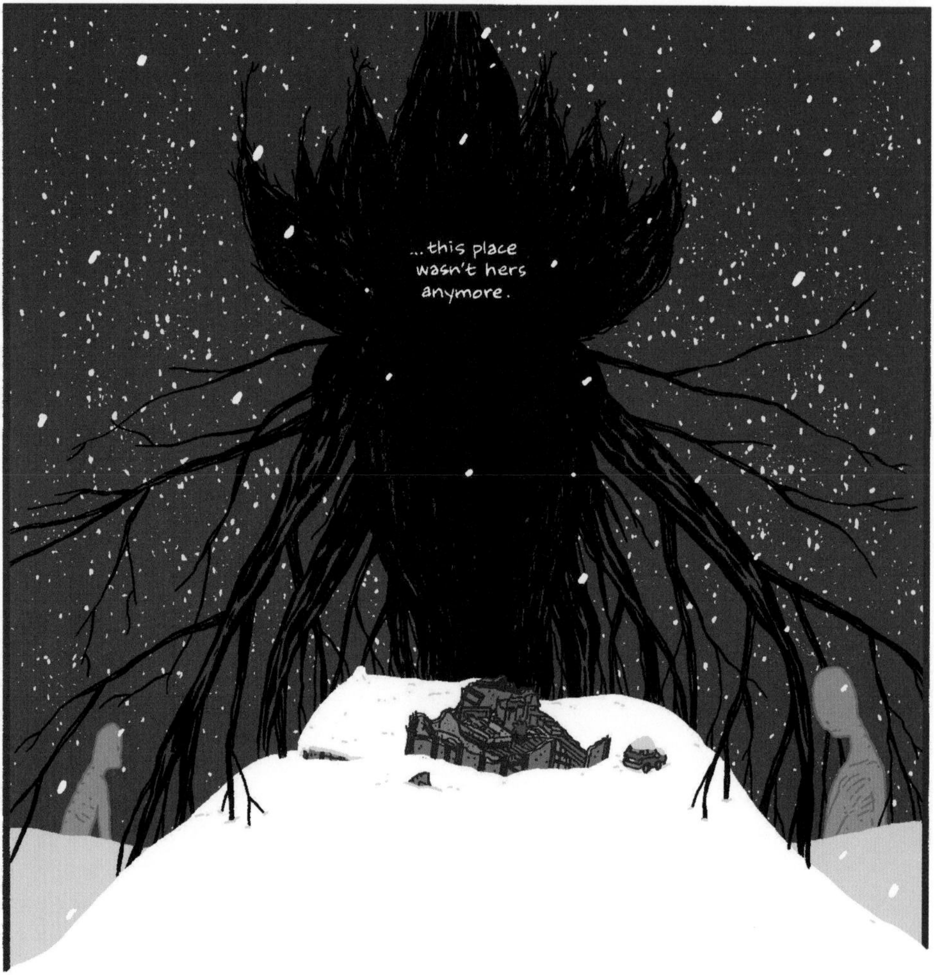
...this place wasn't hers anymore.

EVERY REVISION...

...WAS A WORLD.

And for one second, Katie understood: each point of light, each junction,

was not just a new time,

but a new place.

Another Seconds. Another Katie.

Every time she woke up it was as a different person.

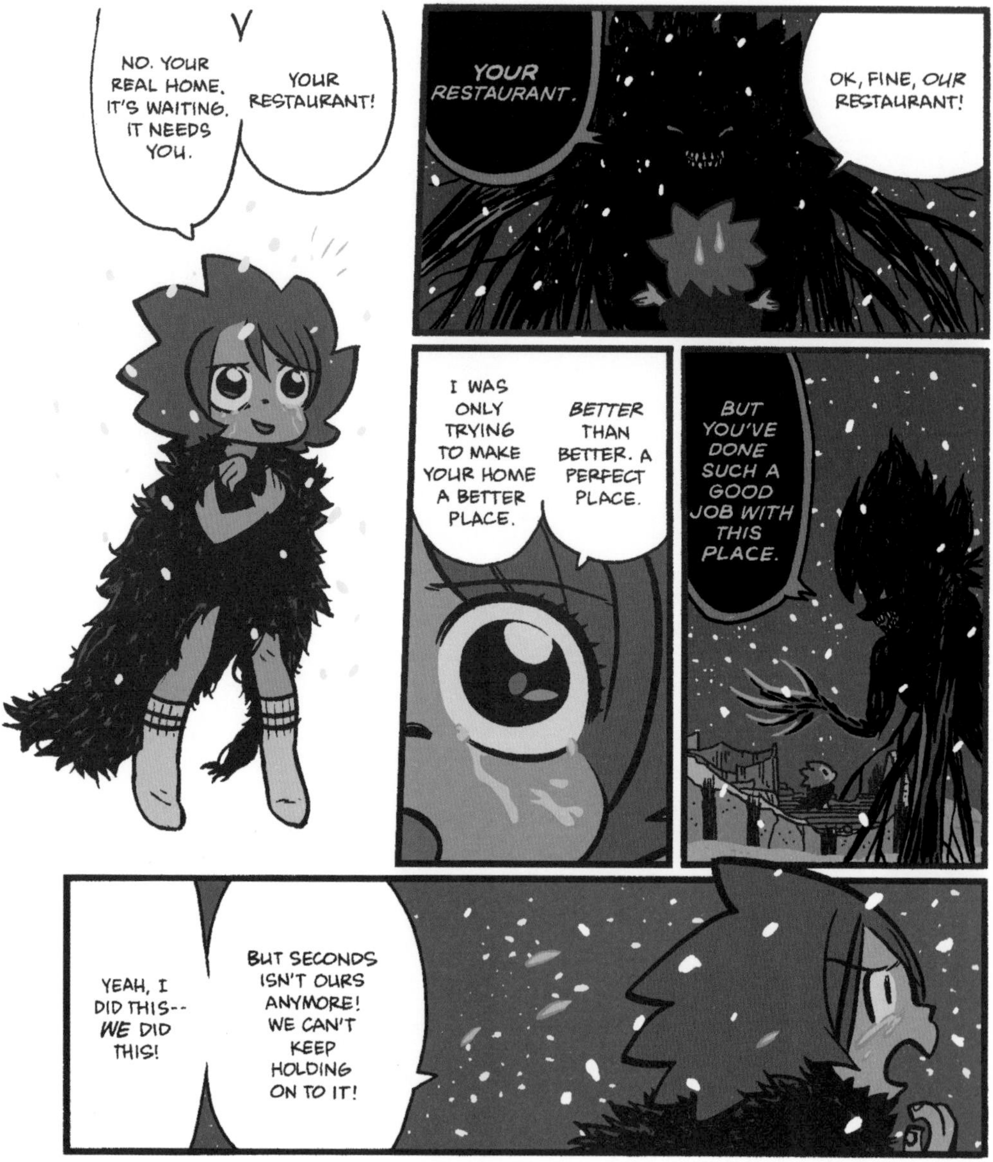
NO. YOUR REAL HOME. IT'S WAITING. IT NEEDS YOU.
YOUR RESTAURANT!
YOUR RESTAURANT.
OK, FINE, OUR RESTAURANT!
I WAS ONLY TRYING TO MAKE YOUR HOME A BETTER PLACE.
BETTER THAN BETTER. A PERFECT PLACE.
BUT YOU'VE DONE SUCH A GOOD JOB WITH THIS PLACE.
YEAH, I DID THIS-- WE DID THIS!
BUT SECONDS ISN'T OURS ANYMORE! WE CAN'T KEEP HOLDING ON TO IT!

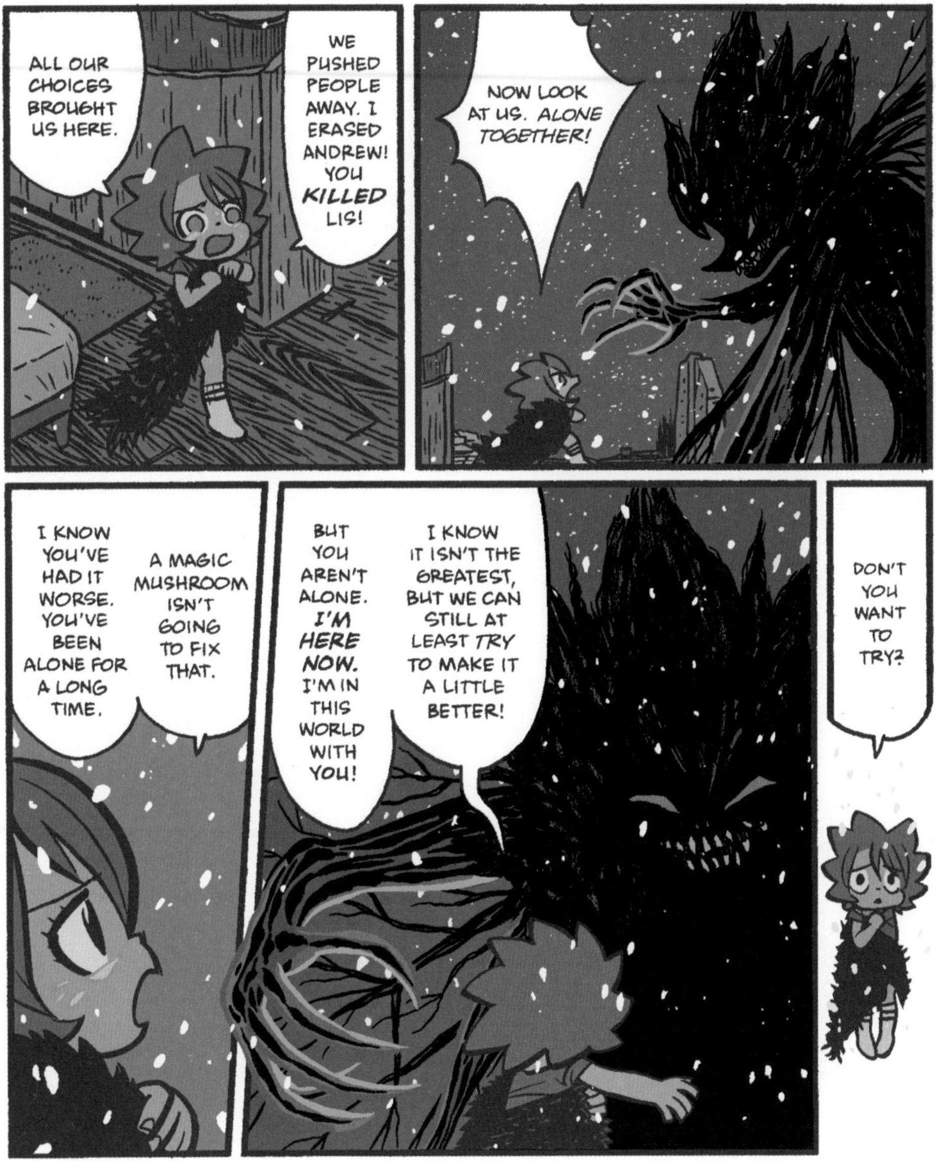

ALL OUR CHOICES BROUGHT US HERE.
WE PUSHED PEOPLE AWAY. I ERASED ANDREW! YOU **KILLED** LIS!
NOW LOOK AT US. *ALONE TOGETHER!*
I KNOW YOU'VE HAD IT WORSE. YOU'VE BEEN ALONE FOR A LONG TIME.
A MAGIC MUSHROOM ISN'T GOING TO FIX THAT.
BUT YOU AREN'T ALONE. ***I'M HERE NOW.*** I'M IN THIS WORLD WITH YOU!
I KNOW IT ISN'T THE GREATEST, BUT WE CAN STILL AT LEAST *TRY* TO MAKE IT A LITTLE BETTER!
DON'T YOU WANT TO TRY?

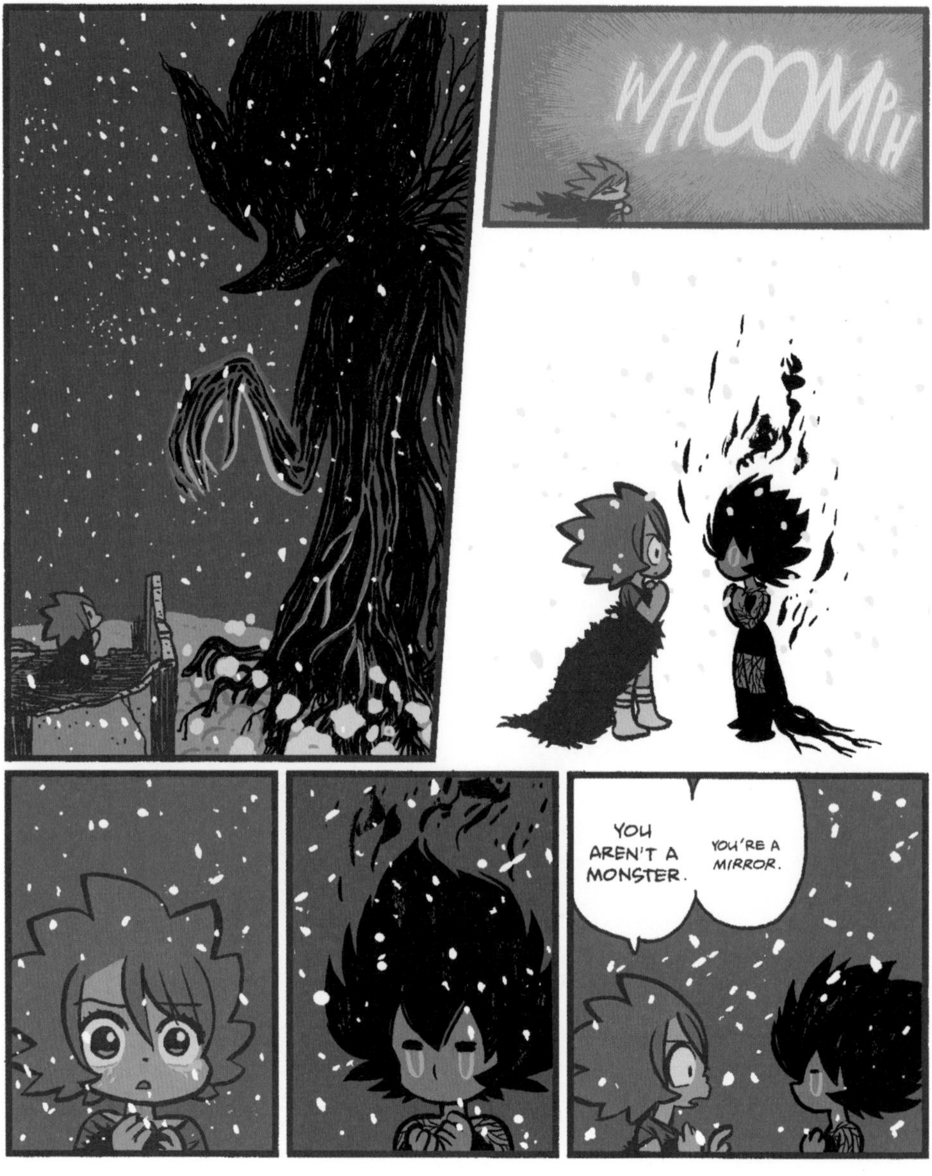
WHOOMPH
YOU AREN'T A MONSTER.
YOU'RE A MIRROR.

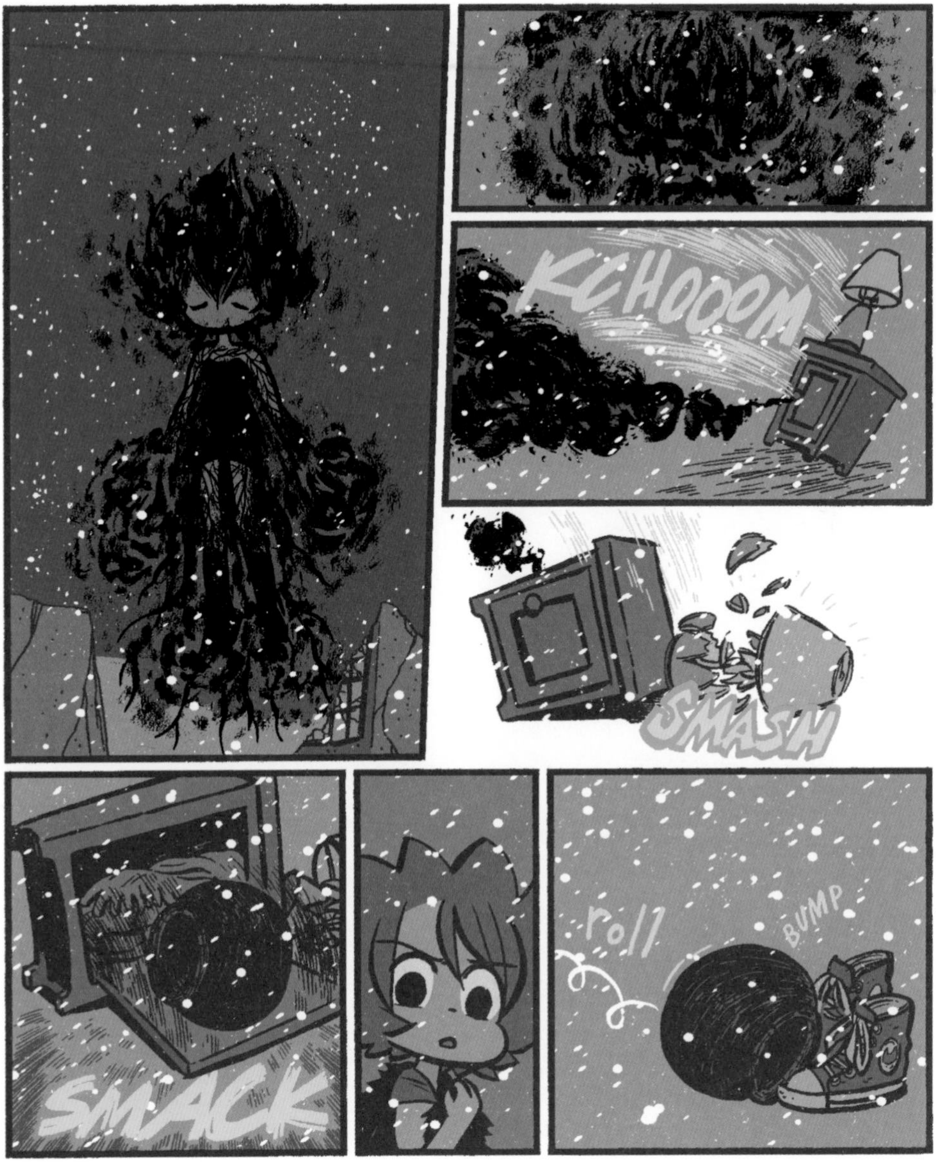
KCHOOOM
SMASH
SMACK
roll
BUMP

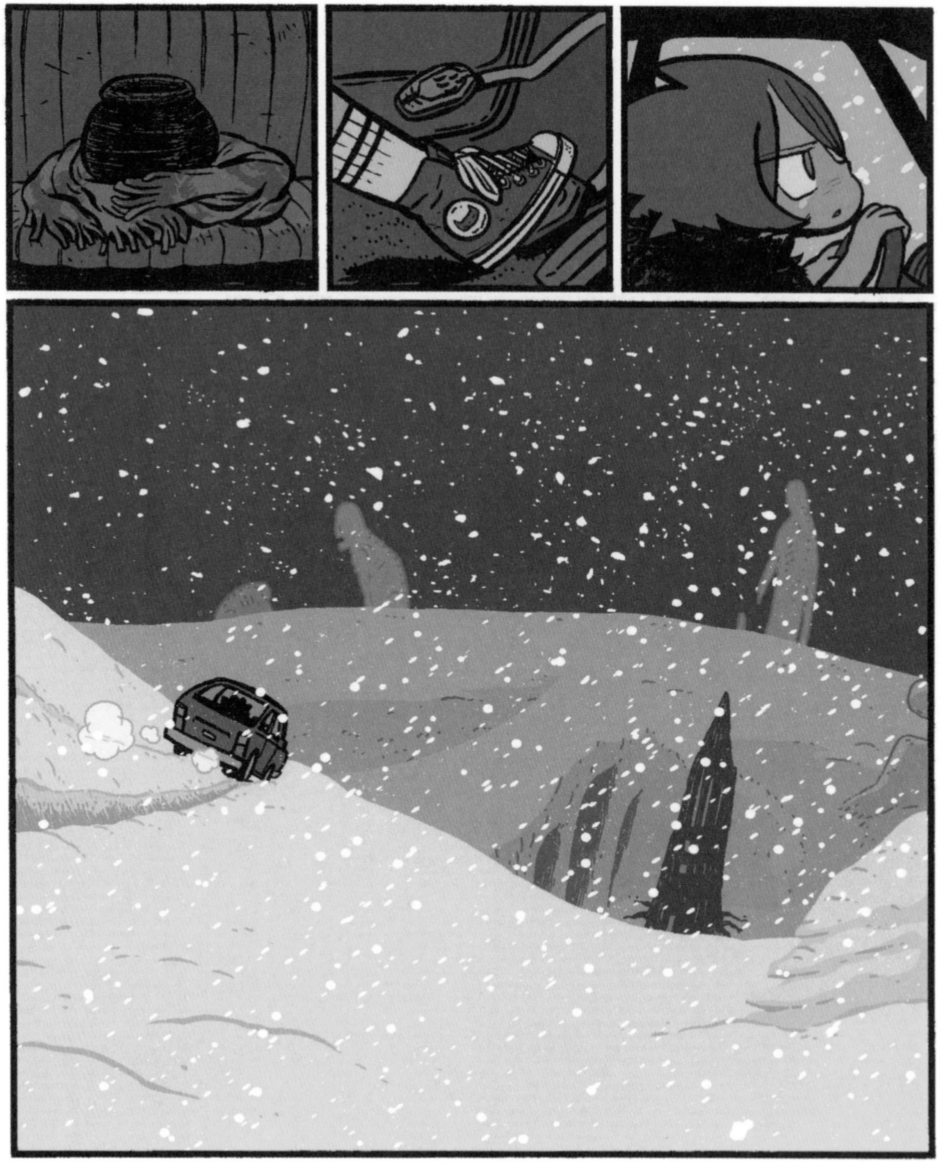

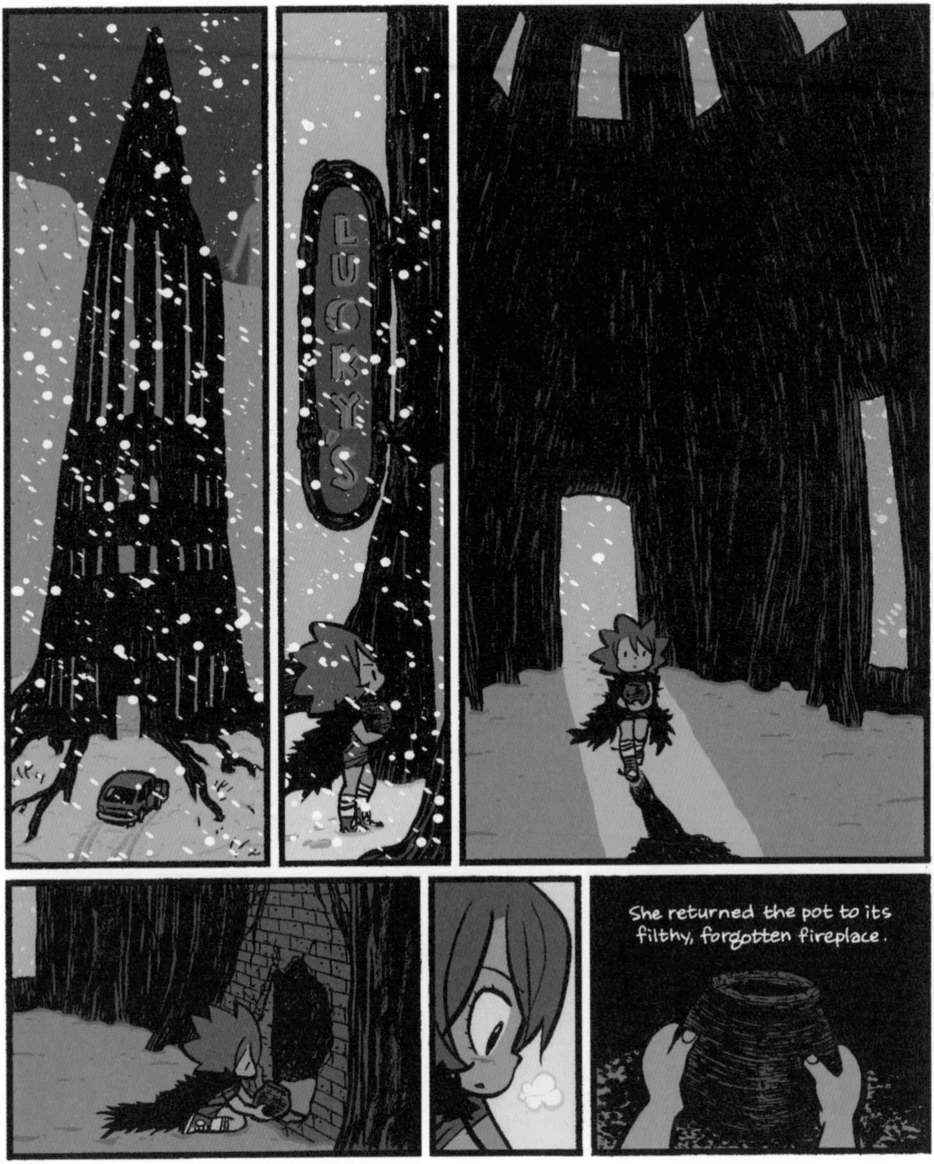
LUCKY'S
She returned the pot to its filthy, forgotten fireplace.

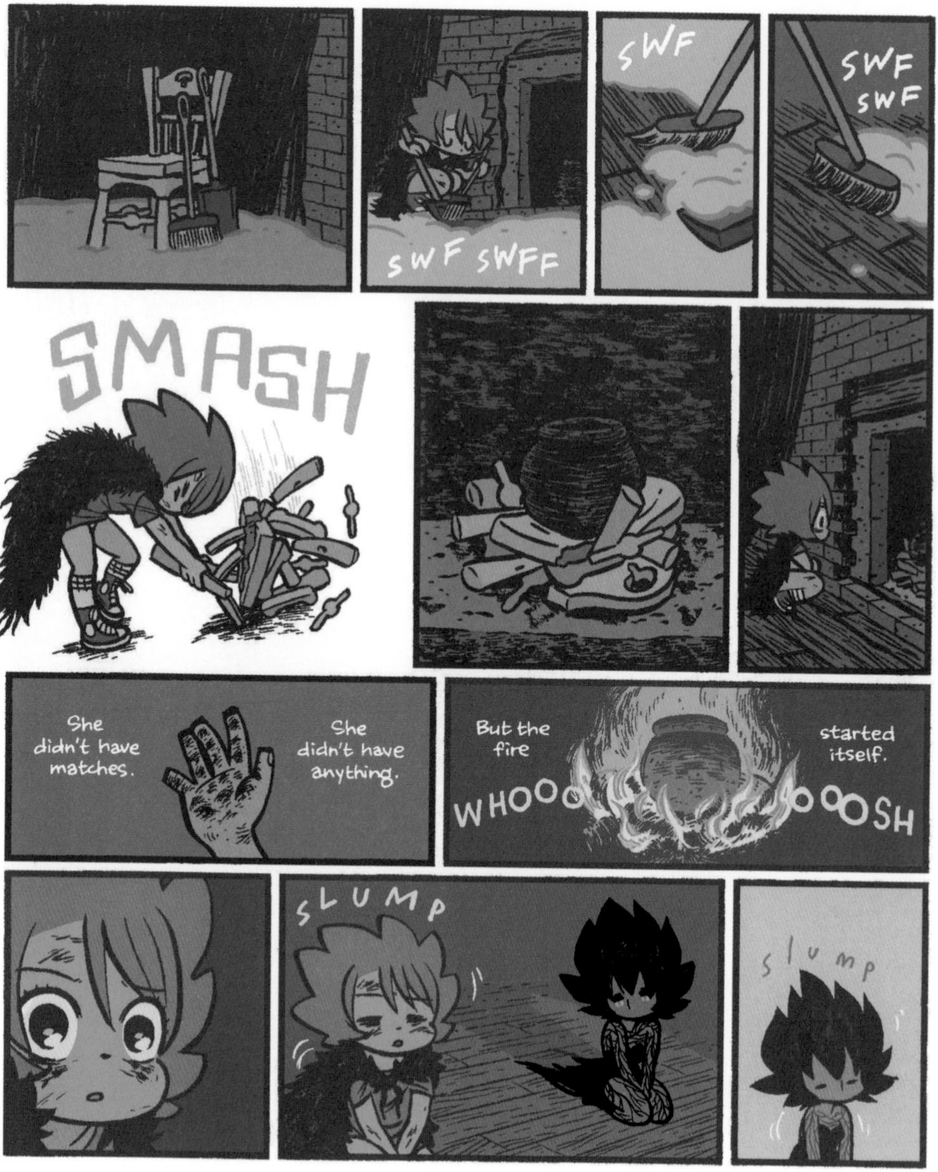
SWF SWFF
SWF
SWF
SWF
SMASH
She didn't have matches.
She didn't have anything.
But the fire
WHOOOOOOOSH
started itself.
SLUMP
slump

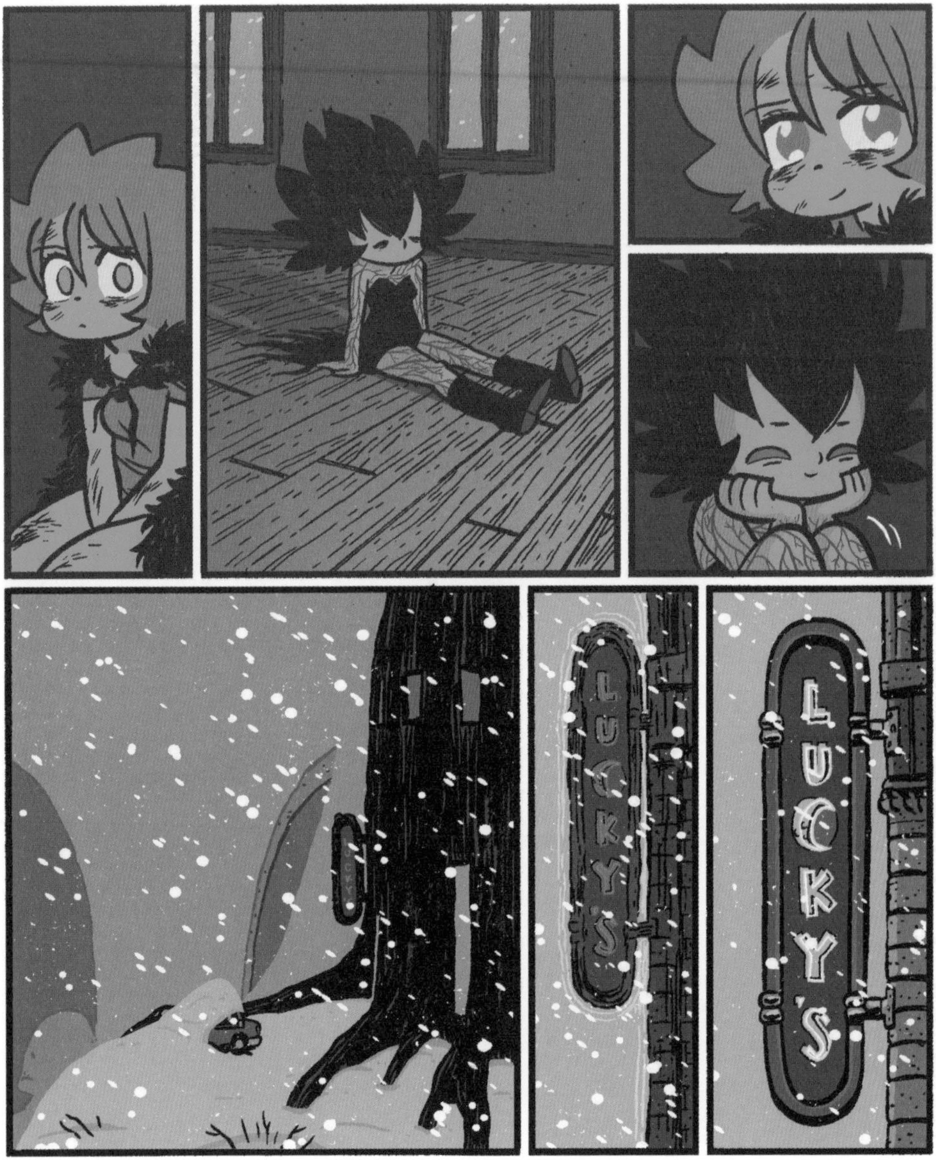
LUCKY'S
LUCKY'S

She'd done the thing, but she was still freezing her butt off in a dead world.

She had to go back. She had to find Lis. Or at least she had to try.

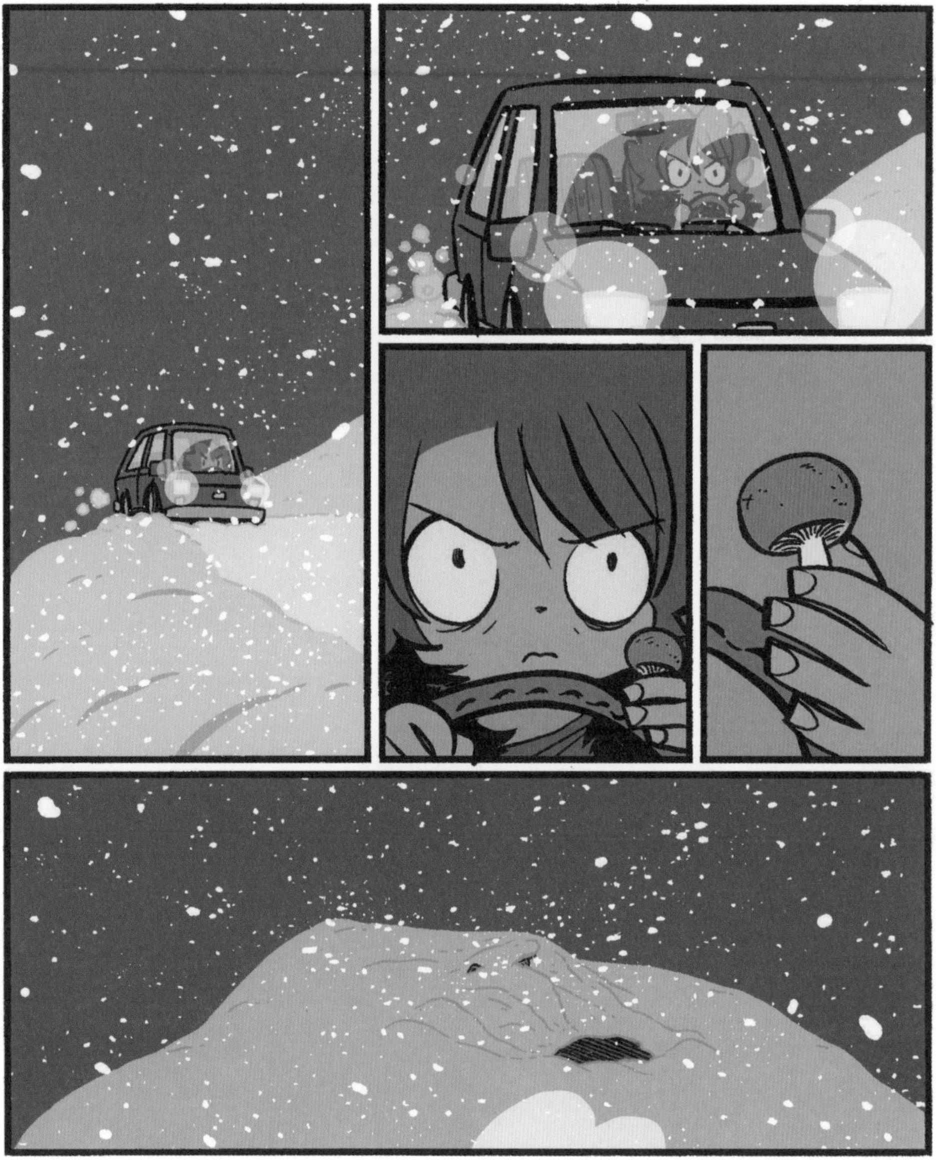

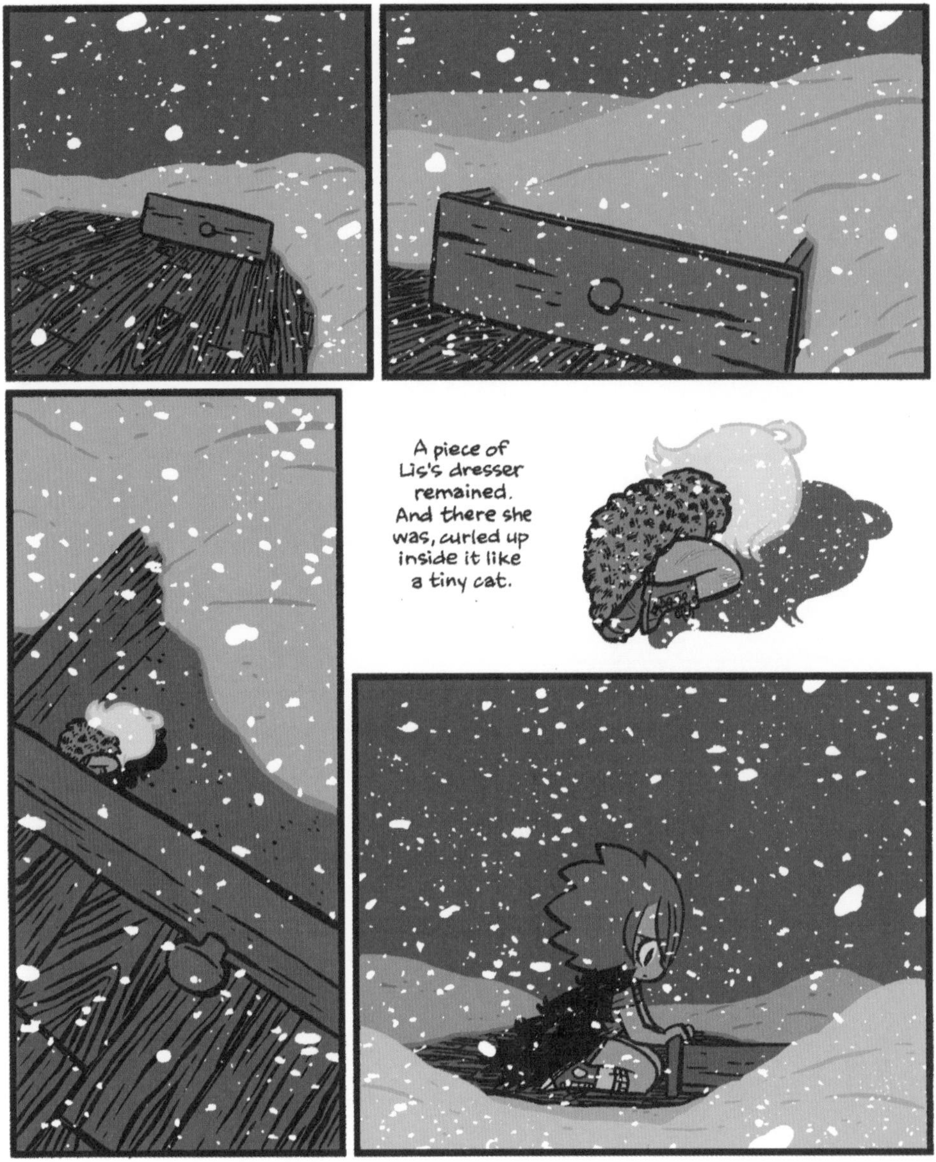
A piece of Lis's dresser remained. And there she was, curled up inside it like a tiny cat.

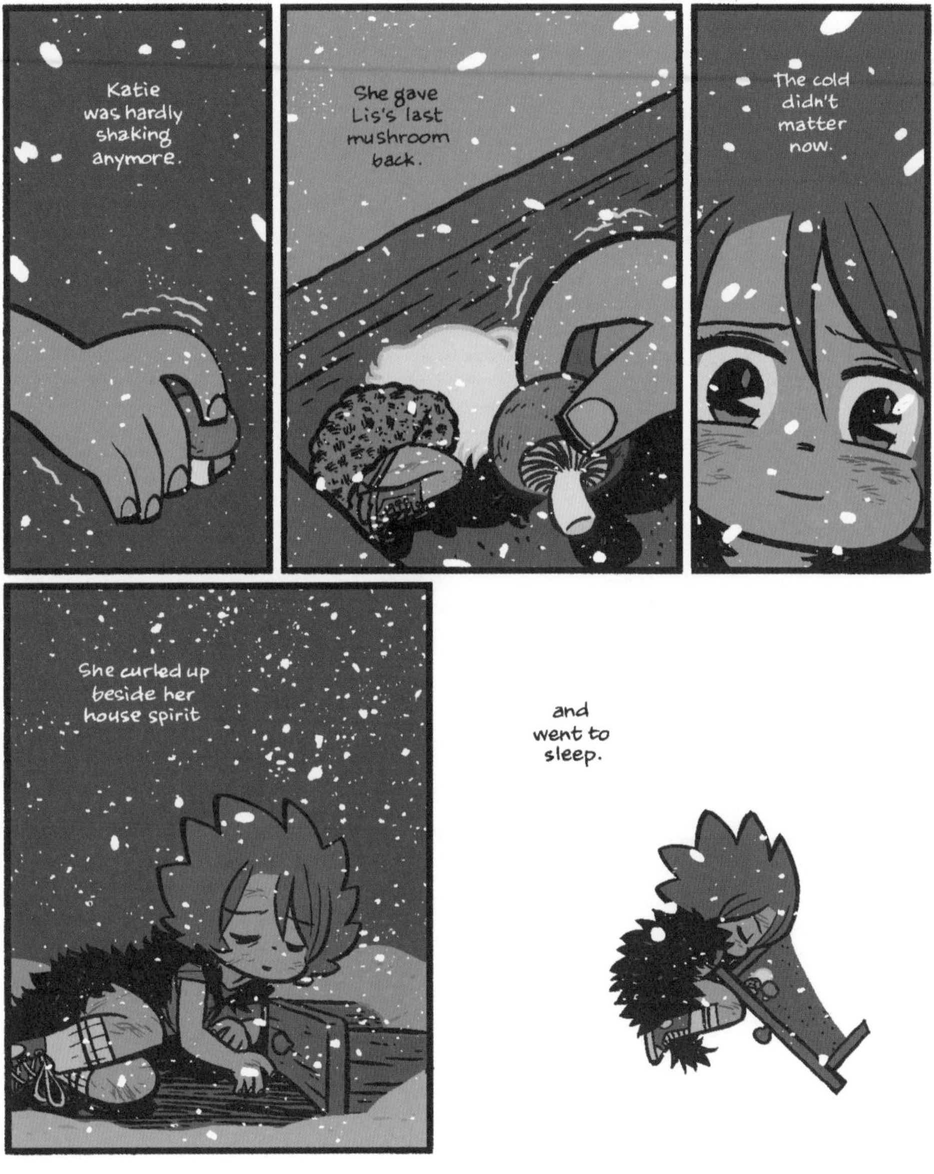
Katie was hardly shaking anymore.
She gave Lis's last mushroom back.
The cold didn't matter now.
She curled up beside her house spirit
and went to sleep.

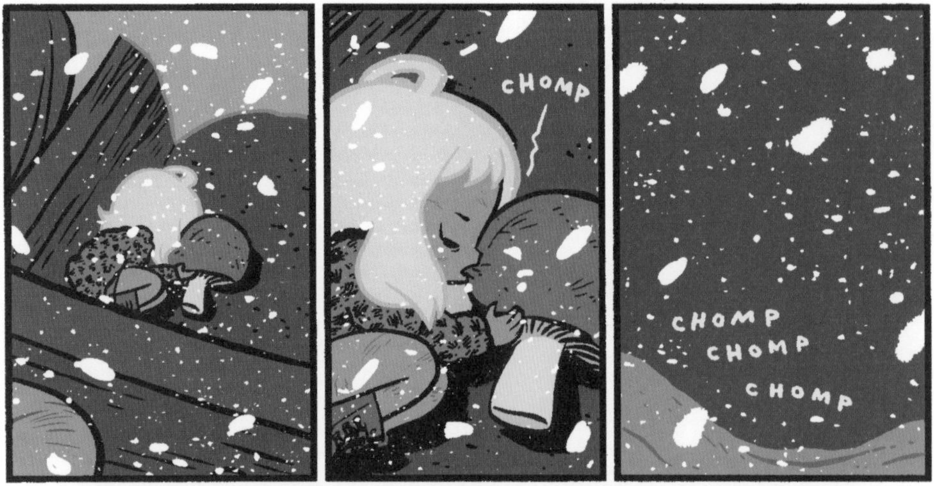
CHOMP
CHOMP
CHOMP
CHOMP

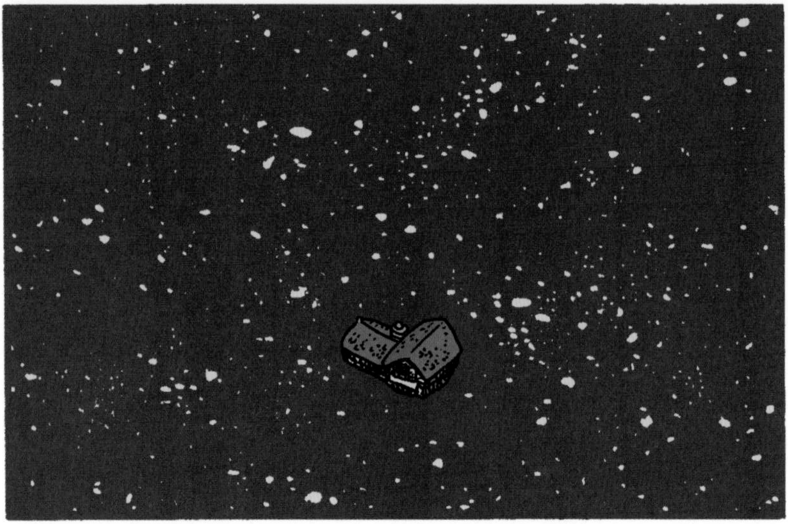

She woke up.

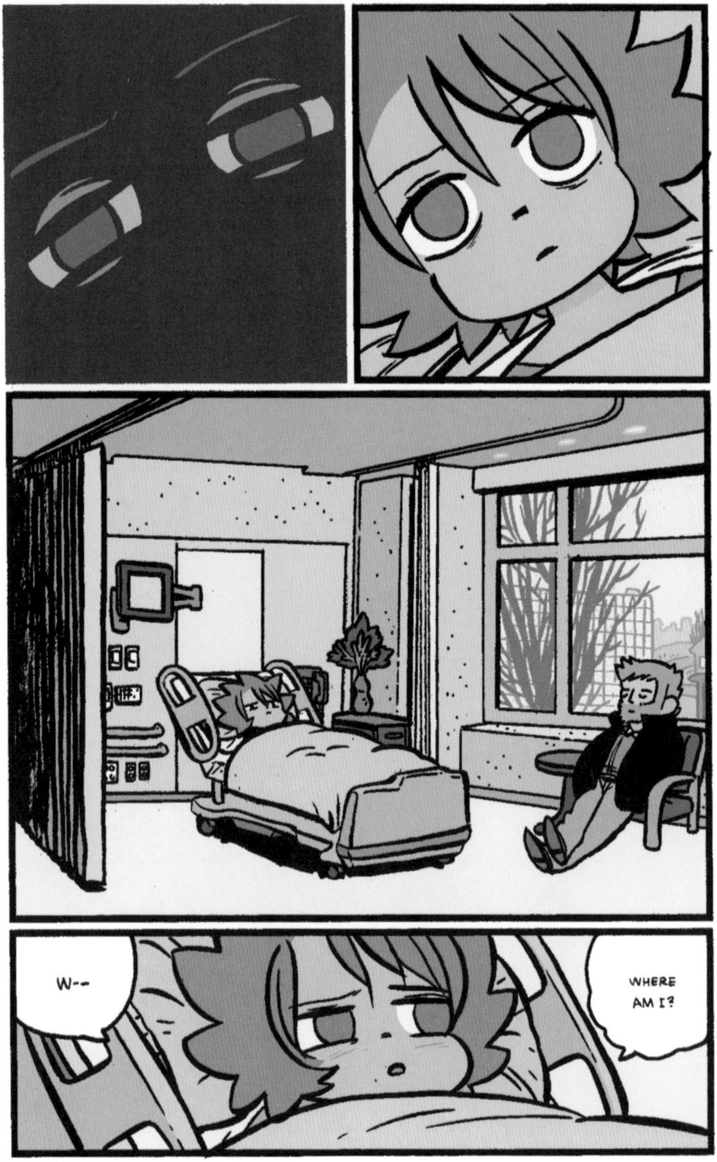
W--
WHERE AM I?

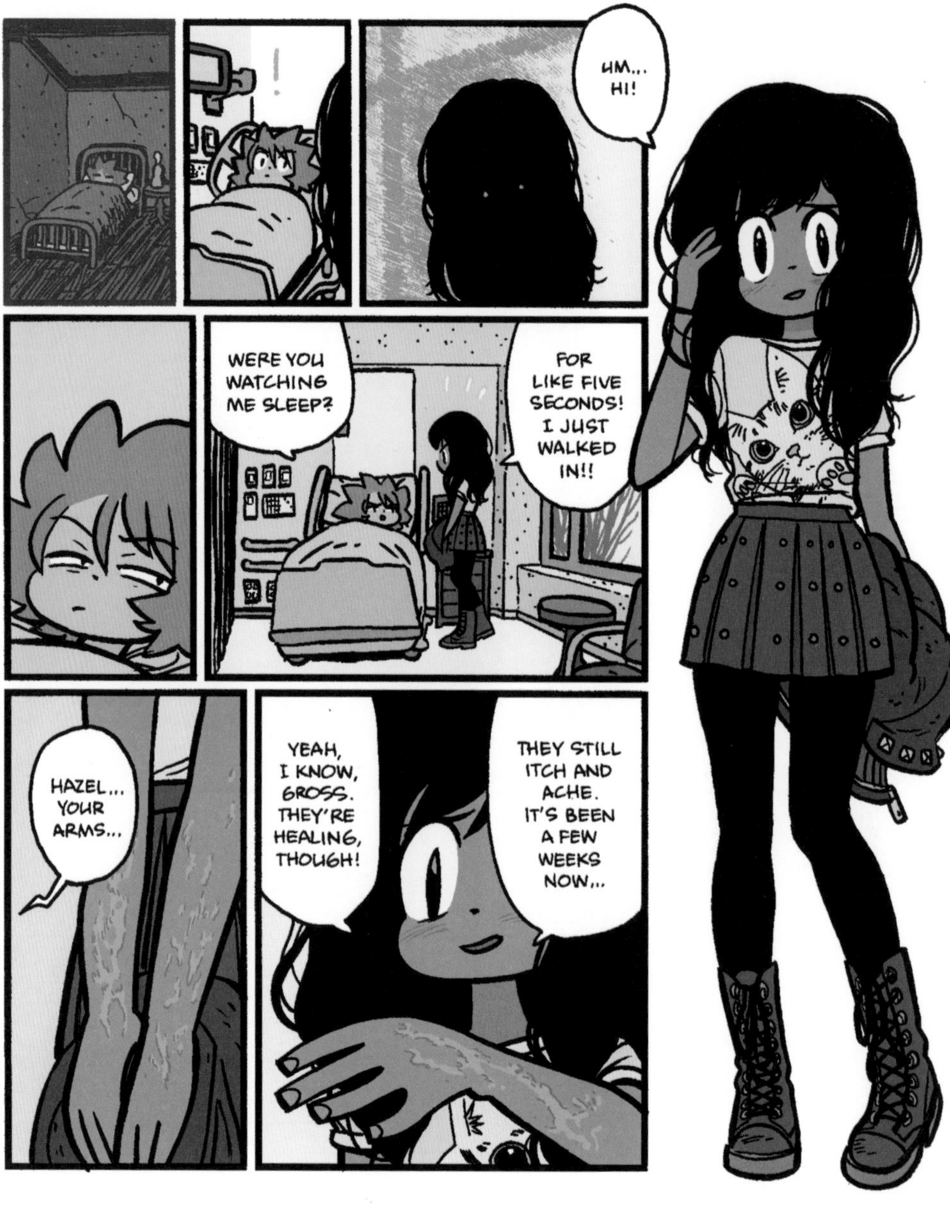
!
UM... HI!
WERE YOU WATCHING ME SLEEP?
FOR LIKE FIVE SECONDS! I JUST WALKED IN!!
HAZEL... YOUR ARMS...
YEAH, I KNOW, GROSS. THEY'RE HEALING, THOUGH!
THEY STILL ITCH AND ACHE. IT'S BEEN A FEW WEEKS NOW...

311

And Hazel told her side of the story:

How one day her weird interests unexpectedly became the focus of conversation with a person who had previously seemed intimidating.

An accidental friendship.

Somehow, through all the changes, this one thing had remained.

Maybe she was still feeling weak, but this was a lot for Katie to take. She got a little sobby.

I NEED TO BECOME A BETTER PERSON, ETC.

SHH, IT'S OKAY.

HAZEL... THANKS.

ANY TIME.

HM... YOUR HAND IS KIND OF... SLIMY.

SHIT, SORRY. OINTMENTS AND STUFF.

IT ACTUALLY KINDA HURTS TO TOUCH YOU...

312

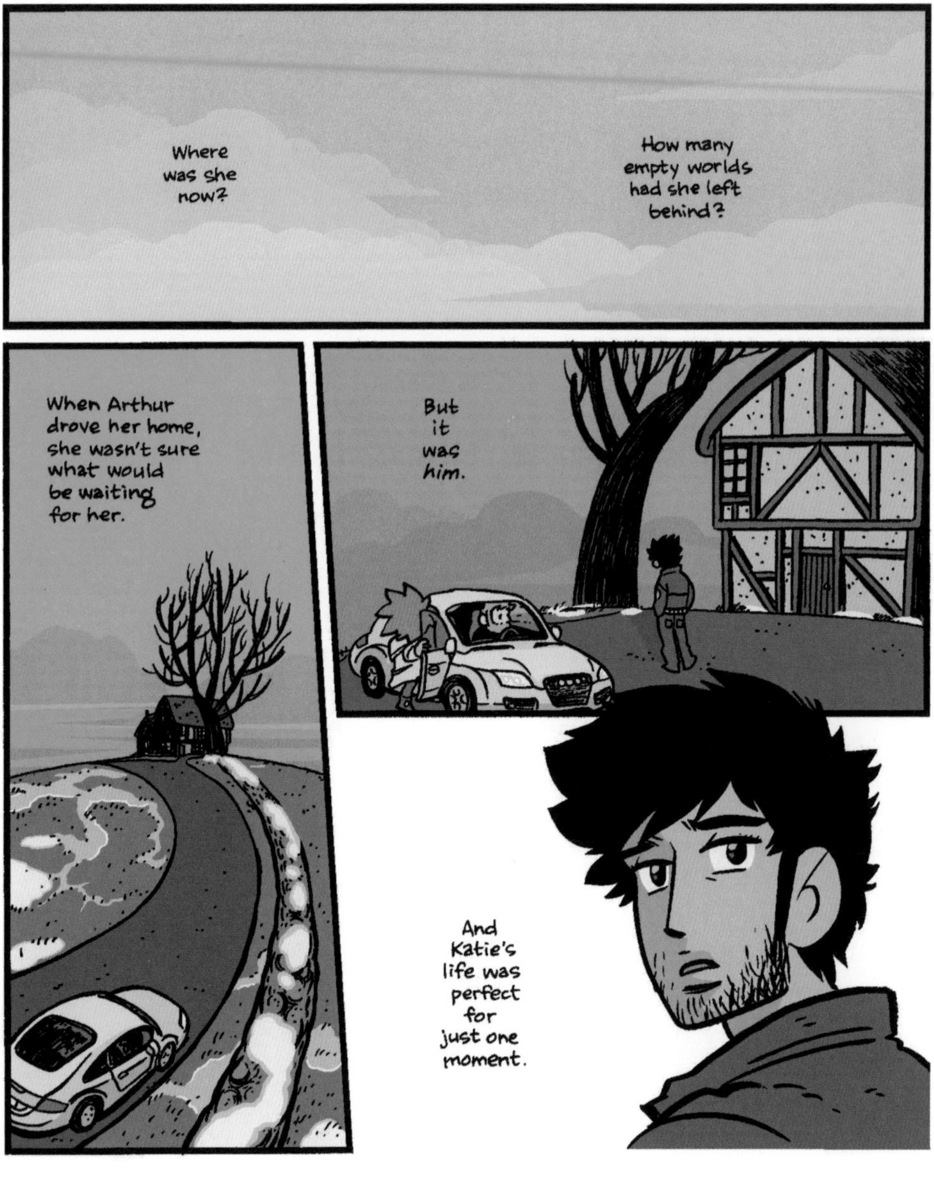
Where was she now?
How many empty worlds had she left behind?
When Arthur drove her home, she wasn't sure what would be waiting for her.
But it was him.
And Katie's life was perfect for just one moment.

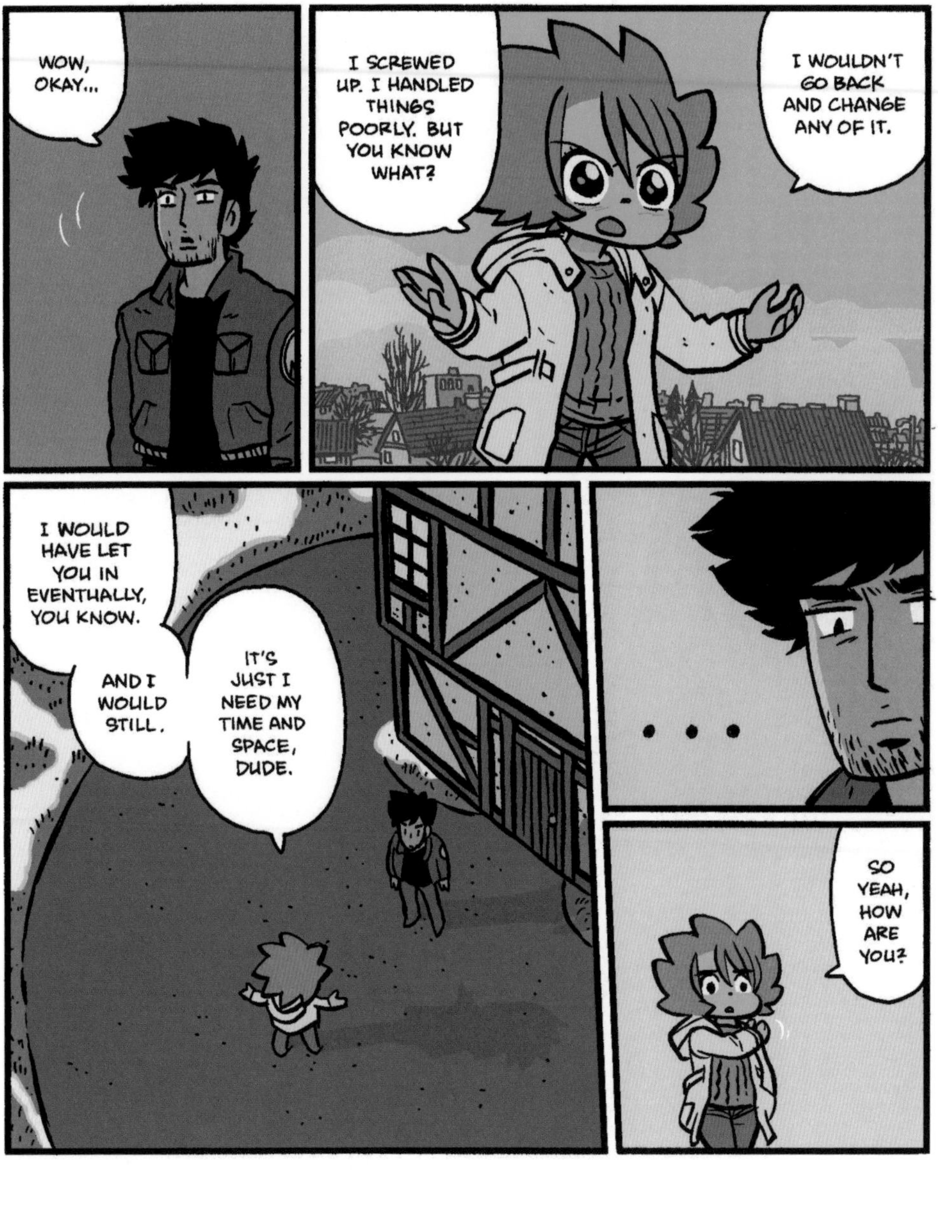
WOW, OKAY...
I SCREWED UP. I HANDLED THINGS POORLY. BUT YOU KNOW WHAT?
I WOULDN'T GO BACK AND CHANGE ANY OF IT.
I WOULD HAVE LET YOU IN EVENTUALLY, YOU KNOW.
AND I WOULD STILL.
IT'S JUST I NEED MY TIME AND SPACE, DUDE.
...
SO YEAH, HOW ARE YOU?

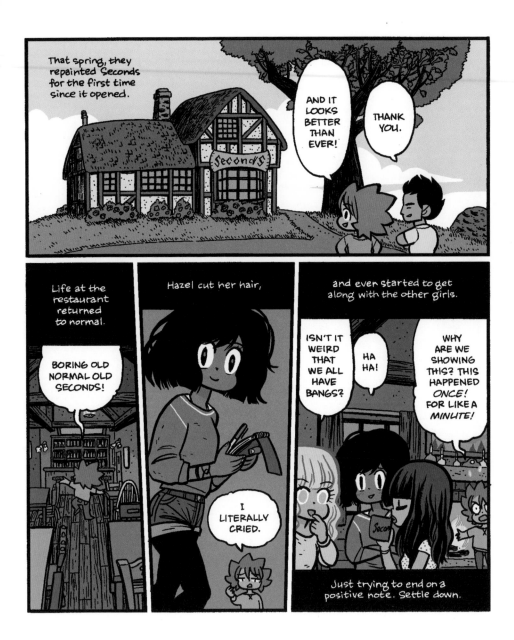

That spring, they repainted Seconds for the first time since it opened.

AND IT LOOKS BETTER THAN EVER!

THANK YOU.

Life at the restaurant returned to normal.

BORING OLD NORMAL OLD SECONDS!

Hazel cut her hair,

I LITERALLY CRIED.

and even started to get along with the other girls.

ISN'T IT WEIRD THAT WE ALL HAVE BANGS?

HA HA!

WHY ARE WE SHOWING THIS? THIS HAPPENED ONCE! FOR LIKE A MINUTE!

Just trying to end on a positive note. Settle down.

317

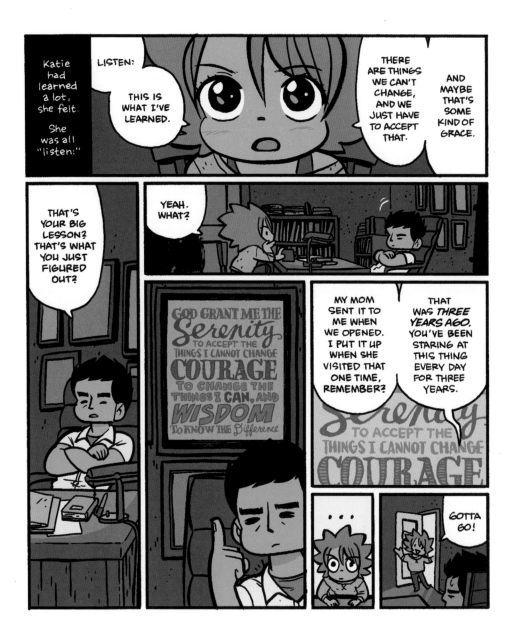

318

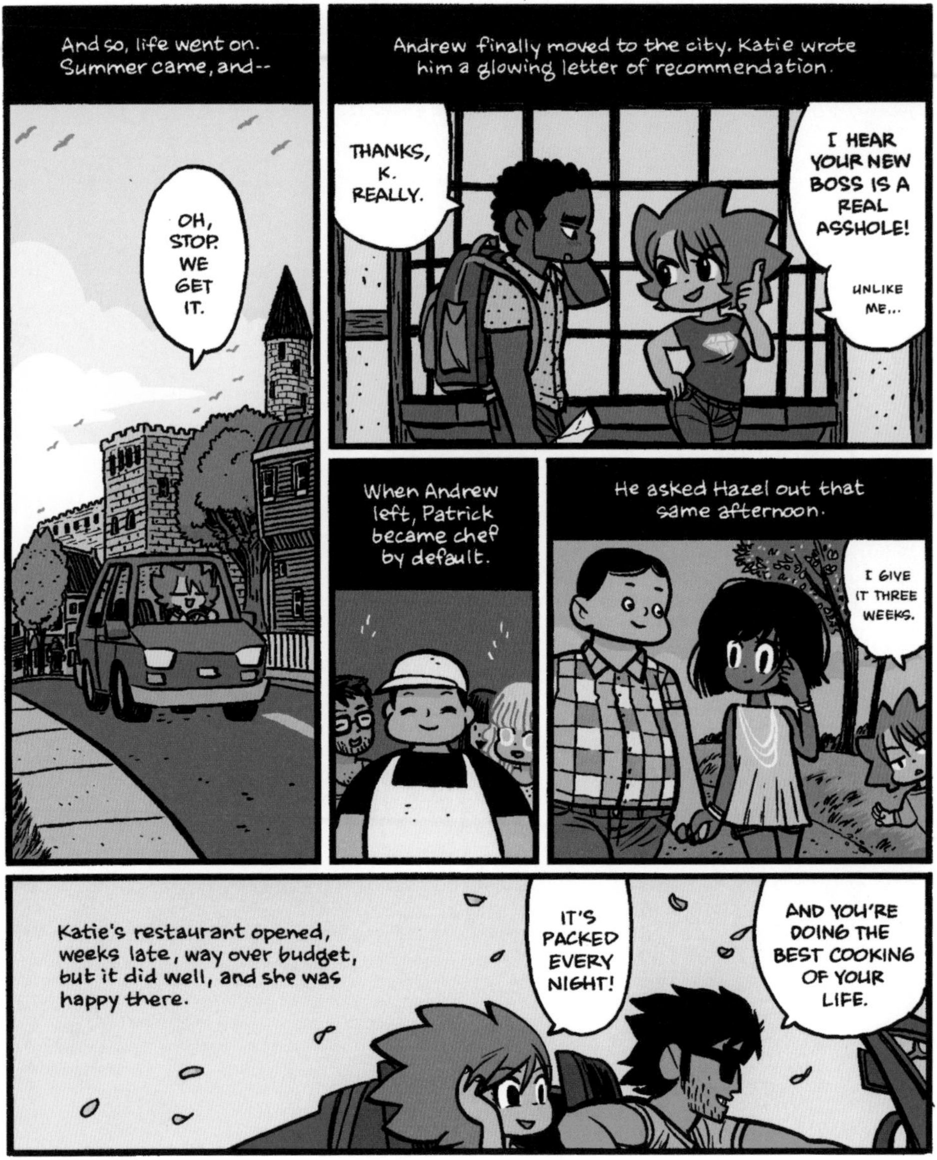
And so, life went on. Summer came, and--
OH, STOP. WE GET IT.
Andrew finally moved to the city. Katie wrote him a glowing letter of recommendation.
THANKS, K. REALLY.
I HEAR YOUR NEW BOSS IS A REAL ASSHOLE!
UNLIKE ME...
When Andrew left, Patrick became chef by default.
He asked Hazel out that same afternoon.
I GIVE IT THREE WEEKS.
Katie's restaurant opened, weeks late, way over budget, but it did well, and she was happy there.
IT'S PACKED EVERY NIGHT!
AND YOU'RE DOING THE BEST COOKING OF YOUR LIFE.

It was often said that Lucky's had a real energy to it, that there was something special about it.

UH, YEAH: *MY FOOD.* DUH.

And Katie? She was the same old Katie.

I'M STILL PRETTY YOUNG, BUT THANKS.

Still cooking. Still making people happy.

OR AT LEAST TRYING, EVERY DAY!

...still talking to herself.

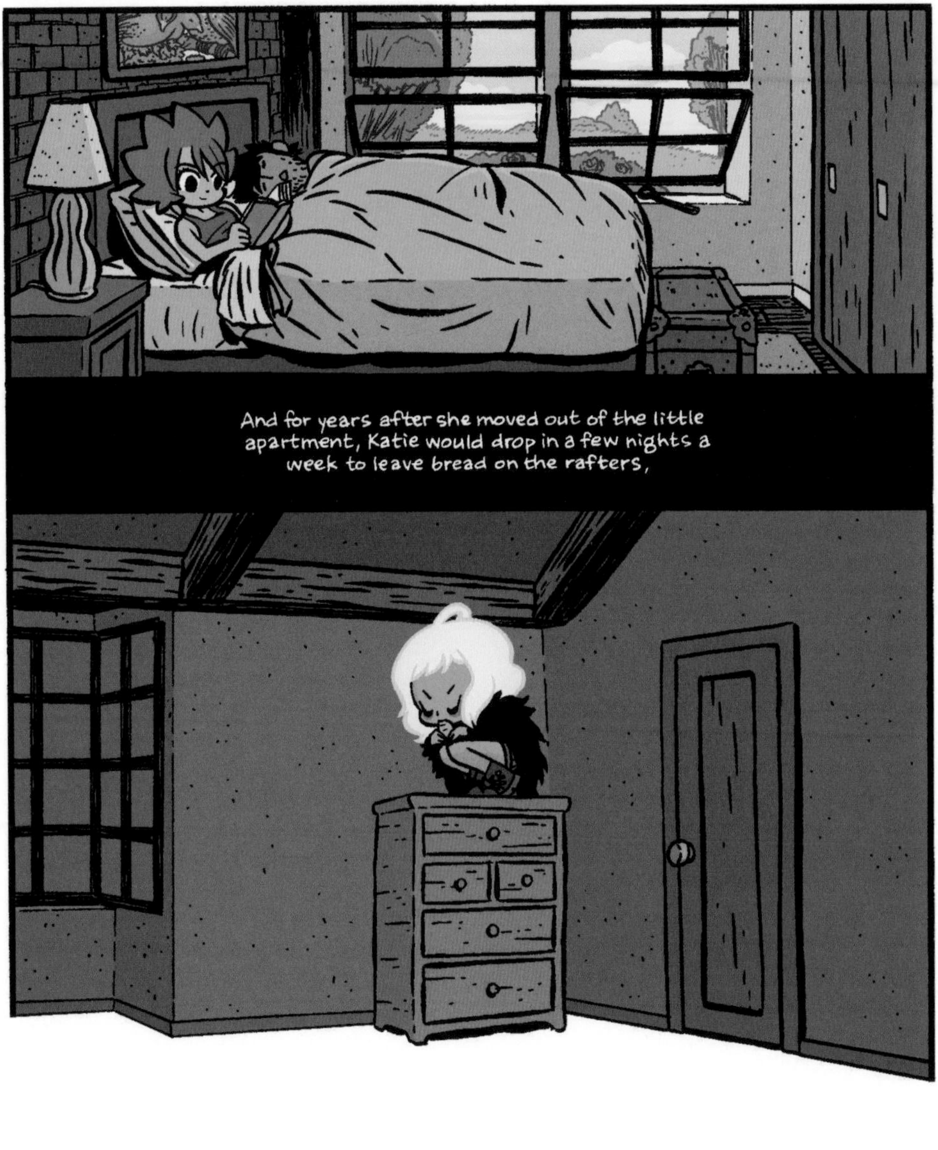
And for years after she moved out of the little apartment, Katie would drop in a few nights a week to leave bread on the rafters,

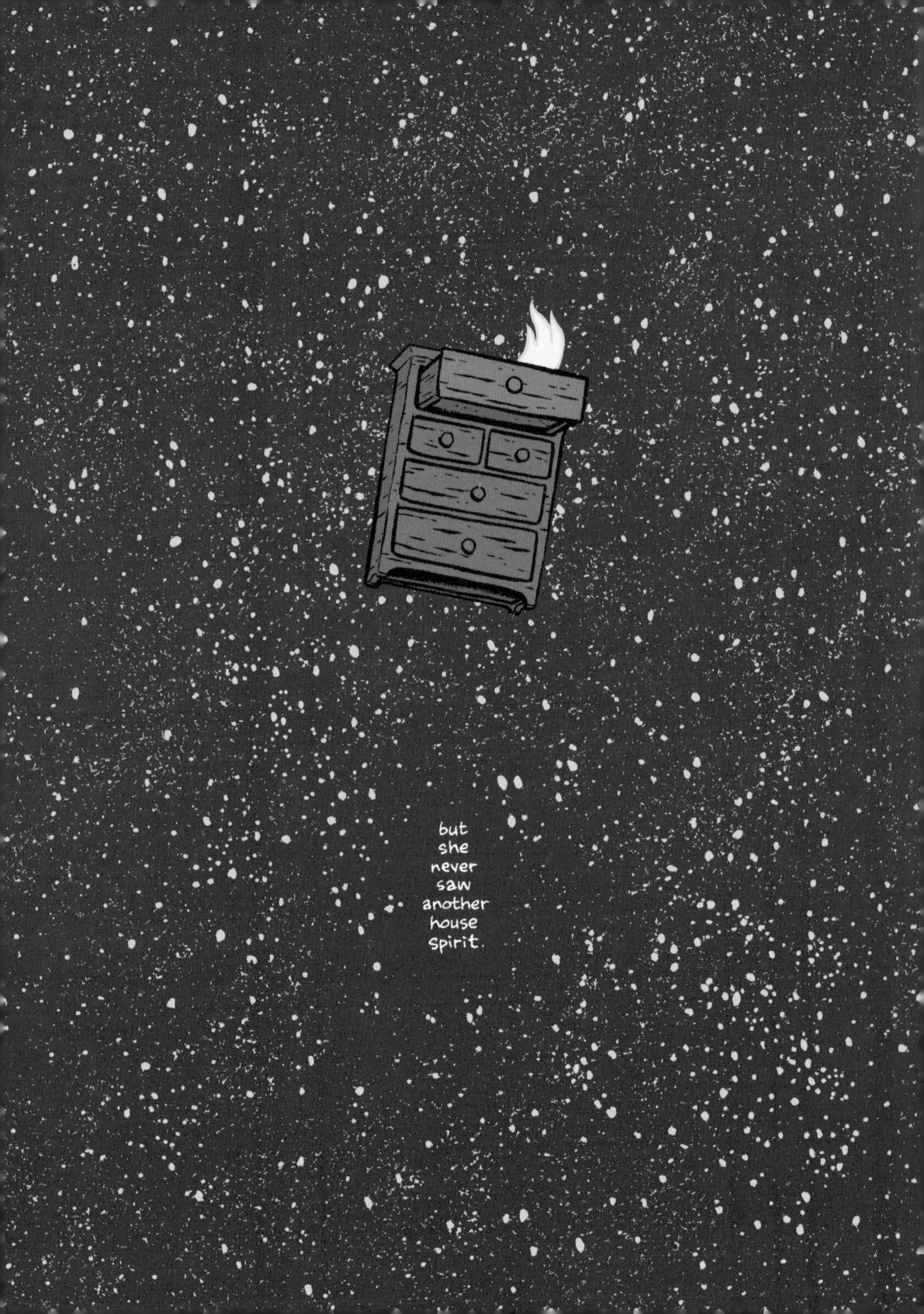
but
she
never
saw
another
house
spirit.

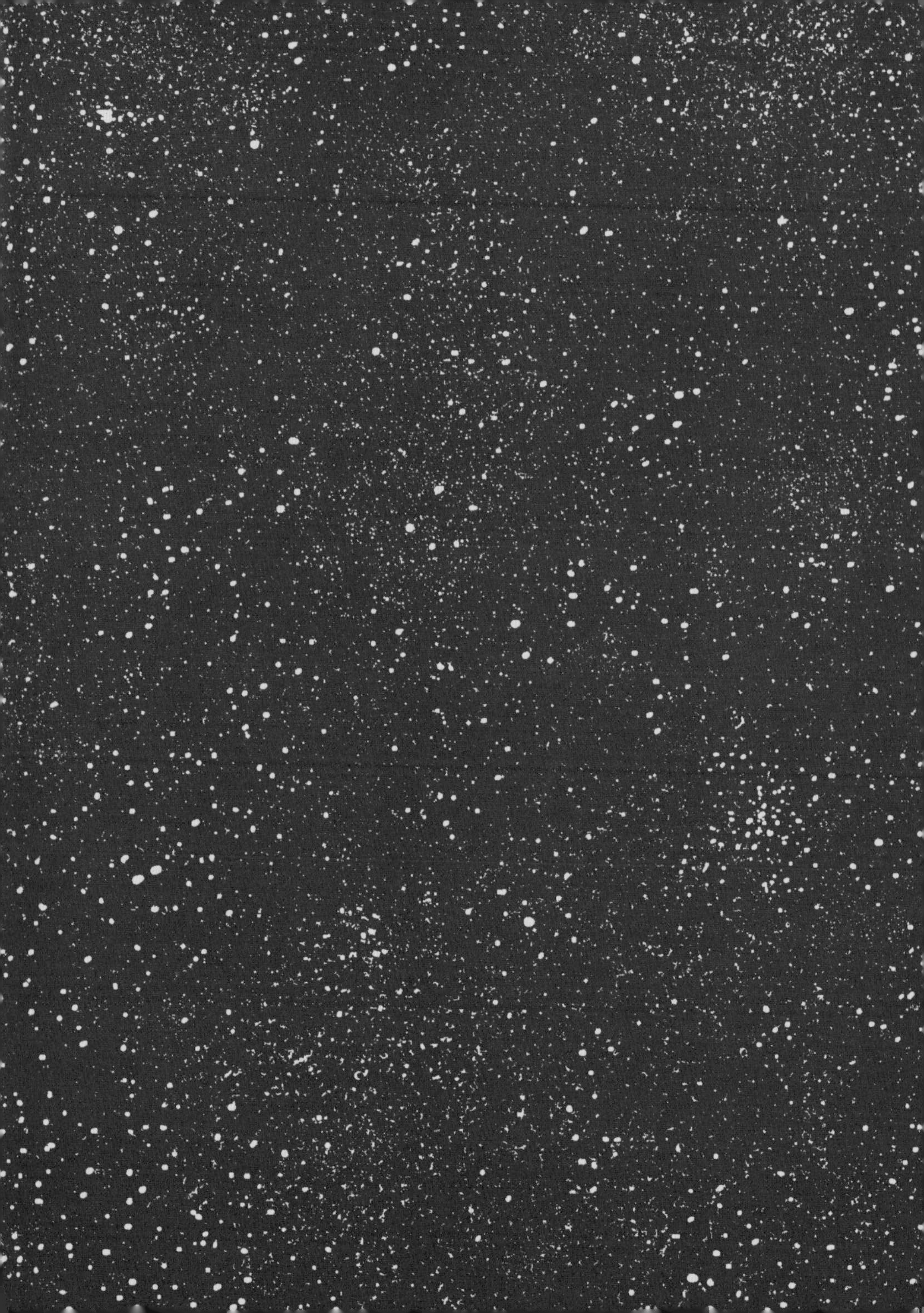

Acknowledgments

There would be no *Seconds* without my team of Jason, Nathan, and Dustin, and without the whole team at Random House/ Ballantine. I have been truly blessed to have all of you with me on this book. All love to my friends and family for all their support during these wild and crazy years. Thanks to Mike S. for providing the recipe in chapter 3—not only did he write it, he actually came to my house and cooked it in front of me, and then we ate it. Additional thanks to Joel and Cory, my food and restaurant consultants, and very special thanks to Heather, Julie, Rosanna, Vili, and Miguel, for helping me to not completely destroy my body during this process.

A Note about the Assistants

Jason Fischer (drawing assistant) is a cartoonist from Los Angeles now living in Portland, Oregon. He loves to draw monsters and food. He enjoys collecting rocks, Daruma dolls, knives, pressed pennies, and Playmobil people.

Nathan Fairbairn (color) is a colorist and writer of comics. He's also a pretty decent cook, despite what his kids might tell you. He lives in Vancouver, Canada.

Dustin Harbin (lettering) is a cartoonist who lives and works in Charlotte, North Carolina. He's too fussy to be a good cook but just fussy enough to be an okay baker.

Additional assistance provided by Megan Messina, Hannah Ayoubi, and Jeremy Arambulo. We love them.

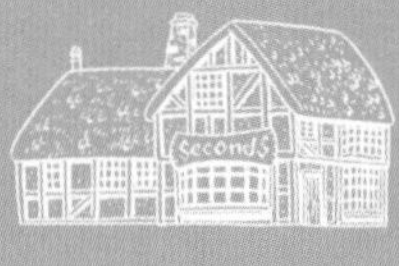
Seconds